TALMUDIC DIALECTICS
Volume I

SOUTH FLORIDA STUDIES IN THE HISTORY OF JUDAISM

Edited by
Jacob Neusner
William Scott Green, James Strange
Darrell J. Fasching, Sara Mandell

Number 127
TALMUDIC DIALECTICS
Volume I
Tractate Berakhot and the Divisions of Appointed Times and Women

by
Jacob Neusner

TALMUDIC DIALECTICS

Volume I

Tractate Berakhot and the
Divisions of Appointed Times and Women

by

Jacob Neusner

Scholars Press
Atlanta, Georgia

TALMUDIC DIALECTICS

Volume I

Tractate Berakhot and the Divisions of Appointed Times and Women

by
Jacob Neusner

©1995
University of South Florida

Publication of this book was made possible by a grant from the Tisch Family Foundation, New York City. The University of South Florida acknowledges with thanks this important support for its scholarly projects.

Library of Congress Cataloging in Publication Data
Neusner, Jacob, 1932–
    Talmudic dialectics / by Jacob Neusner.
       p.   cm. — (South Florida studies in the history of Judaism ; no. 127-128)
    Contents: v. 1. Tractate Berakhot and the Divisions of Appointed Times and Women—v. 2. The Divisions of Damages and Holy Things and Tractate Niddah.
    ISBN 0-7885-0205-0 (v. 1 : cloth : alk. paper). — ISBN 0-7885-0206-9 (v. 2 : cloth : alk. paper)
    1. Talmud—Hermeneutics. I. Title. II. Series.
BM503.7.N48   1995
296.1'2506—dc20   95-39335
                                                                                          CIP

Printed in the United States of America
on acid-free paper

Table of Contents

PREFACE v

INTRODUCTION vii
    i. The Character of the Bavli: A Final Statement vii
    ii. Defining the Dialectical Argument xii
    iii. An Example of a Dialectical Argument xx
    iv. An Example of a Classical Argument of an Other-Than-Dialectical Character xxvi
    v. The Importance of the Dialectical Argument in the Talmud xli
    vi. The Law behind the Laws xliv
    vii. The Unity of the Law xlviii
    viii. Dialectics and the Intellectual Dynamics of Rabbinic Literature .. lii

I.   AN INITIAL PROBE: TYPES AND FORMS OF THE DIALECTICAL ARGUMENT IN BAVLI TO MISHNAH-TRACTATE MOED QATAN 1:1-2 1
    i. Outline of the Talmud 2
    ii. Mishnah-Exegesis the Starting Point 6
    iii. A Limited Instance of the Dialectical-Analytical Argument in Mishnah-Exegesis 9
    iv. The Negligible Role of the Dialectical-Analytical Argument in Mishnah-Exegesis 30

II.   BAVLI TRACTATE BERAKHOT 49
    i. An Exegetical-Dialectical Argument at M. Ber. 1:3 49
    ii. A Source-Critical Dialectical Argument at M. Ber. 2:3 52
    iii. A Mishnah-Exegetical Dialectical Argument at M. Ber. 3:4 55
    iv. An Exegetical-Dialectical Argument at M. Ber. 6:1 57
    v. Proportions 61

III.   BAVLI TRACTATE SHABBAT 63
    i. A Source-Critical Dialectical Argument at M. Shab. 1:1 63
    ii. A Theoretical Question, Worked Out in a Protracted Inquiry, at M.Shab. 2:3A-B 68
    iii. A Theoretical Question, Worked Out in a Systematic Way, at M. Shab. 17:4C-D 74
    iv. Proportions 78

IV.   BAVLI TRACTATE ERUBIN 79
    i. An Analytical Argument on a Principle Deriving from One Instance and Extended to Others at M. Erub. 3:1 79
    ii. Proportions 81

V.	Bavli Tractate Pesahim 83
	i. An Exegetical-Dialectical Argument at M. Pes. 2:1 83
	ii. An Exegetical-Dialectical Argument at M. Pes. 5:3 96
	iii. An Analytical-Dialectical Argument at M. Pes. 7:5 101
	iv. Proportions 105
VI.	Bavli Tractate Yoma 107
	i. Analytical-Dialectical Argument at Mishnah Yoma 1:1 107
	ii. Proportions 129
VII.	Bavli Tractate Sukkah 131
VIII.	Bavli Tractate Besah 133
	i. An Analytical-Dialectical Argument at M. Bes. 2:2-3 133
	ii. Proportions 141
IX.	Bavli Tractate Rosh Hashanah 143
X.	Bavli Tractate Taanit 145
XI.	Bavli Tractate Megillah 147
XII.	Bavli Tractate Moed Qatan 149
XIII.	Bavli Tractate Hagigah 151
XIV.	Bavli Tractate Yebamot 153
	i. An Exegetical-Dialectical and Analogical-Dialectical Argument at M. Yeb. 1:1-2 153
	ii. An Analytical-Dialectical Argument at M. Yeb. 3:9I-L 192
	iii. Proportions 200
XV.	Bavli Tractate Ketubot 201
XVI.	Bavli Tractate Nedarim 203
XVII.	Bavli Tractate Nazir 205
XVIII.	Bavli Tractate Sotah 207
XIX.	Bavli Tractate Gittin 209
	i. An Analytical-Dialectical Argument at M. Git. 5:4G-I 209
	ii. Proportions 217
XX.	Bavli Tractate Qiddushin 219

Preface

This monograph completes my survey of the types and forms of composites that all together comprise the Talmud of Babylonia. It is the logical next step, after the results of *The Initial Phases of the Talmud's Judaism.* Atlanta, 1995: Scholars Press for South Florida Studies in the History of Judaism. I. *Exegesis of Scripture.* II. *Exemplary Virtue.* III. *Social Ethics,* and IV. *Theology.* There I identified and described one of the two kinds of other-than-Mishnah-exegetical composite characteristic of the Bavli, and here I do the same work for the other. I know of no other classes of other-than-Mishnah-exegetical composites (or even compositions) of the Bavli besides those two: the topical (not syllogistic) and the dialectical (not in rhetorical but in logical form, as explained in the Introduction). Of the two, the latter is distinctive and occurs, within the Rabbinic canon, only in the Talmud. So here I address the composite that is unique to the Bavli and that imparts to the Bavli its distinctive, compelling character: the authentically-dialectical argument. All accounts of the Talmud in modern times concur that what makes the Talmud talmudic is the dialectical argument. In the Introduction I place this, my final monograph on the problem of describing the Bavli, into its larger context, and further define the character of that remarkable type of composition and explain what I want to know about it and why I find the issue urgent.

As is my method in approaching every problem, I start with a probe, to establish a hypothesis or definition, as the case may be, and then survey all relevant data; in the Introduction I begin with a sample, in this case, a tractate, and analyze what I find devoted to Mishnah-exegesis; once a hypothesis on the types and forms of Mishnah-exegetical composites has taken shape, I then turn to the entirety of the document and catalogue the exempla. That is what forms the body of the work.

With the conclusion of this monograph I proceed to conduct for the Yerushalmi the systematic inquiry now completed for the Bavli. The academic commentary for the Yerushalmi, complete outline, and then comparison of the two Talmuds for the tractates (Berakhot and Niddah) and the divisions (Moed, Nashim, and Neziqin) at which they overlap, will occupy me for some years. The academic commentary will begin to appear in 1997. For the moment, this monograph thus completes my inquiry into the types and forms of writing in the Bavli.

No work of mine can omit reference to the exceptionally favorable circumstances in which I conduct my research as Distinguished Research Professor in the Florida State University System at the University of South Florida. I wrote this book as part of my long-term labor of research scholarship, expressed through both publication and teaching at the University of South Florida, which has afforded me an ideal situation in which to conduct a scholarly life. I express my thanks for not only the advantage of a Distinguished Research Professorship in the Florida State University System, which for a scholar must be the best job in the world, but also of a substantial research expense fund, ample research time, and stimulating and cordial colleagues.

At the time of this work I also enjoyed a research grant as Fellow of the Bard Center of Bard College, Annandale-on-Hudson, New York. My thanks go to that College for graciously joining in the support of my research and for the remarkable hospitality of my colleagues in the Department of Religion.

JACOB NEUSNER

DISTINGUISHED RESEARCH PROFESSOR OF RELIGIOUS STUDIES
UNIVERSITY OF SOUTH FLORIDA
TAMPA, FLORIDA 33620-5550 U.S.A.

Introduction

I. THE CHARACTER OF THE BAVLI: A FINAL STATEMENT

In the aggregate the Talmud is made up of two types of composites, those devoted to the exegesis of the Mishnah and the amplification of the law, which I call Mishnah-exegetical, and those that address a task other than that of Mishnah-exegesis, which I call other-than-Mishnah-exegetical. The Talmud of Babylonia takes shape principally through the compilation of Mishnah-exegetical composites; the other-than-Mishnah-exegetical ones form a negligible proportion of the whole, I presently estimate no more than 10% in volume. That estimated 10% of the Talmud's composites of an other-than-Mishnah-exegetical character breaks down, into two types, the dialectical argument and the topical composite or appendix; the former comprises at most 1-2% of the Talmud in volume (as the exercises on proportions in this monograph show), and the latter, approximately 8-9% in volume, depending on the tractate. But when we take a second look at the matter, as we do here for tractate Qiddushin, we find that the topical composites are included to supplement the amplification of the Mishnah. Of the other 90% in volume, that devoted to the Mishnah's exegesis, one kind supplies information, the other undertakes sustained analytical argument generated by the Mishnah's formulation or by its law or its case. I have not found necessary, for the present stage of the description of the Bavli, the breakdown of the Bavli's Mishnah-exegesis into types and forms.

The category, "Mishnah-exegetical," encompasses a variety of distinct subdivisions. For the Talmud of Babylonia contains four principal types of systematic discourse on law,

[1] exegetical (explanation of the language, sources, and authorities of the Mishnah),

[2] informative (non-propositional display of information on a given topic set forth in the Mishnah),

[3] syllogistic (presentation of a proposition and the evidence and argumentation therefor), ordinarily in connection with the exegesis of the Mishnah

[4] dialectical (an analytical argument moving from point to point to establish the coherence of diverse data).

Of these the ubiquitous is the first; the least specific to the Mishnah (being topical and not purposive) the second; and the most characteristic and substantively important, the third; and the least common but most influential, the fourth. And, further, the easiest to confuse with one another are the third and fourth. That is because both syllogistic and dialectical discourses utilize the same rhetorical form, the dialogue in the form of question and answer or other kinds of dialogue. But the former sets forth a static demonstration of a set-piece proposition, while the latter undertakes an open-ended exploration of a problem, moving across the boundaries that separate one topic from another.

I have now completed such work as I wish to undertake on the description of all four types of composites in the Bavli, the relevant titles being as follows:

THE TAXONOMY OF THE BAVLI'S COMPOSITES: My basic statement is contained in the following:

> *The Bavli's One Voice: Types and Forms of Analytical Discourse and their Fixed Order of Appearance.* Atlanta, 1991: Scholars Press for South Florida Studies in the History of Judaism.

That is the work that demonstrates the formal cogency of the Bavli, its documentary character, and further indicates the paramount status of Mishnah-exegetical composites in the formation of the whole, showing, also, the fixed order in which the types of Mishnah-exegetical compositions and composites take their place. From that point forward, the case for the Bavli as a planned and deliberate work of literature, not merely a haphazard scrapbook or collection of this, that, and the other thing, thrown together in a disorganized and purposeless manner (such as has been the prior, and ignorant, opinion), was set forth.

THE BAVLI'S MISHNAH-EXEGETICAL DISCOURSE: As to the Mishnah-exegetical compositions and composites — my initial probe is represented by these two items:

> *The Bavli's Primary Discourse. Mishnah Commentary, its Rhetorical Paradigms and their Theological Implications in the Talmud of Babylonia Tractate Moed Qatan.* Atlanta, 1992: Scholars Press for South Florida Studies in the History of Judaism.

> *The Principal Parts of the Bavli's Discourse: A Final Taxonomy. Mishnah-Commentary, Sources, Traditions, and Agglutinative Miscellanies.* Atlanta, 1992: Scholars Press for South Florida Studies in the History of Judaism.

Further, I have taken up the exegetical discourse of the Bavli in the following:

> *The Principal Parts of the Bavli's Discourse: A Final Taxonomy. Mishnah-Commentary, Sources, Traditions, and*

Introduction

> *Agglutinative Miscellanies.* Atlanta, 1992: Scholars Press for South Florida Studies in the History of Judaism.

THE BAVLI'S INFORMATIVE DISCOURSE IN MISHNAIC- AND EXTRA-MISHNAIC CONTEXT: The informative, mainly the other-than-Mishnah-exegetical, composites are set forth as to their classifications, with close attention to [1] the point of intersection between a composite at the context in the Talmud in which said composite is utilized; and [2] the cogency of the composite itself. I have classified the other-than-Mishnah-exegetical composites so as to see whether I could identify points of formal differentiation as well. This work is in the following:

> *The Initial Phases of the Talmud's Judaism.* Atlanta, 1995: Scholars Press for South Florida Studies in the History of Judaism. I. *Exegesis of Scripture.*
>
> *The Initial Phases of the Talmud's Judaism.* Atlanta, 1995: Scholars Press for South Florida Studies in the History of Judaism. II. *Exemplary Virtue.*
>
> *The Initial Phases of the Talmud's Judaism.* Atlanta, 1995: Scholars Press for South Florida Studies in the History of Judaism. III. *Social Ethics.*
>
> *The Initial Phases of the Talmud's Judaism.* Atlanta, 1995: Scholars Press for South Florida Studies in the History of Judaism. IV. *Theology.*

My prior probe of the same type of composites, *The Bavli's Massive Miscellanies. The Problem of Agglutinative Discourse in the Talmud of Babylonia.* Atlanta, 1992: Scholars Press for South Florida Studies in the History of Judaism, has now been replaced, since, over all, I found only a small proportion of miscellanies, but a high proportion of composites that were both formed and then utilized in a highly purposeful manner.

THE SYLLOGISTIC COMPOSITION AND COMPOSITE: My work on specific problems within the framework of syllogistic compositions and composites is contained in the following monographs:

> *The Bavli's One Statement. The Metapropositional Program of Babylonian Talmud Tractate Zebahim Chapters One and Five.* Atlanta, 1991: Scholars Press for South Florida Studies in the History of Judaism.
>
> *How the Bavli Shaped Rabbinic Discourse.* Atlanta, 1991: Scholars Press for South Florida Studies in the History of Judaism.
>
> *The Law Behind the Laws. The Bavli's Essential Discourse.* Atlanta, 1992: Scholars Press for South Florida Studies in the History of Judaism.
>
> *The Bavli's Intellectual Character. The Generative Problematic in Bavli Baba Qamma Chapter One and Bavli Shabbat*

> *Chapter One.* Atlanta, 1992: Scholars Press for South Florida Studies in the History of Judaism.
>
> *Decoding the Talmud's Exegetical Program: From Detail to Principle in the Bavli's Quest for Generalization. Tractate Shabbat.* Atlanta, 1992: Scholars Press for South Florida Studies in the History of Judaism.

In addition, I compare the syllogistic programs of the two Talmuds in the following work:

> *The Bavli's Unique Voice. A Systematic Comparison of the Talmud of Babylonia and the Talmud of the Land of Israel.* Volume Two. *Yerushalmi's, Bavli's, and Other Canonical Documents' Treatment of the Program of Mishnah-Tractate Sukkah Chapters One, Two, and Four Compared and Contrasted. A Reprise and Revision of* The Bavli and its Sources. Atlanta, 1993: Scholars Press for South Florida Studies in the History of Judaism.
>
> *The Bavli's Unique Voice. A Systematic Comparison of the Talmud of Babylonia and the Talmud of the Land of Israel.* Volume Three. *Bavli and Yerushalmi to Selected Mishnah-Chapters in the Division of Moed. Erubin Chapter One, and Moed Qatan Chapter Three.* Atlanta, 1993: Scholars Press for South Florida Studies in the History of Judaism.
>
> *The Bavli's Unique Voice. A Systematic Comparison of the Talmud of Babylonia and the Talmud of the Land of Israel.* Volume Four. *Bavli and Yerushalmi to Selected Mishnah-Chapters in the Division of Nashim. Gittin Chapter Five and Nedarim Chapter One. And Niddah Chapter One.* Atlanta, 1993: Scholars Press for South Florida Studies in the History of Judaism.
>
> *The Bavli's Unique Voice. A Systematic Comparison of the Talmud of Babylonia and the Talmud of the Land of Israel.* Volume Five. *Bavli and Yerushalmi to Selected Mishnah-Chapters in the Division of Neziqin. Baba Mesia Chapter One and Makkot Chapters One and Two.* Atlanta, 1993: Scholars Press for South Florida Studies in the History of Judaism.
>
> *The Bavli's Unique Voice. A Systematic Comparison of the Talmud of Babylonia and the Talmud of the Land of Israel.* Volume Six. *Bavli and Yerushalmi to a Miscellany of Mishnah-Chapters. Gittin Chapter One,*

Qiddushin Chapter Two, and Hagigah Chapter Three.
Atlanta, 1993: Scholars Press for South Florida Studies in the History of Judaism.

The Bavli's Unique Voice. Volume Seven. *What Is Unique about the Bavli in Context? An Answer Based on Inductive Description, Analysis, and Comparison.* Atlanta, 1993: Scholars Press for South Florida Studies in the History of Judaism.

For the syllogistic argument worked out in the Mishnah itself, I have spelled matters out in these works:

The Philosophical Mishnah. Volume I. *The Initial Probe.* Atlanta, 1989: Scholars Press for Brown Judaic Studies.

The Philosophical Mishnah. Volume II. *The Tractates' Agenda. From Abodah Zarah to Moed Qatan.* Atlanta, 1989: Scholars Press for Brown Judaic Studies.

The Philosophical Mishnah. Volume III. *The Tractates' Agenda. From Nazir to Zebahim.* Atlanta, 1989: Scholars Press for Brown Judaic Studies.

The Philosophical Mishnah. Volume IV. *The Repertoire.* Atlanta, 1989: Scholars Press for Brown Judaic Studies.

Judaism as Philosophy. The Method and Message of the Mishnah. Columbia, 1991: University of South Carolina Press.

For the syllogistic argument expressed in Midrash-compilations, I have provided an account in these works:

Uniting the Dual Torah: Sifra and the Problem of the Mishnah. Cambridge and New York, 1989: Cambridge University Press.

Judaism and Scripture: The Evidence of Leviticus Rabbah. Chicago, 1986: The University of Chicago Press. [Fresh translation of -' text and systematic analysis of problems of composition and redaction.] Jewish Book Club Selection, 1986.

For the moment these probes seem to me to suffice for an account of the syllogistic argument, though it is easy to see distinctive nuances and special types and forms that characterize the Bavli in particular.

THE BAVLI'S DIALECTICAL ARGUMENT: It is the *The Principal Parts of the Bavli's Discourse* that leads to the probe undertaken in these pages. For once I have shown, as I have, that Mishnah-commentary in the Talmud falls into two classes, the exegetical and the amplificatory, I have to undertake a sustained study of the second of the two, the syllogistic and the dialectical. This is necessary to find out what I can through systematic taxonomy of the forms and the types of discourse.

II. Defining the Dialectical Argument

Dialectical argument — the movement of thought through contentious challenge and passionate response, initiative and counter-ploy — characterizes the Talmud of Babylonia[1] in particular, and finds a limited place, also, in only two

---

[1] For further reading on dialectics in Rabbinic literature, see my comparison of the two Talmuds in the seven volumes of *The Bavli's Unique Voice. A Systematic Comparison of the Talmud of Babylonia and the Talmud of the Land of Israel*. Atlanta, 1993: Scholars Press for South Florida Studies in the History of Judaism. Of special relevance is Volume Seven. *What Is Unique about the Bavli in Context? An Answer Based on Inductive Description, Analysis, and Comparison*. Atlanta, 1993: Scholars Press for South Florida Studies in the History of Judaism. Note also my *Invitation to the Talmud. A Teaching Book*. Second edition, completely revised, San Francisco, 1984: Harper & Row; and, especially, the pair of theological works that identify dialectics as the key to the hermeneutics that forms the theological medium of the Judaism set forth in Rabbinic literature: *Judaism States its Theology: The Talmudic Re-Presentation* (Atlanta, 1993: Scholars Press), *and Judaism's Theological Voice: The Talmudic Melody* (Chicago, 1995: University of Chicago Press). I find it significant that in the index to Stemberger-Strack, there is no entry for "dialectic," and the topic addressed in its own terms, as a major category of the intellectual world of Judaism, does not occur elsewhere, e.g., in *Encyclopaedia Judaica*. Stemberger discusses "rabbinical hermeneutics," pp. 17-34, but this pertains to the "middot," or exegetical principles. See H. L. Strack and Günter Stemberger, *Introduction to the Talmud and Midrash* (Minneapolis, 1992: Fortress Press), translated by Markus Bockmuehl. General Introduction, pp. 1-118; on oral and written tradition, pp. 35-50. The other introductions in the English language that treat the Talmud ignore the dialectical argument altogether, as the following brief summary shows: John Bowker, *The Targums and Rabbinic Literature. An Introduction to Jewish Interpretations of Scripture* (Cambridge, 1969: Cambridge University Press), pp. 40-93: a brief introduction to rabbinic literature; halakah and haggadah, Midrash and Mishnah, pp. 40-48; the transmission of Oral 'Torah, pp. 48-53; Rabbinic literature in general, pp. [illegible line] Tanna debe Eliyyahu; etc.; Hyam Maccoby, *Early Rabbinic Writings* (Cambridge, 1988: Cambridge University Press). *Cambridge Commentaries on Writings of the Jewish and Christian World, 200 BC to AD 200*. Edited by P. R. Ackroyd, A. R. C. Leaney, and J. W. Packer. Volume III. pp. 1-30: "a corporate literary effort, in which a large number of experts...is engaged in a common enterprise: the clarification of Scripture and the application of it to everyday life;" the oral Torah, pp. 3-5; canonicity, pp. 5-7; the style of Rabbinic writings, pp. 8-9; Pharisees and Sadducees, pp. 9-11; Pharisees and rabbis, pp. 11-16; historical background; halakhah and haggadah, pp. 16-22; haggadah and Midrash, pp. 22-25; Mishnah and Midrash, pp. 25-29; the Targums, pp. 29-30. Note also under "miscellaneous works," Maccoby discusses Seder Olam and "the mystical literature," pp. 38-39; the main rabbinic figures, pp. 39-46; "the main ideas of the early Rabbinic literature," e.g., the nature of God, the covenant-people, the Land, the promise of a transformed world, pp. 46-48. General characterization (p. 48): "Thus the rabbinical literature, though wholly subordinating itself to Scripture, which it endeavors to 'search' and explicate, in fact contains great originality arising from the struggle to make biblical values actual in the times in which the rabbis found themselves." Maccoby treats in the rubric of Rabbinic literature the synagogue liturgy as well, pp. 204-217; "history," pp. 218-229, gives samples of Megillat Ta'anit and

Introduction xiii

other Rabbinic documents.² But, even though it occurs in only a few documents, and even there, in only a limited proportion,³ the dialectical, or moving, argument is important because, in the sustained conflict provoked by the testing of proposition in contention, argument turns fact into truth. Making a point forms of data important propositions. The exchanges of propositions and arguments, objects and ripostes, hold together, however protracted.

A preliminary and rather general definition of the mode of writing set forth as a dialectical argument is called for.⁴ The Rabbinic dialectical argument,

---

Seder 'Olam Rabbah; Shmuel Safrai, editor; Peter J. Tomson, Executive Editor, *The Literature of the Sages*. First Part: *Oral Tora, Halakha, Mishna, Tosefta, Talmud, External Tractates* In the series, *Compendia Rerum Iudaicarum ad Novum Testamentum*. Section Two. *The Literature of the Jewish People in the Period of the Second Temple and the Talmud* (Assen/ Maastricht and Philadelphia, 1987: Van Gorcum and Fortress Press): "Halakhah" (general characteristics, origins of the halakhah, the origin of independent halakhah, sources of the halakha of the sages, stages in the history of Tannaitic halakhah), in Safrai, *Literature of the Sages*, pp. 121-210; "Oral Tora" (the scope of oral Tora, origin and nature of oral Tora, ways of literary creation, oral Tora and rabbinic literature, terminology of oral Torah, central religious concepts developed in oral Tora), in Safrai, *Literature of the Sages*, pp. 35-120. This survey of the program of the several introductions leaves no doubt that none addresses the critical component of the Talmudic literature, the source of its dynamism and the kind of writing that is unique to the Talmud.

² The outstanding case is Sifra, which sets forth a vast repertoire of dialectical arguments, as shown in my *Sifra. An Analytical Translation*. Atlanta, 1988: Scholars Press for Brown Judaic Studies. I. *Introduction* and *Vayyiqra Dibura Denedabah* and *Vayiqqra Dibura Dehobah; Sifra. An Analytical Translation*. Atlanta, 1988: Scholars Press for Brown Judaic Studies. II. *Sav, Shemini, Tazria, Negaim, Mesora,* and *Zabim; Sifra. An Analytical Translation*. Atlanta, 1988: Scholars Press for Brown Judaic Studies. III. *Aharé Mot, Qedoshim, Emor, Behar,* and *Behuqotai; Uniting the Dual Torah: Sifra and the Problem of the Mishnah*. Cambridge and New York, 1989: Cambridge University Press; and *Sifra in Perspective: The Documentary Comparison of the Midrashim of Ancient Judaism* Atlanta, 1988: Scholars Press for Brown Judaic Studies. Besides Sifra and the Yerushalmi (to be dealt with in future studies of mine), however, I do not know any other Rabbinic compilation that sustainedly utilizes the dialectical argument. The Tosefta contains nothing of consequence. It does not appear in any Midrash-compilation (besides Sifra), e.g., Genesis Rabbah, Leviticus Rabbah, Pesiqta deRab Kahana, Mekhilta, or the late Midrash-compilations; or in The Fathers, or in The Fathers According to Rabbi Nathan. Future work will tell us whether the types and forms of the dialectical argument in the Bavli govern in the Yerushalmi as well. My impression is that they do not, but I have not yet done the hard work of finding out the facts.

³ That statement will require refinement when Yerushalmi and Sifra are subjected to the detailed academic commentary that I plan for them. But I cannot identify any other document that contains dialectical-analytical arguments, properly construed, though the rhetoric of dialectics occurs here and there.

⁴ Only when we have examined the repertoire of cases will a clear and reliable definition emerge.

— the protracted, sometimes meandering, always moving flow of contentious thought, — raises a question and answers it, then raises a question about the answer, and, having raised another question, it then gives an answer to that question, and it continues in the same fashion. So it moves hither and yon; it is always one, but it is never the same, and it flows across the surface of the document at hand. "Dialectical" means, moving, and a dialectical argument is a systematic exposition, through give and take, moving from point to point; the argument is the thing, since the dialectical argument strays from its original, precipitating point and therefore does not ordinarily undertake the demonstration of a fixed proposition. Rather, it moves along, developing an idea through questions and answers, sometimes implicit, but commonly explicit. The dialectical character derives not from the mere rhetorical device of question and answer, but from the pursuit of an argument, in a single line, but in many and diverse directions: not the form but the substantive continuity defines the criterion. And the power of the dialectical argument flows from that continuity. We find the source of continuity in the author's capacity to show connections through the momentum of rigorous analysis, on the one side, and free-ranging curiosity, on the other.

Those second and third and fourth turnings[5] differentiate a dialectical from a static argument, much as the bubbles tell the difference between still and sparkling wine. The always-sparkling dialectical argument is one principal means by which the Talmud or some other Rabbinic writing accomplishes its goal of showing the connections between this and that, ultimately demonstrating the unity of many "thises and thats." These efforts at describing the argument serve precisely as well as program notes to a piece of music: they tell us what we are going to hear; they cannot play the music. What "moves" therefore is the flow of argument and thought, and that is — by definition — from problem to problem. The movement is generated specifically by the raising of contrary questions and theses. What characterizes the dialectical argument in Rabbinic literature is its meandering, its moving hither and yon. It is not a direct or straight-line movement, e.g., the dialectical argument with which we are familiar in the modern West, thesis, antithesis, synthesis. It also does not correspond to any propositional or syllogistic argument, even though such arguments may take place in three or more steps, inclusive of counter-arguments.[6]

---

[5] And one of the tasks of form-analysis will be to identify the components of a moving argument and see whether patterns govern the secondary and tertiary articulation of the analytical inquiry and argument.

[6] The comparison of Talmudic dialectics to Platonic dialectics in the Dialogues has not taken place, so far as I know. I have in mind an elementary effort in that regard in the planned study, presently under way, which I call, *Why the Talmud Works*. There I argue that the power of the Talmud lies in its translation into concrete and everyday matters of the two most powerful intellectual components of Western civilization from its roots to our own time, science and philosophy, specifically, [1] Aristotle's principles of knowledge and [2] Socrates' (Plato's) principles of rational inquiry and argument. The modes of scientific inquiry of the one and of reasoned analysis of the other are translated by the Talmud into

Introduction   xv

    An important qualification is in order, and that concerns the exclusion from consideration of protracted presentations of data, in the form of questions and answers, that simply set forth a mass of well-crafted information, but no sustaining and continuous proposition. Such agglutinations of compositions and even composites prove informative; they collected information, much of it serving as on-site footnotes; but they follow no analytical problem, and they aim at little more than the provision of information. Readers who follow the survey with the text in hand and wish to know why I have not referred to a given item may appeal to the present criterion: an analytical program or a merely illuminating collection of information. Both will exhibit connections from one item to the next, but the dialectical-analytical argument will always pursue an abstract and generalizing question, and the agglutinative composite will ordinarily turn out to be a set of footnotes. To be sure, reasonable people can disagree in specific problems of classification. But the general distinction will stand.

    Let me give one example of discourse that moves forward through rhetorical questions and answers but does not demand classification as dialectical, in that the movement proves superficial, the basic argument static and narrowly propositional. In the following case we see how a dialectical form conceals a perfectly standard exchange of information, nothing more:

I.6   A.   Said R. Huna, "He who enters the synagogue and finds the community saying the Prayer, if he can begin and complete the Prayer before the leader of the community in his repetition, reaches the blessing, 'We acknowledge...,' should say the Prayer, and if not, he should not say the Prayer."

        B.   And R. Joshua b. Levi said, "If he can begin and complete the Prayer before the leader of the community in his repetition reaches the Sanctification, he should say the Prayer, and if not, he should not say the Prayer."

---

everyday terms, so that the experience of the everyday is turned into the academy for reasoned explanation of how things are: a book that turns concrete facts of the home and street into propositions of scientific interest and problems of philosophical inquiry. The Talmud turns the world into a class room, people into disciples, and culture into a concrete exemplification of abstract and reliable truth. Specifically: the Talmud is made up of two components, a philosophical law code, the Mishnah, which, in concrete ways, inculcates the principles of rational classification that Aristotle stated in abstract form; and a commentary to the Mishnah, called the Gemara (or simply, the Talmud proper), which, through the utilization of applied reason and practical logic, forms a moving ("dialectical") and analytical argument about the working of those principles in concrete cases. The importance of the moving argument lies in its open-endedness, so that successive generations found themselves not merely invited, but empowered, to join in the argument and so assume the disciplines of rational argument that the Talmud exemplifies. In both aspects, therefore, the document serves as the medium of inductive instruction into the principles of science and philosophy that define the structure of the well-ordered society.

xvi   *Talmudic Dialectics*

    C. *Concerning what principle do they differ?*
    D. *One master [A] takes the view that an individual may say the Sanctification-prayer [by himself].*
    E. *The other [B] takes the view that the individual may not say the Sanctification-prayer [by himself].*
    F. So too [D] did R. Ada bar Ahba say, "How do we know on the basis of Scripture that an individual [praying by himself] does not say the Sanctification-prayer? As it is said, 'And I shall be sanctified among the children of Israel' (Lev. 22:32). Every matter involving sanctification may be conducted among no fewer than ten men."
    G. *How does the besought proof derive from the cited verse?*
    H. *It accords with that which Rabbinai, brother of R. Hiyya bar Abba, taught on Tannaite authority,* "An analogy is drawn on the use of the word 'among.'
    I. "Here it is written, 'And I shall be sanctified among the children of Israel' (Lev. 22:32), and elsewhere it is written, 'Separate yourselves from among this congregation' (Num. 16:21). Just as, in the latter instance, 'among' involves ten men, so here ten are required."
    J. *Both authorities concur, in the end, that one does not interrupt [the Prayer. If a person has begun to recite the Prayer, when the congregation comes to recite the Sanctification, the person does not interrupt his prayer to recite the Sanctification with the congregation.]*

What we have is little more than a first-rate exposition of the point at issue in a dispute, followed by a secondary datum, which shows how a proposition emerges from a proof-text. Merely presenting a dispute in a fair and balanced way, utilizing the form of question and answer, does not lead us into the realm controlled by authentic dialectics. We cannot confuse the deft presentation of conflicting propositions, along with required information, with the rich intellectual movement, hither and yon, that dialectics involves.

    This distinction, between the rhetoric of dialectics and the logic thereof, forms so central a point of differentiation in all that follows as to justify introducing a second example of what I class as other than an analytical-dialectical argument. It is a case in which the formal utilization of questions and answers masks a quite static argument, in which set-piece positions are intertwined, compared and contrasted, without a trace of movement from one point to some other:

SERVING MISHNAH-TRACTATE ERUBIN 6:3-4

VI.2   A.   Abbayye asked Rabbah, "Five tenants lived in a single courtyard, and one of them forgot and did not participate in the fusion meal —when he renounces his rights of access, does he have to

Introduction xvii

- renounce it in favor of each and every tenant or does he not have to do so?"
- B. He said to him, "He has to renounce his right in favor of each and every tenant."
- C. *An objection was raised:* One party who did not participate in the fusion meal abrogates his right in favor of one party who did participate in the fusion meal; two persons who participated in the fusion meal assign their right to one who didn't, and two who didn't participate in the fusion meal abrogate their right to two who did participate in the fusion meal or to one who did not participate in the fusion meal. But one who participated in the fusion meal doesn't abrogate his right to one who didn't participate, and two who participated in the fusion meal do not abrogate their right in favor of two who didn't participate, and two who didn't participate in the fusion meal don't abrogate their right in favor of two who didn't participate in the fusion meal. *Now the Tannaite formulation in any event states at the outset,* one party who did not participate in the fusion meal abrogates his right in favor of one party who did participate in the fusion meal. *Now how are we to imagine the case? If there is no other with him, then with whom might he have joined in the fusion meal? So it must follow, there must have been another tenant alongside, and yet it is stated,* one party who did participate in the fusion meal! [Slotki: How could Rabbah maintain that renunciation must be made in favor of each and every tenant individually?]
- D. And Rabbah?
- E. *Here with what situation do we deal? It is a case in which there was a tenant with whom the fusion meal was made, but who died* [Slotki: by the time the third party presented his share; so there were only two tenants in the courtyard, and one may renounce in favor of the other].
- F. *Well, then, what about what follows:* But one who participated in the fusion meal doesn't abrogate his right to one who didn't participate? *Now, if he had been there but died, why shouldn't it be permitted* [for the survivor to renounce his share (Slotki)]? *So it's obvious that the tenant with whom the meal was prepared was still around, and, since the final clause takes for granted that he was still around, the initial clause also deals with a case in which he was still around [and Rabbah's got a problem]!*
- G. *What makes you see things that way? The one clause deals with its case, the other deals with its situation. You may know that*

that is the case, for the concluding part of the opening formulation says, two who didn't participate in the fusion meal abrogate their right to two who did participate in the fusion meal. *So to two they may do so, but not to one.*

H. And Abbayye?

I. *He may say, what is the meaning of "to two"? It is "to one of the two."*

J. *If so, why instead of "two" wasn't it said, "To one who joined in the fictive fusion meal or to one who did not"* [Slotki: since one tenant cannot join in a fictive meal with himself, it would then be obvious that the sense was, to one of two]?

K. *Well, that's a legitimate problem.*

L. ...one party who did not participate in the fusion meal abrogates his right in favor of one party who did participate in the fusion meal –

M. *in Abbayye's view, this speaks of a case in which the other tenant* [who joined in the fiction meal with the one mentioned] *was still alive, and so we are informed that it is not necessary to renounce one's rights in favor of each and every tenant.*

N. *In Rabbah's view, it is a case in which he was around but then died, and so we are informed that no precautionary decree is enacted to deal with the possibility that someone may yet be around [and yet the same procedure might be followed].*

O. ...two parsons who participated in the fusion meal assign their right to one who didn't –

P. *So that's pretty obvious.*

Q. *What might you otherwise have imagined? That since he did not participate in the fusion meal, an extrajudicial penalty is to be imposed on him? So we are informed that that is not the case.*

R. ...and two who didn't participate in the fusion meal abrogate their right to two who did participate in the fusion meal –

S. *In Rabbah's view, the Tannaite formulation of the concluding clause was meant to clarify the sense of the opening clause. To Abbayye, it was necessary to include the clause concerning two who didn't participate in the fusion meal. For it might have entered your mind that we should make a precautionary decree, to cover the possibility that they may come and renounce in their favor [which is forbidden[, but so we are informed that that is not the case.*

T. ...or to one who did not participate in the fusion meal –

U. *What do I need this item for?*

V. *What might you otherwise have supposed? That the rule applies to a case in which some of the tenants participated in the fusion meal and some didn't, but in a case in which all of them didn't, we impose a penalty, so that the rule of the fusion meal should not be forgotten? So we are informed that that is not so.*

W. But one who participated in the fusion meal doesn't abrogate his right to one who didn't participate –

X. *From Abbayye's perspective, the Tannaite formulation of the concluding clause serves to explain the sense of the opening one. From Rabbah's perspective, since the opening clause was set forth, the closing clause was put in to match it.*

Y. ...and two who participated in the fusion meal do not abrogate their right in favor of two who didn't participate –

Z. *So for what do I need to be told this again?*

AA. *It was necessary to cover the case in which one of them renounced his share in favor of the other [of those who didn't share in the fusion meal]. What might you have supposed? That the latter should then have the right to use the courtyard? So we are informed that that is not the case, since at the time the former renounced his share, he had no right to use the courtyard.*

BB. ...and two who didn't participate in the fusion meal don't abrogate their right in favor of two who didn't participate in the fusion meal –

CC. *So for what do I need to be told this again?*

DD. *It was necessary to cover even the case in which they said to him, "Acquire our share on the stipulation that you transfer them."*

Here is a superb exercise in fair and equitable presentation of two positions; but the positions stand still and the argument leads no where; without motion, the dialectic or movement proves merely formal but in no way substantive, the basic point at issue being made manifest but not made to move. Time and again, a closer look at what appears to be a moving argument shows us that all we have is a rhetorical device to secure the proper and orderly balance between two contradictory positions. We shall return to this point once more, to underscore the contrast between rhetorical and logical dialectics.

The dialectical argument opens the possibility of reaching out from one thing to something else, not because people have lost sight of their starting point or their goal in the end, but because they want to encompass, in the analytical argument as it gets underway, as broad and comprehensive a range of cases and rules as they possibly can. The movement from point to point in reference to a single point that accurately describes the dialectical argument reaches upward toward a goal of proximate abstraction, leaving behind the specificities of not only cases but laws,

xx   *Talmudic Dialectics*

carrying us upward to the law that governs many cases, the premises that undergird many rules, and still higher to the principles that infuse diverse premises; then the principles that generate other, unrelated premises, which, in turn, come to expression in other, still-less intersecting cases. The meandering course of argument comes to an end when we have shown how things cohere. Or, sometimes, the argument simply stops, leaving open possibilities for coming generations to take up

III. AN EXAMPLE OF A DIALECTICAL ARGUMENT

The passage that we consider occurs at the Babylonian Talmud Baba Mesia 5B-6A, which is to say, Talmud to Mishnah Baba Mesia. 1:1-2. Our interest is in the twists and turns of the argument and what is at stake in the formation of a continuous and unfolding composition:

[5B] **IV.1. A. This one takes an oath that he possesses no less a share of it than half, [and that one takes an oath that he possesses no less a share of it than half, and they divide it up]:**

The rule of the Mishnah, which is cited at the head of the sustained discussion, concerns the case of two persons who find a garment. We settle their conflicting claim by requiring each to take an oath that he or she owns title to no less than half of the garment, and then we split the garment between them.

Our first question is one of text-criticism: analysis of the Mishnah-paragraph's word choice. We say that the oath concerns the portion that the claimant alleges he possesses. But the oath really affects the portion that he does not have in hand at all:

B. *Is it concerning the portion that he claims he possesses that he takes the oath, or concerning the portion that he does not claim to possess?* [Daiches: "The implication is that the terms of the oath are ambiguous. By swearing that his share in it is not 'less than half,' the claimant might mean that it is not even a third or a fourth (which is 'less than half'), and the negative way of putting it would justify such an interpretation. He could therefore take this oath even if he knew that he had no share in the garment at all, while he would be swearing falsely if he really had a share in the garment that is less than half, however small that share might be].

C. *Said R. Huna, "It is that he says, 'By an oath! I possess in it a portion, and I possess in it a portion that is no more than half a share of it.'"* [The claimant swears that his share is at least half (Daiches)].

Having asked and answered the question, we now find ourselves in an extension of the argument; the principal trait of the dialectical argument is now before us: [1] but [2] maybe the contrary is the case, so [3] what about — that is, the setting aside of a proposition in favor of its opposite. Here we come to the definitive trait of the

Introduction xxi

dialectic argument: its insistence on challenging every proposal with the claim, "maybe it's the opposite?" This pestering question forces us back upon our sense of self-evidence; it makes us consider the contrary of each position we propose to set forth. It makes thought happen. True, the Talmud's voice's "but" — the whole of the dialectic in one word! — presents a formidable nuisance. But so does all criticism, and only the mature mind will welcome criticism. Dialectics is not for children, politicians, propagandists, or egoists. Genuine curiosity about the truth shown by rigorous logic forms the counterpart to musical virtuosity. So the objection proceeds:

C. *Then let him say, "By an oath! The whole of it is mine!"*

Why claim half when the alleged finder may as well demand the whole cloak?

D. *But are we going to give him the whole of it?* [Obviously not, there is another claimant, also taking an oath.]

The question contradicts the facts of the case: two parties claim the cloak, so the outcome can never be that one will get the whole thing.

E. *Then let him say, "By an oath! Half of it is mine!"*

Then — by the same reasoning — why claim "no less than half," rather than simply, half.

F. *That would damage his own claim* [which was that he owned the whole of the cloak, not only half of it].

The claimant does claim the whole cloak, so the proposed language does not serve to replicate his actual claim. That accounts for the language that is specified.

G. *But here too is it not the fact that, in the oath that he is taking, he impairs his own claim?* [After all, he here makes explicit the fact that he owns at least half of it. What happened to the other half?]

The solution merely compounds the problem.

H. *[Not at all.] For he has said,* "The whole of it is mine!" [And, he further proceeds,] "And as to your contrary view, By an oath, I do have a share in it, and that share is no less than half!"

We solve the problem by positing a different solution from the one we suggested at the outset. Why not start where we have concluded? Because if we had done so, we should have ignored a variety of intervening considerations and so should have expounded less than the entire range of possibilities. The power of the dialectical argument now is clear: it forces us to address not the problem and the solution alone, but the problem and the various ways by which a solution may be reached; then, when we do come to a final solution to the question at hand, we have reviewed all of the possibilities. We have seen how everything flows together, nothing is left unattended.

The dialectical argument in the Talmud and in other Rabbinic writings therefore undertakes a different task from the philosophical counterpart. What we have here is not a set-piece of two positions, with an analysis of each, such as the staid philosophical dialogue exposes with such elegance; it is, rather, an analytical argument, explaining why this, not that, then why not that but rather this; and onward to the other thing and the thing beyond that — a linear argument in constant motion. When we speak of a moving argument, this is what we mean: what is not static and merely expository, but what is dynamic and always contentious. It is not an endless argument, an argument for the sake of arguing, or evidence that important to the Talmud and other writings that use the dialectics as a principal mode of dynamic argument is process but not position. To the contrary, the passage is resolved with a decisive conclusion, not permitted to run on.

But the dialectical composition proceeds — continuous and coherent from point to point, even as it zigs and zags. We proceed to the second cogent proposition in the analysis of the cited Mishnah-passage, which asks a fresh question: why an oath at all?

2.   A.   [It is envisioned that each party is holding on to a corner of the cloak, so the question is raised:] Now, since this one is possessed of the cloak and standing right there, and that one is possessed of the cloak and is standing right there, why in the world do I require this oath?

Until now we have assumed as fact the premise of the Mishnah's rule, which is that an oath is there to be taken. But why assume so? Surely each party now has what he is going to get. So what defines the point and effect of the oath?

        B.   Said R. Yohanan, "This oath [to which our Mishnah-passage refers] happens to be an ordinance imposed only by rabbis,

        C.   "so that people should not go around grabbing the cloaks of other people and saying, 'It's mine!'" [But, as a matter of fact, the oath that is imposed in our Mishnah-passage is not legitimate by the law of the Torah. It is an act taken by sages to maintain the social order.]

We do not administer oaths to liars; we do not impose an oath in a case in which we may end up one of the claimants would take an oath for something he knew to be untrue, since one party really does own the cloak, the other really has grabbed it. The proposition solves the problem — but hardly is going to settle the question. On the contrary, Yohanan raises more problems than he solves. So we ask how we can agree to an oath in this case at all?

        D.   *But why then not advance the following argument: since such a one is suspect as to fraud in a property claim, he also should be suspect as to fraud in oath-taking?*

Yohanan places himself into the position of believing in respect to the oath what we will not believe in respect to the claim on the cloak, for, after all, one of the parties before us must be lying! Why sustain such a contradiction: gullible and suspicious at one and the same time?

        E.   *In point of fact, we do not advance the argument: since such a one is suspect as to fraud in a property claim, he also should be*

Introduction   *xxiii*

> *suspect as to fraud in oath-taking, for if you do not concede that fact, then how is it possible that the All-Merciful has ruled,* "One who has conceded part of a claim against himself must take an oath as to the remainder of what is subject to claim"?

If someone claims that another party holds property belonging to him or her, and the one to whom the bailment has been handed over for safe-keeping, called the bailee, concedes part of the claim, the bailee must then take an oath in respect to the rest of the claimed property, that is, the part that the bailee maintains does not belong to the claimant at all. So the law itself — the Torah, in fact — has sustained the same contradiction. That fine solution, of course, is going to be challenged:

    F.   *Why not simply maintain, since such a one is suspect as to fraud in a property claim, he also should be suspect as to fraud in oath-taking?*

    G.   *In that other case, [the reason for the denial of part of the claim and the admission of part is not the intent to commit fraud, but rather,] the defendant is just trying to put off the claim for a spell.*

We could stop at this point without losing a single important point of interest; everything is before us. One of the striking traits of the large-scale dialectical composition is its composite-character. Starting at the beginning, without any loss of meaning or sense, we may well stop at the end of any given paragraph of thought. But the dialectics insists on moving forward, exploring, pursuing, insisting; and were we to remove a paragraph in the middle of a dialectical composite, then all that follows would become incomprehensible. That is a mark of the dialectical argument: sustained, continuous, and coherent — yet perpetually in control and capable of resolving matters at any single point.

Now, having fully exposed the topic, its problem, and its principles, we take a tangent indicated by the character of the principle before us: when a person will or will not lie or take a false oath. We have a theory on the matter; what we now do is expound the theory, with special reference to the formulation of that theory in explicit terms by a named authority:

    H.   This concurs with the position of Rabbah. [For Rabbah has said, "On what account has the Torah imposed the requirement of an oath on one who confesses to only part of a claim against him? It is by reason of the presumption that a person will not insolently deny the truth about the whole of a loan in the very presence of the creditor and so entirely deny the debt. He will admit to part of the debt and deny part of it. Hence we invoke an oath in a case in which one does so, to coax out the truth of the matter."]

    I.   For you may know, [in support of the foregoing], that R. Idi bar Abin said R. Hisda [said]: "He who [falsely] denies owing money on a loan nonetheless is suitable to give testimony, but he who denies that he holds a bailment for another party cannot give testimony."

The proposition is now fully exposed. A named authority is introduced, who will concur in the proposed theoretical distinction. He sets forth an extra-logical consideration, which of course the law always will welcome: the rational goal of finding the truth overrides the technicalities of the law governing the oath

Predictably, we cannot allow matters to stand without challenge, and the challenge comes at a fundamental level, with the predictable give-and-take to follow:

J. But what about that which R. Ammi bar. Hama repeated on Tannaite authority: "[If they are to be subjected to an oath,] four sorts of bailees have to have denied part of the bailment and conceded part of the bailment, namely, the unpaid bailee, the borrower, the paid bailee, and the one who rents."

K. *Why not simply maintain, since such a one is suspect as to fraud in a property claim, he also should be suspect as to fraud in oath-taking?*

L. *In that case as well, [the reason for the denial of part of the claim and the admission of part is not the intent to commit fraud, but rather,] the defendant is just trying to put off the claim for a spell.*

M. *He reasons as follows: "I'm going to find the thief and arrest him." Or: "I'll find [the beast] in the field and return it to the owner."*

Once more, "if that is the case" provokes yet another analysis; we introduce a different reading of the basic case before us, another reason that we should not impose an oath:

N. *If that is the case, then why should one who denies holding a bailment ever be unsuitable to give testimony? Why don't we just maintain that the defendant is just trying to put off the claim for a spell. He reasons as follows: "I'm going to look for the thing and find it."*

O. *When in point of fact we do rule,* He who denies holding a bailment is unfit to give testimony, *it is in a case in which witnesses come and give testimony against him that at that very moment, the bailment is located in the bailee's domain, and he fully is informed of that fact, or, alternatively, he has the object in his possession at that very moment.*

The solution to the problem at hand also provides the starting point for yet another step in the unfolding exposition. Huna has given us a different resolution of matters. That accounts for No. 3, and No. 4 is also predictable:

3. A. *But as to that which R. Huna has said [when we have a bailee who offers to pay compensation for a lost bailment rather than*

Introduction xxv

        swear it has been lost, since he wishes to appropriate the article by paying for it, (Daiches)], "They impose upon him the oath that the bailment is not in his possession at all,"

    B. *why not in that case invoke the principle, since such a one is suspect as to fraud in a property claim, he also should be suspect as to fraud in oath-taking?*

    C. *In that case also, he may rule in his own behalf, I'll give him the money.*

4. A. Said R. Aha of Difti to Rabina, "But then the man clearly transgresses the negative commandment: 'You shall not covet.'"

    B. "You shall not covet" *is generally understood by people to pertain to something for which one is not ready to pay.*

Yet another authority's position now is invoked, and it draws us back to our starting point: the issue of why we think an oath is suitable in a case in which we ought to assume lying is going on; so we are returned to our starting point, but via a circuitous route:

5. A. [6A] *But as to that which R. Nahman said,* "They impose upon him [who denies the whole of a claim] an oath of inducement," *why not in that case invoke the principle, since such a one is suspect as to fraud in a property claim, he also should be suspect as to fraud in oath-taking?*

    B. *And furthermore, there is that which R. Hiyya taught on Tannaite authority*: "Both parties [employee, supposed to have been paid out of an account set up by the employer at a local store, and store-keeper] take an oath and collect what each claims from the employer," *why not in that case invoke the principle, since such a one is suspect as to fraud in a property claim, he also should be suspect as to fraud in oath-taking?*

    C. *And furthermore, there is that which R. Sheshet said,* "We impose upon an unpaid bailee [who claims that the animal has been lost] three distinct oaths: first, an oath that I have not deliberately caused the loss, that I did not put a hand on it, and that it is not in my domain at all," *why not in that case invoke the principle, since such a one is suspect as to fraud in a property claim, he also should be suspect as to fraud in oath-taking?*

We now settle the matter:

    D. *It must follow that we do not invoke the principle at all, since such a one is suspect as to fraud in a property claim, he also should be suspect as to fraud in oath-taking?*

What is interesting is why walk so far to end up where we started: do we invoke said principle? No, we do not. What we have accomplished on our wanderings is a survey of opinion on a theme, to be sure, but opinion that intersects at our particular problem as well. The moving argument serves to carry us hither and yon; its power is to demonstrate that all considerations are raised, all challenges met, all possibilities explored. This is not merely a set-piece argument, where we have proposition, evidence, analysis, conclusion; it is a different sort of thinking altogether, purposive and coherent, but also comprehensive and compelling for its admission of possibilities and attention to alternatives. What we shall see, time and again, is that the dialectical argument is the Talmud's medium of generalization from case to principle and extension from principle to new cases.

IV. AN EXAMPLE OF AN ARGUMENT OF AN OTHER-THAN-DIALECTICAL CHARACTER

The survey that follows excludes merely-rhetorical dialectics, that is, arguments framed in terms of sequences of questions and answers, since, in my judgment, such compositions and composites set forth exchanges of information and principle, but do not establish that wide-ranging analytical inquiry that encompasses within an extending frontier broad areas of law. Another rhetorical argument that serves only to set forth information in a balanced and proportionate manner takes an important role in the Talmud but in no way constitutes that logical marvel of dialectics that the Talmud occasionally creates. Readers who follow the Talmud along with my survey will note that I have not included numerous examples of exquisite exposure of balanced opposites. Two or more positions will be set forth, amplified, analyzed, without the intrusion of that logic of dialectics that requires us to move beyond the limits of the case. Here is a single example, and an especially lucid and appealing one, of how the Talmud's sense of equity and classicism comes to expression in the orderly representation of conflicting views:

I.1   A.   [Mishnah-tractate Erubin 4:7A: **He who was coming along the way and darkness overtook him, and who knew about a certain tree or a fence and said, "My place of residence for the Sabbath will be under it," has said nothing at all:**] *What is the meaning of* **he has said nothing at all**?

       B.   Said Rab, "**He has said nothing at all** in any way, shape, or form, *so that he may not even continue to the space under the tree.*" [Slotki: He must not move from his position until after the Sabbath, since he has acquired no place for his Sabbath rest, from which he could be entitled to walk within a permitted Sabbath limit; his right to the place on which he stood when the Sabbath came into effect has been expressly renounced by his choosing another one, and the area under the tree couldn't be acquired by him, since he had not specified which particular four cubits of that space he chose.]

       C.   And Samuel said, "**He has said nothing at all** in respect to going on to his home. *But he may go to the space under the tree.*"

Introduction

D. The space under the tree is treated as in the case of an ass driver and a camel driver [so the man can't move in any direction for very far]. If he wanted to measure from the north side of the tree, they tell him to begin measuring from the south side. [Slotki: In appointing the tree as his Sabbath base, he didn't specify which particular four cubits of space under the tree he wanted to acquire, so any four cubits of space within the circumference of the tree and the branches may be assumed to be the appointed spot. In measuring the distances, therefore, a course must be adopted that under all circumstances could not possibly lead to an infringement of any of the restrictions involved. If the diameter of the circumference of the tree and its branches measured twenty cubits, and the distance from the northern point to the man's house was exactly two thousand cubits, the measuring must not begin from that point, but from the southern point of the diameter, which is two thousand and twenty cubits distant from the house. And since it is forbidden to proceed beyond two thousand cubits, the man's Sabbath limit would terminate at a point twenty cubits away from his house, which, in consequence, he would not be able to enter during the Sabbath.] So, too, if he came to measure from the south side of the tree, they tell him to measure from the north side.

E. [50A] Said Rabbah, "What is the operative consideration behind the ruling of Rab? Because the man didn't specify the exact spot."

F. There are those who say: Said Rabbah, "What is the operative consideration behind the ruling of Rab? Because he takes the view, in any case in which if a statement would not be valid if one statement followed another, then even if the statements are made simultaneously, they are also null." [Freedman, Nedarim 69B: Whatever is not valid consecutively is not valid even simultaneously.] [Slotki: The man's appointment of the entire area under the tree, including both the northern and southern sides, is therefore null; an area of four cubits on the northern side of the tree cannot be acquired after such an area had been acquired on the southern side or vice versa.]

G. *What's the difference between these two explanations?*

H. *At issue between the two explanations would be a case in which someone said, "Let me acquire an area of four cubits out of eight." One who has said that the operative consideration is that the man didn't specify the exact spot will hold that here he didn't specify the spot. And one who said that the operative consideration is, In any case in which if a statement would not be valid if one statement followed another, then even if the statements are made simultaneously, they are also null, lo, such a statement is valid if an area of four cubits has been specified, for here the man said he wanted to acquire no more than four cubits.*

I.2 A. *Reverting to the body of the foregoing:* Said Rabbah, "In any case in which if a statement would not be valid if one statement followed another, then even if the statements are made simultaneously, they are also null" –

B. Objected Abbayye to Rabbah, "**He who gave too much tithe —while the produce is properly tithed, the tithe is ruined [since part of what is included within the tithe is in fact not tithe at all]** [T. Dem. 8:13A-B]. *But why should this be the case? Why not say, 'What cannot be done consecutively also cannot be done simultaneously'?*

C. *He said to him,* "That case is exceptional, because, as to tithes, it is possible in the case of half-grain to do it, for if one said, 'Let half of each grain be sanctified,' it is indeed sanctified; but as to tithes of cattle, it is impossible to do it by halves, and it is also impossible to do it consecutively; and yet Rabbah has said, 'If two animals came out of the corral simultaneously as tenth, and he called them tenth, the tenth and the eleventh are treated as a group together [the tenth is actually tithe, the eleventh is a peace-offering].'" [If he had declared them so in sequence, the second would be invalid; why is the simultaneous declaration valid? (Freedman)].

D. *The tithing of cattle is exceptional, since it is valid even when done in error, for we have learned in the Mishnah:* **[If] he called the ninth, tenth, and the tenth, ninth, and the eleventh, tenth, all three are sanctified [M. Bekh. 9:8D].**

E. *Lo, what about the matter of the thanksgiving-offering, which cannot be designated in error nor consecutively [that is, the thanksgiving-offering was accompanied by forty loaves that were sanctified; if the animal was sacrificed to sanctify certain loaves, which weren't the intended ones, they are not sanctified; if after forty loaves are sanctified, another forty are declared holy, the declaration is null (Freedman)], and yet it has been stated:* A thank-offering that one slaughtered in connection with eighty loaves of bread –

F. Hezekiah said, "Forty of the loaves among the eighty have been sanctified."

G. R. Yohanan said, "Forty of the loaves among the eighty have not been sanctified."

H. *Hasn't it been stated in that connection: Said Zira, "All concur that if the officiating priest said, 'Let forty out of the eighty be sanctified,' they are sanctified. 'The forty shall not be sanctified unless all eighty are sanctified,' they are not sanctified. Where they differ is only when the matter has not been made explicit. One authority takes the view that the unstated intention of the donor in presenting eighty loaves was to make sure that at least forty would be found suitable,* **[50B]** *and the other authority maintains that the intention was merely to provide a very large offering [so all eighty have to be valid]"?*

I.3 A. [With reference to the statement, said Rab, "**He has said nothing at all** in any way, shape, or form, *so that he may not even continue to the space under the tree,*"] said Abbayye, "That has been taught only with regard to a tree with a diameter underneath of no less than twelve cubits [Slotki: the length comprising no less than three sections of four cubits each, so it is impossible to ascertain whether it was the middle section or one of the outer ones that the man wanted to acquire as his Sabbath base]. But in the case of a tree with a diameter underneath of less than twelve cubits, at least part of the man's house is well marked out." [Slotki: If the diameter was only eleven cubits, each four cubits at either of the extremities must inevitably overlap half a cubit with the middle four cubits; if the man chose the middle section, all of his Sabbath base is obviously well defined; but even if he intended one of the outer sections to be his Sabbath base, each of them is at least partially defined in that part where it overlaps with the middle sections; his base may therefore be regarded as located in full or in part in that section.]

B. *Objected R. Huna b. R. Joshua, "But how do you know that he ever intended to utilize the middle four cubits? Maybe he intended to utilize either the four cubits on one side or the four on the other!"*

C. Rather, said R. Huna b. R. Joshua, "That has been taught only with regard to a tree with a diameter underneath of no less than eight cubits [where we don't know what section he intended], but if it has seven cubits underneath, then in such a situation at least part of the man's house is well marked out."

I.4 A. [With regard to the statements above, said Rab, "**He has said nothing at all in any way, shape, or form, so that he** *may not even continue to the space under the tree.*" And Samuel said, "**He has said nothing at all** in respect to going on to his home. *But he may go to the space under the tree,*"] *it has been taught on Tannaite authority in accord with the position of Rab, and it has been taught on Tannaite authority in accord with the position of Samuel.*

B. *It has been taught on Tannaite authority in accord with the position of Rab:* He who was going along the way and it got dark and he knew a certain tree or fence and said, "My place of Sabbath rest will be under it," has said nothing at all. But if he said, "My place of Sabbath rest will be in such and such a place," he may continue the trip till he gets to that place. Once he has gotten to that place, he may walk throughout the place and outside of it for two thousand cubits. Under what circumstances? If it is a place that is well defined, for instance, a mount ten handbreadths high and from four cubits to two bet seahs in area, or a valley ten handbreadths deep and from four cubits to two bet seahs in area; but if it was a place that was not well defined, he is not allowed to move for more than four cubits. If there were two people traveling together, and one of them knows of a well-delineated spot and the other doesn't, the latter assigns to the former his right to choose a place for Sabbath rest, and the other says, "My place of Sabbath rest will be in such and such a place." Under what circumstances? Where the man indicated the four cubits he selected by a clearly defined landscape marker. But if he did not define the four cubits by a clearly defined landscape marker, he may not move from his place.

C. *May we then say that this is a refutation of the position of Samuel?*

D. *Samuel may say to you, "Here with what case do we deal? It would be one in which from the place where the man stood to the root of a tree were two thousand four cubits, so that if you set him up on the far side of the tree, he would be standing outside of his permitted limit; so, if he indicated that the spot was four cubits on the hither side of the tree, he may go there, but otherwise, not."*

E. *And it has been taught on Tannaite authority in accord with the position of Samuel:* If someone erred and made fusion meals in two opposite directions in the belief that it is permitted to set out fusion meals in two opposite directions, or if he said to his servants, "Go and set out a fusion meal for me," and one of them set out a fusion meal to the north and the other to the south, he may go northward as far as the limit of the southern fusion meal, and southward up to the limit of the northern fusion meal. But if they measured each limit exactly, he may not stir from the place.

F. *May we then say that this is a refutation of the position of Rab?*

G. Well, not exactly: Rab has the standing of a Tannaite authority and so has every right to differ from this Tannaite formulation.

This argument stands still, a static presentation of beautifully articulated and amplified exchanges of principles. The argument utilizes the rhetoric of question and answer but does not move. In Hegelian terms, we have a thesis, an antithesis, but no synthesis, hence, no dialectics of logic, merely of rhetoric. The balance between B and its articulation against C, then the introduction in Rabbah's name, of the consideration underlying Rab's position, simply deepens the presentation, but does not expand it in any way. The same static trait characterizes G-H. I:2 forms nothing more than a footnote. That is shown by I:3, which simply reverts to our starting point; I:4 follows suit. And the appendix at I:4B draws us back to the contrary position of Samuel. So, as I said, what we have is balanced, orderly, fair — but in the end merely an exercise in paraphrase, recapitulation, and amplification. And these valued modes of clarification of conflicting principles stand still and find no resolution, such as dialectics effects. Within this classification of rhetorical dialectics falls the bulk of the cases that are not reproduced here and that play no role in my account of matters.

The Talmud presents a vast quantity of exquisitely balanced expositions of various positions, that is, essentially syllogistic arguments, in which two contrary propositions are argued. These exhibit a pure classicism, according to each party to a proposition a balanced and proportionate share of the whole, with both sides given equal opportunity to answer one another. The result is the construction, in words, of a discourse that compares in balance and order and exact proportion to the Parthenon. Here is yet another instance of that perfection of presentation that may readily be confused with a dialectical argument, but that is not, in fact, dialectical at all.

I.1 A. *It has been stated:*
    B. He who enters into the rite of removing the shoe with a pregnant woman who then miscarried —
    C. R. Yohanan said, "She does not perform the rite of removing the shoe [with the brothers]."
    D. And R. Simeon b. Laqish said, "She does perform the rite of removing the shoe [with the brothers]."
        E. R. Yohanan said, "She does not perform the rite of removing the shoe [with the brothers]:" the rite of removing the shoe performed by a pregnant woman who has miscarried is classified as a valid rite of removing the shoe, and the act of sexual relations of a pregnant woman is classified as a valid act of sexual relations.
        F. And R. Simeon b. Laqish said, "She does perform the rite of removing the shoe [with the brothers]:" the rite of

removing the shoe performed by a pregnant woman who has miscarried is not classified as a valid rite of removing the shoe, and the act of sexual relations of a pregnant woman is not classified as a valid act of sexual relations.

G. *What is at stake in this dispute?*

H. *If you wish, I shall say that at issue is the interpretation of a verse of Scripture, and if you wish, I shall say that at issue is a matter of reasoning.*

I. *If you wish, I shall say that at issue is the interpretation of a verse of Scripture: "R. Yohanan takes the view that the language, "And have no child" is what Scripture has said, and lo, this one has no child. And R. Simeon b. Laqish maintains that the language, "And have no child" implies, "look into the matter" [and find out whether there has been any kind of offspring; here the miscarriage then qualifies].*

J. *and if you wish, I shall say that at issue is a matter of reasoning. R. Yohanan takes the view that, if Elijah should come and say that the woman is going to miscarry, would she not in any event have been subject to the rite of removing the shoe or levirate marriage? [She most certainly would.] So here too, it is a fact that is subject to retrospective clarification. And R. Simeon b. Laqish maintains that we do not invoke the principle that a fact is subject to retrospective clarification [but we settle matters as they are at the moment of decision].*

K. *R. Yohanan objected to R. Simeon b. Laqish, "* **[If] the offspring is not timely, he is prohibited from marrying her relatives, and she is prohibited from marrying his relatives, and he has invalidated her from marrying into the priesthood.** *Now from my perspective, in holding that* the rite of removing the shoe performed by a pregnant woman who has miscarried is classified as a valid rite of removing the shoe, and the act of sexual relations of a pregnant woman is classified as a valid act of sexual relations, *that explains why he renders her unfit. But from your perspective, in holding that,* the rite of removing the shoe performed by a pregnant woman who has miscarried is not classified as a valid rite of removing the shoe, and the act of sexual relations of a pregnant woman is not classified as a valid act of sexual relations, *why in the world can he have* **invalidated her from marrying into the priesthood**?"

L. *He said to him, "It is based on rabbinical authority and represents merely a stricter ruling than the law would require"* [Slotki: one not knowing the circumstances of this particular case would erroneously assume that any other woman who has performed the rite of removing the shoe likewise may be married to a priest].

M. *There are those who represent matters as follows: R. Simeon b. Laqish objected to R. Yohanan, "* **[If] the offspring is not timely, he is prohibited from marrying her relatives, and she is prohibited from marrying his relatives, and he has invalidated her from marrying into the priesthood.** *Now from my perspective, in holding that* the rite of removing the shoe performed by a pregnant woman who has miscarried is not classified as a valid rite of removing the shoe, *that explains why he renders her unfit — that is, as a strict interpretation of the law. But it is not taught as the Tannaite rule,* she does not have to undergo the rite of removing the shoe with the brothers. *But from your perspective, the rule should be stated:* she does not have to undergo the rite of removing the shoe with the brothers."

N. *He said to him, "True enough. But since the Tannaite formulation in the first clause is,* **and he has not invalidated her from marrying into the priesthood,** *it is stated in the second clause,* **and he has invalidated her from marrying into the priesthood."**

O. *R. Yohanan objected to R. Simeon b. Laqish, "* **[If] the offspring is not timely, he may confirm [the marriage]:** *now from my perspective, in holding that* the rite of removing the shoe performed by a pregnant woman who has miscarried is classified as a valid rite of removing the shoe, and the act of sexual relations of a pregnant woman is classified as a valid act of sexual relations, *that explains why* **he may confirm [the marriage]**. *But from your perspective, in holding that,* the rite of removing the shoe performed by a pregnant woman who has miscarried is not classified as a valid rite of removing the shoe, and the act of sexual relations of a pregnant woman is not classified as a valid act of sexual relations, *why in the world [can he* **confirm the marriage]***? Rather, the rule should state,* he must go and have sexual relations with her again, and only then may he confirm the marriage!'"

P. "*But what is the meaning of,* **he may confirm [the marriage]***? It is,* he must go and have sexual relations with her again, and only then may he confirm the marriage. That is, it is not sufficient [without doing so]."

Q. *There are those who represent matters as follows: R. Simeon b. Laqish objected to R. Yohanan,* " **[If] the offspring is not timely, he may confirm [the marriage]:** *now from my perspective, in holding that* the rite of removing the shoe performed by a pregnant woman who has miscarried is not classified as a valid rite of removing the shoe, and the act of sexual relations of a pregnant woman is not classified as a valid act of sexual relations, *that explains why* **he may confirm [the marriage]** — *meaning:* he must go and have sexual relations with her again, and only then may he confirm the marriage. That is, it is not sufficient [without doing so]. *But from your perspective, the rule should be,* if he wants, he may divorce her, but if he wants, he may confirm the marriage with her."

R. *He said to him,* "True enough. But since in *the prior clause it says,* **he must put her away,** *in the following clause it says,* **he may confirm [the marriage].**"

S. *An objection was raised:* He who marries his deceased childless brother's widow and she turns out to be pregnant, lo, her co-wife should not remarry, lest the offspring turn out to be viable. *To the contrary, what it should say is this: if the offspring is viable, her co-wife is exempt [and free to marry, so none of the widows of the deceased is subject to the levirate connection is any form]. So rather read:* it is possible that the offspring will not be viable. *Now, if it should enter your mind that* the act of sexual relations of a pregnant woman is classified as a valid act of sexual relations, *why is the rule that* her co-wife should not remarry, lest the offspring turn out to be viable? *Let her be freed of the levirate connection through the act of sexual relations of her fellow!"*

T. *Said Abbayye, "As to the sexual relations, both parties concur that she does not exempt her co-wife. What separates them is only the question of the rite of removing the shoe. R. Yohanan maintains that that* the rite of removing the shoe performed by a pregnant woman who has miscarried is classified as a valid rite of removing the shoe but the act of sexual relations of a pregnant woman is not classified as a valid act of sexual relations, *and R. Simeon b. Laqish holds the view that that* the act of sexual relations of a pregnant woman is not classified as an act of sexual relations, and the rite of removing the shoe performed by a pregnant woman who has miscarried is not classified as a valid rite of removing the shoe."

U. *Said to him Raba, "Well, how do you want it?* If the act of sexual relations of a pregnant woman is classified as an act of sexual relations, then the rite of removing the shoe performed by a pregnant woman should be regarded as valid, and if the act of sexual relations of a pregnant woman is not classified as an act of sexual relations, then the rite of removing the shoe performed by a pregnant woman should not be regarded as valid. *For we have it as an established rule* **[36A]** that anyone who is subject to marriage with the levir is subject to the rite of removing the shoe, and anyone who is not subject to marriage with the levir is not subject to the rite of removing the shoe."

V. *Rather, said Raba, "This is the sense of the matter:* 'He who marries his deceased childless brother's widow and she turns out to be pregnant, lo, her co-wife should not remarry, lest the offspring turn out to be viable, and sexual relations with a pregnant woman are not classified as sexual relations, and the rite of removing the shoe done with a pregnant woman is not classified as a valid rite of removing the shoe, and the offspring does not exempt the co-wives from the levirate connection until it is actually born.'"

W. *It has been taught on Tannaite authority in accord with the position of Raba:* He who marries his deceased childless brother's widow and she turns out to be pregnant, lo, her co-wife should not remarry, lest the offspring turn out to be viable, and sexual relations with a pregnant woman or the rite of removing the shoe does not exempt the co-wives from the levirate connection, but only the offspring exempts the co-wives, and the offspring does not exempt the co-wives from the levirate connection until it is actually born.

X. *The operative consideration therefore in exempting the co-wives from the levirate connection is,* lest the offspring turn out to be viable. *But then, if the offspring is not viable, the co-wife is exempt* [Slotki: on the strength of the sexual relations that took place prior to the miscarriage of the child, no repeated sexual relations being necessary]. *May we then say that this refutes the position of R. Simeon b. Laqish?*

Y. *R. Simeon b. Laqish will say to you, "This is the sense of the statement:* He who marries his deceased childless brother's widow and she turns out to be pregnant, lo, her co-wife should not remarry, lest the offspring not turn out to be viable, and sexual relations with a pregnant woman are not classified as valid sexual relations, and the rite of removing the shoe performed with her is not classified as a valid rite of removing the shoe. And if you should say, 'well, follow the rule governing the majority of women, and the majority of women produce perfectly healthy offspring,' still it is the fact that an offspring exempts the co-wives from the levirate connection only when it is actually born."

Z. Said R. Eleazar, "Well, how is it possible that there should be such a ruling as that which R. Simeon b. Laqish has laid down, and yet we have not learned it as a Tannaite formulation in our Mishnah?" He went forth and took a close look, and found the following, which we have learned in the Mishnah: **A woman whose husband and co-wife went overseas and they came and said to her, "Your husband has died," should not remarry [without the rite of removing the shoe or enter into levirate marriage, until she ascertains whether her co-wife is pregnant [M. 16:1A-B].** *Now it is easy to understand why she should not enter into levirate marriage, lest the offspring be viable, so the levir would violate the Torah's prohibition against marrying a brother's wife. But why should she not perform the rite of removing the shoe? Now there is no problem in understanding why she should not perform the rite of removing the shoe within the nine months after the husband's death, and not contract a marriage in that same period, on account of doubt [as to whether the offspring is viable; if it is, the rite and the levirate marriage would be invalid; the exemption is brought into force by the actual birth]. But why should she not* perform the rite of removing the shoe within the nine months of the husband's death and enter into marriage after nine months?" [Slotki: this should be permitted by Yohanan in any event: if the rival had been pregnant and miscarried or had not been pregnant at all, the rite of removing the shoe was valid; if a viable child had been born, the exemption took effect at his birth, and the subsequent marriage would be lawful; since the rule forbids the rite of removal and marriage even after nine months unless definite information about the rival has been received, it must be assumed to represent the view of Simeon b. Laqish, who deems the rite of removal invalid wherever the child is not viable and the ceremony took place during pregnancy.]

AA. *But even in accord with your position* [the rite of removal is forbidden because the co-wife may have been pregnant when the rite took place (Slotki)], let her perform the rite of removal and then marry after nine months [when there will be no doubt on the pregnancy; why wait to find out whether the co-wife has been pregnant at all]? *So this passage must be excluded from consideration, for Abbayye and Bar Abba and R. Hinena bar Abbayye all maintained, "It is possible that the offspring of the co-wife might be viable, and you would then make it necessary to proclaim concerning her with regard to the priesthood [that the rite of removal was unnecessary and therefore null, so she remains eligible to the priesthood]."*

BB. *So make it necessary to issue such a proclamation!*

CC. *There may be someone who witnessed the rite of removing the shoe but did not hear about the proclamation and so would imagine that a woman who has performed the rite of removing the shoe may marry a priest [which is not the case].*

DD. *Said to him Abbayye, "Now has it been said, 'She should not carry out the rite of removing the shoe nor enter into levirate marriage'? What is stated is, 'She shall not be married nor enter into levirate marriage' that is, without the rite of removing the shoe. But if the rite of removing the shoe was carried out [even within the nine months of the death of the husband], she would be permitted to marry at the end of the period"* [Slotki: and the passage affords no support to Simeon b. Laqish].

EE. *It has been taught on Tannaite authority in accord with the position of R. Simeon b. Laqish:* He who carries out the rite of removing the shoe with a pregnant woman, who subsequently miscarried — she has to enter into the rite of removing the shoe with one of the other brothers.

.2 A. Said Raba, *"The decided law accords with the position of R. Simeon b. Laqish in three matters. The first is the one that we have just now been discussing.*

B. *"The second is in accord with that which we have learned in the Mishnah:* **He who** divides his estate among his sons by a verbal [donation], [and] gave a larger portion to one and a smaller portion to another, or treated the firstborn as equivalent to all the others — his statement is valid. But if he had said, "By reason of an inheritance [the aforestated arrangements are made]," he has said nothing whatsoever. [If] he had written, whether at the beginning, middle, or end, [that these things are handed over] as a gift, his statement is valid [M. B.B.8:5E-J]. [36B] And said R. Simeon b. Laqish, 'Title is not transferred unless he said, "Let Mr. X and Mr. Y will inherit such-and-such a field, which I have assigned to them as a gift, so that they may inherit them."'

C. *"And the third is in line with that which we have learned in the Mishnah:* **He who writes over his property to his son [to take effect] after his death — the father cannot sell the property, because it is written over to the son, and the son cannot sell the property, because it is [yet] in the domain of the father. [If] the father sold [it], the property is sold until he dies. If the son sold the property, the purchaser has no right whatever in the property until the father dies. The father harvests the crops and gives the usufruct to anyone whom he wants. And whatever he left already harvested-lo, it belongs to his heirs** [M. B.B. 8:7]. *And it has been stated:* if the son sold the property in the lifetime of the father and died in the lifetime of the father — R. Yohanan said, "The purchaser has not acquired the property." R. Simeon b. Laqish said, "The purchaser has acquired the property." R. Yohanan said, "The purchaser has not

Introduction

acquired the property," *for the right to the usufruct [such as the step father in our case had] is tantamount in law to the right to the substance of the estate, [so that when the son sold the estate during the lifetime of the father, he sold something that he did not own.]* [R. Simeon b. Laqish said, "The purchaser has acquired the property," for *the right to the usufruct [such as the step father in our case had] is not tantamount in law to the right to the substance of the estate, so that when the son sold the estate during the lifetime of the father, he sold something that he did own."*

The first initiative takes place at 1.E-F, the second at Gff. In the former, each party gets to amplify his position, in the latter, the anonymous voice articulates the principle at issue, and each of the choices is then worked out in detail and in balance. Then each party is given the opportunity to object to the position of the other, with an appropriate rejoinder. Even when we have new versions of the several statements, these exhibit that same proportion and balance. When T-U then introduce a new perspective, the two positions once more are carefully balanced. And so throughout. All of this captures our admiration, but none of it falls into the category of an argument that moves out of its original framework, and, viewed whole, the composition falls into the category of a syllogism, brilliantly executed.

v. THE IMPORTANCE OF THE DIALECTICAL ARGUMENT IN RABBINIC LITERATURE

What then is at stake in the dialectical argument? I see three complementary results. All of them, in my view, prove commensurate to the effort required to follow these protracted, sometimes tedious disquisitions.

First, we test every allegation by a counter-proposition, so serving the cause of truth through challenge and constant checking for flaws in an argument.

Second, we survey the entire range of possibilities, which leaves no doubts about the cogency of our conclusion. And that means, we move out of our original case, guided by its generative principle to new cases altogether.

Third, quite to the point, by the give and take of argument, we ourselves are enabled to go through the thought processes set forth in the subtle markings that yield our reconstruction of the argument. We not only review what people say, but how they think: the processes of reasoning that have yielded a given conclusion. Sages and disciples become party to the modes of thought; in the dialectical argument, they are required to replicate the thought-processes themselves.

Let me give a single example of the power of the dialectical argument to expose the steps in thinking that lead from one end to another: principle to ruling,

expose the steps in thinking that lead from one end to another: principle to ruling, or ruling to principle. In the present instance, the only one we require to see a perfectly routine and obvious procedure, we mean to prove the point that if people are permitted to obstruct the public way, if damage was done by them, they are liable to pay compensation. First, we are going to prove that general point on the basis of a single case. Then we shall proceed to show how a variety of authorities, dealing with diverse cases, sustain the same principle.

TALMUD BABA MESIA 10:5/O-X

O. He who brings out his manure to the public domain —
P. while one party pitches it out, the other party must be bringing it in to manure his field.
Q. They do not soak clay in the public domain,
R. and they do not make bricks.
S. And they knead clay in the public way,
T. but not bricks.
U. He who builds in the public way —
V. while one party brings stones, the builder must make use of them in the public way.
W. And if one has inflicted injury, he must pay for the damages he has caused.
X. Rabban Simeon b. Gamaliel says, "Also: He may prepare for doing his work [on site in the public way] for thirty days [before the actual work of building]."

We begin with the comparison of the rule before us with another Tannaite position on the same issue, asking whether an unattributed, therefore authoritative, rule stands for or against the position of a given authority; we should hope to prove that the named authority concurs. So one fundamental initiative in showing how many cases express a single principle — the concrete demonstration of the unity of the law — is to find out whether diverse, important authorities concur on the principle, each ruling in a distinctive case; or whether a single authority is consistent in ruling in accord with the principle at hand, as in what follows:

I.1   A. *May we say that our Mishnah-paragraph does not accord with the view of R. Judah? For it has been taught on Tannaite authority:*

   B. **R. Judah says, "At the time of fertilizing the fields, a man may take out his manure and pile it up at the door of his house in the public way so that it will be pulverized by the feet of man and beast, for a period of thirty days. For it was on that very stipulation that Joshua caused the Israelites to inherit the land"** [T. B.M. 11:8E-H].

   C. *You may even maintain that he concurs with the Mishnah's rule*

Introduction xliii

        bringing it in to manure his field]. R. Judah concedes that if one has caused damage, he is liable to pay compensation.

In line with the position just now proposed, then Judah will turn out to rule every which way on the same matter. And that is not an acceptable upshot.

    D.   *But has it not been taught in the Mishnah:* **If the store-keeper had left his lamp outside the store-keeper is liable [if the flame caused a fire]. R. Judah said, "In the case of a lamp for Hanukkah, he is exempt"** [M. B. Q. 6:6E-F], because he has acted under authority. *Now surely that must mean,* under the authority of the court [and that shows that one is not responsible for damage caused by his property in the public domain if it was there under the authority of the court]!

The dialectic now intervenes. We have made a proposal. Isn't it a good one? Of course not, were we to give up so quickly, we should gain nothing:

    E.   *No, what it means is, on the authority of carrying out one's religious obligations.*

By now, the reader is able to predict the next step: "but isn't the contrary more reasonable?" Here is how we raise the objection.

    F.   *But has it not been taught on Tannaite authority:*
    G.   in the case of all those concerning whom they have said, "They are permitted to obstruct the public way," if there was damage done, one is liable to pay compensation. But R. Judah declares one exempt from having to pay compensation.
    H.   *So it is better to take the view that our Mishnah-paragraph does not concur with the position of R. Judah.*

The point of interest has been introduced: whether those permitted to obstruct the public way must pay compensation for damages they may cause in so doing. Here is where we find a variety of cases that yield a single principle:

I.2   A.   *Said Abayye, "R. Judah, Rabban Simeon b. Gamaliel, and R. Simeon all take the position that* i n *the case of all those concerning whom they have said, 'They are permitted to obstruct the public way,' if there was damage done, one is liable to pay compensation.*
    B.   *"As to R. Judah, the matter is just as we have now stated it.*

Simeon b. Gamaliel and Simeon now draw us to unrelated cases:

    C.   *"As to Rabban Simeon b. Gamaliel, we have learned in the Mishnah:* **Rabban Simeon b. Gamaliel says, 'Also: He may prepare for doing his work [on site in the public way] for thirty days [before the actual work of building].'**
    D.   *"As to R. Simeon, we have learned in the Mishnah:* **A person should not set up an oven in a room unless there is a space of four cubits above it. If he was setting it up in the upper story,**

there has to be a layer of plaster under it three handbreadths thick, and in the case of a stove, a handbreadth thick. And if it did damage, the owner of the oven has to pay for the damage. R. Simeon says, 'All of these measures have been stated only so that if the object did damage, the owner is exempt from paying compensation if the stated measures have been observed' [M. B.B. 2:2A-F]."

We see then that the demonstration of the unity of the law and the issue of who stands, or does not stand, behind a given rule, go together. When we ask about who does or does not stand behind a rule, we ask about the principle of a case, which leads us downward to a premise, and we forthwith point to how that same premise underlies a different principle yielding a case — so how can X hold the view he does, if that is his premise, since at a different case he makes a point with a principle that rests on a contradictory premise. The Mishnah and the Talmud are comparable to the moraine left by the last ice age, fields studded with boulders. For the Talmud, reference is made to those many disputes that litter the pages and impede progress. That explains why much of the Talmud is taken up with not only sorting out disputes, but also showing their rationality, meaning, reasonable people have perfectly valid reasons for disagreeing about a given point, since both parties share the same premises but apply them differently; or they really do not differ at all, since one party deals with one set of circumstances, the other with a different set of circumstances.

VI. The Law behind the Laws

The dialectical argument proves the ideal medium for the assertion, through sustained demonstration alone, of the union of laws in law. Specifically, if all we know is laws, then we want to find out what is at stake in them? Accordingly, the true issues of the law emerge from the detailed rulings of the laws. Generalization takes a variety of forms, some yielding a broader framework into which to locate a case, others a proposition of consequence. Let me give an obvious and familiar instance of what is to be done. Here is an example of a case that yields a principle:

Talmud Baba Mesia to 9:11

- A. (1) **A day worker collects his wage any time of the night.**
- B. (2) **And a night worker collects his wage any time of the day.**
- C. (3) **A worker by the hour collects his wage any time of the night or day.**

I.1   A.   *Our rabbis have taught on Tannaite authority:*
      B.   How on the basis of Scripture do we know, **A day worker collects his wage any time of the night**?
      C.   "[You shall not oppress your neighbor or rob him.] The wages

Introduction

xlv

of a hired servant shall not remain with you all night until the morning" (Lev. 19:13).

D. And how on the basis of Scripture do we know, **and a night worker collects his wage any time of the day**?

E. "[You shall not oppress a hired servant who is poor and needy]...you shall give him hire his hire on the day on which he earns it, before the sun goes down" (Dt. 23:14-15).

F. *Might I say that the reverse is the case [the night worker must be paid during the night that he does the work, in line with Lev. 19:13, and the day worker by day, in line with Dt. 23:15]?*

G. Wages are to be paid only at the end of the work [so the fee is not payable until the work has been done].

What do we learn from this passage? Specifically, two points.

[1] Scripture yields the rule at hand;

[2] Scripture also imposes limits on the formation of the law; but one generalization, that the law of the Mishnah derives from the source of Scripture.

And, if we take a small step beyond, of course, we learn that the two parts of the Torah are one. The hermeneutics instructs us to ask, how on the basis of Scripture do we know...? Its premise then is that Scripture forms the basis for rules not expressed with verses of the written Torah. The theological principle conveyed in the hermeneutics expressed in the case is that the Torah is one and encompasses both the oral and the written parts; the oral part derives its truths from the written part.

Now if I had to identify the single most important theological point that the Talmud and other writings that use dialectics sets forth, it is that the laws yield law, the truth exhibits integrity, all of the parts — the details, principles, and premises — holding together in a coherent manner. To understand how generalizations are attained, however, we cannot deal only with generalizations. So we turn to a specific problem of category-formation, namely, in the transfer of property, whether or not we distinguish between a sale and a gift. That is, in both instances property is transferred. But the conditions of transfer clearly differ; in the one case there is a quid pro quo, in the other, not. Now does that distinction make a difference? The answer to that question will have implications for a variety of concrete cases, e.g., transfers of property in a dowry, divisions of inheritances and estates, the required documents and procedures for effecting transfer of title, and the like. If, then, we know the correct category-formation — the same or not the same category — we form a generalization that will draw together numerous otherwise unrelated cases and (more to the point) rules.

One way to accomplish the goal is to identify the issue behind a dispute, which leads us from the dispute to the principle that is established and confirmed by a dispute on details, e.g., whether or not the principle applies, and, if it does, how it does. In this way we affirm the unity of the law by establishing that all parties to a dispute really agree on the same point; then the dispute itself underlines the law's coherence:

TALMUD BABA BATRA 1:3
- A. He whose [land] surrounds that of his fellow on three sides,
- B. and who made a fence on the first, second, and third sides —
- C. they do not require [the other party to share in the expense of building the walls].
- D. R. Yosé says, "If he built a fence on the fourth side, they assign to him [his share in the case of] all [three other fences]."

In the following dispute, we ask what is subject to dispute between the two named authorities, B-C.

.2   A. *It has been stated:*
- B. R. Huna said, "All is proportional to the actual cost of building the fence [Simon: which will vary according to the materials used by the one who builds the fence]."
- C. Hiyya bar Rab said, "All is proportionate to the cost of a cheap fence made of sticks [since that is all that is absolutely necessary]."

To find the issue, we revert to our Mishnah-rule. The opinions therein guide the disputing parties. Each then has to account for what is subject to dispute in the Mishnah-paragraph. Then the point is, the Mishnah's dispute is not only rational, but it also rests upon a shared premise, affirmed by all parties. That is the power of D.

- D. *We have learned in the Mishnah:* **He whose [land] surrounds that of his fellow on three sides, and who made a fence on the first, second, and third sides — they do not require [the other party to share in the expense of building the walls].** Lo, if he fences the fourth side too, he must contribute to the cost of the entire fence. *But then note what follows:* **R. Yosé says, "If he built a fence on the fourth side, they assign to him [his share in the case of] all [three other fences]."** *Now there is no problem from the perspective of R. Huna, who has said,* "All is proportional to the actual cost of building the fence [Simon: which will vary according to the materials used by the one who builds the fence]." *Then we can identify what is at issue between the first authority and R. Yosé. Specifically, the initial authority takes the view that we proportion the costs to what they would be if a cheap fence of sticks was built, but not to what the fence-builder actually spent, and R. Yosé maintains that under all circumstances, the division is proportional to actual costs. But from the perspective of Hiyya bar Rab, who has said,* "All is proportionate to the cost of a

Introduction

xlvii

cheap fence made of sticks [since that is all that is absolutely necessary]," *what can be the difference between the ruling of the initial Tannaite authority and that of R. Yosé? If, after all, he does not pay him even the cost of building a cheap fence, what in the world is he supposed to pay off as his share?*

We now revert to the dialectics, but a different kind. Here we raise a variety of possibilities, not as challenges and responses in a sequence, but as freestanding choices; the same goal is at hand, the opportunity to examine every possibility. But the result is different: not a final solution but four suitable ones, yielding the notion that a single principle governs a variety of cases. That explains why we now have a set of four answers, all of them converging on the same principle:

E. *If you want, I shall say that what is at issue between them is the fee to be paid for a watchman. The initial authority holds that he pays the cost of a watchman, not the charge of building a cheap fence, and R. Yosé says that he has to pay the cost of building a cheap fence.*

F. *But if you prefer, I may say that at issue between them is the first, second, and third sides, in which instance the initial Tannaite authority has the other pay only the cost of fencing the fourth side, not the first three, and R. Yosé maintains he has to pay his share of the cost of fencing the first three sides too.*

G. *And if you prefer, I shall maintain that at issue between them is whether the fence has to be built by the owner of the surrounding fields or the owner of the enclosed field if the latter pays the cost of the whole. The initial Tannaite authority says that the consideration that leads the owner of the enclosed field to have to contribute at all is that he went ahead and built the fourth fence, so he has to pay his share of the cost of the whole; but if the owner of the surrounding fields is the one who went ahead and did it, the other has to pay only the share of the fourth fence. For his part, R. Yosé takes the position that there is no distinction between who took the initiative in building the fourth fence, whether the owner of the enclosed field or the owner of the surrounding field. In either case the former has to pay the latter his share of the whole.*

H. *There are those who say, in respect to this last statement, that at issue between them is whether the fourth fence has to be built by the owner of the enclosed field or the surrounding fields so that the former has to contribute his share. The initial Tannaite authority holds that, even if the owner of the surrounding fields makes the fourth fence, the other has to contribute to the cost, and R. Yosé maintains that if the owner of the enclosed field*

xlviii   *Talmudic Dialectics*

> *takes it on himself to build the fourth fence, he has to pay his share of the cost of the whole, because through his action he has shown that he wants the fence, but if the owner of the surrounding fields builds the fourth side, the other pays not a penny [since he can say he never wanted a fence to begin with].*

The premise of E is that the owner of the land on the inside has a choice as to the means of guarding his field; but he of course bears responsibility for the matter. F agrees that he bears responsibility for his side, but adds that he also is responsible for the sides from which he enjoys benefit. And of course G concurs that the owner of the inner field is responsible to protect his own property. H takes the same view. What we have accomplished is, first, to lay a foundation in rationality for the dispute of the Mishnah-paragraph, and, further, demonstrate that all parties to the dispute affirm the responsibility to pay one's share of that from which one benefits. Justice means, no free lunch.

VII. THE UNITY OF THE LAW

In what follows, the unity of the law extends from agreements behind disputes to a more fundamental matter: identifying the single principle behind many, diverse cases. What do diverse cases have in common? Along these same lines, that same hermeneutics wants us to show how diverse authorities concur on the same principle, dealing with diverse cases; how where there is a dispute, the dispute represents schism vs. consensus, with the weight of argument and evidence favoring consensus; where we have a choice between interpreting an opinion as schismatic and as coherent with established rule, we try to show it is not schismatic; and so on and so forth. All of these commonplace activities pursue a single goal, which is to limit the range of schism and expand the range of consensus, both in political, personal terms of authority, and, more to the point, in the framework of case and principle. If I had to identify a single hermeneutical principle — that is, defining melody — that governs throughout, it is, the quest for harmony, consensus, unity, and above all, the rationality of dispute: reasonable disagreement about the pertinence or relevance of established, universally-affirmed principles.

Here is a fine instance of the working of the hermeneutics that tells us to read the texts as a single coherent statement, episodic and unrelated cases as statements of a single principle. The principle is: it is forbidden for someone to derive uncompensated benefit from somebody else's property. That self-evidently valid principle of equity — "thou shalt not steal" writ small — then emerges from a variety of cases; the cases are read as illustrative. The upshot of demonstrating that fact is to prove a much-desired goal. The law of the Torah — here, the written Torah, one of the ten commandments no less! — contains within itself the laws of everyday life. So one thing yields many things; the law is coherence in God's mind, and retains that coherent as it expands to encompass the here and the now of the social order. The details as always are picayune, the logic practical, the reasoning

Introduction xlix

concrete and applied; but the stakes prove cosmic in a very exact sense of the word. The problem involves a two-story house, owned by the resident of the lower story. The house has fallen down. The tenant, upstairs, has no where to live. The landlord, downstairs, does not rebuild the house. The tenant has the right to rebuild the downstairs part of the house and to live there as long as the landlord does not complete the rebuilding of the house and also refund to the tenant the cost of rebuilding the part that the tenant has reconstructed for himself. Judah rejects this ruling, and, in doing so, invokes a general principle, by no means limited to the case at hand. Then the Bavli will wish to show how this governing principle pertains elsewhere.

MISHNAH-TRACTATE BABA MESIA 10:3
AND TALMUD BABA MESIA 117A-B

A. A house and an upper story belonging to two people which fell down —
B. [if] the resident of the upper story told the householder [of the lower story] to rebuild,
C. but he does not want to rebuild,
D. lo, the resident of the upper story rebuilds the lower story and lives there,
E. until the other party compensates him for what he has spent.
F. R. Judah says, "Also: [if so,] this one is [then] living in his fellow's [housing]. [So in the end] he will have to pay him rent.
G. "But the resident of the upper story builds both the house and the upper room,
H. "and he puts a roof on the upper story,
I. "and he lives in the lower story,
J. "until the other party compensates him for what he has spent."

At issue is a principle, which settles the case at hand. It is whether or not one may gratuitously derive benefit from someone else's property. We shall now show that Judah repeatedly takes that position in a variety of diverse cases:

I.1 A. [117B] Said R. Yohanan, "In three passages R. Judah has repeated for us the rule that it is forbidden for someone to derive benefit from somebody's else's property. *The first is in the Mishnah passage at hand. The next is in that which we have learned in the Mishnah.*"

The case that is now introduced involves an error in dyeing wool. The premise of the rulings is that dyeing always enhances the value of the wool, whether it is dyed of one color or some other. On that basis, the following is quite clear:

B. He who gave wool to a dyer to dye it red, and he dyed it black, or to dye it black, and he dyed it red —

1 Talmudic Dialectics

C. R. Meir says, "The dyer pays him back the value of his wool."
D. And R. Judah says, "If the increase in value is greater than the outlay for the process of dyeing, the owner pays him back for the outlay for the process of dyeing. And if the outlay for the process of dyeing is greater than the increase in the value of the wool, the owner pays him [the dyer] only the increase in the value of the wool" [M. B.Q. 9:4G-K].
E. *And what is the third? It is as we have learned in the Mishnah:*
F. **He who paid part of a debt that he owed and deposited the bond that has been written as evidence covering the remaining sum with a third party, and said to him, "If I have not given you what I still owe the lender between now and such-and-such a date, give the creditor his bond of indebtedness," if the time came and he has not paid,**
G. R. Yosé says, "He should hand it over."
H. And R. Judah says, "He should not hand it over" [M. B.B. 10:5A-E]"
I. *Why [does it follow that Judah holds that it is forbidden for someone to derive benefit from somebody's else's property]? Perhaps when R. Judah takes the position that he does here, it is only because there is blackening of the walls.*
J. [Freedman: the new house loses its newness because the tenant is living there, so the house owner is sustaining a loss, and that is why the tenant has to pay rent];
K. as to the case of the dyer who was supposed to dye the wool red but dyed it black, *the reason is that he has violated his instructions, and we have learned in the Mishnah:*
L. **Whoever changes [the original terms of the agreement] — his hand is on the bottom [M. B.M. 6:2E-F].** [That is to say, the decision must favor the other party, the claim of the one who has changed the original terms being subordinated.]
M. *And as to the third case,* **the one who has paid part of his debt,** *here we deal with an enticement, and we infer from this case that R. Judah takes the position that in the case of a come-on, there is no transfer of title.*

Yohanan's observation serves the purpose of showing how several unrelated cases of the Mishnah really make the same point: you shall not steal. The voice of the Talmud — that is to say, the dialectics itself — then contributes an objection and its resolution, making Yohanan's statement plausible and compelling, not merely an observation that may or may not be so.

An ideal way of demonstrating the unity of the law is to expose the abstract premise of a concrete rule, and that without regard to the number of discrete cases

Introduction li

that establish the same rule. Here is a case in which the theological principle, a stipulation made not be made contrary to what is written in the Torah, is shown to form the premise of a concrete case; then the case once more merely illustrates the principle of the Torah, which delivers its messages in just this way, through exemplary cases. 2.A commences with a common attributive formula, said x...said y.... This bears the meaning, said x in the name of y (and on his authority). Judah is then the tradent of the opinion or ruling, and Samuel the original source. Such an attributive formula may encompass three or more names and is common in both Talmuds.

.2 A. And said R. Judah said Samuel, "He who says to his fellow, '...on the stipulation that the advent of the Seventh Year will not abrogate the debts' — the Seventh Year nonetheless abrogates those debts."

B. *May one then propose that Samuel takes the view that that stipulation represents an agreement made contrary to what is written in the Torah, and, as we know, any stipulation contrary to what is written in the Torah is a null stipulation? But lo, it has been stated:*

C. He who says to his fellow, "[I make this sale to you] on the stipulation that you may not lay claim of fraud [by reason of variation from true value] against me" —

D. Rab said, "He nonetheless may lay claim of fraud [by reason of variation from true value] against him."

E. Samuel said, "He may not lay claim of fraud [by reason of variation from true value] against him."

F. *Lo, it has been stated in that connection: said R. Anan, "The matter has been explained to me such that Samuel said, 'He who says to his fellow, "[I make this sale to you] on the stipulation that you may not lay claim of fraud [by reason of variation from true value] against me" — he has no claim of fraud against him. [If he said,] "...on the stipulation that in the transaction itself, there is no aspect of fraud," lo, he has a claim of fraud against him.'"*

G. Here too, the same distinction pertains. If the stipulation was, "on condition that you do not abrogate the debt to me in the Sabbatical Year," then the Sabbatical Year does not abrogate the debt. But if the language was, "on condition that the Sabbatical Year itself does not abrogate the debt, the Sabbatical Year does abrogate the debt."

TALMUD TO MAKKOT 1:1L-N, 1:2, 1:3/I.2

What is at stake in this issue is of course not only jurisprudential principles but theological truth, concerning the power of language. In the Torah, language is enchanted; it serves, after all, for the principal medium of the divine self-manifestation: in words, sentences, paragraphs, a book: the Torah. So what one says forms the foundation of effective reality: it makes things happen, not only records what has happened.

But what happens if one makes a statement that ordinarily would prove effective, but the contents of the statement contradict the law of the Torah? Then such a stipulation is null. Why? Because the Torah is what makes language work, and if the Torah is contradicted, then the language is no more effective — changing the world to which it refers, the rules or conditions or order of existence — than it would be if the rules of grammar were violated. Just as, in such a case, the sentence would be gibberish and not convey meaning, so in the case at hand, the sentence is senseless and null.

VIII. DIALECTICS AND THE INTELLECTUAL DYNAMICS OF RABBINIC LITERATURE

The main consequence for the Rabbinic literature of formation through dialectical arguments more than through any other mode of thought and writing is simply stated. It is the power of that mode of the representation of thought to show us — as no other mode of writing can show — not only the result but the workings of the logical mind. By following dialectical arguments, we ourselves enter into those same thought processes, and our minds then are formed in the model of rigorous and sustained, systematic argument. The reason is simply stated. When we follow a proposal and its refutation, the consequence thereof, and the result of that, we ourselves form partners to the logical tensions and their resolutions; we are given an opening into the discourse that lies before us. As soon as matters turn not upon tradition, to which we may or may not have access, but reason, specifically, challenge and response, proposal and counter-proposal, "maybe matters are just the opposite?" we find an open door before us.

For these are not matters of fact but of reasoned judgment, and the answer, "well, that's my opinion," in its "traditional form," namely, that is what Rabbi X has said so that must be so, finds no hearing. Moving from facts to reasoning, propositions to the process of counter-argument, the challenge resting on the mind's own movement, its power of manipulating facts one way rather than some other and of identifying the governing logic of a fact — that process invites the reader's or the listener's participation. The author of a dialectical composite presents a problem with its internal tensions in logic and offers a solution to the problem and a resolution of the logical conflicts.

What is at stake in the capacity of the framer of a composite, or even the author of a composition, to move this way and that, always in a continuous path, but often in a crooked one? The dialectical argument opens the possibility of

Introduction

reaching out from one thing to something else, and the path's wandering is part of the reason. It is not because people have lost sight of their starting point or their goal in the end, but because they want to encompass, in the analytical argument as it gets underway, as broad and comprehensive a range of cases and rules as they can. The movement from point to point in reference to a single point that accurately describes the dialectical argument reaches a goal of abstraction. At the point at which we leave behind the specificities of not only cases but laws, sages carry the argument upward to the law that governs many cases, the premises that undergird many rules, and still higher to the principles that infuse diverse premises; then the principles that generate other, unrelated premises, which, in turn, come to expression in other, still-less intersecting cases. The meandering course of argument comes to an end when we have shown how things cohere that we did not even imagine were contiguous at all.

The dialectical argument forms the means to an end. The distinctive character of the Talmuds' and other documents' particular kind of dialectical argument is dictated by the purpose for which dialectics is invoked. Specifically, the goal of all argument is to show in discrete detail the ultimate unity of the law. The hermeneutics of dialectics aims at making manifest how to read the laws in such a way as to discern that many things really say one thing. The variations on the theme then take the form of detailed expositions of this and that. Then our task is to move backward from result to the reasoning process that has yielded said result: through regression from stage to stage to identify within the case not only the principles of law that produce that result, but the processes of reasoning that link the principles to the case at hand. And, when we accomplish our infinite regression, we move from the workings of literature to its religious character and theological goal: it is to know God in heaven, represented, on earth, by the unity of the law, the integrity of the Torah.

I

An Initial Probe: Types and Forms of the Dialectical Argument in Bavli to Mishnah Tractate Moed Qatan 1:1-2

The purpose of this probe is to establish hypothesis on the types and forms of the dialectic argument. We shall work our way through the opening component of the chapter, the part that serves Mishnah-paragraph 1:1-2, paying attention only to the kind of writing that concerns us in this study. This will provide our initial entry into such questions as the proportion of dialectical argument in the larger Talmudic discussion of a given Mishnah-paragraph; the participants; the occasion for formulating such a composition or composite; and similar issues of context, form, and function. The passage chosen is my favorite starting point for probes of the Talmud; it is neither more nor less representative than any other.

In order to take a fix on the proportions of the Talmud supplied by dialectics I present the chapter whole. It is in the form given it by my academic commentary, that is, with clear markings on the relationship of one component of the writing to another, indicating what is primary, secondary, tertiary; what is basic and what is inserted, and other indications of how the chapter has been put together. This permits us to locate the dialectical argument within the larger framework of the Talmud's composite character and to find out whether the argument takes its place only in the primary and definitive component of the whole, the Mishnah-commentary and amplification, or in relationship to other elements of the Talmud's re-presentation of the materials it has chosen to place on display. I discuss only the constructions that I classify as dialectical arguments within the general definition given in the Introduction.

The topic of the tractate is conduct on the intermediate days of the festivals of Passover and Tabernacle, that is, the days between the opening and closing festival days, on which servile labor is forbidden. In the interval certain forms of labor may be carried on, and the tractate through cases defines the principles that govern what may or may not be done in accord with the lower level of sanctity that applies between the first and the last days of the eight-day festival season.

i. Outline of the Talmud

To understand what is to follow, we do well to examine my outline of the Talmud's treatment of the opening stichs of the Mishnah-paragraph.[1] In bold face type is Mishnah-citation; principal rubrics not in bold face type represent composites formed around other theories of agglutination or composition than Mishnah-commentary.

I. MISHNAH-TRACTATE MEGILLAH 1:1-2
   A. **THE MEGILLAH MAY BE READ ON THE ELEVENTH, ON THE TWELFTH, ON THE THIRTEENTH, ON THE FOURTEENTH, AND ON THE FIFTEENTH OF THE MONTH OF ADAR, NOT BEFORE AND NOT AFTER.**
      1. I:1: From where do we know that the Megillah is read on the eleventh ...of Adar (M 1:1A)? Since, further on, we find it necessary to state, "The sages ruled leniently regarding the villages, allowing them to advance the Megillah reading to the day of assembly, in order that they could provide water and food for their relatives in the walled cities" thereby advancing the date to as early as Adar 11 and extending the celebration to five days in contrast to the two that appear to be intended in Est. 9:31, we therefore rule as follows: In fact, the Men of the Great Assembly instituted all five of them.
      2. I:2: Where is this notion that Esther may be read on five different days, M 1:1A, hinted at in Scripture?
      3. I:3: Said Rabbah bar Bar Hanna, said R. Yohanan: This (M 1:1) is the words of R. Aqiba, the anonymous one, who expounded "time," "their time," "their times." But the sages say: One does not read it the Megillah other that at its proper time i.e., Adar 14 or 15.
      4. I:4: From where do we derive these words? Said Raba, Scripture has said: "Therefore, the Jews who live in the unwalled cities observe the fourteenth of the month of Adar..." (Est. 9:19). Since the unwalled cities read Esther

---

[1] *The Talmud of Babylonia. A Complete Outline.* Atlanta, 1994-1995: Scholars Press for USF Academic Commentary Series. I. *Tractate Berakhot and the Division of Appointed Times.*

Chapter One. Initial Probe 3

        on the fourteenth, the walled cities read on the fifteenth.
- B. **CITIES THAT HAVE BEEN SURROUNDED BY A WALL SINCE THE TIME OF JOSHUA BIN NUN READ ON THE FIFTEENTH. VILLAGES AND LARGE TOWNS READ ON THE FOURTEENTH:**
  1. II:1: What is the scriptural source of this rule?
  2. II:2: The Mishnah 1:1A is not in accordance with this next quoted Tannaite authority, as is taught: R. Joshua ben Qorha says: Cities that have been surrounded by a wall since the time of Ahasuerus read on the fifteenth (cf. T Meg. 1:1A).
- C. **GLOSSING B.2. AND FOUR TEACHINGS OF RABBI YERMIAH OR RABBI HIYYA BAR ABBA**
  - a. II:3: Glossing the concluding statement of the foregoing, B.2: said R. Joshua ben Levi: A city, and everything near it, and everything seen together with it, are considered like the city for purposes of determining the date of reading, How far does this area around the city extend? Said R. Yermiah, or, if you prefer, R. Hiyya bar Abba: About the distance from Hamtan to Tiberias, a mil."
    - I. II:4: And said R. Yermiah, or, if you prefer, R. Hiyya bar Abba: The seers (sofim) the biblical prophets established the double forms of the letters Mem, Nun, Sadi, Pe, and Qof.
    - II. II:5: And said R. Yermiah, or, if you prefer, R. Hiyya bar Abba: Onkelos the proselyte translated the Aramaic rendition of the Torah following R. Eliezer and R. Joshua.
    - III. II:6: "And I alone, Daniel, saw the vision; and the men who were with me did not see the vision, but a great trembling fell upon them, and they fled into hiding" (Dan. 10:7). Who are the men? Said R. Yermiah, or, if you prefer, R. Hiyya bar Abba: Haggai, Zechariah, and Malachi.
- D. **REVERTING TO B.2'S PROOF. THE IMPORTANCE OF READING THE MEGILLAH**
  1. II:7: And now that you have said that "...province by province and city by city..." (Est. 9:28) is to be used for midrashic exposition (V.M), why is "...family by family..." included?
     - a. II:8: Gloss of a tangential detail of the foregoing.
- E. **GLOSSING B. 2. AND FURTHER TEACHINGS OF RABBI JOSHUA BEN LEVI ON MATTERS RELATED TO PURIM**

1. II:9: Said R. Joshua ben Levi: A city (kerakh), and all that is near it, and all that is seen with it is considered like the city.
2. II:10: And said R. Joshua ben Levi: A city that was settled and later surrounded by a wall is considered like a village.
3. II:11: And said R. Joshua ben Levi: A city (kerakh) in which there are not ten idle men is considered like a village.
4. II:12: And said R. Joshua ben Levi: A city (kerakh) that was destroyed and subsequently resettled is treated like a city.
5. II:13: And said R. Joshua ben Levi: Lod, and Ono, and Gei HaHarashim have been surrounded by a wall since the time of Joshua bin Nun.
6. II:14: And said R. Joshua ben Levi: Women are obligated to observe the reading of the Megillah, because they, too, were included in that miracle.
7. II:15: And said R. Joshua ben Levi: When Purim falls on the Sabbath, one asks about and expounds the matters of the day even though the Megillah is read on a different day.
8. II:16: And said R. Joshua ben Levi: One is required to read the Megillah at night of the appropriate day and to go over it in the daytime, as is said, "My God, I will read in the daytime, even though you do not answer, and at night, I am not quiet. (Ps. 22:3).

F. BUT THE VILLAGES MAY ADVANCE TO THE PRECEDING DAY OF ASSEMBLY
1. III:1: Said R. Hanina: The sages ruled leniently regarding the villages, allowing them to advance the Megillah reading to the day of assembly, in order that they could provide water and food for their relatives in the walled cities.

G. HOW DOES THIS HAPPEN? IF THE FOURTEENTH FALLS ON THE SECOND DAY, VILLAGES AND LARGE TOWNS READ ON THAT VERY DAY, AND WALLED CITIES ON THE NEXT DAY ADAR 15. IF ADAR 14 FALLS ON THE THIRD OR ON THE FOURTH DAY OF THE WEEK, VILLAGES ADVANCE TO THE DAY OF ASSEMBLY MONDAY, ADAR 13 OR 12, RESPECTIVELY; AND LARGE TOWNS READ ON THAT VERY DAY TUESDAY OR WEDNESDAY, ADAR 14; AND WALLED CITIES ON THE NEXT DAY WEDNESDAY OR THURSDAY, ADAR 15. IF ADAR 14 FALLS ON THE FIFTH DAY, VILLAGES AND LARGE TOWNS READ ON THAT VERY DAY, AND WALLED CITIES ON THE NEXT DAY FRIDAY, ADAR 15.
1. IV:1: Why is the first part of the Mishnah, which follows the sequence of the days of the month, different from the last part of the Mishnah, which follows the sequence of the days of the week?

H. If Adar 14 falls on the eve of the Sabbath, villages advance to the day of assembly Thursday, Adar 13, and large towns and walled cities read on that very day Friday. If Adar 14 falls on the Sabbath, villages and large towns advance and read it on the day of assembly Thursday, Adar 12, and walled cities on the next day Sunday, Adar 15. If Adar 14 falls after the Sabbath on Sunday, villages advance to the day of assembly Thursday, Adar 11, and large towns read on that very day, and walled cities on the next day Monday, Adar 15.

1. V:1: According to whom is the Mishnah formulated, R. Judah the Patriarch or R. Yosé?
   a. V:2: Gloss of a detail of the foregoing. Does R. Judah the Patriarch really think that we never reschedule the towns back to the preceding day of assembly
2. V:3: In any case, everyone agrees that we do not read the Megillah on the Sabbath. What is the reason? Said Rabbah: Everyone is obligated to hear the reading of the Megillah and the blowing of the Shofar, but not everyone is expert in the way to do the reading of the Megillah, so we prohibit reading it on the Sabbath, lest one take it in his hand and go to an expert to learn how to read it and carry it four cubits in a public domain in violation of the Sabbath law. R. Joseph said: Because the eyes of the poor are lifted up during the reading of the Megillah to await the distribution of the gifts for the poor, which cannot be done on the Sabbath.
3. V:4: Said Rab: At the proper time, one may read the Megillah, even in private; not at the proper time, it may be read only among ten people; i.e., in public. R. Asi said: Whether at the proper time or not at the proper time, one reads the Megillah only among ten people.

Nothing in the outline points toward the presence of dialectical arguments; the outline portrays a systematic commentary to the Mishnah, enriched with composites that are inserted as appendices or supplements. It raises the unanticipated possibility that the dialectical-analytical argument forms only a modest proportion of the Talmud overall; only our complete survey can provide the facts of the matter.

II. Mishnah-Exegesis the Starting Point

We shall now see that the treatment of the opening rule, Outline reference I.A, is exegetical; there is no broadening of interest, and we find no dialectical argument, just the formal organization of discourse into questions and answers. But the examination of Outline reference B involves precisely such an argument, as we shall discern. That is, B.1 involves a flow of argument over a variety of fields.

1:1-2
1:1

- A. They water an irrigated field on the intermediate days of a festival and in the Sabbatical Year [when many forms of agricultural labor are forbidden],
- B. whether from a spring that first flows at that time, or from a spring that does not first flow at that time.
- C. But they do not water [an irrigated field] with (1) collected rainwater, or (2) water from a swape well.
- D. And they do not dig channels around vines.

1:2

- A. R. Eleazar b. Azariah says, "They do not make a new water channel on the intermediate days of a festival or in the Sabbatical Year."
- B. And sages say, "They make a new water channel in the Sabbatical Year, and they repair damaged ones on the intermediate days of a festival."
- C. They repair damaged waterways in the public domain and dig them out.
- D. They repair roads, streets, and water pools.
- E. And they (1) do all public needs, (2) mark off graves, and (3) go forth [to give warning] against [maintaining a field that is planted with] Diverse Kinds [or species of crops].

I.1   A. [They water an irrigated field on the intermediate days of a festival and in the Sabbatical Year, whether from a spring that first flows at that time, or from a spring that does not first flow at that time:] *since it is explicitly stated that they may water a field from a spring that flows for the first time, which may damage the soil by erosion [making necessary immediate repair of the damage during the intermediate days of the festival], is it necessary to specify that they may water from a spring that does not first flow at that time, which is not going to cause erosion?*

Chapter One. Initial Probe

B. *One may say that it is necessary to include both the latter and the former, for if the Tannaite framer had given the rule only covering a spring that first flows on the intermediate days of the festival, it is in that case in particular in which it is permitted to work on an irrigated field, but not for a rain-watered field, because the water is going to cause erosion, but in the case of a spring that does not first flow on the intermediate days, which is unlikely to cause erosion, I might have said that even a rain-watered field may be watered. So by specifying both cases the framer of the Mishnah-paragraph informs us that there is no distinction between a spring that flows for the first time and one that does not flow for the first time. The rule is the same for both: an irrigated plot may be watered from it, but a rain-watered plot may not be watered from [either a new or an available spring].*

I.2 A. *And on what basis is it inferred that the meaning of the words* "**irrigated field**" *is, a thirsty field [which has to be irrigated]?*

B. *It is in line with that which is written:* "When you were faint and weary" (Dt. 25:18), *and the Hebrew word for weary is represented in Aramaic by the word that means, "exhausted."*

C. *And how do we know that the words translated rain-watered field refers to a well-fucked field?*

D. "For as a man has sexual relations with a maiden, so shall your sons be as husbands unto you" (Is. 62:5), *and the word in Aramaic is rendered,* "Behold, as a boy fucks a girl, so your sons shall get laid in your midst."

I.3 A. *Who is the Tannaite authority who takes the position that work on the intermediate days of a festival is permitted if it is to prevent loss, but if it is to add to gain it is not permitted, and, further, even to prevent loss, really heavy labor is forbidden?*

B. *Said R. Huna, "It is R. Eliezer b. Jacob, for we have learned in the Mishnah:* **R. Eliezer b. Jacob says, 'They lead water from one tree to another, on condition that one not water the entire field. Seeds which have not been watered before the festival one should not water on the intermediate days of the festival'** [M. 1:3]."

C. *Well, I might concede that there is a representation of R. Eliezer's position that he prohibits work to add to one's gain, but have you heard a tradition that he disallows work in a situation in which otherwise loss will result?*

D. *Rather, said R. Pappa, "Who is the authority behind this rule? It is R. Judah, for it has been taught on Tannaite authority:* **'From** a spring that first flows on the intermediate days of a festival they irrigate even a rain watered field,' the words of R. Meir. And sages [=Judah vis à vis Meir] say, 'They irrigate from it only a field that depends upon irrigation, which has gone dry.' R. Eleazar b. Azariah says, "Not this nor that, [[but they do not irrigate a field from it [namely, a field the spring of which has gone dry] even in the case of an irrigated field]' [T. Moed 1:1A-C]. Even further, said R. Judah, 'A person should not clean out a water channel and with the dredging on the intermediate days of a festival water his garden or seed bed.'"

E. *Now what is the meaning of "that has gone dry"? If you say that it really has dried up, then what is going to be accomplished by watering it?*

F. *Said Abbayye, "The point is that this former water source has gone dry and another has just emerged."*

G. **R. Eleazar b. Azariah says, "Not this nor that:"** *there is no difference between the case of an old spring that has gone dry or that has not gone dry, in any event a spring that has just flowed may not be utilized on the intermediate days of the festival.*

H. *And how to you know [that it is Judah in particular who takes the position that work on the intermediate days of a festival is permitted if it is to prevent loss, but if it is to add to gain it is not permitted, and, further, even to prevent loss, really heavy labor is forbidden]? Perhaps R. Judah takes the position that he does, that is, that it is permitted to use the water for an irrigated field but not for a field that depends on rain, only in the case of a spring that has just now begun to flow, [NB] since it may cause erosion, [hence, that may cause damage, as stipulated], but in the case of a spring that has not just now begun to flow and will not cause erosion, such a spring might be permitted for use even on a field that depends on rain?*

I. *If so, then in accord with which authority will you assign our Mishnah-paragraph? For in fact, in R. Judah's view, there is no distinction between a spring that has just now flowed and one that has not just now flowed; in either case, an irrigated field may be watered, while one that depends on rain may not. And the reason that the passage specifies the spring that has just now flowed is only to show the extend to which R. Meir was prepared to go, even a spring that has just now flowed may be used, and that is, even for a field that depends upon rain.*

Chapter One. Initial Probe

The foregoing presents Mishnah-commentary and amplification. While the form is superficially dialectical, in that the rhetoric involves questions and answers, the episodic character of the discussion in no way corresponds to the large-scale and sustained mode of composition that the analytical-dialectical argument sets forth.

III. A Limited Instance of the Dialectical-Analytical Argument in Mishnah-Exegesis

The next unit, which is a free-standing discussion pursuing its own interest and in no way a formal comment on our Mishnah-paragraph, cites our Mishnah-paragraph in the context of its pursuit of a solution to its problem. That formally accounts for the introduction of the passage into the amplification of our Mishnah-paragraph. But, as I shall explain at the end, introducing the composition into our composite serving M. 1:1 profoundly deepens our grasp of the law, not just the case and ruling, before us. Our concern in the Mishnah-paragraph before us has been to specify those interstitial acts that are neither heavy labor nor optional, but of moderate difficulty and necessary to preserve the value of the crop. Much then has to do with the character of the act. This yields an interest in the character and classification of agricultural labor: how hard, and for what purpose, is the work done. In what follows, we take up a free-standing composition that analyzes the classification of agricultural labor, once more with special reference to watering the field. Since what follows is a free-standing discussion that does not pursue the program of Mishnah-exegesis or continue the secondary implications of that program, and indeed does not even intersect with the law or principle before us, I indent the passage. The citation, later on, of a sentence of our Mishnah-passage provides the formal explanation for the inclusion of the following composition, but, as I shall propose at the end, reading the Mishnah-paragraph in light of what follows yields a profound grasp of the law, not only the rule, to which the Mishnah-paragraph's statement points. This is how the compositors of the Talmud move our vision from the rule to the laws, and from the laws to law.

> I.4 A. *It has been stated:*
> B. He who on the Sabbath weeds a field or waters his seedlings
> — *on what count is he to be admonished [not to do so]?*
> C. Rabbah said, "On the count of plowing."
> D. R. Joseph said, "On the count of sowing."

One who violates the law of the Sabbath is admonished that he is violating the law, being told specifically what law he is violating, and on what count. Here the act or weeding or watering is classified among the classes of forbidden labor. Is watering an act of plowing or of sowing? The point of intersection is now clear. Our Mishnah-paragraph has dealt with irrigating a field, which is a marginal activity; under some conditions it may be performed on the intermediate days of the festival. Can we sow? Certainly not. Can we plow? As we shall now see, there is an aspect of plowing that pertains to the intermediate days of the festival, namely, softening the soil.

E. *Said Rabbah, "It is more reasonable to see matters as I do. For what is the purpose of plowing, if not to loosen the soil, and, here too, he loosens the soil."*

F. *Said R. Joseph, "It is more reasonable to see matters as I do. For what is the purpose of sowing? It is to make produce sprout up. And here too, he makes produce sprout up."*

Here is a point of intersection with our rule, since we recall we may save the crop but not enhance its growth. Joseph's thinking, then, intersects with the problem before us, when he introduces the notion that plowing is forbidden on the count of enhancing the crop's growth. But how will Rabbah differ, since plowing a crop enhances its growth by aerating the roots. Keeping in mind that we deal with a free-standing composition, we cannot find surprising the systematic analysis of the dispute just now introduced:

G. *Said Abbayye to Rabbah, "There is a problem in your position, and there also is a problem in the position of R. Joseph.*

  H. *"There is a problem in your position: does this act come only under the classification of plowing and not sowing?*

  I. *"And there also is a problem in the position of R. Joseph: does this act come only under the classification of sowing and not plowing?*

We are now on quite familiar ground, namely, the area where we deem a given action to fall into two distinct classifications. Yet, if the issue is crop-enhancement, then distinguishing one position from the other produces a distinction that makes slight difference.

  J. *"And should you say that in any place in which an act may be classified under two taxa, one is subject to liability on only one count, has not R. Kahana said, 'If one pruned his tree but requires the wood for fuel, he is liable on two counts, one on the count of planting, the other on the count of harvesting'?"*

  K. *That's a problem.*

  L. Objected R. Joseph to Rabbah, "**He who weeds or covers with dirt diverse seeds is flogged. R. Aqiba says, 'Also one who preserves them'** [T. Kil. 1:15A-B]. *Now from my perspective, in that I hold that one is liable on the count of sowing, that explains the penalty, since sowing is forbidden in connection with mixed seeds in the vineyard; but from your perspective, in that you say that the count is plowing, is there any prohibition of plowing in connection with mixed seeds?"*

If plowing is classified as crop-enhancing, then on what basis is it forbidden to plow when the taboo against mixed seeds has been violated? That is an easy question to answer. Preserving the crop is a form of enhancing it.

Chapter One. Initial Probe

M. He said to him, "The count is that he has preserved them."
N. "But lo, since the concluding clause states, **R. Aqiba says, 'Also one who preserves them,'** *it must follow that the initial Tannaite authority maintains that the count for sanction is not that of preserving the crop of mixed seeds!*"
O. "The whole of the statement represents the position of R. Aqiba, and the sense of the passage is to explain the operative consideration, specifically: what is the reason that **he who weeds or covers with dirt diverse seeds is flogged**? *It is because one is thereby preserving them, since* **R. Aqiba says, 'Also one who preserves them.'**"

We now add a gloss to the foregoing, of which we may rapidly dispose; it is simply a scriptural foundation for a rule.

P. *What is the basis in Scripture for the position of R. Aqiba?*
Q. *It is in line with that which has been taught on Tannaite authority:*
R. "You shall not sow your field with two kinds of seed" (Lev. 19:19) —
S. I know only that sowing is forbidden. How do we know that preserving the sown seed is forbidden?
T. Scripture says, "Mixed seeds in your field not....," [meaning: it is the mixing of seeds that is emphatically forbidden, and you may have no share by your action in producing such a situation (Lazarus)].

We revert to the discussion broken off at U. We continue our interest in the intersecting issues, first, grounds for prohibiting watering a field — plowing vs. sowing; and, second, the matter of the sanctification expressed through prohibition of labor on the Sabbath and the Festival day, as against the sanctification expressed through that same prohibition on days that are comparable to the Sabbath and the Festival but of a diminished level of sanctification. For that purpose, we revert to our Mishnah-paragraph. And that in a formal sense accounts for the inclusion here of the entire, massive composition, together with its inserted and appended supplements. But, as I shall explain at the end, the result of the insertion of the discussion is greatly to deepen our understanding of the context in which the law of our Mishnah-paragraph finds its place. So we grasp not merely the rule, but the law, when we have read our Mishnah-paragraph as part of a larger essay of thinking about labor, sanctification, the Sabbath and Festivals, and spells of time that are comparable to the Festival or to the Sabbath. Since we have dealt with the intermediate days of festivals, comparable to the Festival day, we turn now to the Sabbatical Year, that is to say, the seventh year of a seven-year cycle, which, as its name states, is comparable to the Sabbath, in bearing prohibitions as to acts of labor by reason of Sabbath rest, but at the same time is subject to a lesser degree of sanctification than the Sabbath.

U. *We have learned in the Mishnah:* **They water an irrigated field on the intermediate days of a festival and in the Sabbatical Year [M. 1:1A]:**

The reason for the introduction of the Mishnah paragraph's rule on the Sabbatical Year is immediately articulated:

V. [With respect to the inclusion of **in the Sabbatical Year:**] *Now there is no difficulty understanding the rule concerning the intermediate days of the festival, which pertains to a situation in which there is substantial loss, on account of which rabbis have permitted irrigation.* [We simply repeat the result of the opening exegetical discussion, without citing it verbatim. Our passage's author need not have known Nos. 1-3 above. Now reference is made to the present composition's important question, now linked to the Mishnah-rule before us:] *But as to the Sabbatical Year, whether one holds that watering is classified as sowing or that watering is classified as plowing, is it permitted either to sow or to plow in the Sabbatical Year [that it should be permitted to water the field]?*

The question is a powerful one and brings to the surface the premises of our entire discussion, which are, we compare days that are comparable to the Sabbath or Festival, therefore we invoke the rule governing the one for the law that prevails on the other, here, intermediate days of the festival, there, the Sabbatical Year. Once we have asked the question in this way, the answer is obvious, and Abbayye can be relied upon, as always, to see it:

W. Said Abbayye, "It is concerning the Sabbatical Year at this time that the rule speaks, and the rule represents the position of Rabbi."

X. *For it has been taught on Tannaite authority:*

Y. Rabbi says, "'This is the manner of release: release [by every creditor of that which he has lent his neighbor' (Dt. 15:2) — it is of two different acts of release that Scripture speaks, one, the release of lands, the other, the release of debts. When you release lands you release debts, and when you do not release lands, you do not release debts." [The prohibition of agricultural labor in the Sabbatical Year now that the Temple is destroyed is merely by reason of rabbinical authority, and that prohibition is not enforced where loss is involved (Lazarus). Therefore, from our perspective, the lenient

Chapter One. Initial Probe

ruling for the intermediate days of the festival applies also to the Sabbatical Year in the present age.]

Z. *Raba said, "You may even maintain that the rule before us represents the position of rabbis [vis à vis Rabbi]. It is the generative categories of labor that the All-Merciful has prohibited,* **[3A]** *but the subsidiary classes of labor* [such as the ones we are considering as analogous to the generative category, that is, watering is either in the class of plowing or in the class of sowing] *have not been forbidden. For it is written, 'But in the seventh year shall be a Sabbath of solemn rest for the land...you shall neither sow your field nor prune your vineyard. That which grows of itself of your harvest you shall not reap and the grapes of your undressed vine you shall not gather'* (Lev. 25:4-5). *Since pruning falls within the generative category of sowing, and grape gathering falls within the generative category of reaping, for what concrete legal purpose did the All-Merciful make written reference to these items? It is to present the inference that it is to these particular derivative classes of generative categories of labor that liability pertains, but to all others, there is no liability."*

AA. *So they don't, don't they? But has it not been taught on Tannaite authority:*

We now adduce evidence that the subsidiary acts of labor do fall under the same restrictions as the generative acts of labor, and this is explicit. The evidence is from Sifra and is marked as Tannaite in attribution. Spelling out the evidence is not critical to the exposition and I treat it as a footnote or appendix. The concluding sentence disposes of the whole, as we shall see presently.

BB. **["The Lord said to Moses on Mount Sinai, Say to the people of Israel, When you come into the land which I give you, the land shall keep a Sabbath to the Lord. Six years you shall sow your field, and six years you shall prune your vineyard and gather in its fruits; but in the seventh year there shall be a Sabbath of solemn rest for the land, a Sabbath to the Lord; you shall not sow your field or prune your vineyard. What grows of itself in your harvest you shall not reap, and the grapes of your undressed vine you shall not gather; it shall be a year of solemn rest for the land. The Sabbath of the land shall provide food for you, for yourself and for your male and female slaves and for your hired servant and the** sojourner who lives with you; for your cattle also and for the beasts that are in your land all its yield shall be for food" (Lev. 25:1-7):] "you shall not sow your field or prune your vineyard:"

CC. the Torah forbids me only to sow or prune,

DD. And how do we know that farmers may not fertilize, prune trees, smoke the leaves or cover over with powder for fertilizer?

EE. Scripture says, "your field you shall not...." — no manner of work in your field, no manner of work in your vineyard, shall you do.

FF. And how do we know that farmers may not trim trees, nip off dry shoots, trim trees?

GG. Scripture says, "your field you shall not...." — no manner of work in your field, no manner of work in your vineyard, shall you do.

HH. And how do we know that one may not manure, remove stones, dust the flower of sulphur, or fumigate?

II. Scripture says, "your field you shall not...." — no manner of work in your field, no manner of work in your vineyard, shall you do.

JJ. Since Scripture says, "you shall not sow your field or prune your vineyard,"

KK. might one suppose that the farmer also may not hoe under the olive trees, fill in the holes under the olives trees, or dig between one tree and the next?

LL. Scripture says, "you shall not sow your field or prune your vineyard" —

MM. sowing and pruning were subject to the general prohibition of field labor. Whey then were they singled out?

NN. It was to build an analogy through them, as follows:

OO. what is distinctive in sowing and pruning is that they are forms of labor carried on on the ground or on a tree.

PP. So I know that subject to the prohibition are also other forms of labor that are carried on on the ground or on a tree, [excluding from the prohibition, therefore, the types of labor listed] [Sifra CCXLV:I.3-6].

QQ. *What we have here is a rule made by rabbinical authority, for which support is adduced from Scripture.*

Chapter One. Initial Probe

The solution to the problem at QQ is a simple one. The prohibition derives from rabbis, who then can release it on their own; the role of Scripture is not to declare the rule but only to provide support for rabbis' opinion. We have now completed our exposition. So much for 1.4.

Now to the issue at hand: how come I maintain that we have an authentic dialectical-analytical argument? The turning point comes at U. Had we stopped at T, we should have been left with a fine exposition of the dispute of Rabbah and Joseph. A-D set forth the dispute, E-F amplify the operative considerations, G+H-I then present a challenge to each of the positions, and J-K complete the challenge. Then L-O present an objection by one party to the argument to the other. P-T form an interpolated gloss and do not disrupt matters. That concludes the entire composition, a beautiful articulation of a single dispute. As I said, the mere utilization of the rhetoric of questions and answers does not signify that a dialectic argument is underway.

Then we come to U. Here we introduce a problem that is hardly required to resolve the matter presented up to T. Our problem is now a fresh one, namely, the Sabbatical year and the classification of watering therein. The issue is fresh, and this is the point at which the argument veers off in its own, unpredictable direction: On what basis have we treated the intermediate days of the festival as comparable to the Sabbatical Year, even though they share the classification of spans of time that are comparable to the Sabbath or Festival day but at a diminished level of sanctification. Once we introduce Rabbi's position as a solution to our problem, we work on the exposition of that position. Then Raba rejects the proposed solution and his solution has to be amplified, BBff. What we have is not one of those sustained and penetrating dialectical-analytical compositions, but it also is not a simple and cogent exegetical proposition in its own terms.

To proceed to the conclusion: The foregoing insertion has alleged at KK-LL that it is permitted in the Sabbatical Year to aerate the soil under an olive tree. That matter is now treated on its own; the composition that follows is then an appendix to an appendix. The indentation is meant to show the relationship of the following composition to the foregoing.

    I.5   A. *And is it permitted to stir the soil under an olive tree in the Sabbatical Year? Has it not been taught on Tannaite authority:*

            B. *Now it is permitted to hoe [in the Sabbatical Year]? And has it not been written, "*

            C. *"But the seventh year you shall let [the land] rest and lie still" (Ex. 23:11).*

            D. *"You shall let it rest" from hoeing,*

            E. *"and lie still" from having stones removed.*

            F. *Said R. Uqba bar Hama, "There are two kinds of hoeing. In one kind one closes up the holes [around*

> the roots of a tree], and in the other, he aerates the soil [around the roots of a tree].
>
> G. "Aerating the soil is forbidden, closing up the holes is permitted [since the former serves the roots of the tree, the latter merely protects the tree]."

Yet another free standing composition is appended. We have dealt with plowing and sowing on the intermediate days of the festival, which we have treated as comparable to the Sabbatical Year. So it is natural to pursue the rules of the Sabbatical year as these have been introduced. Is it then permitted at all to plow in the Sabbatical Year? The next appendix follows.

> **I.6** A. *It has been stated:*
> B. He who plows in the Sabbatical Year —
> C. R. Yohanan and R. Eleazar —
> D. One said, "He is flogged."
> E. The other said, "He is not flogged."

Clearly, there is debate on the matter, and the premise of our discussion, comparing the two types of diminished sanctification, depends upon the opinion of the one who says he is not flogged. Were we to conclude here, we should have an ample presentation of our free-standing composition, as well as its secondary accretions. But we proceed to expand upon the expansion, in fresh commentary to what has just preceded.

It answers, specifically, the question, hence the basis for the division? At stake for us is a rational reading of the law; we wish to show that both parties to a dispute have ample basis for their opinions, and, ideally, the basis for the dispute will be a deeper, more systematic conflict on how, exactly, we interpret Scripture. The issue in its own terms has been set forth. What is the basis in a more encompassing reading of matters? What underlies the dispute is now spelled out, in an appended commentary on the dispute itself.

> **I.7** A. *May we say that the dispute concerns that which R. Abin said R. Ilaa said, for* said R. Abin said R. Ilaa, "In any passage in which you find a generalization concerning an affirmative action, followed by a qualification expressing a negative commandment, people are not to construct on that basis an argument resting on the notion of a general proposition followed by a concrete exemplification only the substance of the concrete exemplification." [Freedman, *Sanhedrin*, p. 777-8, n. 8: The rule in such a case is: the general proposition includes only what is enumerated in the particular specification. But when one is

thrown into the form of a positive command and the other stated as a negative injunction this does not apply.]

B. *By this theory of what is at issue, one who says he is flogged does not concur with what R. Abin said R. Ilai said, and one who said, "He is not flogged," concurs with what R. Abin said.* [Lazarus: The general rule in positive terms: "The land shall keep a Sabbath..." (Lev. 25:2-5); the particulars in negative terms, "You shall neither sow..." (Lev. 25:4-5); the general rule again in positive form, "It shall be a year of solemn rest...." Then the particulars are considered typical as illustrations, serving to include in the general rule all such items as are similar to the particulars. If the particulars are typical of the general rule, one who does any of these would break the law. In the case of the former, he takes sowing, pruning, reaping, and gleaning as typical illustrative instances, and plowing is covered and is punishable. In the case of the latter, plowing is not included among the forbidden processes and is not punishable.]

C. *No, all parties reject the position stated by R. Abin in R. Ilai's name. One who says he is flogged has no problems anyhow.*

D. *The one who says he is not flogged may reply in this way:*

E. *Since pruning falls within the generative category of sowing, and grape gathering falls within the generative category of reaping, for what concrete legal purpose did the All-Merciful make written reference to these items? It is to present the inference that it is to these particular derivative classes of generative categories of labor that liability pertains, but to all others, there is no liability."*

Following the printed text, we now go over the previously-introduced demonstration that for the purposes of the Sabbatical Year we treat as uniform, under the same law and penalty, an entire class of acts of labor.

F. *So they don't, don't they? But has it not been taught on Tannaite authority:*

G. ["The Lord said to Moses on Mount Sinai, Say to the people of Israel, When you come into the land which I give you, the land shall keep a Sabbath to the Lord. Six years you shall sow your field, and six years you shall prune your vineyard and gather in its fruits; but in the seventh year there shall be a Sabbath of solemn rest for the land, a Sabbath to the Lord; you shall not sow your field or prune your vineyard. What grows of itself in your harvest you shall not reap, and the grapes of your undressed vine you shall not gather; it shall be a year of solemn rest for the land. The Sabbath of the land shall provide food for you, for yourself and for your male and female slaves and for your hired servant and the sojourner who lives with you; for your cattle also and for the beasts that are in your land all its yield shall be for food" (Lev. 25:1-7):] "you shall not sow your field or prune your vineyard:"
H. the Torah forbids me only to sow or prune,
I. And how do we know that farmers may not fertilize, prune trees, smoke the leaves or cover over with powder for fertilizer?
J. Scripture says, "your field you shall not...." — no manner of work in your field, no manner of work in your vineyard, shall you do.
K. And how do we know that farmers may not trim trees, nip off dry shoots, trim trees?
L. Scripture says, "your field you shall not...." — no manner of work in your field, no manner of work in your vineyard, shall you do.
M. And how do we know that one may not manure, remove stones, dust the flower of sulphur, or fumigate?
N. Scripture says, "your field you shall not...." — no manner of work in your field, no manner of work in your vineyard, shall you do.

Chapter One. Initial Probe

O. Since Scripture says, "you shall not sow your field or prune your vineyard,"
P. might one suppose that the farmer also may not hoe under the olive trees, fill in the holes under the olives trees, or dig between one tree and the next?
Q. Scripture says, "you shall not sow your field or prune your vineyard" —
R. sowing and pruning were subject to the general prohibition of field labor. Whey then were they singled out?
S. It was to build an analogy through them, as follows:
T. what is distinctive in sowing and pruning is that they are forms of labor carried on on the ground or on a tree.
U. So I know that subject to the prohibition are also other forms of labor that are carried on on the ground or on a tree, [excluding from the prohibition, therefore, the types of labor listed] [Sifra CCXLV:I.3-6].
V. *What we have here is a rule made by rabbinical authority, for which support is adduced from Scripture.*

We proceed to a further refinement on the proposition at hand. The Sabbatical Year is augmented by a month fore and aft, during which prohibitions of a diminished order are introduced, on the one side, and continued, on the other. This protects the sanctity of the Sabbatical Year by training the farmers to observe the taboos before the advent of the year, and making certain they continue to observe them for a bit of time after the year has terminated, so that they do not cut the year short. So we ask whether the result just now adduced pertains to these still-less sanctified spells, and that is a gloss upon an appendix, and is so marked:

W. *[3B] When R. Dimi came, he said, "Might one suppose that one is flogged even for doing so during the additional time that has been added to the Sabbatical Year [fore and aft]? But the discussion resolved in favor of exempting one who worked during the addition to the Sabbatical Year."*
X. *But I don't know what is this "discussion" and to what reference*

is made under the category, "addition"!

Y. *R. Eleazar said, "Reference is made to plowing, and this is the sense of the statement: might one suppose that one is flogged on account of plowing in the Sabbatical Year?* For that conclusion would derive from a reading of the relevant verses under the principle of a generalization followed by a particularization of the foregoing followed by another generalization. And the discussion resolved in favor of exempting one who worked during the addition to the Sabbatical Year in the following way: if the flogging were in order, then what is the sense of the many particularizations that the text contains?"

Z. *R. Yohanan said, "Reference is made to* the days that sages added to the Sabbatical Year prior to the advent of the New Year that marks the commencement of the Sabbatical Year proper, *and this is the sense of the statement: might one suppose that one is flogged on account of plowing on the days that sages added to the Sabbatical Year prior to the advent of the New Year that marks the commencement of the Sabbatical Year proper? For that conclusion would derive from the following:* 'In plowing time and in reaping time you shall rest' (Ex. 34:21). *And the discussion resolved in favor of exempting one who did so,"* as we shall have to explain below.

A further appendix is now called for, to explain the reference to days added to the Sabbatical Year.

Chapter One. Initial Probe

AA. *To what is reference made in the allusion to the days that sages added to the Sabbatical Year prior to the advent of the New Year that marks the commencement of the Sabbatical Year proper?*

We now proceed to a secondary development of the statement that has just been made. Were we to stop before what follows, we should suffer no less of sense or meaning. The discussion that follows moreover goes off in its own direction.

BB. *That is in line with what we have learned in the Mishnah:* **Until what time do they plow an orchard during the year preceding the Sabbatical Year? The House of Shammai say, "As long as [the plowing] continues to benefit the produce [of the Sixth Year. Until that year's fruit ripens and is harvested] ." But the House of Hillel say, "Until Pentecost." And the opinion of the one is close to the opinion of the other [M. Sheb. 1:1]. Until what time do they plow in a field of grain (lit.: a white field) during the year preceding the Sabbatical Year? Until the moisture [in the ground] is gone As long as people plow in order to plant chatemelons and gourds. Said R. Simeon, "You have put the law into the hands of each individual. Rather, [one may plow] in a field of grain until Passover [when Israelites offer the first sheaf of new grain at the Temple; cf. Lev. 23:10] and [one may plow] in an orchard until Pentecost [when they present the firstfruits] [M. Sheb. 2:1].**

CC. And said R. Simeon b. Pazzi said R. Joshua b. Levi in the name of Bar Qappara, "Rabban Gamaliel and his court took a vote concerning these two spells and annulled them." [It was permitted to till down to the New Year itself (Lazarus).]

The allegation that has just now been made requires exposition in its own terms. It attracts interest for obvious reasons: how can a later court nullify the actions of an earlier one?

DD. *Said R. Zira to R. Abbahu, and some say, R. Simeon b. Laqish to R. Yohanan, "How could Rabban Gamaliel and his court have annulled an ordinance made by the House of Shammai and the House of Hillel? And lo, we have learned in the Mishnah:* **[And why do they record the opinion of an individual along with that of the majority, since the law follows the opinion of the majority? So that, if a court should prefer the opinion of the individual, it may decide to rely upon it.] For a court has not got the power to nullify the opinion of another court unless it is greater than it in wisdom and in numbers. [If] it was greater than the other in wisdom but not in numbers, in numbers but not in wisdom, it has not got the power to nullify its opinion — unless it is**

Chapter One. Initial Probe

greater than it in both wisdom and numbers [M. Ed. 1:5]!"

EE. *For a moment he was stupefied, but then he said to him, "I say,* this is what they stipulated among themselves: whoever wants to nullify the rule may come along and nullify it."

FF. *Well, did that measure really belong to them? Was it not a law revealed by God to Moses at Mount Sinai? For that is in line with what R. Assi said R. Yohanan said in the name of R. Nehunia of the Valley of Bet Hauran,* "The rules covering ten saplings, [**As regards ten saplings which are spread out within a seah space — they plow the entire seah space for the saplings' sake until the New Year of the Sabbatical Year (M. Sheb. 1:6A-B)**], the willow [carried around the altar during the festival], and the water offering are laws revealed to Moses at Sinai."

GG. *Said R. Isaac, "When we received as a tradition the law adding additional restricted time to the Sabbatical Year as a law revealed to Moses at Sinai, it was only concerning the thirty days prior to the New Year. The House of Shammai and Hillel came along and ordained that* work should case from Passover [for the grain field] and from Pentecost [for an orchard], and, at the same time, they made the stipulation with regard to what they said that, whoever might afterward come along and want to nullify those spells of restricted time may come along and nullify them."

HH. *But are these specified spells of time merely law? Are they not based in fact on explicit verses of Scripture? For has it not been taught on Tannaite authority:*

II. "Six days you shall work but on the seventh day you shall rest, in plowing time and in harvest you shall rest" (Ex. 34:21) [whatever the need, plowing and reaping may not be done on the Sabbath or the Sabbatical Year] —

JJ. R. Aqiba says, "The reference to plowing and reaping is not required to indicate that these actions are forbidden in the Sabbatical Year itself, for that is explicitly covered when Scripture says, 'neither shall you sow your field or prune your vineyard[(Lev. 25:4-5). Rather, the purpose is to impose the restriction of plowing even in the year prior to the Sabbatical Year **[4A]** when the effect of the plowing will extend into the Sabbatical Year, and it is to restrict harvesting produce partly grown in the Sabbatical Year but reaped in the year following the Sabbatical Year."

KK. R. Ishmael says, "Just as plowing is optional, so reaping is optional. Excluded from the prohibition of work on the Sabbath then is the reaping of the first sheaf of barley for the sheaf to be waved, which is a religious duty [and may be done on the Sabbath]."

LL. *Rather, said R. Nahman bar Isaac, "When the law was handed on as a tradition [concerning the time prior to the Sabbatical Year], this concerned permitting tilling to benefit saplings, while the cited verses of Scripture concern prohibiting tilling around old trees."*

MM. *Well, if it was necessary to appeal to a traditional low to allow tilling around saplings up to the advent of the New Year, is it not self-evident that doing so around old trees is going to be forbidden?*

NN. *Rather, when the traditional law was handed down as a prohibition, it was required only from the view of R.*

Ishmael, while the verses of Scripture form the basis of the position of R. Aqiba.

OO. R. Yohanan said, Rabban Gamaliel and his court nullified the restrictions on the authority of the Torah."

PP. What is the scriptural basis for their position?

QQ. They formed a verbal analogy based on the use of the word "Sabbath" with reverence to both the Sabbatical Year, called the Sabbatical Year, and also the Sabbath of Creation, along these lines:

RR. Just as in the case of the Sabbath of Creation, prohibitions pertain to the holy day but not to the time beforehand or afterward, so in the case of the Sabbatical Year, prohibitions pertain to the year but not to the time beforehand or afterward.

SS. Objected R. Ashi, "(In the view of one who maintains that the restriction is a traditional law, can an argument based on verbal analogy come along and nullify a traditional law? And if one says that it is based on a verse of Scripture, along these same lines, can an argument formed of a verbal analogy come along and nullify the result of the reading of a verse of Scripture?"

Chapter One. Initial Probe 27

TT. *Rather, said R. Ashi, "Rabban Gamaliel and his court adopted the reasoning of R. Ishmael, who said, 'The prohibitions of tilling on the spell prior to the actual advent of the Sabbatical Year derives from a traditional law. And to what span of time did that traditional law pertain? It was during the time that the Temple was standing, just as the rule of the water libation [which likewise derived from a traditional law] pertained only during the time that the Temple was standing. But when the Temple is no longer standing, the law received by tradition does not apply.'"*

The final entry clearly serves as a massive appendix; it is intelligently situated for that purpose at the end, since it does not impede the presentation of the whole. In contemporary scholarship we should situate in an appendix at the end of a chapter or of a book such a discussion, only tangentially relevant to the main point. One of the marks of the conclusion of a systematic and cogent presentation of a point is the insertion of such sizable complexes of supplementary data. Whoever wrote up the composition had his own focus and in no way evinces knowledge of the ultimate location of his writing; and whoever inserted the composition selected it for the sake of completeness, even recognizing how the insertion would impart to his composite a discursive character.

The continuation in no way forms a dialectical argument — just a run on exposition. The compositor has paid a heavy price for his decision, since the Talmud before us loses cogency before it has run its course even half way. Then what lesson did he propose to teach by the composition as we have it, in which the opening units pursue a single line of thought, and everything else wanders off hither and yon? To frame the question more concretely: we have now completed the presentation of the entire treatment of M. 1:1A. The run-on effect of the whole proves blatant. Had we stopped at No. 3, we should have found a fairly ample exposition of the Mishnah-passage. Not only so, but Nos. 4-6 really do not address the Mishnah-rule at all; they go their own way, with a focus upon the Sabbatical Year, not the intermediate days of the festival. But the Sabbatical Year in the Mishnah-rule is subordinate, introduced by reason of an analogy that is not spelled out. Any allegation that the Talmud is coherent and well-drafted must address the challenge of the sizable and meandering composite before us.

The secondary expansion, No. 4, drawing in its wake the appended, also free-standing discussions at Nos. 5 and 6, bearing their extensions and accretions, obviously has taken up most of our attention. Together with its enormous amplification in successive appendices, the consideration of that matter has defined the context in which the Talmud wishes us to read the Mishnah-paragraph at hand. So we have now to ask, What has the framer accomplished in introducing the passage into the context of our Mishnah-paragraph? First, he has raised the issue of the Sabbath and its categories of prohibited labor, and therefore he has introduced a complication into our consideration of the Mishnah-passage. We deal here with watering. Watering on the Festival is forbidden, since all acts of labor but cooking that are forbidden on the Sabbath are forbidden on the Festival. Then we forthwith deal with the prohibition of watering on the Sabbath and ask by what reason it is forbidden, with implications for the considerations operative in our Mishnah-rule governing the diminished sanctity of the intermediate days of the festival. In doing so, the compositor who took a free-standing discussion and deposited it here has accomplished a second matter in the exegesis of the theme before us. He has settled the paramount issue of our tractate: to what do we compare the intermediate days of the festival? Are they comparable to the Festival and the Sabbath, only subject to diminished restrictions? Or are they comparable to weekdays, but subject to some restrictions rather than none?

Juxtaposition the exposition of M. 1:1 with a rule concerning the Sabbath (therefore also, the Festival taboo against labor), introducing a case comparable to the Mishnah's, namely, watering the field, the compiler of the set has underscored the theoretical issue that must engage us: the governing analogy, Sabbath-Festival or ordinary week day, that generates the specific rulings at hand. Since I maintain that the juxtaposition makes a point directly pertinent to the theoretical problem our Mishnah states in concrete terms, let me spell out the connections I see to join to the exposition of our Mishnah-rule an otherwise utterly irrelevant passage.

That brings us to the substance of the comment on the Mishnah-passage that is effected by the compositor simply by introducing the present free-standing composition. It is to introduce the complications of classifications of acts of labor into the simple matter at hand. Our Mishnah-paragraph has made the point that we may keep a crop alive through irrigating it, but we may not go to great effort to water the crop, and we may also not do more than keep it alive; that is, we may do nothing to enhance the growth. That point is made explicit in the language, "*work on the intermediate days of a festival is permitted if it is to prevent loss, but if it is to add to gain it is not permitted.*" The free-standing composition then goes over

Chapter One. Initial Probe

the same ground in a different setting. Why? Because the free-standing composition addresses the matter of crop enhancement on the Sabbath; the Festival day is comparable to the Sabbath in every prohibition but that concerning food-preparation. Hence the issue of the Sabbath and the Festival, so far as crop-enhancement is the governing consideration, pertains here. We then draw the contrast between crop-enhancement — watering the crop, the same act the Mishnah-rule has introduced — on the Sabbath or Festival and on the intermediate days of the festival. What we simply may not do on the former occasion we may or may not be permitted to do on the latter. Introducing this discussion has served to remind us that while we deal with the intermediate days of the festival, the diminished sanctity that pertains must be protected, and the very same considerations that govern on the Sabbath (here: crop-enhancement) govern also on the intermediate days of the festival, but in a different way.

The operative principle then is underscored: loss is prevented, gain is not permitted. And that means, what may not be done on the Sabbath or Festival also may not be done on the intermediate days of the festival. By introducing the rule for the Sabbath and producing the explanation that the operative consideration behind the rule is the prohibition against crop-enhancement, the framer has made his main point: the intermediate days of the festival are comparable not to ordinary days, but subject to some restrictions, but to the Festival or Sabbath, and are subject to formidable restrictions. The governing analogy is the Sabbath and Festival, their restrictions diminished only for very special reasons, and not the everyday practices of the unconsecrated week, subject to a few special limitations. If this juxtaposition expresses the point I have spelled out — the priority of the Sabbath-Festival in defining the governing metaphor — then we should have a sustained interest in showing how the intermediate days of the festival really are comparable to the Festival itself, and are not comparable to, and do not follow the rules that pertain on, the ordinary days of the secular calendar. The upshot is that, in introducing an independent composition, with its own focus, the compositor has asked us to read the Mishnah-rule in a more complex way and so made us understand the rule as part of a larger web of law on the comparison of sacred and this-worldly matters.

We then form a preliminary hypothesis that the key to the selection-process is an interest in comparison and contrast of like classes of things, e.g., spans of time that are not sanctified like the Sabbath and Festival but that are in a diminished level of sanctification. Within that category falls each class of data we have worked on. Then the connections that are made yield the conclusions that are drawn, and, inclusive of the supplementary appendices, the whole holds together and imparts a lesson that on their own the parts do not convey. In this way the Talmud vastly transcends the labor of Mishnah-commentary and also enriches our grasp of the law that the Mishnah conveys through detail. We now proceed to the next clause of our Mishnah-paragraph.

IV. THE NEGLIGIBLE ROLE OF THE DIALECTICAL-ANALYTICAL ARGUMENT IN MISHNAH EXEGESIS

We resume the work of Mishnah-commentary, now turning directly to the sense of the statement. We do not understand why the same rule applies to two distinct classes of water-sources. The answer takes the form of a dispute:

II.1 A. **But they do not water [an irrigated field] with (1) collected rain water, or (2) water from a swape well [1:1C]:**

B. *There is no trouble in understanding why water from a swape well should not be used, since watering in that way involves heavy labor. But what objection can there be to using collected rain water, since what heavy labor can possibly be involved in irrigating with rain water?*

C. *Said R. Ilaa said R. Yohanan, "It is a precautionary decree, on account of the possibility of the farmer's going on to make use of water from a swape well."*

D. *R. Ashi said, "Rain water itself can be as hard to draw as the water of a swape well."*

Yohanan concedes the premise of the question, Ashi does not, but insists upon commensurability. Now the dispute is situated on a shared premise, so shown to be rational:

E. *At issue between them is what R. Zira said. For said R. Zira said Rabbah bar Jeremiah said Samuel, "From irrigation streams that draw water from ponds it is permitted to irrigate on the intermediate days of the festival." One authority [Ashi] concurs with the position of R. Zira, and the other authority does not concur with the position of R. Zira.*

The dispute now rests upon whether or not it is permitted to draw water from ponds, as Zira maintains is the case; so the problem is whether or not the rain water is in the same classification as standing water. We proceed to analyze 1.E in its own terms, and since the analysis is not required for the purpose that defines the matter but complements the discussion, in our setting we should footnote what follows, which is therefore indented:

II.2 A. *Reverting to the body of the foregoing:* said R. Zira said Rabbah bar Jeremiah said Samuel, "From irrigation streams that draw water from ponds it is permitted to irrigate on the intermediate days of the festival."

B. *Objected R. Jeremiah to R. Zira, "* **But they do not water [an irrigated field] with collected rain water, or water from a swape well."**

C. *He said to him, "Jeremiah my son, the pools in Babylonia are like water that never languishes."*

Chapter One. Initial Probe

The intersection with the Mishnah-rule is now explicit and shows why the entire composition serves Mishnah-exegesis. What follows are other items that are comparable, namely, bodies of water that draw from a constant source and do not involve physical labor in collecting the water for irrigation. These too form complements to the topic of the Mishnah.

II.3 A. *Our rabbis have taught on Tannaite authority:*
B. Ditches and pools that were filled with water on the eve of the festival may not be used for irrigation on the intermediate days of the festival. But if an irrigation ditch passes between them, they may be used.
C. Said R. Pappa, "But that is so only if the greater part of that field derives its water from that irrigation ditch."
D. R. Ashi said, "Even though the greater part of that field does not derive its water from that irrigation ditch, *since the water flows continuously, the owner concludes, the the field does not get enough water one day, it will get enough two or three days later [and he will not undertake heavy labor during the intermediate days of the festival]."*

The data not only add facts but also receive amplification at 3.D, which shows us the underlying reckoning that leads sages to their rulings. We now move on to Tosefta's complement to the Mishnah, which we analyze just as we do a Mishnah-paragraph. I cite the whole of the passage, though the Bavli gives us only the opening sentence and discusses that alone:

II.4 A. *Our rabbis have taught on Tannaite authority:*
B. **A pool that gets a trickle of water from an irrigated field higher up may be used for watering another field. [R. Simeon b. Menassia says, "Two pools, one above the other — one should not draw water from the lower to water the upper, but he may draw water from the upper to water the lower one. R. Simeon b. Eleazar says, "A furrow, part of which is low and part high — one should not draw water from the lower part for the upper part and irrigate it. But he may draw water from the upper part for the lower part and irrigate by that means" (T. Moed 1:1F-I)].**
C. [With reference to the statement, **A pool that gets a trickle of water from an irrigated field higher up may be used for watering another field**,] *but lo, will it not give out?*
D. Said R. Jeremiah, "In any event at this moment it is still trickling."
E. Said Abbayye, "The rule applies only so long as the first spring has not languished." [Lazarus: but once the trickling has ceased, the pool has lost its supply and becomes like a swape well or stored rain likely to entail exertion.]

The contribution lies in the analysis, which once more underscores the governing principle, for the reason that Lazarus contributes to the elucidation of Abbayye's comment. Now we go forward with further components of the passage just now cited.

II.5   A.   *It has been taught on Tannaite authority:*

B.   R. Simeon b. Menassia says, "Two pools, one above the other — one should not draw water from the lower to water the upper, but he may draw water from the upper to water the lower one.

C.   More than this did R. Simeon b. Eleazar [Bavli: Eleazar b. R. Simon] say, "Even in the case of a furrow, part of which is low and part high — one should not draw water from the lower part for the upper part and irrigate it. [T. adds: But he may draw water from the upper part for the lower part and irrigate by that means"] [T. Moed 1:1F-I].

This completes the citation and amplification of the Tosefta-paragraph. We go on with another rule in the status of Tannaite formulation:

II.6   A.   *Our rabbis have taught on Tannaite authority:*

B.   They may raise up water by buckets from a well during the festival week for vegetables so as to eat them. But if it is only to enhance their growth, it is forbidden to do so [since this is done for profit, not merely for maintaining the crop for the week or preventing loss].

The cited rule is now given amplification through a specific case, which clarifies the sense of the foregoing:

II.7   A.   *Rabina and Rabbah Tosefaah were going along the way. They saw somebody who was drawing buckets of water during the intermediate days of the festival. Said Rabbah Tosefaah to Rabina, "So let's go and excommunicate that man."*

B.   *He said to him, "But has it not been taught on Tannaite authority:* They may raise up water by buckets from a well during the festival week for vegetables so as to eat them. But if it is only to improve their appearance, it is forbidden to do so?*"*

C.   *He said to him, "Do you really think that the meaning of 'raise up' means raise up water? What is the real meaning of 'raise up'?* **[4B]** *it is to pull out vegetables. That meaning of the word is in line with what we have learned in the Mishnah:* "He who thins [using the word at hand] grape vines, just as he [is allowed] to thin his own [produce, the normal clusters], so may he thin [the defective clusters] which belong to the poor," the words of R. Judah. R. Meir says, "He is permitted to thin his own [produce], but he is not permitted [to thin produce] which belongs to the poor" [M. Peah 7:5]."

D. *He said to him, "But has it not been taught on Tannaite authority:* They may raise up water by buckets from a well during the festival week for vegetables so as to eat them?"

E. *He said to him, "So if that has been taught on Tannaite authority, that is what has been taught [and no more discussion]."*

The exposition of the Mishnah-paragraph in dialogue with the Toseftan supplements is now complete, the whole a cogent statement of the principle behind the rule: maintaining the crop, not making a profit, defines the acts that may be performed on the intermediate days of the festival, and how this works in detail is then spelled out for the case at hand. None of the exposition of the Mishnah-stich requires the formation of a dialectical argument.

III.1 A. **And they do not dig channels around vines:**

B. *What are "channels"?*

C. *Said R. Judah, "They are little hollows."*

D. *So too it has been taught on Tannaite authority:*

E. **What are channels dug around a tree? These are ditches dug around the roots of trees [T. Moed 1:2B-C].** They hoe lightly around the roots of olives and vines.

F. *Is that so? But did not R. Judah permit the sons of Bar Zittai to make little hollows in their vineyards?*

G. *That's no problem, the statement of our Mishnah speaks of fresh ones, R. Judah's to established ones.*

The explanation of word-choices is followed by citation and clarification of precedents.

IV.1 A. **R. Eleazar b. Azariah says, "They do not make a new water channel on the intermediate days of a festival or in the Sabbatical Year." And sages say, "They make a new water channel in the Sabbatical Year, and they repair damaged ones on the intermediate days of a festival:"**

We find ourselves thrust once more into the comparison of different spells that are at a lower level of sanctification than the Sabbath or the Festival, namely, the intermediate days of the festival and the Sabbatical Year. Consequently, we resume the task we began earlier, and, specifically, we want to know why the Sabbatical Year is subject to the prohibition at hand, which obviously pertains to the intermediate days of the festival. Here, the Mishnah-rule has dictated its own exegetical problem. The matter is spelled out in so many words in the terms I introduced earlier:

34   *Talmudic Dialectics*

B.   *There is no problem with respect to the prohibition concerning the intermediate days of a festival, since the operative consideration is that this is heavy labor, but why ever not make a channel in the Sabbatical Year?*
C.   *R. Zira and R. Abba b. Mamel differ on the matter —*
D.   One said, "The reason is that the one who digs appears to be hoeing."
E.   And the other said, "The reason is that he looks as though he is preparing the banks for sowing."
F.   *So what's at stake?*
G.   *At issue is a case in which the water comes along immediately. From the perspective of him who has said,* "The reason is that he looks as though he is preparing the banks for sowing," *it is still objectionable. But from the perspective of him who has said,* "The reason is that the one who digs appears to be hoeing," *there is no objection.*
H.   *But should not the one who objects for the reason that it looks as though he is spading also object that he looks as though he is preparing the bank for seed?*
I.   *Rather, this is what's at stake between the two explanations: it would involve a case in which he takes what is in the trench and tosses it out. From the perspective of him who says,* "The reason is that he looks as though he is preparing the banks for sowing," *there is no objection; but from the perspective of him who says,* "The reason is that the one who digs appears to be hoeing," *it is still subject to an objection.*
J.   *But from the perspective of him who says that he appears to be preparing the sides for seed, would he not also admit that he seems to be hoeing?*
K.   *Not really, for one who hoes, as soon as he takes up a spadeful, he puts it down again in place.*

This argument employs the rhetoric of questions and answers but is hardly dialectical in character; it is simply a systematic presentation of the issues at hand, beautifully balanced in classic proportions. What makes the exposition satisfying is that each side is given an opportunity to apply its reasoning at every stage in the argument, hence a full account, through the rhetorical-dialectic of back-and-forth exchange of positions and reasoning, is set forth. We proceed to a secondary analysis of the matter just now spelled out; the whole is continuous and cogent. The next step in the exposition raises the possibility that a given authority has taken two positions that contradict one another in principle.

IV.2   A.   *Amemar repeated the Mishnah's law along with the reason,* The reason is that the one who digs appears to be hoeing, *but this*

Chapter One. Initial Probe 35

presented a problem to him because of a contradiction between two statements of R. Eleazar b. Azariah [in the following language]: "And has R. Eleazar b. Azariah taken the position that any act that looks as if he is hoeing is forbidden? And in contradiction to that position: **A person places [all] the manure in his possession in [one large] pile. R. Meir forbids [the farmer from doing this] unless he either deepens [the ground by] three [handbreadths] or raises [the ground by] three [handbreadths]. If one had a small amount [of manure already piled up in the field], he continually adds to it. R. Eleazar b. Azariah forbids [the farmer from doing so] unless he either deepens [the ground by] three [handbreadths] or raises [the ground by] three [handbreadths] or unless he places [the manure] on rocky ground [M. Shebiit 3:3D-G].** [Lazarus: here Eleazar permits digging in the field in the sabbatical year to prepare a place for the manure store without concern about giving a wrong impression, such as he had in mind when he prohibited making a water channel.]

B. *R. Zira and R. Abba b. Mamel differ on the matter —*
C. One said, "The cited passage speaks of a case in which he had already had the place excavated."
D. And the other said, "The operative consideration is that the manure heap itself shows what his real intention is."

The possibility of Eleazar's adopting contradictory principles — do we take account of the farmer's giving the wrong impression? — is now explored and worked out. The exposition of the Mishnah's rule has given way to a systematic account of the consideration of the Sabbatical Year. Yet this too has a profound bearing on the conduct of the farmer on the intermediate days of the festival. Once more, we find nothing resembling a dialectical argument, such as I have defined.

V.1 A. **and they repair damaged ones on the intermediate days of a festival:**
B. *What is the meaning of* "damaged ones"?
C. Said R. Abba, "If one was only a handbreadth deep, he may restore it to a depth of six handbreadths."

The Mishnah-exegesis is simple and routine. We proceed to an important clarification of the kind of "damaged ones" that the farmer may repair. This imposes a considerable clarification and limitation: the original principle — no heavy labor, no work for enhancing profit — is illustrated once more. We now ask a question that flows from the matter at hand, one that defines an interstitial case.

V.2 A. *It is obvious that restoring the channel from a half handbreadth to three, since there was to begin with hardly any flow of water, is null [and work that is useless and so* forbidden]; to deepen it from two handbreadths to the original twelve involves heavy labor and that is not permitted. But what about deepening it from two to seven? Here he deepens it by five handbreadths, from one to six, so here too he deepens it by five, two to seven? Or perhaps what is going on here is that he is actually deepening it by an extra handbreadth, so that involves heavy and needless labor and is forbidden?

B. *The question stands.*

We proceed to a set of precedents, clarifying the application of the law to real cases.

V.3 A. *Abbayye permitted the people of Harmakh [during the intermediate days of the festival] to clear away the growths obstructing the irrigation ditch.*
B. *R. Jeremiah permitted the people of Sacuta [during the intermediate days of the festival] to dredge a ditch that had been blocked.*
C. *R. Ashi permitted the people of Mata Mehasia to clear obstructions from the Barnis canal, saying, "Since people get their water from it, it is as public domain, and we have learned in the Mishnah:* **And they do all public needs.**"

The Mishnah-sentence has now been fully clarified, and we go on to the next clause.

VI.1 A. **They repair [5A] damaged waterways in the public domain and dig them out:**

We begin by a close reading of the word choice: repair, yielding, but not make new ones. We immediately qualify the result of that reading:

B. *Repairing is all right, but not digging afresh.*
C. Said R. Jacob said R. Yohanan, "They have taught this rule only when the public has no need of the waterways, but if the public needs them, then it is permitted even to dig afresh."

The proposed distinction yields the principle that public welfare overrides the prohibitions of hard labor on the intermediate days of the festival. This is forthwith challenged:

D. *But if the public needs them, is it permitted to do that work? And has it not been taught on Tannaite authority:* Cisterns, pits, and caverns that belong to private property may be cleaned out, and, it goes without saying, those that belong to the public; but cisterns, pits, and caverns belonging to the public may not be dug, and all the more so those of a private person? *Does this not address a case in which the public has need of these facilities?*

Chapter One. Initial Probe

E. *No, it addresses a case in which the public has no need of those facilities.*

F. *Along these same lines with respect to a private party, where the private person has no need of the facility, is repairing allowed? And has it not been taught on Tannaite authority:* As to cisterns, pits, and caverns of a private person, they collect water in them but they may not be cleaned out, nor may their cracks be plastered; but as to those belonging to the public, they may be cleaned out and their cracks may be plastered?

G. *Now what is the point here? It is when a private person has need of the facility. And in that case, in regard to what is required for public use, where the public has need of it the same rule pertains? And where the public has need of the facility, is it forbidden to dig? Has it not been taught on Tannaite authority:* As to cisterns, pits, and caverns belonging to a private person, they collect water in them and clean them out, but they may not plaster their cracks nor put scourings into them to fill cracks; as to those serving the public, they may dig them to begin with and plaster them with cement?

H. *So the initial formulation poses a contradiction.*

I. *This is how to iron out the difficulty:* They may clean out wells, ditches or caverns of a private person, when the private party requires the facility, and, it goes without saying, those that belong to the public *when the public require use of the facility, in which case even digging them out is permitted.* But they may not dig out wells, ditches, or caverns belonging to the public when the public does not require use of the facility, and, it goes without saying, those belonging to a private party. *When the private party does not require using them, then even cleaning them out is forbidden.*

We have now made the necessary distinctions to iron out our problem, leaving open only the question of how to relate our result to the formulation of the rule in the Mishnah.

J. *Said R. Ashi, "A close reading of our Mishnah-paragraph yields the same result:* **And they do all public needs.** *Now what is encompassed within the augmentative formulation,* **all***? Is it not to encompass, also, digging?"*

K. *Not at all, it is to encompass what is covered in that which has been taught on Tannaite authority:* **On the** fifteenth day of Adar agents of the court go forth and dig cisterns, wells, and caves. **And they repair immersion pools and water channels.** Every immersion pool that contains forty seahs of water is suitable for receiving further drawn water if need be, and to every immersion pool that does not contain forty seahs of water they lead a water course and s complete its volume to the measure of forty seahs of water that has not been drawn so that it is suitable to receive further drawn water if need be [T. Sheq. 1:1]. And how on the basis of Scripture do we know that if they did not go forth and carry out all these duties, that any blood that is shed there is credited by Scripture as though they had shed it? Scripture states, "And so blood be upon you" (Dt. 19:10).

L. *Lo, in point of fact the framer of the Mishnah has covered these matters explicitly:* **They repair roads, streets, and water pools. And they do all public needs***! what is encompassed within the augmentative formulation,* **all***? Is it not to encompass, also, digging?*

M. *Yes, that's the proof!*

The exposition has come to a successful conclusion, in that all of the complementary formulations of the rule at hand are held together in a single coherent statement and moreover are shown to accord with Scripture.

The next clause of the Mishnah is linked to Scripture's statements on the same subject.

VII.1 A. **mark off graves**

B. Said R. Simeon b. Pazzi, "Whence do we find an indication in Scripture that it is required to mark off graves? Scripture states, 'And when they pass through the land and one sees a man's bone, then shall he set up a sign by it' (Ez. 29:15)."

C. *Said Rabina to R. Ashi, "So before Ezekiel made that point, how did we know it?"*

H. *Said R. Ashi to Rabina, "So until Ezekiel came along and made that statement, how did we know the correct rule?"*

I. *"According to your reasoning, when R. Hisda made his statement,* 'This matter we have not learned from the Torah of our lord, Moses, but from the teachings of Ezekiel b. Buzi we have learned it, "No alien, uncircumcised in heart and uncircumcised in flesh, shall enter my sanctuary" (Ez. 44:9),' — *until Ezekiel came along and made that statement, how did we know the correct rule? Rather, it is a tradition that was handed on, and Ezekiel came*

Chapter One. Initial Probe 39

> *along and supplied it with support from Scripture. Here too, it is a tradition that was handed on, and Ezekiel came along and supplied it with support from Scripture."*

The relationship of Ezekiel's prophecy to the Torah of Moses is worked out as a byproduct of our interest in Scripture's allusions to the rule of the Mishnah. We now go off on a tangent and address the issue of VII.1.I: the source of the rule that aliens may not enter the sanctuary.

VII.2 A. R. Abbahu said, "It derives from the following: 'And he shall cry, unclean, unclean' (Lev. 13:45) — the uncleanness affecting him cries out for him and says, 'Keep away.'"
    B. And so said R. Uzziel, grandson of Rabbah, "'...the uncleanness affecting him cries out for him and says, 'Keep away.'"
    C. *But does that verse serve the specified purpose? It is in point of fact required in line with that which has been taught on Tannaite authority:*
    D. "And he shall cry, unclean, unclean" (Lev. 13:45) — one has to publicize his pain in public, so that the public may seek for mercy on his behalf.
    E. *If that were the case, then Scripture can as well have written,* "Unclean he shall cry out." *Why say,* "Unclean, unclean"? *It is to yield both points.*

VII.3 A. Abbayye said, "It derives from the following: 'And do not put a stumbling block before the blind' (Lev. 19:14)."
    B. R. Pappa said, "It derives from the following: 'And he will say,m Cast you up, cast you up, clear the way' (Is. 57:14)."
    C. R. Hinena said, "It derives from the following: 'Take up the stumbling block out of the way of my people' (Is. 57:14)."
    D. R. Joshua b. R. Idi said, "It derives from the following: 'And you shall show them the way in which they must walk' (Ex. 18:20)."
    E. Mar Zutra said, "It derives from the following: 'And you shall separate the children of Israel from their uncleanness' (Lev. 15:31)."
    F. R. Ashi said, "It derives from the following: 'And they shall have charge of my charge' (Lev. 22:9), meaning, protect my charge [the priesthood]."
    G. Rabina said, "It derives from the following: 'And to him who orders his way will I show the salvation of God' (Ps. 50:23)."

We proceed to a footnote on Rabina's statement, that is, further exposition of Ps. 50:23:

    VII.4 A. And R. Joshua b. Levi said, "Whoever properly sets his ways in this world will have the merit of witnessing the salvation of the Holy One, blessed be he,

B. "as it is said, 'To him who orders his way I will show the salvation of God' (Ps. 50:23).
C. "Do not read 'orders' but 'properly sets' [his] way" [Cohen, *Sotah*, p. 21, n. 6: He calculates the loss incurred in fulfilling a precept against the reward it will bring him.]

VII.5 A. *R. Yannai had a disciple who day by day raised tough questions, but on the Sabbaths of Festivals did not raise tough questions.*
B. *[5B] In his regard he recited the verse,* "And to him who orders his way will I show the salvation of God" (Ps. 50:23).

The composite follows familiar lines of order and structure. We take up the exposition of the Mishnah-rule again, now turning to Tosefta's supplement. It is topical, concerning marking off graves; it has no bearing on the issue of our Mishnah-sentence, which is, labor permitted on the intermediate days of the festival. The framers of the Talmud have in mind not only an exposition of the Mishnah's laws and logic, but also an amplification of the subjects that it covers. But, we note, these amplifications are subordinate, coming later in the sequence of treatments of a Mishnah-sentence or paragraph. Since what follows is topical and in no way clarifies the Mishnah's rule governing the intermediate days of the festival, I treat it as a secondary and subordinate statement.

VII.6 A. *Our rabbis have taught on Tannaite authority:*
B. They do not may a mark to indicate the presence of corpse matter that is not bigger in volume than an olive's bulk, nor a human bone that is not bigger than a barley seed, nor any human remains that would not convey uncleanness when under a tent. But they do make a marking to indicate the presence of a spine, skull, or major limb of a skeleton, or the larger part of the small bones.
C. They make markings not when the matter is certainly known, but only when it is uncertain.
D. What are cases of uncertainty?
E. leafy bowers, jutting ledges, and a grave-area.
F. And they do not make a mark right on the spot of the source of uncleanness, so as not to waste what is unaffected [and so remains] uncontaminated, nor is a mark placed far from the spot, so as not to waste space in the Land of Israel [cf. T. Sheq. 1:5].
G. *But will an olive's bulk of human flesh not convey uncleanness in a tent? Lo, we have learned in the Mishnah:* **These contaminate in the Tent: (1) the corpse, and (2) an olive's bulk [of flesh] from the corpse, [and (3) an olive's bulk of corpse dregs, and (4) a ladleful of corpse mould;**

Chapter One. Initial Probe 41

(5) the backbone, and the skull, and (6) a limb from the corpse, and (7) a limb from the living person on which is an appropriate amount of flesh; (8) a quarter-qab of bones from the larger part of the frame [of the skeleton] or (9) from the larger number; and (10) the larger part of the frame or (11) the larger number of the corpse, even though there is not among them a quarter-qab, are unclean. How much is the "larger number"? One hundred twenty-five] [M. Oh. 2:1]*!*

H. *Said R. Pappa, "Here we deal with a piece of flesh precisely an olive's bulk in size, since ultimately it will be found lacking.* It is better that on its account food in the status of priestly rations and Holy Things should be burned on its account for a little while, but not for all time."

VII.7 A. **What are cases of uncertainty? Leafy bowers, jutting ledges, and a grave-area:**

B. **leafy bowers:** a tree that overshadows the ground near a cemetery.

C. **jutting ledges: Protruding stones that project from a wall** [T. Oh. 9:2].

D. **and a grave-area:** *that is in line with that which we have learned in the Mishnah:* **He who plows up the grave — lo, he makes [the field into] a grave area. How much [space] does he make? The length of a furrow of a hundred cubits, [over] a space of four seahs [M. Oh. 17:1A-B].**

The block of topically-agglutinated materials is itself now subjected to its own amplification.

VII.8 A. *So does dirt deriving from a grave-area convey uncleanness through overshadowing by a common tent? But did not* R. Judah say Samuel said, "One [who wants to remain uncontaminated by corpse matter] in a *beth haperas* [a grave area, an area possibly contaminated by corpse matter] blows away the earth and goes along his way."

B. R. Judah bar Ammi in the name of R. Judah said, "A *beth haperas* [a grave area, an area possibly contaminated by corpse matter] that has been trodden down is no longer a source of uncleanness."

C. Said R. Pappa, *"There is no contradiction.* The one statement speaks of a field in which the location of a grave has been lost" [so the whole field is a source of uncleanness], and the other speaks of a field in which a grave has been turned up by a plow [which crushes the bones so that they are no longer a source of uncleanness]."

D. *But is a field in which a grave has been plowed up even classified as a grave area?*

E. *Yes indeed, for we have learned in the Mishnah:* **There are three kinds of grave areas: [1] He who plows up the grave — it may be planted with any kind of tree, but it may not be sown with any kind of seed, except for seed [the plants of which] are cut. And if one uprooted it, one heaps up the threshing floor in it, and sifts — "the grain through two sieves," the words of R. Meir. And sages say, "The grain with two sieves, and the pulse through three sieves." And one burns the stubble and the stalks [in the grave area]. And it renders unclean through contact and through carrying, and it does not render unclean through the Tent. [2] A field in the midst of which a grave has been lost is sown with any kind of seed but is not planted with any kind of tree. And they do not preserve trees in it, except for a barren tree, which does not produce fruits. And it renders unclean through contact and through carrying and through the Tent. [3] A field of mourners/tomb niches is not planted, and is not sown, but its dust is clean. And they make from it ovens for holy [use] [M. Oh. 18:2-4].**

VII.9 A. *What is the definition of A field of mourners?*

B. R. Joshua bar Abba in the name of Ulla said, "It is a field in which they take leave of the dead."

C. *And how come [it is classified as a grave area, imparting uncleanness]?*

D. Said Abimi, "It is because of the contingency of abandonment by the owners [of the limbs that may have been dropped there when collection was made for secondary burial]."

VII.10 A. *And is it not necessary to mark of a field in which a grave has been dug up by a plow? Has it not been taught on Tannaite authority:*

B. If one found a field that is marked off as having corpse matter in its midst, and the nature of the uncleanness is not known, if there is a tree in it, one may be sure that a

Chapter One. Initial Probe

grave has been plowed up in it. If there is no tree in it, one may be sure that a grave has been lost in it.
- C. Said R. Judah, "Under what circumstances? When there is available a sage or a disciple, for not everybody is going to be expert in this matter" [T. Ahilot 17:12].
- D. *Said R. Pappa, "When that passage was repeated on Tannaite authority, it made reference to a field in which a grave had been lost and which therefore had been marked. If, then, there are trees in the field, that means that a grave had been plowed up by a plow thereafter; if there are no trees in it, it means a grave has been lost in it."*
- E. *But should we not take account of the possibility that trees are located in the field but the grave lies outside of it? For that would be in line with what Ulla said,* "We speak of a case in which trees are located at the edges of the field," *so here too,* "We speak of a case in which trees are located at the edges of the field."
- F. **[6A]** *But perhaps the uncleanness is located inside the field and trees are situated outside* [Lazarus: and since corpses are not buried on the road, the grave must be located among the trees and it must have been run over by the plow when the field was tilled for the sake of the trees].
- G. *We deal with a case in which the trees were planted irregularly.*
- H. *If you prefer, I shall say, "It is in line with what we said earlier:* **nor is a mark placed far from the spot, so as not to waste space in the Land of Israel.***"*

VII.11 A. **Said R. Judah, "Under what circumstances? When there is available a sage or a disciple, for not everybody is going to be expert in this matter:"**
- B. *Said Abbayye, "That proves that, when a neophyte rabbi is located in a place, all affairs of the place are assigned to his authority."*

VII.12 A. Said R. Judah, "If one found a stone with a marking, the space under it is deemed to be unclean [with corpse uncleanness]. If there were two such stones, then if there is lime between them, the space between them is deemed unclean. If there is no lime between them, then the space between them is deemed clean."
- B. *But is that the case even if there is no mark of plowing there? And has it not been taught on Tannaite authority:*

C. If one found a single stone marked off, even though it is not to be kept in that way, he who overshadows it is clean. If one found two of them, if there is a mark of plowing between them, the space between them is clean, if not, it is unclean [T. Sheq. 1:5D-E].

D. Said R. Pappa, "Here we deal with a case in which the lime was poured on top of the stones and then spread down on either side. If there is a mark of plowing between them, the space is clean, *for we assume that the lime that splashed was peeled off by the plowing; if there is no mark of plowing, the lime is clearly intended to mark the space between and that space is held to be unclean.*"

VII.13 A. Said R. Assi, "If there is a marking on one side, that side is unclean, the rest of the whole field is clean. it there is marking on two sides, those are unclean, the whole rest of the field is clean; if there was marking on three sides, those are unclean, but the whole rest of the field is clean. If there is a marking on four boundaries, they are then held to be the marks of what is clean, but the entire field inside is unclean."

B. "For a master has said, **nor is a mark placed far from the spot, so as not to waste space in the Land of Israel.**"

If we had a Talmud for Mishnah-tractate Ohalot, we should have found the present composition a likely candidate for inclusion, e.g., in the exposition of Mishnah-tractate Ohalot Chapter Two. Our problem is, why is this excellent composition inserted here? The answer is, the whole is a secondary amplification of other rules that pertain to a topic we treat in the context of our tractate's problem. Topical appendices inserted into the text give the Talmud the appearance of prolixity. In fact, understood for what they are and explained within the technical capacities available to our document's writers, the compositions that add to the exposition of various topics greatly enrich the presentation of the whole and truly belong. The definition of the document as a whole must then encompass a further purpose, besides Mishnah-amplification, which is, the composition of a topical encyclopaedia.

What does belong is a further exposition of the Mishnah-clause that follows: giving a warning that farmers who find in their fields situations in which diverse seeds are sown in the same plot had better remove the inappropriate species:

VIII.1A. **and go forth [to give warning] against Diverse Kinds:**

Here the issue is whether or not on the intermediate days of the festival to go out into the fields to find whether Diverse Kinds are growing there. Opinion on

Chapter One. Initial Probe 45

when this is done contradicts the premise of the rule of the Mishnah, since the following indicates that is done not on the intermediate days of Passover, but long before Passover, some four or so weeks prior, in the middle of the preceding month of Adar:

> B. *But in fact in the intermediate days of a festival do we go about to inspect whether or not there are mixed seeds in a field? But there is the following contradiction:* **On the first day of Adar they make public announcement concerning [payment of] sheqel dues and concerning the sowing of mixed seeds [Lev. 19:19, Dt. 22:9]. On the fifteenth day of that month they read the Megillah [Scroll of Esther] in walled cities. And they repair the paths, roads, and immersion pools. And they carry out all public needs. And they mark off the graves. And they go forth [to inspect the fields] on account of mixed seeds [M. Sheq. 1:1]***!***

The clear contradiction between the two rules, both occurring in the Mishnah, is now resolved:

> C. R. Eleazar and R. Yosé bar Hanina —
> D. One said, "The latter refers to the crops that ripen earlier [in mid-Adar], the other, of late-ripening crops [and our Mishnah-paragraph has a further inspection, now in mid-Nisan, during the intermediate days of the festival of Passover]."
> E. And the other said, "In the one case [in Adar] they go out to inspect the condition of grain fields, in the other, vegetable patches."
> F. Said R. Assi said R. Yohanan, "The rule pertains only in a case in which the sprouts are not yet recognizable [earlier on]; but where it is possible to discern the character of the sprouts early on, they went forth to inspect the situation earlier."

The contradictions as to the facts are now neatly resolved, and we ask a further question as to why it is permitted to do at least part of the work on the intermediate days of the festival. This brings us to the principle of the law, now that we have dealt with a detail of disharmony.

> VIII.2 A. *What makes the festival week special that we go out at that time for the purpose at hand?*
> B. *Said R. Jacob said R. Yohanan, "It is at that time labor is cheap with us [since there is no demand for labor during the intermediate days of the festival]."* [The work is light, and the cost is trivial. So there is no reason to prohibit it.]
> C. *Said R. Zebid, and some say, R. Mesharshayya, "That leads to the inference that, when we pay them, we pay them out of the heave offering taken up from the sheqel-chamber. For if*

you should imagine that the owners of the fields are paid, what difference does it make to us? Pay whatever the workers ask [and don't try to hire workers at a time when wages are low, since the householders are going to have to shell out]!"

We have completed the exposition of the Mishnah-rule, and, as before, we proceed to a topical appendix, on the subject of the law of Mixed Seeds. Here we have a talmud for Mishnah-tractate Kilayim, which in the Bavli lacks one.

VIII.3 A. How much [constitutes a mixture of seeds]?
B. Said R. Samuel bar Isaac, "It is in line with that which we have learned in the Mishnah: **[Concerning] every seah [of one kind of seeds] which contains [6B] a quarter [-qab] of another kind — he shall lessen [the quantity of seeds of the other kind, so that those seeds form less than a quarter-qab] [M. Kil. 2:1A].**"
C. *But has it not been taught on Tannaite authority:* They ordained that they should declare ownerless the crop of the entire field?
D. *There is no contradiction, the Mishnah-rule describes how things were done before the ordinance, the latter tells us how things were done afterward, in line with what has been taught on Tannaite authority:* At first they would uproot the crops and throw them in front of their cattle, but the householders were delighted on two counts, first, that they weeded their fields for them, second, they threw the crop to the cattle. So they ordained that they should uproot the forbidden crop and throw it in the road. So the householders were still delighted, because the court then took care of weeding their field. So in the end they ordained that they should declare ownerless the crop of the entire field.

There clearly is a pattern of Mishnah-exposition followed by Tosefta-exposition followed by topical appendices. A brief summary of the results suffices to show how the work is carried out. **I.1** raises a fundamental question of Mishnah-exegesis. No. 2 proceeds to explain the meanings of words. No. 3 asks a third routine question of Mishnah-exegesis. Nos. 4-5 pursue their own interests, and the composite is included here because of the point of intersection with our Mishnah; this is then an appendix. **II.1** asks an obvious question in clarifying the principle of the Mishnah's rule. No. 2 footnotes the foregoing. Nos. 3, 4, 5, 6+7 provide an anthological supplement, principally deriving from the Tosefta, to the theme of the Mishnah. **III.1** engages in a simple exercise of Mishnah-exegesis. **IV.1** asks a question invited by the point of the Mishnah's rule. No. 2 clarifies the foregoing explanation. **V.1** explains the meaning of the language of the Mishnah, and No. 2

Chapter One. Initial Probe

then builds on the facts given in No. 1. No. 3 then provides case reports on how the law at hand is applied. **VI.1** investigates the implications of the rule of the Mishnah in light of other Tannaite formulations on the subject. **VII.1, 2, 3** ask the familiar question of the scriptural basis for a rule of the Mishnah. No. 4 is tacked on to the foregoing by reason of the shared proof-text. No. 5 is present for the same reason. The Mishnah's theme then accounts for the inclusion of the Tannaite appendix that follows, Nos. 6, 7-13, which is hardly required except for a complete presentation of the topic. **VIII.1** investigates the implications of the framing of the Mishnah's rule and harmonizes them with other rulings. No. 2 continues the exposition of the Mishnah's rule. No. 3 then turns to the theme at hand.

What is the upshot of this little probe? Very little, since a sizable Talmudic passage yields only one example of the kind of writing we seek — and not a very ambitious one at that. So the result is to advance for consideration the hypothesis that the dialectical argument does not define a principal medium of Mishnah-exegesis at all. The small part played by the dialectical-analytical composition I identified earlier proves striking — and the negligible role that that composition plays in the program of the Talmud, which is Mishnah-exegesis and little more than that. On the basis of the instance before us, we cannot even form a hypothesis about the form of the argument — the example is too slight and undeveloped — and we certainly cannot attempt a hypothetical taxonomy of the types of dialectical argument. What we must now do is a systematic survey of the entire Talmud, aiming at a complete catalogue of the significant dialectical-analytical arguments. To that task we now turn.

II

Bavli Tractate Berakhot

I. AN EXEGETICAL-DIALECTICAL ARGUMENT AT M. BER. 1:3

An important task of the dialectical argument is fully to expose the exegetical alternatives that inhere in conflicting positions on a law of the Mishnah (less commonly: of the Tosefta). A vivid grasp of the correct modes of reading Scripture emerges, and the two possibilities are fully exposed.

1:3

A. The House of Shammai say, "In the evening everyone should recline to recite the Shema, and in the morning they should stand.

B. "As it says, 'When you lie down and when you rise up' (Deut. 6:7)."

C. And the House of Hillel say, "Everyone recites according to his usual manner.

D. "As it says, 'And as you walk by the way' (ibid.)."

E. "If so why does [the verse] say, 'When you lie down and when you rise up'?

F. "[It means, recite the Shema] at the hour that people lie down [at night] and at the hour that people rise [in the morning]."

G. Said R. Tarfon, "I was coming on the road and I reclined, so as to recite the Shema, according to the words of the House of Shammai. And I placed myself in danger of [being attacked by] thugs."

H. They said to him, "You have only yourself to blame [for what might have befallen you], for you violated the ruling of the House of Hillel."

I.1 A. [11A] *Now [at M. 1:3C-F] the House of Hillel explain their position and also deal with the reason behind the position of the House of Shammai.*

B. *But what is the reason that the House of Shammai do not rule as do the House of Hillel?*

C. *The House of Shammai will say to you, "If [matters were] as [you state, at M. 1:3D-E], Scripture should say merely, 'In the morning... and at night.' Why does Scripture say, 'When you lie down and when you rise up' (Deut. 6:7)? It is to indicate that one recites the Shema at the time that one actually lies down, and at the time that one actually gets up."*

D. *Then how do the House of Shammai interpret the words, "And when you walk by the way" (Deut. 6:7)?*

E. *They require it for support for the following proposition, which has been taught on Tannaite authority:*

    F. "When you sit in your house" thus excluding [from the requirement to recite the Shema] one who is engaged in carrying out a religious duty.

    G. "When you walk by the way" further is meant to exclude the newly-wed [who does not have to recite the Shema].

    H. On the basis of the foregoing exegesis, sages have ruled:

    I. He who marries a virgin-woman is exempt from the obligation to recite the Shema, but he who marries a widow is obligated.

J. *What is the force of the proof-text at hand?*

K. Said R. Papa, "The word 'way' contains this implication: Just as one goes on the way [and makes a journey] as an optional matter, so anyone involved in a merely optional matter [is obligated to recite the Shema, but one engaged in a religious duty is exempt].

L. *But do we not deal with someone who may be en route to carry out a religious duty, and here too, the All-Merciful has said that such a one should recite the Shema?*

M. *If so, the All-Merciful should have stated, "While sitting... while walking...." Why has it made explicit reference to your sitting and your going? When you are sitting and involved in your own affairs, when you are going on the way for your own purposes, is that point at which you are obligated. But if what you are doing concerns a religious duty, you are exempt.*

N. *If that is the operative consideration, then should not even one who marries a widow also be exempt [from reciting the Shema, since it is a religious duty to engage in procreation]?*

O. *The one who marries a virgin is preoccupied [with the sexual act], and the one who marries a widow is not preoccupied.*

Chapter Two. Berakhot 51

P. *If the operative consideration is whether or not one is preoccupied, then even if one's boat is sinking at sea, he should also be exempt from the obligation to recite the Shema.*

Q. *And if you say, that indeed is the rule, then take account of what* R. Abba bar Zabeda said Rab said, "A mourner is liable to carry out all of the religious duties that are stated in the Torah,

R. "exempt for the duty of putting on phylacteries.

S. "For lo, in their regard, the word 'glory' is used, as it says, 'Put your glory upon you' (Ez. 24:17). [Ezekiel was a mourner but was told, as a matter of exception, to put on his head-covering. What this means is that under ordinary circumstances a mourner does not put on his head-covering, understood to refer to the phylacteries]." [Accordingly, it cannot be the case that one who is preoccupied with a major financial loss is exempt from the obligation to recite the Shema.]

T. *There [with respect to marriage to a virgin], the groom is preoccupied with concerns brought about in the performance of a religious duty, while here [with reference to the one whose ship is sinking], he is preoccupied with concerns brought about by an optional [and personal] matter.*

U. *And how do the House of Shammai [deal with the words, "and when you walk along the way"]?*

V. *That phrase excludes from the requirement to recite the Shema those who are messengers carrying out religious duties.*

W. *And the House of Hillel [deal with the verse in the same way, in which case, how can they also use the verse to prove their point as at M. 1:3D]?*

X. *They will respond, "Quite tangentially the phrase at hand bears the implication that, even when one is on the way, he also has to recite the Shema."*

What characterizes the exegetical-dialectical argument is the acute balance that the framer maintains between the two parties. Each gives its reason and its refutation of the opposite party. If one side puts forth an exegetical argument, the other side is given the opportunity to refute it, e.g.,

> Then how do the House of Shammai interpret the words, "And when you walk by the way" (Deut. 6:7)?
>
> E. *They require it for support for the following proposition, which has been taught on Tannaite authority:*

The proof-texts then are carefully delineated, not merely cited, so that the particular trait of the proof-text that pertains to the besought proposition is made explicit. The secondary development, e.g., from L-M, then works to exclude contrary possibilities, and the amplification and defense of the case, yielding an appeal to an absurd situation ("if that is the operative consideration...") shows the full development of argument to cover all possibilities. At U-V, W-X, we note once more the careful balancing of propositions, each side getting its change both to defend its own view and to counter the opposite one. We note also that the exegetical-dialectical argument holds to a single problem and not only does not wander but exhibits remarkable cogency, beginning to end.

II. A SOURCE-CRITICAL DIALECTICAL ARGUMENT AT M. BERAKHOT 2:3

The same careful balancing of possibilities is exhibited in the inquiry into the named authority behind an anonymous rule. The form — brief, matched sentences — coheres with the foregoing, all the more so the basic attitude of according to both positions a fair hearing.

I.3 A. *We have learned in the following Mishnah-passage:* **All are valid to read the Esther-Scroll on Purim, except for a deaf-mute, an idiot, and a minor. R. Judah declares valid in the case of a minor [M. Meg. 2:4A-B].** *Who takes the view on Tannaite authority that a deaf-mute even de facto may not [read the Esther-scroll]?*

B. *Said R. Matenah, "It is R. Yosé, for we have learned in the Mishnah:*

C. *"'*One who recites the Shema but did not recite it audibly has carried out his obligation,' the words of R. Judah.

D. "R. Yosé says, 'He has not carried out his obligation' [M. 2:3A-B].*"*

E. *Why take the view that it is the position of R. Yosé [that is represented in the anonymous clause of M. Meg. 2:4A], and that even post facto, the deaf-mute also may not read the Esther-scroll?*

F. *[15B] Perhaps the position at hand belongs to R. Judah, and it is de novo that he maintains a deaf-mute may not read the Esther-scroll in public, but de facto it is quite all right.*

G. *Let that proposition not enter your mind! For the passage at hand treats the deaf-mute as equivalent to an idiot and a minor. Just as, in the case of an idiot and a minor, even post facto the action is null, also with respect to the deaf-mute, what is post facto also is invalid.*

H. *And perhaps we may maintain that one category follows the rule applying to that category, and the other the rule applying to a different category.*

I. *But can you actually conclude that the passage at hand is to be assigned to R. Judah? And lo, since the concluding clause of the construction states,* **R. Judah declares valid in the case of a minor,** *surely it follows that the opening clause of the same*

Chapter Two. Berakhot

construction cannot represent the view of R. Judah! [He should not be arguing with himself.]

J. But perhaps the entire construction indeed does follow the view of R. Judah, and at issue are two categories of minor. The passage, then, exhibits a flaw, and this is the way it is to be repeated on Tannaite authority:

K. **"All are valid to read the Esther-scroll except for a deaf-mute, an idiot, and a minor.**

L. "Under what circumstances [may a minor not read the Esther-scroll]? It is a minor who is not yet of age to be taught. But in the case of a minor who has reached the age at which he may be taught, even to begin with he is valid to recite the Esther-scroll," the words of R. Judah.

M. For **R. Judah declares valid in the case of a minor.**

N. *What then is the outcome? It is R. Judah's view, and he takes the position that, post facto, one has [carried out his obligation], while, de novo, he has not.*

O. *Then let us turn to the following teaching on Tannaite authority of R. Judah, son of R. Simeon b. Pazzi:* "A deaf-mute who can speak but not hear may to begin with separate heave-offering."

P. *In accord with which of the two authorities is that teaching? It can be neither R. Judah nor R. Yosé.*

Q. *If it were R. Judah, lo, he has taken the position that, de facto one may indeed do so, but only de novo he may not, and, in the view of R. Yosé, lo, he has said that even de facto one may not do so.*

R. *Then the upshot is that it must accord with R. Judah, and even de novo one may also [carry out the action].*

S. *Then let us consider the following, that is taught on Tannaite authority:*

T. A person should not say the Grace after Meals silently [in his heart], but if he has done so, he has carried [post facto] out his obligation.

U. *According to whom is the cited teaching? It cannot be either R. Yosé or R. Judah.*

V. *For in the view of R. Judah, he has maintained the position that even de novo, one has carried out his obligation [if he has said a prayer silently], while in the view of R. Yosé, he has the position that even post facto one has not carried out his obligation.*

W. *What then is the outcome?*

X. *It is R. Judah's view, and he takes the position that even de novo one has [carried out his obligation if he has said a prayer silently].*

Y. *And there is no contradiction between the versions of R. Judah's views, for the one is his own view, and the other is the view of his master..*

Z. *For we have learned on Tannaite authority:* R. Judah says in the name of R. Eleazar b. Azariah, "He who recites the Shema has to do oo audibly, as it is said, 'Hear O Israel, the Lord our God the Lord is one.'"

AA. Said to him R. Meir, "Lo, Scripture says, 'Which I command you this day shall be upon your heart' (Deut. 6:5).

BB. "Matters follow the intention of the heart."

CC. *Now that you have reached this point, you may take the view that R. Judah concurs with the position of his master. There is, then, no contradiction among the several passages, since, on the one side, we have the view of R. Judah, on the other, R. Meir.*

DD. Said R. Hisda said R. Shila, "The decided law accords with the position of R. Judah stated in the name of R. Eleazar b. Azariah.

EE. "And the law accords with R. Judah."

FF. *And it is necessary to have both statements of the decided law in hand, for had we heard only that the law accords with R. Judah, I might have supposed that that is the case even de novo. Accordingly we are told [that that is not the case], but the decided law accords with R. Judah as he stated matters in the name of R. Eleazar b. Azariah.*

GG. *And had we learned only that the law accords with R. Judah as he stated it in the name of R. Eleazar b. Azariah, I should have reached the conclusion that it is necessary to do things that way, and there is no remedy if one did not do it that way.*

HH. *Accordingly we are informed also that the law accords with R. Judah [so there is a remedy if one has not done things properly].*

The purpose in finding the named authority hardly aims at antiquarian information; it is to formulate the governing principle, which in turn allows us to move from this case to others and to show the unity of the law behind diverse, particular cases. Here what is noteworthy is the specification of equally-valid possibilities, e.g.,

E. *Why take the view that it is the position of R. Yosé [that is represented in the anonymous clause of M. Meg. 2:4A], and that even post facto, the deaf-mute also may not read the Esther-scroll?*

F. **[15B]** *Perhaps the position at hand belongs to R. Judah, and it is de novo that he maintains a deaf-mute may not read the Esther-scroll in public, but de facto it is quite all right.*

Chapter Two. Berakhot 55

That same dialectics recurs at H, where we raise the possibility of a distinction between categories. I objects that, if so, we have a flawed version and the passage has to be reformulated. And this carries us to a review of the upshot and a confrontation with a consequent inconsistency: if we take the view we do, then at an intersecting case, we are left with the anomaly that is spelled out:

    N.   *What then is the outcome? It is R. Judah's view, and he takes the position that, post facto, one has [carried out his obligation], while, de novo, he has not.*

    O.   *Then let us turn to the following teaching on Tannaite authority of R. Judah, son of R. Simeon b. Pazzi:* "A deaf-mute who can speak but not hear may to begin with separate heave-offering."

    P.   *In accord with which of the two authorities is that teaching? It can be neither R. Judah nor R. Yosé.*

This is beautifully articulated at P-Q, with a proposed resolution at R. The same problem recurs, however, at U-V. The outcome is at CC, which allows for a new resolution of matters. And this raises the issue of redundancy, which is worked out at FF, showing that each case had to be articulated, since both cases bear their own distinctive markings.

III. A Mishnah-Exegetical Dialectical Argument at M. Ber. 3:4

We should not suppose that Mishnah-exegesis does not take advantage of the opportunities provided by the protracted argument fully to expose a line of thought, even in its secondary extensions. The following shows the contrary fact:

3:4

    A.   **One who has had a seminal discharge may silently meditate but may not recite the blessings out loud,**

    B.   **either [those blessings] before [the Shema] or [those blessings] after it.**

    C.   **And as to those for the meal, he may recite the blessing after it, but not before.**

    D.   **R. Judah says, "He may say the blessings both before them [i.e., the Shema and the meal] and after them."**

I.1   A.   *Said Rabina,* "That then suggests that meditation is equivalent to speech [since at M. 3:4A, one may say the blessings in his heart but may not say them out loud, yet that suffices for the purpose].

    B.   *"For if you maintain that the meditation does not fall into the classification of actual recitation, then why should one meditate [and say the blessings silently at all]?*

    C.   "So what conclusion is to be drawn? Meditation falls into the same classification as speech."

D. [But if that is the case, then] let the man say the blessings with his lips [out loud]! For so we find at Sinai [Simon, p. 124, n. 1: Moses ordered the Israelites to keep away from woman before receiving the Torah, but those who were unclean could still accept it mentally].

E. *And [contrary to A] R. Hisda said "Meditation is not equivalent to speech. For if you maintain that meditation does fall into the classification of recitation, let someone actually say the blessings with his lips [out loud]!*

F. *"So what conclusion is to be drawn? Meditation does not fall into the same classification as speech."*

G. Why then should one meditate [on the blessings but not say them]?

H. Said R. Eleazar, "It is so that, while everyone is engaged in [the blessings at hand], he should not sit and do nothing."

I. *But let him study some other teaching?*

J. Said R. Adda bar Ahba, "He should be engaged with something with which the community also is dealing."

K. [21A] But there is the matter of the Prayer, which is something with which the community is dealing, *and we have learned in the Mishnah:*

L. One who was standing in recitation of the Prayer and remembered that he had had a seminal emission should not interrupt his recitation. Rather he should shorten the prayer [M. 3:5A-D].

M. *The operative consideration, then, is that he had begun. Lo, if he had not begun, he should not begin [and that is the case even though everyone else is saying the Prayer. That would appear to contradict Adda bar Ahba's view].*

N. *The case of the Prayer is different, because it contains no mention of the dominion of Heaven [on which account it is not essential that a man participate in it when the community says it].*

O. *But lo, there is the matter of the Grace after Meals, which does not contain a mention of the dominion of Heaven, and yet we have learned in the Mishnah:*

P. **As to those for the meal, he may recite the blessing after it but not before [M. 3:4C].** [So that applies even to the one who has had a seminal emission.]

Q. *But the operative distinction is that the recitation of the Shema and the Grace after Meals rests upon the authority of the Torah, while saying the Prayer rests on the authority*

Chapter Two. Berakhot

> *of rabbis [and that is why, in the latter case, one need not engage in the same matter with which the community at large is occupied].*

Rabina's thesis immediately moves from the particular to the general, expressing what he conceives to be the unstated premise of the Mishnah's rule. A mark of the dialectical argument will be the introduction of an argument contrary to fact, which corresponds to our own null-hypothesis: if you maintain that the meditation does not fall into the classification of actual recitation, then why should one meditate [and say the blessings silently at all]?. Another mark of the dialectical argument will be the introduction of an opinion, or premise, contrary to the initial one; it seems self-evident that dialectics requires conflict, but since the dispute-form, whether the Mishnah's or the various forms of the Talmud, does not always, or even often, precipitate the dialectical argument, we have to take note of the contrary fact. We note also at G the commencement of a second unit of thought within the same argumentative setting.

IV. AN EXEGETICAL-DIALECTICAL ARGUMENT AT M. BER. 6:1

Here is another well-articulated and neatly balanced exposition of the scriptural foundations of a Mishnah-rule.

    A.   **[35A] How does one say a blessing over produce?**

I.1   A.   *What is the source of this rule [that one must say a blessing before eating produce]?*

    B.   *It is in accord with what our rabbis have taught on Tannaite authority:*

    C.   *"The fruit thereof shall be holy, for giving praise to the Lord" (Lev. 19:24). [This verse refers to produce in the fourth year after planting a given tree.]*

    D.   *This teaches that [produce] requires the recitation of a blessing, both before and after eating.*

    E.   *On the basis of the foregoing exegesis, R. Aqiba said, "It is forbidden for a person to taste anything before reciting a blessing."*

    F.   *Now does the exegesis, "for giving praise....," serve the purpose just now specified?*

    G.   *It serves [two purposes], for the All-Merciful has stated, "Redeem [the produce of the fourth year, if it is not eaten in Jerusalem], and, second, [to apply the stated rule only to the fruit of the vine by indicating that] what requires a song [of praise] requires redemption, and what does not require a song does not require redemption [thus speaking only of wine, which alone is subject to the rule governing produce of the first year].*

H. *And the foregoing further accords with what R. Samuel bar Nahmani said R. Jonathan said.*
I. For R. Samuel bar Nahmani said R. Jonathan said, "How do we know that a song [of praise] is sung only over wine?
J. "As it is said, 'And the vine said to them, Should I leave my wine, which cheers God and man' (Jud. 9:13).
K. "If wine cheers man, how does it cheer God?
L. "It is on the basis of that statement that we learn that people may sing a song [of praise] only over a cup of wine."

I.2 A. *The foregoing exegesis [proving that we derive the requirement to say a blessing from the use of the word 'praise'] poses no problem to him who repeats the tradition in the form of* "the planting of the fourth year." [Then the cited verse speaks of all produce that reaches the fourth year of growth, and does not refer only to wine. Simon, p. 218, n. 4: In this case the word for praise cannot be used to prove that only the vine requires redemption and is available for teaching that a blessing must be said over fruit.] *But for him who repeats the version as "the vineyard in the fourth year of its growth" [in which case the cited verse speaks only of fruit of the vine, wine], what is there to be said?*
B. *For it has been stated:*
C. R. Hiyya and R. Simeon, son of Rabbi
D. One authority repeated: "Vineyard in the fourth year [speaking then only of wine]."
E. And the other stated, "'the planting in the fourth year of its growth."
F. *Now that poses no problem for one who repeats the Tannaite formulation as "a vineyard in the fourth year after planting, there is no problem," if he derives the rule from an argument by analogy, as has been taught on Tannaite authority:*
G. Rabbi says, "Here it states, 'That it may yield to you more richly the increase thereof' (Lev. 19:25). And elsewhere it says, 'The increase of the vineyard' (Deut. 22:9).
H. "Just as the word 'increase' used in the latter passage refers to the vineyard, so here it refers to the vineyard."

I. *And even if one does derive the required proof from the argument from analogy, then we know only that a blessing has to be said after eating [produce]. How do we prove that one has to say a blessing before eating produce?*

J. That is no problem, for proof derives from an argument a fortiori:

K. Now if one has to say a blessing once he is full, when he is hungry, all the more so!

L. Accordingly, we have found proof that one has to say a blessing before and after consuming produce of the vineyard.

    M. How do we know that one must do so for all other varieties of produce?

    N. It must be derived from the case of fruit of the vineyard.

    O. *For it has been taught on Tannaite authority:*

    P. Just as, in the case of produce of a vineyard, something from which one derives benefit, one has to say a blessing, so in the case of any thing from which one derives benefit, one has to say a blessing.

    Q. No, there is a weak point in that argument:

    R. The distinctive trait of the vineyard [which accounts for the special requirement of saying a blessing] is that it is subject to the rule governing gleanings [which must be left for the poor, so Lev. 19:10].

    S. But then the case of grain will prove the case [since it is not subject to the rule governing gleanings, but is subject to the recitation of a blessing, as stated at Deut. 8:10].

    T. What follows is that one of the meanings to be imputed to the word "praise" remains available to prove that one must recite a blessing.

    U. But the special trait of grain is that it is liable to dough-offering [which must be separated from dough].

    V. The case of the vineyard will prove the matter [since it is not subject to dough-offering].

    W. So we come full circle. The special trait characteristic of the one is not characteristic of the other, and vice versa. What they have in common, then, is that both of them are things from which people derive benefit, and both require the recitation of a blessing. So anything from which people derive benefit demands a blessing.

X. [No, that is not conclusive either, for] what the two [wine, grain] have in common is that both of them are used on the altar. [What is not analogous will not require a blessing.]

Y. *Then there is the case of the olive, which also is offered on the altar.*

Z. *But does proof derive from the fact that the olive is offered on the altar [and that is why we derive the rule that a blessing is required]?*

AA. Lo, in the case of the olive, it is described in Scripture as a "vineyard."

BB. For it is written, "And he burned up the shocks and the standing grain and also the vineyard of olives" (Jud. 15:5).

CC. *Said R. Pappa, "While it may be called 'a vineyard of olives,' it is never called merely, 'a vineyard.'" [When we see the word 'vineyard,' without further reference to olives, we do not imagine that it is a vineyard of olives]."*

DD. *In any event we have a problem, for all that the three have in common is that they are offered on the altar.*

EE. Rather, one must derive [the requirement of saying a blessing] from the case of the seven species [specified at Deut. 8:8 as the produce of the Land of Israel].

FF. Just as, in the case of the seven species, that from which people derive benefit requires a blessing, so any thing from which people derive benefit requires a blessing.

GG. [No, that will not do, for] the distinctive trait of the seven species is that they are liable for the presentation of the first fruits [which must be brought to the priest in the Temple].

HH. And furthermore, [what you could prove in any event] involves the blessing to be said after eating such produce. How do we learn that one has to say a blessing before hand?

II. That indeed is no problem.

Chapter Two. Berakhot 61

>JJ. If when one is full, one says a blessing, when one is hungry, is it not all the more so that one says a blessing?
>
>KK. *For him who repeats the Tannaite tradition as a fourth year planting, there is no problem for what is planted, but for anything that is not planted, such as meat or eggs or fish, how does such a one know the rule at all?*
>
>LL. It is a matter of reasoning: it is forbidden for someone to derive benefit from the world of ours without reciting a blessing of thanks.

We start with a simple declaration of the scriptural source of the rule, but then raise the precipitating question: does the cited verse serve the alleged purpose? For we have reason to suppose that the verse pertains to another problem altogether, F. A further gloss, Hff., extends that point. No. 2 then continues the challenge, by introducing a free-standing dispute and asking how the parties to the first part of the discussion sort out the issues of a separate matter altogether, I.2. The question is pressed at F, and another trait of the dialectics of the Talmud emerges, which is, the clear articulation of the point of a piece of evidence. One of the many results of dialectics is to ascertain that the relevance and point of intersection of a piece of evidence or argument are always articulated; we may lose sight of start and finish, but we never lose sight of where we are at any given point in the discussion. That is the result of the consideration shown by F, which does not take for granted that we know what is in the mind of the person who has introduced the objection and the evidence. The question is then reenforced, and made more complicated, by I. We turn at M to a new problem, which is, the proof for the requirement of a blessing in connection with produce other than that of the vine, and we construct a new dialectical argument to investigate that problem, Off. The mode of extended argument here characterizes Sifra, but we see is not unique to that document.

v. PROPORTIONS

The proportion of dialectical arguments, whether analytical or exegetical or source-critical, to the tractate proves remarkably slight, and even in the chapters in which they occur, the arguments play only a minor role. We establish the proportions in the context of my translation into English by comparing the number of bytes used for the dialectical argument with the number of bytes used for the chapter as a whole,[1] thus dialectical argument/chapter as a whole = percentage:

---

[1] We deal with proportions, not exact numbers, since proportions will prove fairly constant from one language to the other.

An Exegetical-Dialectical Argument
  at M. Ber. 1:3   5019/173872   2.8%
A Source-Critical Dialectical Argument
  at M. Ber. 2:3   5615/76070   7.3%
A Mishnah-Exegetical Dialectical Argument
  at M. Ber. 3:4   3202/136900   2.3%
An Exegetical-Dialectical Argument
  at M. Ber. 6:1   7312/147160   5.0%

Now if we add, further, all of the bytes of the chapters of the tractate, as against the bytes required for the dialectical arguments of the tractate, we find the following:

$$21158/979981 = 2.1\%$$

The proportion of dialectical argument to the whole overstates matters, since, in five of the tractates nine chapters, including the enormous Chapter Nine, there are no such arguments at all. The hypothesis now comes to the fore that what makes the Talmud talmudic is, in the end, not very much.

III

Bavli Tractate Shabbat

I. A Source-critical Dialectical Argument at M. Shab. 1:1

What makes this dialectical argument interesting is its capacity to solve a problem of logical analysis, B, by appeal to the premised principle and assigning the anonymous rule to the authority behind the premise, C. This is then not only worked out — which would represent a first-rate piece of Mishnah-exegesis — but spun out in interesting and new directions.

IV.1 A. [If on the Sabbath the beggar stands outside and the householder inside, and] the beggar stuck his hand inside [and put a beggar's bowl] into the hand of the householder, or if he took something from inside it and brought it out, the beggar is liable, the householder is exempt]:

B. *But why should he be liable, for lo, we require that the removing of the object and the depositing of the object must involve a space four by four handbreadths square, and that condition has not been met here?*

C. *Said Rabbah, "But who is the authority behind this rule? It must be R. Aqiba, who maintains that we do not require that the removing of the object and the depositing of the object must involve a space four by four handbreadths square, for we have learned in the Mishnah:* **He who throws [an object] from private domain to public domain, [or] from public domain to private domain, is liable. [He who throws an object] from private domain to private domain, and public domain intervenes — R. Aqiba declares [him] liable [to a sin-offering]. And sages exempt [him] [M. 11:1].** *R. Aqiba maintains the theory that an object that is intercepted by the air through which it passes is as though it has come to rest there [so when it crosses the public domain, it is as though it had come to rest there, and liability is incurred], and sages take the view that an object that* is intercepted by the air through which it passes is not as though it has come to rest there."

IV.2 A. *But is that to say that it is self-evident to Rabbah that an object that is intercepted by the air through which it passes is as though it has come to rest there?* **[4B]** *And that is so when it is within ten handbreadths of the ground?* [Freedman: The space above ten handbreadths is not classified as public domain.] *But surely Rabbah raised a question on that very matter! For Rabbah raised the question: "If the object passes through the space below ten handbreadths of the ground, do they really disagree? It is in this matter that they disagree: R. Aqiba maintains that in that area, an object that is intercepted by the air through which it passes is as though it has come to rest there [so when it crosses the public domain, it is as though it had come to rest there, and liability is incurred], and sages take the view that an object that is intercepted by the air through which it passes is not as though it has come to rest there. But as to the space above ten handbreadths, all concur that he is not liable. They hold in common — so this theory goes — that we do not we do not treat as comparable the act of throwing and the act of reaching an object across a space.* [Freedman: If one reaches over an object from private domain to private domain across public domain, even if it is above ten handbreadths, he is liable.] *Or perhaps they differ as to the space above ten handbreadths, and what is at issue is this: R. Aqiba maintains that we do treat as comparable the act of throwing and the act of reaching an object across a space. Sages, by contrast, take the view that we do not treat as comparable the act of throwing and the act of reaching an object across a space. But as to the situation prevailing for the space lower than ten handbreadths, all would concur that he is liable. How come? We concur in the principle that an object that is intercepted is treated as though it has come to rest.* [Since Rabbah has phrased the question in that way, it is not so clear that Rabbah treats as self-evident the proposition that an object that is intercepted by the air through which it passes is as though it has come to rest there.]"

B. *No, that's not a serious problem: After raising the question, he resolved it: R. Aqiba indeed does maintain that an object that is intercepted by the air through which it passes is as though it has come to rest there.*

Chapter Three. Shabbat

IV.3 A. *But maybe — responding to Rabbah's theory that R. Aqiba maintains that we do not require that the removing of the object and the depositing of the object must involve a space four by four handbreadths square — while [Aqiba] doesn't require the deposition of the object in a space four handbreadths square [for liability to be incurred,] he does require removal from such a confined space?*

B. *Rather, said R. Joseph, "Who is the authority behind the cited passage? It is Rabbi."*

C. *So which ruling of Rabbi is supposed to be invoked here? Should we say it is the following ruling of Rabbi:* If one tossed an object and it came to rest on a projection, if it is a small projection, Rabbi declares him liable, and sages declare him exempt? *But surely in that case — as we shall point it in context — it is in accord with what Abbayye said, for said Abbayye, "Here, with what situation do we deal? It is a tree that stands in private domain, with its foliage extending into public domain, and one tossed the object, and it landed in the foliage. In that case, Rabbi takes the view that we do invoke the conception, we assign the foliage to the status of the trunk of the tree, and rabbis hold the position that we don't invoke the conception of assigning the foliage to the status of the stock of the tree." [So it cannot be that case at all.] Rather, it has to be the following ruling of Rabbi, which has been taught on Tannaite authority:* If one tossed an object from public domain to public domain, with private domain intervening — Rabbi declares the act liable. And sages declare it exempt. [In that context] said R. Judah said Samuel, "Rabbi would impose liability on two counts, one on the count of removing the object from the one domain, the other on the count of bringing it in to the other domain." *Therefore, it follows, a place four by four is not required either for removal of the object nor for the deposit of the object.*

D. *But lo, in that same matter, it has been said: Both Rab and Samuel say,* **[5A]** "Rabbi imposed liability only in the case of a private domain that was roofed over, *in which instance we invoke the principle, the house is as though it were full of objects [and so had no air space at all, thus as soon as the object enters the space, it is as though it has come to rest].* But that rule would not apply to a space that is not roofed over." *And should you say, here, too, it is a case in* which it is roofed over, then that poses no problem in the case of private domain that is roofed over, but in the case of public domain that is roofed over, does one incur liability in that same way? And hasn't R. Samuel bar Judah said R. Abba said R. Huna said Rab said, "If someone transfers an object through four cubits of public domain that is roofed over, he is exempt for liability, since that area is not comparable to the case of the flags of the wilderness." [Freedman: The definition of what constitutes forbidden work on the Sabbath depends on the work that was done in connection with the tabernacle in the wilderness; carrying was necessary, so carrying an object four cubits is work. But there it was done under the open sky, hence Rab's statement; the same applies here. By 'flags of the wilderness' is meant the whole disposition and encampment of the Israelites; they didn't have any cover in public ground.]

E. *Rather*, said R. Zira, "Lo, who is the authority behind our rule? It is 'others.' For it has been taught on Tannaite authority: Others say, 'If someone stood still in place and caught a tossed object, the one who threw the object is liable; if he moved from his place to catch the tossed object, the one who threw it is exempt.' [If the catcher didn't move, the one who threw is liable, being regarded as having both removed the object and also deposited it; but if the catcher moved and caught the object, the thrower didn't deposit the object, since it doesn't come to rest where it would have solely on the strength of his having tossed the object.] *If someone stood still in place and caught a tossed object, the one who threw the object is liable*: Lo, we require that the object come to rest in a space of four cubits, and that condition has not been met. So it must follow that we do not require that the object come to rest in a space of four cubits."

F. *But maybe it is coming to rest in such a space that we don't require, but removal from a space of four cubits we do require [for liability to be incurred on the part of the one who tossed the object]? And even in regard to depositing the object, maybe the sense is that he spread out his cloak and caught the object, in which case, the depositing also has taken place in a space of four cubits?*

G. Said R. Abba, "Our Mishnah paragraph likewise means that he removes the object from one basket and puts it into another basket, so that there is depositing in a place four cubits square."

Chapter Three. Shabbat

H. *But the language that is used in our Mishnah paragraph is* **his hand**!

I. *Repeat it as:* A basket in his hand.

IV.4 A. *Well, o.k., forget about a basket in private domain, but a basket located in public domain is classified itself as private domain [so why should one be liable in regard to carrying the basket out of private domain]?*

B. *Then don't we have to say that the Mishnah paragraph is not in accord with the view of R. Yosé b. R. Judah? For it has been taught on Tannaite authority:* R. Yosé b. R. Judah says, "If one stuck a reed in public domain, with a basket on the top of it, and one tossed an object, which landed on it, he is liable [for the object is regarded as private domain]. *But if the passage concurred with R. Yosé b. R. Judah, how could the rule be that he is liable* **[if] the householder stuck his hand outside and put [something] into the hand of the beggar [the householder is liable]**? *What he is doing is moving an object from private domain to private domain!*

C. *You may even take the view that the passage accords even with R. Yosé b. R. Judah, for in that case, the basket is above ten handbreadths, here it is lower than that [and so is classified as public domain].*

IV.5 A. *This presented a problem to R. Abbahu: Is the language that is used in our Mishnah paragraph a basket in his hand? The language that is used is,* **his hand**!

B. *Rather, said R. Abbahu, "It is a case in which he lowered his hand to within three handbreadths of the ground and received the object"* [Freedman: everything within three handbreadths of the ground is regarded as part of the ground itself, so the hand becomes a place four cubits square].

C. *But the language that is persistently used in the Mishnah is* **standing**!

D. *It refers to his bending over; or, if you prefer, he is standing, but in a pit; or, if you prefer, it is a very short person.*

E. *Said Raba, "Oh come on, is a Tannaite authority going to go to the trouble of telling us about all these weird cases?"*

F. Rather, said Raba, "A person's hand is reckoned as though it were a space of four by four cubits."

G. *And so when Rabin came,* he said R. Yohanan [said], "A person's hand is reckoned as though it were a space of four by four cubits."

IV.6 A. Said R. Abin said R. Ilai said R. Yohanan, "If someone threw an object and it landed in the hand of a second party, he is liable."

B. *Well, then, what is he telling us? That a person's hand is reckoned as though it were a space of four by four cubits? Lo, R. Yohanan said that once!*

C. *What might you otherwise have maintained? That is the case where the man himself reckons his hand in such a way, but where he doesn't reckon his hand in such a way, I might say that is not so; thus we are informed that that is not the case.*

It is at C that the Mishnah-exegesis reaches its point, linking the rule at hand to another rule and showing the foundations of both in a single thesis in physics. IV.2 then goes off in its own direction, raising a complication not required to solve the problem if IV.1 and showing how the dialectical argument works. A solution precipitates its own problem, and the solution to that problem, yet another. IV.3 then takes up the solution of IV.2 and proposes a different solution, and this leads to the further problem that is pursued at C-D. E then offers yet a third solution, and that too involves its own principle. IV.4 goes in its own direction; we have asked in accord with what authority the rule is laid forth, so we now ask, the opposite question: who would not concur? And, as we see, at IV.5 this bears its own gloss. While, in the aggregate, the composite works its way through problems of Mishnah-exegesis, the problems are so framed as to lead us through diverse, generative principles, and that is why I classify the discussion as a systematic, dialectical one, rather than an episodic and exegetical one.

II. A Theoretical Question, Worked Out in a Protracted Inquiry, at M.Shab. 2:3A-B

The formation of a protracted and wide-ranging argument commonly takes place in response to a problem of theory, even though at the surface the problem is formulated as a question addressed to Scripture: how on the basis of Scripture do we know such and so? In the present instance the theoretical problem transcends that question, since it concerns whether what is unclean can contract uncleanness, that is, a question that shades over into the metaphysics of purity-law. Our portion commences at II:2.

II.1 A. **And nothing which exudes from a tree contracts uncleanness [as a tent] through overshadowing [a corpse] except for flax:**

B. *How do we know this on the basis of Scripture?*

C. Said R. Eleazar, "One derives the meaning of the word 'tent' from its use in connection **[28A]** with the tabernacle in the

Chapter Three. Shabbat 69

wilderness. *Here it is written,* 'This is the Torah. As to a man, when he dies in a tent' (Num. 19:14). *And elsewhere it is written,* 'And he spread the tent over the tabernacle' (Ex. 40:19). Just as, in that later passage, the covering of linen is classified as a tent, so here, too, the covering of linen must be such as to be classified as a tent."

D. Well, then, just as in that case, it was twisted, its thread was doubled six times, so here, too, mustn't it be twisted with its thread doubled six-fold [and otherwise there should be no uncleanness]?

E. Scripture uses the language, "tent" repeatedly, and that serves to augment the coverage of the law.

F. Then, if Scripture uses the language, "tent" repeatedly, which serves to augment the coverage of the law, *everything else [of any material] also should be covered by the rule!*

G. *If that were the case, what purpose would the verbal analogy just now given have served?*

H. *But say:* Just as in the case of the tabernacle, it was made of boards, so here, too, a tent of boards was meant?

I. Said Scripture, "And you shall make boards for the tabernacle" (Ex. 26:15): It is the tabernacle itself [Freedman: twelve joined strips passing over the boards and forming the roof] that falls into the classification of a tabernacle, but boards on their own don't fall into the classification of a tabernacle.

J. *Well, then, what about the following possibility:* "And you shall make a covering for the tent" (Ex. 26:14) — *here, too, isn't a covering classified as a tent?*

K. *So, when R. Eleazar raised the question,* "What is the law as to the hide of an unclean beast becoming unclean when it overshadows a corpse" — *why should he have been in doubt, since the hide of a clean animal cannot contract uncleanness* [Freedman: on the present hypothesis, that the covering, which included ram skins, which are clean, is not a tent, it is excluded from the rule of overshadowing a corpse at Num. 19:14]? *So if the hide of a clean beast does not contract uncleanness, is there any doubt as to the rule covering the hide of an unclean beast?*

L. *There is an exceptional situation there, for Scripture went and restored [under the category of tent] the hide of an unclean animal, as it is written,* "they shall bear the curtains of the tabernacle and the tent of meeting, its covering and the covering of sealskin that is above it" (Num. 4:25), meaning: there is an analogy drawn between the upper covering and the lower one, so that, just as the lower one is classified as a tent, so the upper one is classified as a tent.

II.2 A. *Reverting to the body of the foregoing: R. Eleazar raised the question,* "What is the law as to the hide of an unclean beast becoming unclean when it overshadows a corpse" —

B. *So what is he asking?* [Freedman: How can he think that it is subject to such uncleanness, seeing that he derives the definition of "tent" from the tabernacle, where the skins of clean animals alone were used?]

C. *Said R. Adda bar Ahbah, "What he is asking about is* the badger that existed in the time of Moses, specifically, was it unclean or clean?"

D. *Said R. Joseph, "What's sort of a problem is that? We have learned as a Tannaite statement:* Validated for the sacred work is only the skin of a clean animal."

E. *Objected R. Abba,* "R. Judah says, 'There were two coverings, one of dyed rams' hides, the other of badger hides.' R. Nehemiah says, 'There was one covering, and it was like a squirrel's hide.' But the squirrel is unclean!"

F. *This is the sense of the statement:* Like a squirrel's hide, which has many colors, *but not really a squirrel, for the squirrel in general is unclean, but here, only a clean animal is under discussion."*

G. *Said R. Joseph, "If so, that's why we render the word sasgawna as* 'that it rejoices in having many colors.'"

II.3 A. *Raba said, "The fact that the hide of an unclean animal is made unclean when it overshadows a corpse derives from the following, which was taught on Tannaite authority:*

B. "Since Scripture could have said, 'skin,' when it says, 'or in skin' (Lev. 13:48) it serves to extend susceptibility to uncleanness to the hide of an unclean beast or one that was smitten with the skin ailment while subject to the examination of a priest. If someone cut off a piece of any of these materials listed in that verse, and made one piece of them all, how do we know that the composite is subject to uncleanness? Scripture says, 'or in any thing made of hide' (Lev. 13:48)."

C. *But there is the following flaw in the proposed proof [deriving in particular from the uncleanness of the skin ailment, for the proposition that concerns uncleanness deriving from overshadowing a corpse, namely:]* what

Chapter Three. Shabbat

distinguishes what is affected by the skin ailment is that the warp and woof would be made unclean through that form of uncleanness [which is not the case of corpse uncleanness].

D. *Well, then, derive the same fact from the case of dead creeping things, for it has been taught on Tannaite authority:*

E. Scripture says, "skin" (Lev. 11:32). I know only that the hide of a clean beast is affected by the uncleanness of a dead creeping thing. How do I know that the same is so for the hide of an unclean beast? Scripture says, "or skin" (Lev. 11:32) [and that extends the law to the hide of an unclean beast].

F. *But here, too, there is the following flaw:* What distinguishes uncleanness deriving from dead creeping things is that the minimum volume that suffices for uncleanness is a lentil in bulk [which is not the same for a corpse, which must be the volume of an olive, much bigger than a lentil]. [Freedman: Since the defilement of dead creeping things is stricter in that respect, it may also be stricter in respect of the skin of an unclean animal.]

G. But the uncleanness of the skin ailment proves the contrary.

H. So we find ourselves going about in a circle, for the governing taxonomic trait of the one is not the same as that of the other, and that of the other is not the same as that of the one, but what they have in common is that the hide in both cases may contract uncleanness, and the hide of an unclean animal is treated as equivalent to the hide of a clean animal. So I introduce the matter of the overshadowing of a corpse, in which the hide is unclean in that case, so that the hide of an unclean animal should be treated as equivalent to the hide of a clean animal.

I. *Said Raba of Barnesh to R. Ashi, "But there is the following flaw in the proposed argument:* The common taxonomic trait among them is that these sources of uncleanness impart uncleanness in less than the volume of an olive. But will you say the same of a corpse, which imparts uncleanness only if it is of the volume of an olive?"

J. Rather, said Raba of Barnesh, **[28B]** "The proposition derives from an argument a fortiori from the case of goats' hair: That is not subject to uncleanness deriving from the skin ailment, yet it does contract uncleanness when it overshadows a corpse; so the hide of an unclean animal, which does contract uncleanness via the skin ailment, surely should contract uncleanness when it overshadows a corpse."

II.4 A. *Now then, when R. Joseph stated as a Tannaite teaching,* "Validated for the sacred work is only the skin of a clean animal," *for what concrete purpose did he make that statement?* [Freedman: It does not teach that the hide of an unclean animal is not defiled by overshadowing the dead, so what is the point?]

B. It pertains to phylacteries [showing that the parchment must derive from a clean animal].

C. *But that fact is stated in so many words with regard to phylacteries:* "That the Torah of the Lord may be in your mouth" (Ex. 13:9), meaning something that is permitted in your mouth.

D. Rather, it has to do with the hide [that makes the capsules for the parchment].

E. But didn't Abbayye say, "The law governing the hide of the phylacteries is revealed by God to Moses at Sinai"?

F. But it has to do with tying the phylacteries with the hair and sewing it with the tendons of a clean beast and not an unclean beast.

G. *This, too, is a law revealed by God to Moses at Sinai, for it has been taught on Tannaite authority:*

H. The fact that the boxes containing the prayer parchments have to be square is a law revealed to Moses at Sinai. They must be tied with their hair and sewn with their tendons [that is, those of the same type of animal that proves the parchment and the leather, a clean animal].

I. Rather it pertains to the straps.

J. But didn't R. Isaac say, "The fact that the straps of the prayer parchments must be black is a law given to Moses at Sinai"?

Chapter Three. Shabbat

K. *Well, granted that we have learned from that source the fact that they have to be black, have we learned from that source that they must derive from a clean beast?*

II.5 A. *So what's the upshot with respect to the badger that existed in the time of Moses?*

B. Said R. Ilaa said R. Simeon b. Laqish, "R. Meir would say, 'The badger that existed in the time of Moses was sui generis, and sages did not settle the question of whether it was assigned to the genus of wild beasts or to the genus of domesticated animals; it was a unicorn, and it was just for the occasion that it was prepared for Moses, so that he could make the tabernacle from its hide. He hid it away.'"

C. *Now since it is stated, it was a unicorn, it follows that it was clean. For* said R. Judah, "The ox that the first man offered was a unicorn, as it is said, 'And it shall please the Lord better than an ox whose horns extend beyond its hooves' (Ps. 69:32)."

D. *But does not the language "horns" mean that there were two?*

E. *Said R. Nahman b. Isaac, "The word for horns is spelled defectively."*

F. *Well, then, why not solve the problem from that fact, to determine that it was a domesticated animal [an ox or a bullock, such as Adam offered]?*

G. *Since there is the unicorn, which is a species of wild beast, which has only one horn, one may also imagine that this was a species of wild beast too.*

The question is initially formulated at II.1, but we see that the analytical argument commences when we treat the question as not tangential but critical. Our interest, II:3, is to derive the rule from Scripture, and the proof is rejected because of a distinction drawn between two classes that are alleged to be comparable; once the distinction is drawn, the argument from analogy collapses. II:4 then proceeds in a new direction, introducing the result of II:3 to a different context altogether. That is the mark of the dialectical argument, one that allows for the maximum movement over the surface of the law. II:5 then reverts to its own problem; here too is another mark of the dialectical composite, the possibility of coming to a full stop at a variety of points in sequence without a loss of sense of meaning. Where the composite disappoints is not at the joining-points but at the net-result, which involves a sweep over topics rather than a penetration beneath the surface of matters.

III. A THEORETICAL QUESTION, WORKED OUT IN A SYSTEMATIC WAY, AT M. SHAB. 17:4C-D

In the elegant composition that follows, Mishnah-exegesis itself provokes the systematic analysis of a theoretical question. We ask for definitions of basic Mishnah-terminology, and a carefully balanced response generates a considerable, protracted and penetrating secondary analysis, all tightly linked from beginning to end.

17:4C-D

C. **All utensils are handled in case of need and not in case of need.**

D. **R. Nehemiah says, "They are handled only in case of need."**

I.1 A. *What is the definition of,* **in case of need,** *and what is the definition of* **not in case of need***?*

B. Said Rabbah [better: Abbayye], "…**in case of need** means, an object the work of which is permitted on the Sabbath, and when it is required for its intrinsic purpose. …**not in case of need** means, an object the work of which is permitted on the Sabbath, but handling it is required only so that one may make use of the space that it occupies. But as to an object, the work of which is forbidden on the Sabbath, one may handle it if one requires it for use of the object itself [for some subsidiary purpose that is legitimate on the Sabbath, but not when the location where the object is situated is needed. *And R. Nehemiah comes along to say,* even if it is an object, the ordinary purpose of which is permitted on the Sabbath, if it is for the necessity of using the object for its own purpose, it is permitted to move it, but if it is only to clear away the place where it is located, it may not be handled."

C. *Said to him Raba, "But do you really classify* handling an object so as to clear away the space it occupies as **not in case of need**?"

D. Rather, said Raba, "…**in case of need** means, it is permitted to handle an object the work of which is permitted on the Sabbath, whether it is because of the need to use the object itself or because of the need for the space where the object is located; …**not in case of need** means, even if it is to move the object from the sun to the shade. And as to an object the ordinary use of which is forbidden on the Sabbath, …**in case of need** means, it is permitted to handle the object to use it for its ordinary purpose or because of need of the space where it is occupied; but if it is to move it from sun to shade, it is not permitted to move it. *Then R. Nehemiah comes along to say,* even if it is an object the work of

Chapter Three. Shabbat

which is permitted, and even if it is for the use of the object itself or for the space that it occupies, it is permitted to move the object, but if it is to move it from sun to shade, it is not permitted to move the object."

E. *In session, R. Safra, R. Aha bar Huna, and R. Huna bar Hanina stated to Rabbah [better: Abbayye], "From the perspective of R. Nehemiah, as to plates, how come we handle them?"*

F. *Said to them R. Safra, "By analogy to a pot of shit."*

G. *Said Abbayye to Rabbah [better: Raba] "From the master's viewpoint, from the perspective of R. Nehemiah, as to plates, how come we handle them?"*

H. *He said to him, "Our colleague, R. Safra, has already explained the matter: by analogy to a pot of shit."*

I. *Objected Abbayye to Raba, "As to a mortar, if it contains garlic, it may be handled, and if not, it may not be handled."*

J. *"Here with what situation do we deal? The rule concerns moving it from sun to shade."*

K. *He raised this objection: "Yet the Houses agree that if one has cut meat on a pestle, it may not be handled."*

L. *"Here with what situation do we deal? The rule concerns moving it from sun to shade."*

M. *"But lo, we have learned in the Mishnah:* **And they do not prop up a pot with a log, and so is the rule for a door [M. Bes. 4:5F-G].** *But lo, on a festival day, a log is an object that serves a permitted purpose, and that shows that a utensil that serves a permitted purpose may not be handled whether it is required for its own ordinary use or whether moving it is needed to free up the space that it occupies! Therefore a utensil the function of which is for a permitted purpose may not be handled, whether it is needed for itself or for the space that it occupies."*

N. *"There, what is the operative consideration? Since on the Sabbath it is forbidden to move an object the ordinary purpose of which cannot be carried out, there is a precautionary decree covering the festival on account of the Sabbath. And should you say that handling it on the Sabbath should be forbidden, lo, since an article the purpose of which is forbidden on the Sabbath may be handled when it is needed for its own use or when its place is needed, in fact, that is only where the object is to begin with classified as a utensil, not where it does not enter the classification of a utensil at all [and the log is no utensil]."*

O. *"But do we make such a decree at all? And haven't we learned in the Mishnah:* **They let down produce [from a roof] through a hatchway on a festival, but not on the Sabbath [M. Bes. 5:1A-B]***?"*

P. *"But don't we make such a precautionary decree? And haven't we learned in the Mishnah:* **The sole difference between the festival and Sabbath is the preparation of food alone, [which is permitted on the festival but forbidden on the Sabbath [M. Bes. 5:2J]***?"*

Q. *Said R. Joseph, "There is no real problem here; the one statement represents the position of R. Eliezer, the other, R. Joshua, for it has been taught on Tannaite authority:* **'A dam and its offspring which fell into a pit'** (Lev. 22:28) — **R. Eliezer says, 'One raises up the first with the intention of slaughtering it and does slaughter it, and, for the second, one provides food while it is in its present location, so that it not die.'** [Freedman: On the Sabbath no animal may be raised up; on a festival an animal may be raised up only to be slaughtered. In the case at hand, Eliezer applies to the second animal the usual rule for the Sabbath. Since it may not be slaughtered, it may not be raised up.] **R. Joshua says, 'One raises up the first one with the intention of slaughtering it but does not slaughter it, and, practicing deception, one then raises up the second, [claiming he wishes to slaughter it instead]. If he wants one, he slaughters it. If he wants the other, he slaughters it' [T. Y.T. 3:2]."**

R. *On what grounds [can you claim that Eliezer holds that what is prohibited on the Sabbath is prohibited on the festival as well]? Perhaps R. Eliezer stated this view, only for a case [such as that at T. Y.T. 3:2] in which [it is possible to avoid monetary loss] by feeding [the animal in the pit]. But [it may be the case that], if it were impossible to feed [the animal so as to avoid monetary loss, that Eliezer would] not [hold the view attributed to him]. In the same way, perhaps R. Joshua holds [the position assigned to him] only in a case in which it is possible to use deception, [so as to make it seem that the second animal is being raised for a permitted purpose]. But here [in a different case], in which it is impossible to use deception [so as to make it seem that the action is permitted, Joshua would] not [permit performing on the festival day an action that is forbidden on the Sabbath].*

Chapter Three. Shabbat

S. Rather, said R. Pappa. "There is no contradiction. This is the opinion of the House of Shammai. This is the opinion of the House of Hillel. As we have learned in the Mishnah: **The House of Shammai say, [124B] '[On a festival day] they do not take out into public domain a minor, a lulab or a scroll of the Torah.' And the House of Hillel permit'** [M. Bes. 1:5]." [Avery-Peck, *Besah* to 37A: The assumption is that, just as the Shammaites prohibit carrying into public domain items not needed for the preparation of food, so they would prohibit handling these things on a festival simply to prevent monetary loss. The Hillelites by contrast permit handling non-food items on a festival. They presumably permit carrying these things for purposes of avoiding monetary loss. But such handling is not permitted on the Sabbath.]

T. *But how so? [Perhaps] the House of Shammai forbids [this] only here, with regard to taking out [of one's house objects not associated with the preparation of food]. But they would not [forbid] handling [such objects within the house].*

U. *But is handling the object itself not forbidden on account of carrying out? [Carrying out involves handling, and handling is forbidden on account of carrying out.]*

I.2   A. *And furthermore, Rab, too, holds this view of Raba, for* said Rab, "Moving a hoe so that it not be stolen is handling that is not necessary and it is forbidden." *So the operative consideration is that it* not be stolen, but if it were for use for some purpose that the object ordinarily can serve and that is permitted on the Sabbath, or if it were to clear away the place at which it is located, it would be permitted.

  B. *Well, now, is that so!? But as a matter of fact, R. Kahana visited the household of Rab, and he said, "Bring a log of wood for Kahana's seat." But that's something the function of which is for a forbidden purpose [for example, fuel], and it is something that ought to be handled only when needed for its own ordinary purpose and not merely because its place is needed!*

  C. *This is the sense of his instructions to them: "Take the log away from Kahana's presence [so he can sit where it is located]." Or, they moved it from sun to shade.*

I.3   A. R. Mari bar Rahel had some pillows lying in the sun. He went to Raba and asked him, "What is the rule about handling these things?"

B. *He said to him, "It is permitted."*
C. *"But you should know that I have others [and don't need these]."*
D. *"They can be used for guests."*
E. *"But you should know that I have some for guests, too."*
F. *"Well, what you've accomplished is to show that you concur with Rabbah [better: Abbayye]. So to everybody else it is permitted, but to you it is forbidden."*

The issue is quickly recast through the introduction of several distinct variables, B, with its match at D. The mark of a highly formalized statement is in the exact balance between B and D, item for item, so that the points at issue emerge with clarity. That exposition completed, E then introduces a practical problem, deriving from the ruling on an independent case. The possibility of moving from case to unrelated case through the recognition of the principles common to both is exploited at M, and N then proposes to identify distinctions to set apart one case from another. Q accomplishes that same labor of extension and, through the recognition of commonality and contrast, differentiation, that all in all demonstrates the unity of the law by reason of the coherent principles that pervade the diverse cases. I:2, I:3 then put the finishing touches on a highly coherent statement.

IV. PROPORTIONS

What portion of the chapters and tractate as a whole is taken up with dialectical-analytical arguments as defined here?

A SOURCE-CRITICAL DIALECTICAL ARGUMENT
   AT M. SHAB. 1:1   11557/178606 = 6.4%

A THEORETICAL QUESTION, WORKED OUT IN A PROTRACTED INQUIRY,
   AT M.SHAB. 2:3A-B   10332/170077 = 6%

A THEORETICAL QUESTION, WORKED OUT IN A SYSTEMATIC WAY,
   AT M. SHAB. 17:4C-D   9483/39688 = 23.8%

These figures take on greater significance when we move from the chapter to the tractate. The ratio between the number of bytes consumed by the dialectical arguments and the total number of bytes in the tractate is as follows:

$$31372/2028000 = 1.5\%$$

The proportion of the tractate taken up with the specified type of composite is somewhat understated here, but the basic result is reliable: the dialectical-analytical argument, as defined here, plays a negligible role in the tractate, which is taken up with the exposition of materials that pertain either to Mishnah-exegesis or to the instantiation of certain themes of theology, morality, and exegesis of Scripture. The extent to which any of these demonstrations relies upon dialectics, apart from the formal repertoire of rhetoric, is inconsequential.

IV

Bavli Tractate Erubin

I. ANALYTICAL ARGUMENT ON A PRINCIPLE DERIVING FROM ONE INSTANCE AND EXTENDED TO OTHERS AT M. ERUB. 3:1

Here is a first-rate example of how a generalization, attached to a single case, will serve as the pretext for assembling a variety of other cases illustrative of the same point.

- A. With any [food] do they prepare a fictive fusion meal to unite courtyards into a single domain [= erub] or a fictive boundary meal to establish one's point of residence for the Sabbath,
- B. except for water and salt.
- C. And any [food] is purchased with money set aside as [second] tithe,
- D. except for water and salt.
- E. He who vows [to abstain] from food is permitted [to make use of] water and salt.
- F. They prepare a fictive fusion meal to unite courtyards into a single domain [= erub] for a Nazir with wine [which he is forbidden by his vow to drink],
- G. and for an Israelite with heave-offering [which he is forbidden by reason of his caste status to eat].
- H. Sumkhos says, "With unconsecrated produce."
- I. And for a priest [they prepare a fictive fusion meal to unite courtyards into a single domain [= erub] and locate it] in a grave area.
- J. R. Judah says, "Even in a graveyard [which he is forbidden by his caste status to enter], [27A] because he can go outside and eat."

I.1 A. Said R. Yohanan, "We may not establish analogies resting on encompassing principles, and that is so even though exceptions are explicitly stated."

B. *Now, since he has said, and that is so even though exceptions are explicitly stated, it follows that he does not make reference to our Mishnah paragraph. Then to what passage does he make reference?*

C. *He makes reference to the following passage:* **For every commandment concerning the son to which the father is subject, men are liable, and women are exempt. And for every commandment concerning the father to which the son is subject, men and women are equally liable. For every positive commandment dependent upon the time [of year], men are liable, and women are exempt. And for every positive commandment not dependent upon the time, men and women are equally liable. [For every negative commandment, whether dependent upon the time or not dependent upon the time, men and women are equally liable, except for not marring the corners of the beard, not rounding the corners of the head (Lev. 19:27), and not becoming unclean because of the dead (Lev. 21:1)] [M. Qid. 1:7].**

D. *So is it a governing rule that* **for every commandment concerning the son to which the father is subject, men are liable, and women are exempt**? *Is this an encompassing generalization here? But what about unleavened bread, rejoicing on the festivals, and assembly on the festival of Sukkot in the Seventh Year (Deut. 31:12) [which include women, but which] depend on a particular time, and for which women are obligated! And furthermore:* What about study of the Torah, procreation, and the redemption of the firstborn, which are not religious duties that depend on a particular time, and yet women are exempt from these?

E. Said R. Yohanan, "We may not establish analogies resting on encompassing principles, and that is so even though exceptions are explicitly stated."

I.2 A. *Said Abbayye, and some say, R. Jeremiah, "So, too, we have learned in the Mishnah:* **And further: Another general rule did they state: Whatever is carried above the Zab is unclean. And whatever the Zab is carried upon is clean, except for something which is suitable for sitting and lying, and [except for] man [M. Zab. 5:2]."**

Chapter Four. Erubin 81

    B. *But aren't there any more exceptions? What about what may be used for riding [a saddle]?*

    C. *But what is the point of the item that may be used for riding? If he sits on it, then it is something he uses for sitting [and is no exception]!*

    D. *This is what we mean to say: Isn't there the upper part of a saddle, on which we have learned on Tannaite authority:* **The saddle is subject to uncleanness on account of sitting, and its handle is subject to uncleanness on account of that which is ridden upon [T. Kel. B.B. 2:7A]**? *So it must follow, We may not establish analogies resting on encompassing principles, and that is so even though exceptions are explicitly stated.*

    E. *Said Rabina, and some say, R. Nahman, "So, too, we learn in the Mishnah passage at hand:* **With any [food] do they prepare an erub and a shittuf [partnership meal], except for water and salt [M. Er. 3:1A]**. *But aren't there any more items? Aren't there also morrils and truffles? So it must follow, We may not establish analogies resting on encompassing principles, and that is so even though exceptions are explicitly stated."*

The issue of the composite is a general one, namely, rules of analogies. We may not treat an encompassing principle as the occasion for the definition of generative analogies. That point requires that we review a number of cases, Cff., which allow for the inspection of the proposition. What is interesting is how the cases themselves are analyzed, each in detail, from the announced perspective. I:2 proceeds along the same line, once more attending to pertinent details, but treating them in their own terms. Admittedly, what we have is hardly one of the great dialectical inquiries, there being little forward movement in the unfolding of the argument, but the interest in transcending a single case in the quest for a governing principle justifies classifying the composite in the present manner.

II. PROPORTIONS

The proportion of 1,356,000 bytes comprised by 4,356 bytes is negligible. The tractate's framers have found little purpose in composing dialectical-analytical arguments.

V

Bavli Tractate Pesahim

I. AN EXEGETICAL-DIALECTICAL ARGUMENT AT M. PES. 2:1

Our first composite pursues the exegetical foundation of a stated position, and what makes the presentation dialectical is the movement out of the original framework of argument:

V.1 A. **And one should not kindle an oven or a double stove with it:**

     B. *That's obvious!*

     C. *No, it was necessary to teach the rule in accord with R. Judah, who has said,* **"The only valid form of removal of leaven is through burning.** *It might have entered your mind to suppose, since R. Judah has said, properly performing the commandment concerning it requires burning it, then, along with burning it, he may as well derive benefit from it. So we are informed that that is not the case.*

V.2 A. Said Hezekiah, "How on the basis of Scripture do we know that, on Passover, it is forbidden to derive benefit from leaven? As it is said, 'There shall be no leavened bread be eaten' (Ex. 13:3) — in it there will be no aspect in which eating may be permitted."

     B. *The operative consideration, therefore, is that it is written,* "There shall be no leavened bread be eaten" (Ex. 13:3), *but if it had not been written,* "There shall be no leavened bread be eaten" (Ex. 13:3), *I might have supposed that while there is an implication that eating it is prohibited, there is no implication that deriving benefit from it is prohibited. Then he differs from R. Abbahu, for* said R. Abbahu, "In any passage in which it is stated, 'it shall not be eaten,' or 'you shall not eat,' or 'you [pl.] shall not eat,' all the same are the prohibitions against eating and against deriving benefit, unless Scripture expressly spells out the contrary, as is the case with carrion. *For it has been taught on Tannaite authority:* '"You shall not eat of anything that dies of itself; to the stranger that is within your gates you may give it that he may eat it; or you may sell it to a gentile" (Dt. 14:21) ["stranger" is one who has renounced idolatry but does not yet observe the food taboos]. I know only that one may give it to a stranger or sell it to a gentile. How on the basis of Scripture do I know that it may be sold to a gentile? Scripture says, "You may give it...or sell it." How do we know that you may give it to a gentile? Because Scripture says, "You may give it that he may eat it or you may sell it to a gentile." So it follows that both giving and selling pertain to both a stranger and a gentile,' the words of R. Meir. R. Judah says, 'Matters are just as they are written out: to a foreigner the food is transferred as a gift, and to a gentile, through sale.'"

V.3   A. *What is the scriptural basis for R. Judah's view?*
       B. *If you think that matters are as R. Meir has stated them,k then the All-Merciful ought to have written, 'you shall give it and he may eat, and sell it....' Why does Scripture say, 'or sell it'? It is to indicate that matters are just as they are written out."*
       C. *And R. Meir?*
       D. *The formulation we have indicates that it is a priority to give it away to a stranger rather than sell it to a gentile.*
       E. *And R. Judah?*
       F. *Since in the case of a stranger, you are commanded to keep him alive, and concerning a Canaanite you are not commanded to keep him alive, it is hardly necessary to have a verse of Scripture to tell us to give priority to the stranger.*

V.4   A. *Not there is no problem from the perspective of R. Meir, who has said,* So it follows that both giving and selling pertain to both a stranger and a gentile, *since a verse of Scripture is required to permit deriving benefit [through sale to a gentile] of carrion, then* everything else forbidden in the Torah would be covered by a prohibition as to both eating and deriving benefit. *But from the perspective of R. Judah, who has said,* Matters are just as they are written out, *then how does he know concerning* everything else forbidden in the Torah would be covered by a prohibition as to both eating and deriving benefit?
       B. *He derives that proposition from the verse,* "You shall not eat any meat that is torn of beasts in the field, **[22A]** you shall cast it to the dogs" (Ex. 22:30) — "it" you cast to the dogs, but you don't cast to the dogs anything else that is

Chapter Five. Pesahim

forbidden in the Torah [but you may derive benefit from it, e.g., by selling it to a gentile].

C. And R. Meir?

D. "it" you cast to the dogs, but you don't cast to the dogs unconsecrated meat from animals slaughtered in the Temple courtyard.

E. *And the other party?*

F. Not deriving benefit from unconsecrated meat from animals slaughtered in the Temple courtyard *is a negative commandment that derives from the Torah itself.*

G. *Objected R. Isaac Nappaha, "Lo, there is the matter of the sciatic nerve! Even though the All-Merciful has said,* 'Therefore the children of Israel do not eat the sinew of the thigh vein' Gen. 32:33), *yet we have learned in the Mishnah:* **A man sends to a gentile a thigh in which the sinew of the hip [is located], because its place [presence] is known [M. Hul. 7:2A]."**

H. *R. Abbahu takes the view that* when carrion was permitted, permissibility extended to it, its forbidden fat, and its thigh sinew [and that's why one may derive benefit from these, by selling them to gentiles].

   I. *That poses no problem to him who has said* the sinews impart flavor [if boiled with meat, so the meat would be forbidden as well]. *But from the perspective of him who has said* that the sinews don't impart a flavor, *what is to be said?* [Freedman: on that view the sinews are as meat and therefore when carrion was permitted the permission included the sinews.]

   J. *Of whom have you heard who takes the view that* the sinews don't impart a flavor? *It is R. Simeon, for it has been taught on Tannaite authority:* He who eats of the thigh sinew of an unclean animal — R. Judah declares him liable on two counts, and R. Simeon declares him exempt [on account of eating meat of an unclean animal, since there is no taste in the sinew, and he is not liable on the sinew, because he would be liable on that count only if the meat of the beast were permitted, but not when the meat also is forbidden (Freedman)].

   K. *But R. Simeon too declares it is forbidden for benefit, for it has been taught on Tannaite authority:* "The sinew of the thigh is permitted as to benefit," the words of R. Judah. And R. Simeon prohibits it.

L. *But then there is the matter of blood, of which the All-Merciful has said,* "No soul of you shall eat blood" (Lev. 17:12), *and yet we have learned in the Mishnah:* [**He tossed the blood on the top of the altar seven times. Then did he pour out the residue of the blood onto the western base of the outer altar. And that [the residue of the blood sprinkled on] the outer altar he poured out on the southern base.] The two streams of blood then mingled together in the [flow of the] surrounding channel and flowed down into the Qidron brook. They are sold to gardeners for fertilizer. And the law of sacrilege applies to them [until the sale] [M. Yoma 5:6].**

M. *The case of blood is exceptional, since it is treated as comparable to water, as it is written,* "You shall not eat it, you shall pour it out upon the earth as water" (Dt. 12:24) — just as water is permitted, so blood is permitted.

N. But say: like water that is poured out as a libation on the alter?

O. Said R. Abbahu, "'like water' means, like water in general."

P. *Yeah, sure, and is it written,* "like water in general"*?*

Q. Rather, said R. Ashi, "Like water that is poured out, but not like water that is presented as a libation."

R. *Well, then, why not say,* "like water that is poured out before an idol"*?*

S. There too it's still called a libation: "They drank the wine of their drink offering" (Dt. 32:38).

T. **[22B]** *And from the perspective of Hezekiah, for what practical purpose is blood treated as comparable to water?* [Freedman: since he holds that only the passive form, "shall not be eaten," implies a prohibition of all benefit, but not the active, "you shall not eat," benefit from blood is permitted in any case, for the prohibition is not expressed in the passive; then what is the purpose of treating blood as equivalent to water?]

U. *It is in accord with R. Hiyya bar Abba, for* said R. Hiyya bar Abba said R. Yohanan, "How on the basis of Scripture do we know that blood of Holy Things does not make anything susceptible to uncleanness?

As it is said, 'You shall pour it on the earth as water' (Dt. 12:24) — blood that is poured out like water imparts susceptibility to uncleanness, blood that is not poured out does not impart susceptibility to uncleanness."

V. *But what about the limb of a living animal, for, although it is written, "You shall not eat the life with the meat" (Dt. 12:23), yet it has been taught on Tannaite authority:* said R. Nathan, "How on the basis of Scripture do we know that one should not extend a cup of wine to a Nazirite [who is forbidden to drink wine] or a limb cut from a living beast to a child of Noah [who may not eat such meat, and that means, anybody]? Scripture states, "you shall not put a stumbling block before the blind" (Lev. 19:14)" — *lo, it is permitted to give it to dogs?*

W. *The limb from the living animal is exceptional, for it is compared to blood, as it is written, "Only be steadfast in not eating the blood, for the blood is the life" (Dt. 12:23).*

X. *And from the perspective of Hezekiah, for what practical purpose is blood treated as comparable to water?*

Y. *He may say to you:* blood is comparable to the limb from the living animal and not vice versa, thus: just as a limb from a living animal is forbidden [only as to eating], so blood from a living animal is forbidden, and what blood is that? It is the blood of arteries from which life flows out.

Z. *But what about the ox that is to be stoned, for though the All-Merciful has said, "its meat shall not be eaten" (Ex. 21:28) [so benefit in general is forbidden, not only eating], yet it has been taught on Tannaite authority:*

AA. Since Scripture is explicit, "The ox will certainly be stoned" (Ex. 21:28), do I not know that the carcass is carrion, and it is forbidden to eat carrion? So why in the world does Scripture find it necessary to state explicitly, "And its meat shall not be eaten" (Ex. 21:28)?

BB. Scripture thereby informs you that if after the court decree has been issued, the beast was properly slaughtered [rather than stoned], it is forbidden to eat it.
CC. I know only that the prohibition extends to eating it, how do I know that it is prohibited also to derive benefit from the carcass [e.g., by selling it as dog food]?
DD. Scripture states, "But the owner of the ox shall be clean" (Ex. 21:28).
EE. *How does that prove the point?*
FF. Simeon b. Zoma says, "It is like someone saying to another, 'So-and-so has gone forth clear of all his property and can get no benefit from anything.'"
GG. *So the operative consideration is that Scripture has said,* "But the owner of the ox shall be clean" (Ex. 21:28). *But if we had deduced the rule from the language,* "And its meat shall not be eaten" (Ex. 21:28), *that would have implied that it is prohibited to eat it but not to derive benefit from it!*
HH. *In point of fact, the language,* "And its meat shall not be eaten" (Ex. 21:28) *bears the meaning that it is forbidden for eating and also for benefit, and the statement,* "But the owner of the ox shall be clean" (Ex. 21:28) *serves the purpose of dealing with its hide [that too is forbidden]. And it was necessary to cover all this ground in so many words. For it might have entered your mind to suppose that since it is written,* "And its meat shall not be eaten" (Ex. 21:28), *the meaning is, that covers the meat but not the hide. So we are informed that it covers the hide as well.*
II. *But from the perspective of those Tannaite authority who read the verse in a different context altogether, namely, to cover half ransom and damages for minors [indicating that half ransom would be payable even when the damage is done by an ox, not by a person], how we know that use of the hide is forbidden?*

Chapter Five. Pesahim

JJ. *They derive it from the use of the accusative particle prior to the noun,* "its meat," meaning to encompass under the prohibition what is secondary to the meat, which is the hide.

KK. *And the other party?*

LL. *He does not derive lessons from the appearance of the accusative particle. That is in accord with what has been taught on Tannaite authority:*

MM. Simeon the Imsonite — some say, Nehemiah the Imsonite — would derive a lesson from the use of every accusative particle that is in the Torah. When he reached the verse that places the accusative particle before the word "Lord," namely, "the Lord your God you shall fear" (Dt. 10:20), he refrained from doing so [since he did not wish to suggest there was more than one God]. He disciples said to him, "My lord, what then will be the fate of all the other accusative particles from which you have drawn lessons [if you pick and choose among them]?"

NN. He said to them, "Just as I have received a reward for the lessons that I have derived, so I shall receive a word for refraining from deriving a lesson."

OO. [And that was the situation that prevailed] until R. Aqiba came along and taught concerning the verse that places the accusative particle before the word "Lord," namely, "the Lord your God you shall fear" (Dt. 10:20), "The accusative particle serves to encompass within the commandment the disciples of sages themselves."

PP. *But what about produce of a tree in the first three years after planting, for though the All-Merciful has said,* "Three years shall it be forbidden unto you, it shall not be eaten" (Lev. 19:23), *yet it has been taught on Tannaite authority:* "Uncircumcised: it shall not be eaten of" (Lev. 19:23) — I know only the prohibition concerning eating it. How do I know that one may derive no benefit from it or use it for dye or light a candle with it? Scripture says, "You shall count the fruit thereof as uncircumcised; uncircumcised it shall not be eaten of" — encompassing all these other usages."

QQ. *So the operative consideration is that Scripture has said, "You shall count the fruit thereof as uncircumcised; uncircumcised it shall not be eaten of." Then if Scripture had not said so, I would have supposed that the prohibition covers eating but not deriving benefit!*

RR. *In point of fact, the language here,* it shall not be eaten, *implies a prohibition of both eating and deriving benefit. But the case at hand is exceptional, since the language,* unto you, *is stated, and necessitates that explicit specification. For otherwise I might have argued, since it is written,* unto you, *the meaning is,* it shall be yours [as to benefit]. *So we are informed that that is not the case.*

SS. *So then, with all of the cited verses [in which the phrase forbidden is repeated, extending the prohibition to benefit, not just eating], what's the point of* "unto you"?

TT. *It is in line with that which has been taught on Tannaite authority.*

UU. **"for you:"**

VV. **this encompasses what is planted [23A] for public use.**

WW. **R. Judah says, "'for you,' excluding what one plants for public use.**

XX. **R. Simeon b. Eleazar says in his name, "He who plants a fruit tree for public use — it is liable to the laws of orlah. If the tree sprouted by itself for public use, it is exempt from the laws of orlah" [T. Orl. 1:2A-G=Sifra CCII:II.1/Parashat Qedoshim Parashah 3].**

YY. *What is the scriptural basis for the position of the initial Tannaite authority?*

ZZ. *It is written, "And you shall have planted," meaning, the law pertains to the individual but not to the public, so the All-Merciful wrote,* "unto you," *to include what is planted for public use.*

AAA. *And R. Judah?*

BBB. *"And you shall have planted," meaning, the law pertains both to the individual and to the public. So too,* "unto you," *bears the meaning, the law pertains both to the individual and to the public. Thus you have an augmentative clause following another augmentative clause, in which case the function is only to impose a limitation.*

CCC. *But what about priestly rations, for though the All-Merciful has said,* "There shall no common person eat of the holy thing" (Lev. 22:10) *yet we have learned in the Mishnah:* **They prepare a fictive fusion meal to unite courtyards into a single domain [=erub] for a Nazir with wine [which he is forbidden by his vow to drink], and for an Israelite with heave offering [which he is forbidden by reason of his caste status to eat] [M. Er. 3:1F-G]**?

DDD. *Said R. Pappa, "That case is exceptional, since Scripture has said, 'your priestly rations"* (Num. 18:27), *meaning, it shall be yours."*

EEE. *And the other party?*

FFF. *"It is your priestly rations," meaning, belonging to all Israel.*

GGG. *But what about the Nazirite, for though the All-Merciful has said,* "From the kernels even to the husk he shall not eat" (Num. 6:4), *yet we have learned in the Mishnah:* **They prepare a fictive fusion meal to unite courtyards into a single domain [=erub] for a Nazir with wine [which he is forbidden by his vow to drink] [M. Er. 3:1F]**?

HHH. *Said Mar Zutra, "That case is exceptional, since Scripture has said, 'all the days of his Naziriteship'* (Num. 6:4) — *it shall be his."*

III. R. Ashi said, "'He shall be holy, he shall let the locks of the hair of his head grow long' (Num. 4:5) — the growth of his hair is holy, but nothing else is holy."

JJJ. *So is* "nothing else" *stated in so many words?*

KKK *Rather, the better reply is Mar Zutra's.*

LLL. *But what about new produce prior to the presentation of the first sheaf of new barley on the fifteenth of Nisan, for though the All-Merciful has said,* "And you shall eat neither bread nor parched corn nor fresh ears until this selfsame day" (Lev. 23:14), *yet we have learned in the Mishnah:* **[Before the presentation of the first sheaf of barley,] one reaps unripe grain and feeds it to cattle [M. Men. 6:8E]***?*

MMM. *Said R. Shemayyah, "That case is exceptional, for Scripture has said,* 'You shall bring the sheaf of the firstfruits of your harvest' (Lev. 23:10) — what you harvest shall belong to you."

NNN. *And the other party?*

OOO. "of your harvest" — *belonging to all Israel.*

PPP. *But what about creeping things, for though the All-Merciful has said,* "It is a detestable thing, it shall not be eaten" (Lev. 23:10), *yet we have learned in the Mishnah:* **Hunters of wild animals, fowl or fish who accidentally caught unclean animals are permitted to sell [such unclean animals] to gentiles [M. Sheb. 7:4C]***?*

QQQ. *That case is exceptional, for Scripture says,* "They are detestable to you" — it shall be yours.

RRR. *If so, then even to begin with it should be permitted [to hunt unclean animals]!*

SSS. *This case is exceptional, since Scripture has said,* "They shall be...," meaning, they shall remain in their forbidden state to begin with [but only if they happen to fall into the trap may they be sold].

TTT. *And from Hezekiah's perspective, what need is there to say* "shall not be eaten," *bearing in its wake* "for you" *so as to teach that it is permitted? Let the All-Merciful not write,* "shall not be eaten," *so that there will be no need to say the words,* "unto you"?

UUU. *Hezekiah may say to you, "The scriptural basis for my view too is right here!"*

VVV. *But what about leaven, for though the All-Merciful has said,* "There shall no leavened bread be eaten" (Ex. 13:3) *yet it has been taught on Tannaite authority:* R. Yosé the Galilean says, "You should find it surprising that leaven is forbidden for general use [not just for eating] for all seven days!"

WWW. *That case is exceptional, since Scripture says,* "Neither shall leaven be seen unto you" (Ex. 13:7) — it shall belong to you.

XXX. And rabbis?

YYY. What is yours you shall not say, but you may say what belongs to others or what belongs to the Most High.

ZZZ. *And the other party?*

AAAA. *The word* "unto you" *is written two times.*

BBBB. *And the other party?*

CCCC. *One pertains to the gentile who is subject to your authority, the other to a gentile who is not subject to your authority.*

DDDD. *And the other party?*

EEEE. *The word* "unto you" *is written three times [including Dt. 16:4].*

FFFF. *And the other party?*

GGGG. *The second one pertains to leaven, the third one to leavened bread, and both classes of leaven had to be specified.*

V.5 A. May we say that at issue is what divides Tannaite authorities as well?

B. **"[Fat from animals that died or were torn by beasts may be put to any use, but] you must not eat it" (Lev. 7:24)] "...may be put to any use:" What is the purpose of this statement?**

C. "One might have maintained that while for the uses of the sanctuary, the fat is permitted, for the use of unconsecrated purposes, it should not be permitted. Accordingly, Scripture says, '...may be put to any use,'" the words of R. Yosé the Galilean.

D. R. Aqiba says, "One might have thought that for purposes of secular use the fat should be regarded as clean, while for purposes of consecrated use it should not be regarded as clean.

E. "Accordingly, Scripture says, '...may be put to any use'" [Sifra XCIII:III.2/Parashat Sav Parashah 102].

F. *R. Yosé the Galilean maintains that a verse is not required to deal with uncleanness or cleanness, but only to deal with what is forbidden or what is permitted, while R. Aqiba maintains that for what is forbidden or permitted no verse of Scripture is required, but a verse of Scripture is regard to deal with what is unclean or clean.*

G. [23B] *Now isn't this what is subject to dispute: R. Yosé maintains that the language, "you shall not eat," pertains to both eating and deriving benefit, so when there is a verse that permits carrion, it has to do with deriving benefit, and R. Aqiba maintains that the language, "you shall not eat," bears the sense of a prohibition as to eating, but not a prohibition as to deriving benefit, so for what purpose is the verse introduced? It has to do with uncleanness and cleanness?*

H. *Not at all. All parties concur that the language, "you shall not eat," pertains to both eating and deriving benefit, and here, this is what is subject to dispute: R. Yosé the Galilean maintains that,* when carrion was permitted [as to benefit] it was permitted, but its fat and sinews were not, *and when the verse was required, it was required to accord permission to derive benefit from these other classes of carrion. And R. Aqiba maintains that* when carrion was permitted [as to benefit] it was permitted, but its fat and sinews were permitted too, and when a verse of Scripture was required, *it was required to deal with uncleanness and cleanness.*

I. *Now as to the position of R. Yosé the Galilean, we have found evidence as to fat that the All-Merciful has permitted it for benefit, but perhaps, as to the sinew, we should say that it is forbidden?*

J. *If you wish, I shall say, true enough, it is forbidden. If you wish, I shall say, the proposition derives from an argument a fortiori: if fat, which is subject to the penalty of extirpation, is permitted for use, then sinew, which is not subject to the penalty of extirpation, all the more so should be permitted for use!*

K. *But from the perspective of R. Simeon, who forbids it, may maintain: one may show a flaw in this argument, namely: the indicative taxon of fat is that it has been released from the generally prevailing prohibition when it comes to the case of a wild beast, but will you say the same of the sinew, which has not been released from the generally prevailing prohibition when it comes to the case of a wild beast?*

L. *And the other party?*

M. *We are speaking of domesticated cattle, and even in the case of domesticated cattle, in any event, the fat was not permitted.*

V.6 A. *Now [regarding the items of No. 4,] we have presented objections deriving from all of these verses and we have answered those objections, so on what do Hezekiah and R. Abbahu differ in the end?*

B. *They differ with respect to leaven on Passover in the framework of the position of rabbis [that deriving benefit from it is forbidden], and with respect to the ox that is to be stoned, in the framework of the position of all authorities [benefit in general is forbidden, not only eating]. Hezekiah derives the view that benefit is forbidden from the phrase, "it shall not be eaten," while R. Abbahu derives the same principle from the analogy of carrion.*

C. *Now note: both authorities maintain that use is forbidden, so in practice, where is there a difference?*

D. *There is a difference between them when it comes to unconsecrated animals that were slaughtered in the Temple courtyard. Hezekiah maintains that the language, "it shall not be eaten" excludes these two items, and "it" serves to exclude unconsecrated animals* slaughtered in the Temple courtyard. R. Abbahu maintains that "it" excludes these two items, and benefit from unconsecrated beasts slaughtered in the Temple courtyard in fact is not forbidden by the Torah at all.

What is important for our repertoire begins at No. 2, because of the interest in finding a scriptural foundation for the position of Judah. This introduces the problem of a case, No. 3, and that requires us at No. 4 to find a derivation for Judah's exegetical principle. The movement then at I is to a new case, which then brings us to a third authority, and the back-and-forth argument on his position. T then provides yet another initiative, this time reverting to the initial authority, Hezekiah. Time and again we pursue the issue of the exegetical basis for a newly-introduced position. At No. 5 we introduce a free-standing dispute and ask whether the same exegetical dispute explains what is at issue there. This carries us to No. 6, a superb conclusion to the whole and evidence that we deal with a unitary composition with a clear direction and purpose.

II. AN EXEGETICAL-DIALECTICAL ARGUMENT AT M. PES. 5:3

What makes the following composition important is the close balance in the exposition of the several positions, which leads to the consideration of a broad range of topics:

- A. **[If] one slaughtered it not for those who [can] eat it or not for those who are registered for it,**
- B. **for uncircumcised men or for unclean ones,**
- C. **it is invalid.**

I.3 A. [61B] If one slaughtered the animal designated as a Passover-offering for circumcised persons, on the stipulation that uncircumcised persons also should gain atonement [that is, should be registered for the beast] with the blood of the beast when it is sprinkled –
- B. R. Hisda said, "It is invalid."
- C. Rabbah said, "It is valid."
  - D. R. Hisda said, "It is invalid": intentionality expressed in connection with sprinkling having to do with an uncircumcised male takes effect.
  - E. Rabbah said, "It is valid": intentionality expressed in connection with sprinkling having to do with an uncircumcised male does not take effect.
    - F. *Said Rabbah, "On what basis do I take that position? It is in line with that which has been taught on Tannaite authority:* Might one suppose that an uncircumcised male should disqualify the association that comes along with him to register for the animal?

Chapter Five. Pesahim

G. "For it is a matter of logic that that should be the case: Since uncircumcision invalidates [one's right to share in] the Passover-offering, and uncleanness invalidates as well, just as in the case of uncleanness, Scripture has not treated uncleanness of part of those who register for the animal as equivalent to uncleanness of all of those who do [in the former case, the offering is valid], so the uncircumcision of some of those who register for an animal should not be treated as equivalent to the uncircumcision of them all.

H. "Or take this route: Since uncircumcision invalidates and improper intentionality to eat part of the sacrifice after the time in which it is permitted to do so, since even intentionality to eat only part of the offering at the improper time invalidates the entire offering, so uncircumcision of only part of those registered for the animal should be treated as equivalent to uncircumcision in respect to the entire group.

I. "Then we have to determine the governing analogy: You should draw an analogy between a trait that does not apply to all sacrifices and another trait that does not apply to all sacrifices [uncircumcision and uncleanness do not apply to other sacrifices, for these may be sacrificed even if the owners were uncircumcised or unclean], but the consideration of improper intentionality as to the time of eating the meat of the offering should not contribute an analogy, for that serves as a disqualification in the case of all sacrifices.

J. "Or perhaps take this route: You should draw an analogy for something that has not been exempted from the general rule that would otherwise govern, from a matter that has not been exempted from the general rule that would otherwise govern [an offering may not be eaten by an uncircumcised person nor may it be eaten after the permitted time], but the consideration of uncleanness should not contribute the governing analogy, since it has been exempted from the general rule that would otherwise govern [if the whole community is unclean, the Passover lamb is sacrificed for them all].

K. "Since logical argument leads to no clear conclusion, Scripture stated, 'This is the ordinance of the Passover' (Ex. 12:43) [which proceeds to disqualify an uncircumcised person; 'this' teaches that an uncircumcised person would not, however, disqualify others who register with him (Freedman)].

L. *"Now what is the force of this 'this'? Should I say, it is to teach that if all the signatories to the offering are uncircumcised, the offering is invalidated, but if part of them are, it is not invalidated? That fact derives from* 'and all uncircumcised persons shall not eat thereof' (Ex. 12:48) [meaning: when all who have signed up are uncircumcised, none may eat of it, but if only part of them are, the circumcised members may eat (Freedman)]. *So isn't this the sense of the Tannaite statement:* Scripture states, 'and all uncircumcised shall not eat thereof,' meaning, if everybody signed up is uncircumcised, the offering is invalidated, but if part are, the offering is not invalidated.

M. *"And should you say, that is the same rule also for tossing the blood, so that, if the intentionality is to do so for a group that is wholly made up of uncircumcised males, that intentionality would invalidate the offering,* Scripture states, 'this,' *meaning: only in connection with slaughtering the sacrifice does the state of uncircumcision of all of those signed up for the animal affect the validity of the rite, but that is not the case in respect to sprinkling the blood, where, even if the intentionality covers the uncircumcision of all of the group signed up for the animal, the offering is not invalidated.*

N. *"And should you say,* [since you assume that 'this' teaches a further leniency in respect to uncircumcision (Freedman)], *then what further lenient aspect is there to the rule here when it has to do with sprinkling? The answer is,* intentionality expressed in connection with sprinkling having to do with an uncircumcised male does not take effect."

O. And R. Hisda?

P. *"To the contrary! We must take the opposite route, namely: Scripture states,* 'and all uncircumcised persons shall not eat thereof,' meaning, if the entire group of registrants is uncircumcised, that invalidates the offering, but if part of it is uncircumcised, that doesn't invalidate the offering; but when it comes to sprinkling

Chapter Five. Pesahim

the blood, even if part of it is uncircumcised, the offering is invalidated.

Q. *"And should you say, that same law would indeed apply to sprinkling, so that, unless everyone among the registrants is uncircumcised, the beast is not invalidated,* Scripture states, 'this,' teaching, only in connection with slaughtering the animal would the fact that part is not circumcised not invalidate the offering, but at the matter of sprinkling, intentionality covering a group, part of which is uncircumcised, would disqualify the offering. *And should you ask, then what further stringency pertains to sprinkling along with this one? it is that the prohibition of rendering the offering refuse by improper intentionality applies only as to intentionality in respect to sprinkling the blood [but if some improper intention applied to some other act of service, that is null; only if the intentionality involves sprinkling is the status fixed and permanent, being the last act of service in the rite]."*

R. *Objected R. Ashi, "But how do you know that the language, 'and all uncircumcised persons' refers to the entirety of the group? Maybe the statement,* 'and all uncircumcised persons,' *speaks of any group in which there is any uncircumcision at all [even a single uncircumcised male would invalidate the sacrifice for them all]? Then it would follow that the All-Merciful used the word 'this' to teach that unless the entire group is uncircumcised, the sacrifice is not invalidated, since there is no difference between whether the intentionality of the priest to cover such a situation affects slaughtering or sprinkling the animal* [there being no basis to intimate a distinction between the one and the other (Freedman)]*?"*

S. *Rather, said R. Ashi, "R. Hisda and Rabbah* **[62A]** *dispute the following verse of Scripture:* 'And it [sprinkling the blood] shall be accepted for him to make atonement for him' (Lev. 1:4) — *for him, not for his fellow. Rabbah reasons that 'his fellow' is comparable to him: just as he must be subject to atonement, so his fellow must be subject to atonement, excluding an uncircumcised male, who is not subject to atonement. And R. Hisda takes* the view that, as to this uncircumcised person, too, since he is subject to the obligation to make the offering, he also is subject to atonement, for, if he wants, he can make himself fit."

T. *But does R. Hisda accept an argument based on an argument from "since"? And hasn't it been stated:*

U. One who baked [bread] on a festival day for use on a [following] weekday –

V. R. Hisda says, "He receives stripes."

W. Rabbah says, "He does not receive stripes."

X. Rabbah said, "He does not receive stripes. *[For] we do invoke the argument, Since, if [visitors dropped by, he may use the bread for them, therefore, even though no visitors came, he may use the bread on a festival day and is not culpable for baking it]."*

Y. R. Hisda says, "He [is deemed a transgressor and] receives stripes. *[This is because] we do not invoke the argument: since, if visitors dropped by, [the bread] would be permitted for him [to serve to them on the festival day itself, therefore], even though [he does not have visitors, the bread] is permitted for use by him."*

Z. *For Rabbah there is no problem, he is consistent: Here, with respect to circumcision, a concrete action is required [circumcision, then he will be fit, and we do not regard his potential action as an actual one], and there, no concrete action that the man can take is required. But for R. Hisda, isn't there a problem of self contradiction?*

AA. *Say: When R. Hisda does not invoke the argument from "since...," it is where it would produce a lenient ruling, but where it would produce a strict ruling, he does invoke such an argument!*

The important side comes at D-E, the formulation of the issue in terms of a broad principle, following by the exegetical foundations for the respective positions, F-K+L-N, balanced, by O-R. Then R moves in a different direction by raising a challenge to the foregoing, and that is emblematic of the exegetical-dialectical argument. T then takes another turn and requires us to consider a new case to test a principle introduced in the established connection. We see, then, that a key to the dialectical argument, as distinct from the syllogistic one, lies in the testing of allegations by appeal to otherwise-unconnected cases.

Chapter Five. Pesahim 101

III. AN ANALYTICAL-DIALECTICAL ARGUMENT TO M. PES. 7:5

What makes the following composite dialectical, not merely exegetical, is the movement out of the limits of Mishnah-exegesis and toward the identification of secondary data introduced in that primary setting. The first step comes at No. 1.J, the second at No. 2.

7:5

A. [If] the meat [of the Passover, offered by clean sacrificers] was made unclean but the fat continued [clean],
B. one does not toss the blood.
C. [If] the fat was made unclean but the meat continued [clean],
D. one does toss the blood.

I.1 A. Said R. Giddal said Rab, "If the blood was tossed, the Passover-offering is made acceptable [and no other is required]. *But lo, we require the possibility of eating the meat [and the owner can't eat unclean meat]!"*
   B. *The act of eating is not indispensable to the rite.*
   C. *But lo, it is written, "According to every man's eating you shall make your count for the lamb" (Ex. 12:4)!*
   D. *That has to do with the proper fulfillment of the religious duty in the best possible manner, but it is still not indispensable.*
   E. *But has it not been taught on Tannaite authority:*
   F. "Then he and his neighbor next to him shall take one according to the number of souls" (Ex. 12:4) — this teaches that the animal designated as a Passover offering is slaughtered only in behalf of those who are registered for it.
   G. Might you suppose that if one slaughters the beast in behalf also of those who are not registered for it, he should be classified as one who has violated the religious duty, [which is to say, the offering nonetheless is fit]?
   H. Scripture states, "You shall make your count" (Ex. 12:4) — in this way Scripture goes over the same matter a second time, to indicate that this provision of the law is indispensable, *and so treated as analogous the matter of those who eat the meat and those who sign up on the beast.*
   I. *Rather, Rab made his statement in accord with the position of R. Nathan, who said, "Eating the Passover offering is not indispensable to the rite."*
      J. *Which statement of R. Nathan is under discussion? Should we say it is the following, as has been taught on Tannaite authority:*

K. R. Nathan says, "How on the basis of Scripture do we know that every Israelite, all together, may carry out their obligation to the Passover offering on the basis of a single Passover offering? 'And the whole assembly of the congregation shall kill the Passover sacrifice at evening' (Ex. 12:6) — now does the entire assembly actually slaughter the Passover offering? And is it not the fact that only a single individual does it? But on the basis of this formulation, we learn that every Israelite, all together, may carry out their obligation to the Passover offering on the basis of a single Passover offering."

L. *But maybe that case is exceptional, because, if some sign off, it is fit for the others, and if others sign off, it is fit for some. So rather, it is the following statement of R. Nathan, which has been taught on Tannaite authority:*

M. If one association signed up on the beast, and then another association signed up on it, the former, for whom there is as much as an olive's bulk per person, may eat from that beast and are not required to sacrifice another Passover offering, but the latter, for whom there is not enough for an olive's bulk of meat per person, cannot eat of it and they are required to make another Passover offering.

N. R. Nathan says, "These and those alike are exempt from having to make another Passover offering. For the blood has already been tossed."

O. *Still, maybe that case is exceptional, since, if these sign off, it is suitable for the others* [so that it is fit for all, but in this case, it's not fit for anybody (Freedman).

P. *If so, let him state as the Tannaite rule: since they are eligible to withdraw. Why use the language, For the blood has already been tossed? That proves that everything depends on sprinkling the blood, and eating the meat is not indispensable to the rite.*

I.2   A. *Now what has forced Rab to interpret our Mishnah to speak of the situation prevailing at the outset, and so in accord with the position of R. Nathan? Why not assign our Mishnah to the authorship of rabbis, and impute the principle that even if the blood was sprinkled post facto it is unfit?*

B. *Rab found a problem in our Mishnah-rule, namely: why use the language,* **one does not toss the blood**? *Rather say,* it is invalid. *So that implies, to begin with* **one**

Chapter Five. Pesahim

does not toss the blood, *but after the fact, it is perfectly all right to do so.*

I.3   A.   *And for what purpose does R. Nathan require the verse, "According to every man's eating you shall make your count for the lamb" (Ex. 12:4)?*

       B.   *It is to indicate that we require a man who is capable of eating.*

I.4   A.   *In accord with what authority is the following, which our rabbis have taught on Tannaite authority:*

       B.   *If one slaughtered the beast in behalf of those who are to eat it but tossed its blood in behalf of those who are not going to eat it, the Passover offering itself is valid, and someone carries out his obligation to make such an offering through that beast.*

       C.   *Now in accord with which authority is that statement made? Should we say that it is R. Nathan but not rabbis?*

       D.   *You may even say that it is in accord with rabbis.* The intentionality as to who is or is not going to eat the meat of the Passover has no bearing upon the act of tossing the blood.

I.5   A.   *In accord with what authority is the following, which our rabbis have taught on Tannaite authority:*

       B.   *Lo, if someone was sick at the time of the act of slaughter but well at the time of tossing of the blood, well at the time of the act of slaughter but sick at the time of the tossing of the blood, they do not slaughter and toss the blood in his behalf — that is done only when he is well enough to eat the meat from the time of slaughtering the beast until the time of tossing the blood.*

       C.   *Now in accord with which authority is that statement made? Should we say that it is rabbis but not R. Nathan?*

       D.   *You may even say that it is in accord with R. Nathan. We require a man who is capable of eating.*

I.6   A.   *In accord with what authority is the following, which our rabbis have taught on Tannaite authority:*

       B.   *If he slaughtered the Passover in a state of cleanness and afterward the owner became unclean, the blood should be tossed in a state of cleanness, but the owner should not eat the meat in a condition of uncleanness.*

       C.   *Now in accord with which authority is that statement made?*

D. Said R. Eleazar, "This was taught in the context of a dispute and represents the position of R. Nathan."

E. *And R. Yohanan said, "You may even say that it represents the view of rabbis, but here, with what case do we deal? It is a communal offering, in which case it may be offered even in a state of uncleanness."*

F. *If it speaks of a communal offering, then* why isn't the meat eaten in a condition of uncleanness?

G. It is a precautionary decree, lest the owner contract uncleanness after the tossing of the blood, and people might then say, "Last year weren't we unclean and yet ate the meat," *This year too we will eat it,"* and they won't know that last year the owner was unclean when the blood was sprinkled, but this year the own was clean when the blood was sprinkled.

I.7 A. [79A] *And if you prefer, I shall say, Rab [who does not consider eating indispensable to the rite] made his statement in accord with the position of R. Joshua, for it has been taught on Tannaite authority:*

B. R. Joshua says, "With respect to all other offerings that are specified in the Torah, whether the offering contracted uncleanness at the sacrificial fat, while the meat remained valid, the priest sprinkles the blood, or the offering contracted uncleanness at the meat but the sacrificial fat is intact, the priest sprinkles the blood. In the case of a Nazirite or someone who is offering a Passover, if the fat became unclean and the meat remains, one sprinkles the blood; if the meat became unclean and the fat remained, one doesn't sprinkle the blood. But if he sprinkled the blood, it is accepted. If the owner contracted corpse uncleanness, he should not sprinkle the blood, and if he sprinkled the blood, it is not accepted." [Freedman: eating is not indispensable in general; but here eating is not indispensable, but the people registered for it must be fit to eat it, and Scripture itself has assigned such a person to the second Passover, so Num. 9:10.]

The argument takes off in its own direction when we ask what statement of Nathan is subject to discussion, and then, why the exegete of the Mishnah has chosen Nathan's schismatic position rather than rabbis' normative one. We then move in yet a new direction at Nos. 3-4, which carry us into the exegesis of the verses that sustain Nathan's and sages' positions. But this requires us to take an anonymous rule and ask about its origins, within the now-established premise, so Nos. 5, 6.

Chapter Five. Pesahim

No. 7 then offers a whole new perspective. What we have, in the aggregate, is a moving inquiry, not a static one; an exploration of a number of related issues, not a syllogistic demonstration of a proposition.

IV. PROPORTIONS

The place of the analytical-dialectical argument in the tractate is roughly indicated when we ask how large a position in the respective chapters is occupied by the several composites we have examined:

AN EXEGETICAL-DIALECTICAL ARGUMENT AT M. PES. 2:1:   24736/226193 = 10.9%
AN EXEGETICAL-DIALECTICAL ARGUMENT AT M. PES. 5:3:   9253/89063 = 10.3%
AN ANALYTICAL-DIALECTICAL ARGUMENT AT M. PES. 7:5:   8222/154588 = 5.3%

The place of the selected items in the tractate as a whole is as follows:

42211/1252459 = 3.3%

That figure conforms to the impression left by the tractate when examined in a cursory way, which is that the tractate presents a considerable corpus of exegetical compositions and composites; I listed only those that conform to the definition that governs here. One may make a case that other items belong in our repertoire. The main point stands firm: the tractate calls upon exegetical-dialectical arguments to accomplish its framers goal.

VI

Bavli Tractate Yoma

I. ANALYTICAL-DIALECTICAL ARGUMENT AT MISHNAH YOMA 1:1

A secondary inquiry into the problem of comparison of rites of consecration and atonement, the composite contains vast amplifications of its own. The whole gives a somewhat run-on impression, but in fact the single problem predominates as indicated above. What we have therefore is an enormous reflection on the basic problem of the comparison and contrast of rites of a single classification, a handsome beginning to our tractate, because the tractate's particular topic is now broaden and deepened into an account of what is encompassing and general.

I.5. A. *How do we know [that for the rite of burning the red cow and for the rites of atonement on the Day of Atonement, it is required to set apart the officiating priest for a period of time]?*

B. Said R. Minyumi bar Hilqiah said R. Mehassaya bar Idi said R. Yohanan, "Said Scripture, 'As has been done this day, so the Lord has commanded to do, to make atonement for you' (Lev. 8:34) —

C. "the word, 'to do' refers to the red cow, and the words 'to make atonement for you' speak of the rites of the Day of Atonement."

D. *Now it is obvious that the entirety of the passage of Scripture cannot be assigned to the matter of the red cow, since the language, "to atone," is used, and the rite of the red cow does not involve atonement. But might one say that the entirety of the passage may speak solely of the Day of Atonement?*

E. *Say: we draw an analogy between passages in which the word "has commanded" is written, that is, here, we find the language, "the Lord has commanded to do" (Lev. 8:34), and there, we find the same language, namely, "This is the statue of the law that the Lord has commanded" (Num. 19:2). Just as in the latter passage, the context concerns the red* cow, so here, reference is made in addition to the red cow, and just as in the present case, there must be separation of the priest for purposes of purification, so in the other case, the priest must be separated for the same purpose.

F. *[2B] Then might one say, we establish the link between the usages of "has commanded" in connection with the Day of Atonement with the result that the passage speaks only of that matter, since we find the language,* "and he did as the Lord has commanded Moses" (Lev. 16:34)?

G. We draw an analogy between a usage of the word "has commanded" that speaks of the situation prior to actually doing the action {Lev. 8:34: "he commanded to do"] from a similar such usage [as at Num. 19:4, where the same formulation occurs], but we do not draw an analogy between the usage of "has commanded" that appears after the actual doing of the rite from the rule governing the case where the language, "has commanded" occurs prior to the doing of the rite [as in the present instance].

H. *Might one say that "has commanded" speaks of sacrifices, where we find the language,* "On the day of the Lord's commanding of the children of Israel" (Lev. 7:38)?

I. We draw analogies between two usages of the language "has commanded," but not between "has commanded" and "his commanding...."

J. *But what difference does the formal variation make anyhow, since a Tannaite statement of the household of R. Ishmael [maintains],* "'The priest shall return' and 'the priest shall come in' (Lev. 14:39) — 'returning' and 'coming in' mean the same thing anyhow"?

K. *The ruling of the household of R. Ishmael pertains to a case in which there is no comparably identical usage, but here, where we find a similar word used in the same way, we do draw an analogy only when the utilization is formally identical.*

I.6 A. "...and the words 'to make atonement for you' speak of the rites of the Day of Atonement:"

B. *But might one say that reference is made here to the atonement that derives from a sacrifice [in general, in behalf of individuals, so that all priests must be set apart for an equivalent period prior to performing the everyday rites]?*

C. *Well, then, do we know which priest is going to be assigned a given rite, that he in particular should be separated for the requisite span of time?*

Chapter Six. Yoma

D. *Say: well, therefore, should we not in fact set apart for the specified span of time the entire priestly division that serves in a given period?*

E. We draw an analogy between the rule governing a matter for which a specific time is designated and another matter for which a specific time is designated, *and that would then eliminate from consideration ordinary offerings, which take place every day.*

F. *Then might one say that priests who are assigned the offerings for the Pilgrim Festivals should be separated for the specified span of time?*

G. We draw an analogy between the rule governing a matter that takes place once a year and the one governing another such matter that takes place just once a year, *and that would then eliminate from consideration the Pilgrim Festivals, which do not take place only one time a year.*

H. *Well, then, might one say that the rule would apply to the priests assigned the offerings for one particular festival [analogous to the Day of Atonement]? And should you say, but we don't know which one of them might be the specified festival,* whether it is the Festival of Unleavened bread, because it is with that Festival that Scripture commenced its exposition of the festivals, or whether it is the Festival of Tabernacles, since the religious duties that apply to that Festival are many —

I. we draw an analogy for the rule governing the separation of the priest for seven days before the rite is to be carried out on a single day from another case in which the priest is separated from his household for seven days for the service of a single day; but we do not draw an analogy from the case of a priest that must be removed for seven days for the rite to be carried out for seven days from the law that governs the case of a priest's being separated from his household for seven days for the service that is performed on only a single day.

J. *But might one then say that* the Eighth Day of Solemn Assembly would come under consideration, for there we should have separation from the household of the officiating priest for seven days for the purpose of carrying out the rite for a single day [and the analogy then would be a valid one].

K. We draw an analogy concerning a matter before which there is no span of sanctification to another matter before which there is no span of sanctification, but we do not draw an analogy for a matter before which there is a spell of sanctification from a matter prior to which there is no spell of sanctification.

L. Well, then, would that very argument not yield a probative argument a fortiori to the contrary? Namely: If a matter prior to which there is no spell of sanctification still requires that the priest be separated for a week before the right, then should not the same rule all the more so apply to a matter prior to which there is a spell of sanctification?

M. Said R. Mesharshayya, "Not at all, for Scripture says in so many words, 'this day' (Lev. 8:34), which means, 'a day like this.'"

N. *[Offering a better answer,] R. Ashi said, "But is it conceivable that there should be a case in which the principal portion of the festival's rites are performed by priests who have not been separated, while the subsidiary portion of the same festival's rites should have to be performed by priests who have been separated from their households? And even from the perspective of him who has said, 'The Eighth day of Solemn Assembly is a festival entirely distinct unto itself,' that is the case so far as the rites of* **[3A]** *dividing the offerings by lot, the recitation of the blessing, 'who has kept us in life...,' the fact that the holiday has its own distinct name, the fact that the festival has its own number of sacrifices, the fact that the festival has its own Psalm, the fact that the festival has its own blessing. But so far as its relationship to the prior days, that festival day serves quite nicely to make up a festival sacrifice that one did not offer on the first day, as much as all the other successive days may serve to make up that offering, inclusive of the last day, the Eighth Day of Solemn Assembly. For we have learned in the Mishnah:* **He who did not make a festal offering on the first festival day of a festival makes festal offerings throughout the entire festival, including the last festival day of the Festival [of Tabernacles] [M. Hag. 1:6A]***."*

I.7 A. *Well, perhaps reference is made to Pentecost [Shabuot], since it would qualify, being a case in which* the priest would have to separate from his household for seven days in preparation for a rite that is carried out for one day only?

B. Said R. Abba, "We draw an analogy between a holy day that is observed through offering one bullock and one ram

Chapter Six. Yoma *111*

from a holy day that is observed by offering one bullock and one lamb, *but that then excludes the matter of Pentecost, which involves an offering of two rams."*

C. *That response poses no problems to him who has said that the offering for the Day of Atonement is a single ram. But from the perspective of him who says that it involves two rams, what is to be said? For it has been taught on Tannaite authority:*

D. Rabbi Says, "The ram to which reference is made here in Leviticus is the one to which reference is made in the book of Numbers."

E. R. Eliezer b. R. Simeon says, "They are two distinct rams, one that is stated here and the other in the book of Numbers." [Eliezer then would reject Abba's solution to the problem.]

F. *You may even say that R. Eliezer b. R. Simeon would concur here. In that case, one of the rams serves to meet the requirement of the holy day,l the other, the requirement of the additional offerings, which then excludes Pentecost, on which occasion both of the rams meet the requirement of the holy day itself.*

I.8 A. *Well, perhaps reference is made to the New Year, which would then require separation of the priest for seven days prior to a one-day rite?*

B. Said R. Abbahu, "We draw an analogy between a case in which a bullock is offered along with a ram deriving from his own resources from another case in which the priest presents a bullock and a ram from his own resources, *which then excludes both Pentecost and the New Year, on which occasions both offerings derive from public funds."*

C. *Well, now, that reply poses no problems for him who interprets the language,* "Take for yourself" (Lev. 9:2) to mean, "from your own resources, **[3B]** and "make for yourself" (Num. 10:2) means, "from your own property." *But from the perspective of him who says that these derive from public funds, what is to be said? For it has been taught on Tannaite authority:*

D. "'Take for yourself' (Lev. 9:2) to mean, 'from your own resources,' and 'make for yourself' (Num. 10:2) means, 'from your own property.' 'And they shall take for you' (Ex. 27:20) means, from the funds of the community," the words of R. Josiah.

E. R. Jonathan says, "Whether the usage is 'take for yourself' or 'they shall take for you,' the source is communal funds. And how come Scripture says, 'Take for yourself'? It is as if to say,m 'What belongs to you I desire more than what belongs to them.'"

F. Abba Hanan said in the name of R. Eleazar, "One verse of Scripture says, 'Make yourself an ark of wood' (Dt. 10:1), and another verse, 'And they shall make an ark of acacia wood' (Ex. 25:10). How so? The one speaks of an age in which the Israelites carry out the will of the Omnipresent, the other of an age in which they do not carry out the will of the Omnipresent."

G. *Now at issue in the dispute is the generic sense of the word "for you" in the usage, "take" or "do," "take for you" in the generic sense:* as in "take for you also the chief spices" (Ex. 30:34), or "Make for yourself" in the generic sense: as in "Make for yourself two trumpets of silver" (Num. 10:2). *But in the matters of the offerings of the high priest on the Day of Atonement and on the eighth day of consecration, by contrast, there is an explicit statement that these derive from the resources of the priest himself. In the case of the consecration of the priests:* "And to the children of Israel you shall speak, saying, Take for yourself a he-goat for a sin offering" (Lev. 9:3). *Now why state,* "And he said to Aaron, take for yourself a bull calf for a sin offering" (Lev. 9:2)? *That surely yields the inference,* "Take for yourself," *that which derives from your own resources. And with reference to the Day of Atonement, we have,* "Herewith shall Aaron come into the holy place, with a young bullock for a sin offering" (Lev. 16:3). *Then why proceed,* "And he shall take of the congregation of the children of Israel" (Lev. 16:5), *and* "And Aaron shall present the bullock of the sin offering which is for himself" (Lev. 16:6)? *Surely that bears the inference,* "for himself,"*from his own resources.*

I.9 A. R. Ashi said, "We draw an analogy from a rite that requires a bullock for a sin offering and a ram for a burnt offering to another in which the bullock is for a sin offering and the ram for a burnt offering, *which then excludes both the New Year and Pentecost, in which case both beasts serve as burnt offerings.*"

I.10 A. Rabina said, "We draw an analogy from a rite that is performed by the high priest to another rite that is performed by the high priest, *then excluding all of the other rites subject to the questions that have been raised, since the rites on those other occasions are not necessarily performed by the high priest."*

B. *There are those who say,* said Rabina, "We drawn an analogy from a rite that is held for the first time to a rite that is held for the first time, *excluding the cases raised earlier, since none of them is classified as a rite that took place for the first time."*

C. *What is the meaning of* "a rite that took place for the first time"? *Should I say, a rite that was performed for the first time ever by the high priest? Then that would go over Rabina's argument in the first version!*

D. *No, the phrase means,* we draw an inference from a rite that was the first service of its classification held in its place for a rite that is the first service held in its place. [The first rite for the Day of Atonement took place in the Holy of Holies, which prior to that time had never been entered, and this was on the first Day of Atonement; the Consecration service involved the first sacrifice on the outer altar, in priestly garments (Jung)].

I.11 A. When R. Dimi came, he said, *"R. Yohanan repeated as a Tannaite statement one thing, R. Joshua b. Levi repeated as a Tannaite statement two things.*

B. *"R. Yohanan repeated as a Tannaite statement one thing:* 'the words, to do, to atone for,' speak of the rite of the Day of atonement.

C. *"R. Joshua b. Levi repeated as a Tannaite statement two things:* to do refers to the rites involving the bullock, to atone for refers to the rites of the day of atonement."

D. *R. Yohanan repeated as a Tannaite statement one thing? And lo, we have learned in the Mishnah in two distinct passages:* **Seven days before the Day of Atonement they set apart the high priest from his house to the councillors' chamber...Seven days before the burning of the cow, they separate the priest who burns the cow from his house***!*

E. *In the latter case, it is merely a general distinction accorded to the latter rite* [as an ad hoc regulation (Jung)].

F. But lo, said R. Minyumi bar Hilqiah said R. Mehassaya bar Idi said R. Yohanan, "Said

Scripture, 'As has been done this day, so the Lord has commanded to do, to make atonement for you' (Lev. 8:34) — the word, 'to do' refers to the red cow, and the words 'to make atonement for you' speak of the rites of the Day of Atonement." [Here he clearly differentiates, like Joshua b. Levi above.]

G. *That statement belongs to his master [whom he cites here].* For when Rabin came, he said R. Yohanan [said] in the name of R. Ishmael, "...the word, 'to do' refers to the red cow, and the words

I.12 A. [Reverting to the basic proof, just now cited, in the context of 5.B, we take up the proof in its own terms, thus:] *said R. Simeon b. Laqish to R. Yohanan, "From what analogy have you drawn your interpretation? It is from the consecration service. But then, by the same analogy, just as in the case of the consecration service, leaving out any of the required rites would invalidate the service, so too here, would omission of any of the details invalidate the service? And should you say that it really would, have we not learned in the Mishnah:* **And they [also] appoint another priest as his substitute, lest some cause of invalidation should overtake him**? *But the Tannaite statement does not use the language also,* **Seven days before the Day of Atonement they set apart the high priest from his house to the councillors' chamber.** *And should you claim, what is the meaning of* **appoint**? *It is,* **they set apart** *— then the framer of the passage surely should be expected to make use in both passage of either the word* appoint *or* set apart!"

B. *He said to him, "Then how does the master draw an appropriate analogy?"*

C. *He said to him, "From the case of Sinai, in which case Scripture states,* 'And the glory of the Lord abode upon Mount Sinai, and the cloud covered him [Moses] for six days, and he called to Moses on the seventh day' (Ex. 24:16). *Since Scripture says,* and he called to Moses on the seventh day, *what is the point of referring also to* for six days? *That serves as the generative metaphor to indicate that whoever enters the camp of the Presence of God has to be set apart for six days."*

D. *Well and good, but in our Mishnah-passage we repeat the formulation,* **Seven days before the Day of Atonement they set apart**!

E. *Our Mishnah-paragraph represents the view of R. Judah b. Betera, who takes account of* **[4A]** *the high priest's becoming unclean through sexual relations with his wife [should her period begin during sexual relations, which case he is unclean for seven days and so cannot officiate].*

I.13 A. Said R. Yohanan to R. Simeon b. Laqish, "Now, from my perspective, there are no problems, for I invoke the analogy of the rite of consecration. That is in line with what has been taught on Tannaite authority:

B. "On both of the priests [the one for the Day of Atonement, the other for the burning of the red cow], they sprinkle purification water all seven days, the water deriving from the remains of all of the sin offerings that they had there.

C. *"That then indicates that there was a rite of sprinkling purification water in connection the the consecration of the priests. But from your perspective, deriving the relevant analogy from the encounter at Sinai itself, was there any rite of sprinkling in connection with Moses's sojourn on Sinai? [Obviously not.]"*

D. He said to him, "Well, now, from your perspective, are matters so flawless? In the rite of consecration, the sprinkling was done with blood, and here it was done with water!"

E. He said to him, "But that's no problem! For R. Hiyya stated as a Tannaite teaching, Water takes the place of blood. *But from your perspective, was there any sprinkling at all at Sinai!?"*

F. He said to him, "It was merely a generic distinction [marking off the rite of the red cow and of the Day of Atonement]."

I.14 A. *It has been taught on Tannaite authority in accord with the position of R. Yohanan, it has been taught on Tannaite authority in accord with the position of R. Simeon b. Laqish.*

B. *It has been taught on Tannaite authority in accord with the position of R. Yohanan:*

C. "With this shall Aaron come into the holy place" (Lev. 16:3) — with that which has been specified in context. *What might that be?* In the context of the consecration. Just as what is stated in the context of the consecration, specifying that Aaron is to separate himself from his household for seven days and serve in the priesthood for one day, and Moses gave him all seven days in order to inform himself for the act of service, so in generations to come, the high priest is set apart for seven days and performs the act of service in the priesthood for one day.

D. And two disciples of sages from among the disciples of sages of Moses [are assigned to his case]. That is done to show rejection of the opinion of the Sadducees. They give him all seven days in order to inform himself for the act of service. On this basis they have said, **Seven days before the Day of Atonement they set apart the high priest from his house to the councillors' chamber.**

E. And just as they separate the high priest, so [**seven days before the burning of the cow,**] **they separate the priest who burns the cow from his house, [bringing him] to the chamber that faces the northeast corner of the Temple building, [and it was called the stone house] [M. Par. 3:1A-C].**

F. All the same is the rule applying to the one and to the other: they sprinkle upon him purification water every day of the seven days from the remains of all sin purification rite ash and water that were there.

G. And should you say, in connection with the consecration blood was used for the rite of purification, while here it was water, you may say: water comes instead of blood.

H. And Scripture further says, "As has been done this day, so the Lord has commanded to do to make atonement for you" (Lev. 8:34) — "to do" speaks of the rite of burning the red cow, "to atone" speaks of the rite of the Day of Atonement.

   I. *But the phrase "with this" is required to make reference to that to which it obviously speaks in any event, namely,* "with a young bullock for a sin offering and a ram for a burnt offering"!

   J. *Say: if that word made reference solely to the offering, Scripture could as well has said* "with this" [in the masculine form, not in the feminine form, as is used], or, it could as well has said, "with these...." *Why the specific utilization of "with this" in the feminine singular? It bears two meanings.*

K. *And what is the point of adding as well,* And Scripture further says, "As has been done this day, so the Lord has commanded to do to make atonement for you" (Lev. 8:34) — "to do" speaks of the rite of burning the red cow, "to atone" speaks of the rite of the Day of Atonement?

L. *Should you say that it was only the first and original Day of Atonement on which the high priest has to be removed, as we find on the occasion of the consecration [the first and only such occasion], but for the Day of Atonement in general thereafter, that is not required, or if you should say that it was only the first high priest who had to be set apart for seven days, but future high priests do not have to be set apart, come and pay attention to the verse:* "As has been done this day, so the Lord has commanded to do to make atonement for you" (Lev. 8:34) — "to do" speaks of the rite of burning the red cow, "to atone" speaks of the rite of the Day of Atonement.

I.15 A. ...*it has been taught on Tannaite authority in accord with the position of R. Simeon b. Laqish:*

B. "Moses ascended in a cloud, was covered by a cloud, was sanctified by a cloud, so as to receive the Torah for Israel in sanctity, as it is written, 'And the glory of the Lord abode upon Mount Sinai' (Ex. 24:16). This event took place after the pronouncement of the Ten Commandments, which came first in the forty days of revelation," the words of R. Yosé the Galilean.

C. R. Aqiba says, "'And the glory of the Lord abode upon Mount Sinai' (Ex. 24:16) — this began at the beginning of the third month.

'And the cloud covered it' — namely, the mountain, **[4B]** Then 'he called to Moses on the seventh day' — Moses and all Israel standing there. But the purpose of the Scripture is solely to pay special respect to Moses."

D. R. Nathan says, "The purpose of Scripture was only to clean Moses of all the food and drink in his bowels, to put him at the same level as the ministering angels."

E. R. Matia b. Heresh says, "It was only the purpose of Scripture only to arouse in him awe, so that the Torah would be given only in awe and in dread and trembling, as is is said, 'Serve the Lord with awe and rejoice with trembling' (Ps. 2:11)."

F. *What is the meaning of* "...rejoice with trembling" (Ps. 2:11)?

G. Said R. Ada bar Matenah said Rab, "Where there is rejoicing, there should also be trembling."

H. *What is at issue in the cited passage?*

I. *R. Yosé the Galilean and R. Aqiba engaged in precisely what is at issue in the following Tannaite conflict, as has been taught on Tannaite authority:*

J. On the sixth of the month [of Sivan] the Ten Commandments were given to Israel.

K. R. Yosé says, "On the seventh of that month."

L. *The one who says that* it was on the sixth of the month holds that on the sixth it was given, and on the seventh he ascended. *The one who says that* it was given on the seventh holds that on the seventh the Torah was given and Moses ascended, as it is written, "And he called to Moses on the seventh day" Ex. 24:16).

M. *R. Yosé the Galilean then sees matters as does the first of the two Tannaite authorities, who has said,* On the sixth of the month [of Sivan] the Ten Commandments were given to Israel. Therefore this event took place after the Ten Commandments, thus: "And the glory of the

Chapter Six. Yoma

Lord abode upon Mount Sinai. And the cloud covered it' — namely, Moses. "And he called to Moses on the seventh day" — *so as to receive the rest of the Torah. For if it should enter your mind to suppose that the sense is, "And the glory of the Lord abode upon Mount Sinai" (Ex. 24:16) — this began at the beginning of the third month. "And the cloud covered it" — namely, the mountain, Then "he called to Moses on the seventh day" — so as to receive the Ten Commandments, well, as a matter of fact, Moses had already received them on the sixth day, and the cloud had departed on the sixth day!*

N. And R. Aqiba sees matters as does R. Yosé, who has said, "On the seventh of that month the Torah was given to Israel."

O. *Well, now, from the perspective of R. Aqiba, we have no problem in understanding the fact that* **on the seventeenth of Tammuz the Tablets were broken [M. Ta. 4:6B].** *Then the twenty-four days of Sivan and the sixteenth of Tammuz make up the forty days on which he was on the mountain, and on the seventeenth of Tammuz he went down and broke the Tablets. But from the perspective of R. Yosé the Galilean, who maintains that there were six days of separation from his household in addition to the forty days Moses spent on the mountain, the Tablets would not have been broken prior to the twenty-third of Tammuz!*

P. *R. Yosé the Galilean may say to you, "The forty days on the mountain include the six days of separation from his household."*

I.16 A. The master has said, "Then 'he called to Moses on the seventh day' — Moses and all Israel standing there:"

B. *That supports the position of R. Eleazar, for* said R. Eleazar said, "Then 'he called to Moses on the seventh day' — Moses and all Israel standing there. But the purpose of the Scripture is solely to pay special respect to Moses."

C. *An objection was raised:* [He heard the voice speaking] "toward him" but not "to him," so we know that Moses heard the voice, but the rest of Israel did not hear the voice [and that interpretation would contradict the claim that all Israel was standing there but Scripture wished to pay special respect to Moses].

D. *No problem! The one refers to the situation at Sinai, the other, to the situation in the Tent of Meeting [where only Moses heard the voice].*

E. *And if you prefer, I shall say, no problem! The one speaks of the call, the other, of the act of speech [the former having been heard solely by Moses, the latter, by all Israel].*

I.17 A. *In the presence of R. Eleazar R. Zeriqa juxtaposed and contrasted verses of Scripture, and some say, said R. Zeria, R. Eleazar juxtaposed and contrasted verses of Scripture, as follows:* "'And Moses was not able to enter into the tent of meeting because the cloud abode thereon' (Ex. 40:35) versus 'And Moses entered into the midst of the cloud' (Ex. 24:18). This contrast teaches that the Holy One, blessed be he, grabbed Moses and poked him into the cloud."

B. *A member of the household of R. Ishmael repeated as a Tannaite statement,* "Here is is said, 'in the midst,' and the same word appears elsewhere, 'and the children of Israel went into the midst of the sea' (Ex. 40:35, Ex. 14:22, respectively). Just as in the latter case there was a demarcated path, so in the case of the cloud there was a demarcated path."

I.18 A. "And the Lord called to Moses and spoke to him [saying]" (Lev. 1:1):

Chapter Six. Yoma

B. Why does the call take precedence over the act of speech?

C. The Torah thereby gives instruction on dignified conduct, that someone should not say something to another person without first calling to him.

D. *That supports the view of R. Hanina, for* said R. Hanina, "Someone should not say something to another person without first calling to him."

E. "...saying," (Lev. 1:1):

F. Said Rabbah, "How on the basis of Scripture do we know that if someone tells something to his fellow, the latter may not repeat it unless the former says to him, 'Go, say it'? As it is said, 'And the Lord called to Moses and spoke to him saying...'"

I.19 A. [Reverting to 12.A, said R. Simeon b. Laqish to R. Yohanan, "From what analogy have you drawn your interpretation? It is from the consecration service. But then, by the same analogy, just as in the case of the consecration service, leaving out any of the required rites would invalidate the service, so too here, would omission of any of the details invalidate the service?"] *it must follow that both authorities take the view that* in the case of the rites of consecration, every detail that Scripture introduces in their regard is essential to the rite [and if omitted, invalidates it].

B. *For it has been stated on Amoraic authority:*

C. As to the rite of consecration —

D. R. Yohanan and R. Hanina —

E. One said, "In the case of the rites of consecration, every detail that Scripture introduces in their regard is essential to the rite [and if omitted, invalidates it]."

F. And the other said, "Whatever matter would invalidate the rite in generations to come if it is omitted invalidates in that connection too, and any matter that would not invalidate the rite if omitted in generations to come would not invalidate in that case either."

G. *Now, on the basis of what has been said here, may you draw the conclusion that it is R. Yohanan who takes the view,* "In the case of the rites of consecration, every detail that Scripture introduces in their regard is essential to the rite [and if omitted, invalidates it]," *in light of the fact that R. Simeon b. Laqish said to R. Yohanan, "From what analogy have you drawn your interpretation? It is from the consecration service. But then, by the same analogy, just as in the case of the consecration service, leaving out any of the required rites would invalidate the service, so too here, would omission of any of the details invalidate the service?" and the other said nothing by way of retort or denial?*

H. *You may indeed draw that conclusion.*

I.20 A. *Now what is the practical issue about which the dispute rages?*

B. **[5A]** *Said R. Joseph, "At issue between them is the rite of laying on of hands on the head of the sacrifice. In the view of him who has said,* 'In the case of the rites of consecration, every detail that Scripture introduces in their regard is essential to the rite [and if omitted, invalidates it],' omitting the laying of hands on the head of the sacrifice would invalidate the rite. *In the view of him who has said,* 'Whatever matter would invalidate the rite in generations to come if it is omitted invalidates in that connection too, and any matter that would not invalidate the rite if omitted in generations to come would not invalidate in that case either,' omitting the laying of hands on the head of the sacrifice would not invalidate the rite."

C. *And as to the generations to come, how do we know that the omission of the laying on of hands would not invalidate the rite?*

D. *As has been taught on Tannaite authority:*

E. **"And he shall lay his hand upon the head of the burnt-offering, and it shall be accepted for him to make atonement for him" (Lev. 1:4): does the atonement come about in consequence of the laying on of hands? And is it not the fact that the atonement comes about only because of the blood rite, as it is said, "For it is the blood that makes atonement by reason of the life" (Lev. 17:11)? So what purpose is served when Scripture states, "And he shall lay his hand upon the head of the burnt-offering, and it shall**

Chapter Six. Yoma

be accepted for him to make atonement for him" (Lev. 1:4)? It is to show that if the owner regarded the laying on of hands as the mere afterthought of the religious duty of making the offering, Scripture regards him as though he did not make atonement, even though he did make atonement [Sifra VI.V.4].

I.21 A. *R. Nahman bar Isaac said, "Waving the offering is at issue between them. In the view of him who has said,* 'In the case of the rites of consecration, every detail that Scripture introduces in their regard is essential to the rite [and if omitted, invalidates it],' omitting the waving of the sacrifice would invalidate the rite. *In the view of him who has said,* 'Whatever matter would invalidate the rite in generations to come if it is omitted invalidates in that connection too, and any matter that would not invalidate the rite if omitted in generations to come would not invalidate in that case either,' omitting the waving of the sacrifice would not invalidate the rite."

B. *And as to the generations to come, how do we know that the omission of the waving of the offering would not invalidate the rite?*

C. *As has been taught on Tannaite authority:*

D. "To be waved, to make atonement for him" (Lev. 14:21):

E. Is it the fact that the waving effects atonement? And is it not the fact that atonement is only through the blood, as it is said, "For the blood is what makes atonement by reason of the life" (Lev. 17:11)?

F. It is to teach the rule that if one has treated the waving as a mere minor detail of the religious duty, Scripture regards it as though he has not achieved atonement.

G. But in point of fact, he has made atonement.

I.22 A. *R. Pappa said, "At issue between them is separating the officiating priest for seven days prior to the rite. In the view of him who has said,* 'In the case of the rites of consecration, every detail that Scripture introduces in their regard is essential to the rite [and if omitted, invalidates it],' not doing so would invalidate the rite. *In the view of him who has said,* 'Whatever matter would invalidate the rite in generations to come if it is omitted invalidates in that connection too, and any matter that would not invalidate the rite if omitted in generations to come would not invalidate in that case either,' not doing so would not invalidate the rite."

D. *And as to the generations to come, how do we know that the omission of the separation of the officiating priest would not invalidate the rite?*

C. *Since the Tannaite formulation uses the language of appoint, and not the language of set apart, [that point follows] [thus:* **And they [also] appoint another priest as his substitute, lest some cause of invalidation should overtake him***? But the Tannaite statement does not use the language also,* **Seven days before the Day of Atonement they set apart the high priest from his house to the councillors' chamber]**.

I.23 A. *Rabina said, "At issue between them are use of the larger number of garments that are used in the rite [eight for the high priest, rather than the four of the ordinary priest] and also the application of the larger number of anointments of oil that are required during the seven days. In the view of him who has said, 'In the case of the rites of consecration, every detail that Scripture introduces in their regard is essential to the rite [and if omitted, invalidates it],' not doing so would invalidate the rite. In the view of him who has said, 'Whatever matter would invalidate the rite in generations to come if it is omitted invalidates in that connection too, and any matter that would not invalidate the rite if omitted in generations to come would not invalidate in that case either,' not doing so would not invalidate the rite."*

B. *And as to the generations to come, how do we know that the omission of these details would not invalidate the rite?*

C. *As has been taught on Tannaite authority:*

D. "And the priest who shall be anointed and who shall be consecrated to be priest in his father's stead shall make atonement" (Lev. 16:32) —

E. What is the point of this verse of Scripture?

F. Since Scripture states, "Seven days shall the son who is priest in his stead put them on" (Lev. 16:32),

I know only that the priest who has put on the greater number of priestly vestments and who has been anointed on each of the seven days might then "minister in the holy place" [on the Day of Atonement]. If the priest put on the larger number of garments for seven days but was anointed for only one, put on the larger number of vestments on one day but was anointed for seven, how do I know that he too could conduct the rite?

G. Scripture says, "And the priest who shall be anointed and who shall be consecrated to be priest in his father's stead shall make atonement" (Lev. 16:32) — meaning, under all circumstances.

H. *Now we have found the basis for the rule that, to begin with, the priest must be distinguished by the larger number of vestments for seven days, but whence do we know the rule that, to begin with, the priest must be anointed for seven days?*

I. *If you wish, I shall say that that is the case since a verse of Scripture was required to exclude that case [I know that to begin with, it was required], or, if you wish, I shall say that it is because Scripture stated, ""And the holy garments of Aaron shall belong to his sons after him, to be anointed in them, and to be consecrated in them" (Ex. 29:29). That verse then establishes an analogy between anointing and the provision of the larger number of garments.* Just as the larger number of vestments is to be worn for seven days, so the anointing is to take place for seven days.]

J. *And what is the foundation in Scripture for the view of him who has said,* "Whatever is written with regard to those forms is indispensable [so that the omission of a given detail invalidates the rite]"?

K. Said R. Isaac bar Bisna, "Said Scripture, 'And thus you shall do to Aaron and his sons' (Ex. 29:29). The use of 'thus' indicates an indispensable detail of the rite."

L. *Well, now that solves the problem with respect to any* **[5B]** *detail that is discussed by Scripture in particular. How do we know that the details [specified at Ex. 29:4] but not articulated there [at*

Lev. 8:33] also are indispensable to the conduct of the rite?

M. *Said R. Nahman bar Isaac, "An analogy is drawn between the two passages on the basis of the occurrence of the word* petah *in both of them* [at Ex. 29:4 and Lev. 8:33]"

N. R. Mesharshayya said, "'And keep the charge of the Lord' (Lev. 8:35) indicates the indispensability [of the details covered by that clause]."

O. R. Ashi said, "'For so am I commanded' (Lev. 8:35) indicates the indispensability [of the details covered by that clause]."

I.24 A. *Our rabbis have taught on Tannaite authority:*
B. "For so I am commanded [in connection with the meal offering]," "as I commanded [in connection with the sin offering]," "as the Lord commanded [in connection with the peace offering]" (Lev. 10:13, 18, 15) — [These were presented in connection with the consecration of the priesthood by Moses, and Moses instructed the priests to eat them, even though they were unclean, "for so I am commanded" (Freedman)].
C. "For so I am commanded [in connection with the meal offering]" — in all instances, the commandment was that the priests eat the sacrificial meat assigned to them even though they had just been bereaved [after the death of the sons of Aaron].
D. "as I commanded [in connection with the sin offering]" — just at the time that the death took place.
E. "as the Lord commanded [in connection with the peace offering]" (Lev. 10:13, 18, 15) — "It is not on my own authority that I say it."

I.25 A. Said R. Yosé bar Hanina, "There is no reference in the passage to the priest's trousers [in Lev. 8-9, on the consecration of the priests]."
B. When Scripture states, "And this is the thing that you shall to to them to consecrate them to minister" (Ex. 29:1), that statement encompasses the matters of both the trousers and the tenth of an ephah.

Chapter Six. Yoma

    C. *Well, now, there is no problem with respect to the trousers, since they are covered by the generic, "garments." But how do we know that the tenth ephah of fine flour offering also is involved?*

    D. It derives from the analogy effected by the occurrence of the word "this" both here and in the verse, "this is the offering of Aaron and his sons that they shall offer to the Lord...the tenth of an ephah" (Lev. 6:13).

I.26 A. Said R. Yohanan in the name of R. Simeon b. Yohai, "How on the basis of Scripture do we know that even the public declamation of the Scriptural passage on the Consecration is essential to the rite [so that if it is omitted, the rite is invalidated]?

    B. "Scripture states, 'This is the matter that the Lord has commanded to be done' (Lev. 8:5) — even an act of speech [the word for 'matter' and 'speech' utilizing the same consonants] is indispensable to the rite.

I.27 A. "How did he put the garments on them?"

    B. "How did he put the garments on them"*!! What was was!*

    C. Rather, "How did he put the garments on them in time to come?"

    D. "How did he put the garments on them in time to come?"!! In time to come too, when Aaron and his sons will come back, so Moses will come right along with them!

    E. Rather, "How in line with the verses of Scripture before us did he put the garments on them?" [Jung: There are apparent contradictions between the command as given in Ex. 29 and the account of the ceremony in Lev. 8. In Ex. 29:9: "And you shall gird them with a girdle, Aaron and his sons" intimates that this girding of father and sons took place in close succession to one another, while Lev. 8:7, "And girded him with the girdle and clothed him with the robe" shows that the girding of Aaron took place before the clothing of the sons had even begun.]

    F. *There was a dispute on that matter involving the sons of R. Hiyya and R. Yohanan.*

    G. One said, "Aaron and afterward his sons."

    H. The other said, "Aaron and his sons simultaneously."

I. *Said Abbayye, "All parties concur that the order was Aaron and then his sons, for whether it involved the commandment of the actual deed, Aaron is mentioned first of all. What is subject to dispute is the order of putting on the girdle. He who says,* 'Aaron and afterward his sons' cites the verse of Scripture, 'And he girded him with the girdle' (Lev. 8:7), only after which it is written, 'And he girded them with a girdle' (Lev. 8:13). *He who says,* 'Aaron and his sons simultaneously' cites the verse of Scripture, 'And you shall gird them with girdles, Aaron and his sons' (Ex. 29:9)."

J. *But in the view of him who says,* "Aaron and his sons simultaneously," *does not Scripture say,* "Aaron and afterward his sons' cites the verse of Scripture, 'And he girded him with the girdle" (Lev. 8:7), only after which it is written, "And he girded them with a girdle" (Lev. 8:13)?

K. **[6A]** He will say to you, "That speaks of the girdle of the high priest, indicating that it is not the same as the girdle of the common priest."

L. *But in the view of him who says,* "Aaron and afterward his sons," *does not Scripture say,* "And you shall gird them with girdles, Aaron and his sons" (Ex. 29:9)?

M. *He will say to you, "That verse serves to teach you that* the girdle of the high priest was the same as that of the common priest."

N. In that case, what need do I have for the statement, "And he girded him with a girdle" and then "and he girded them"?

O. *That yields the conclusion,* Aaron and afterward his sons.

P. *And anyhow, can you find a way in which this can have been done simultaneously?*

Q. *It means to indicate that Aaron came first [in a procedure the steps of which were uninterrupted; Aaron enjoyed priority].*

Chapter Six. Yoma

A sequence of comparisons, I:6-27, execute the required work of detailed comparison. The aim is to prove that the present rite is unique and beyond comparison with any other. The dialectic is spun out of the work of comparison and contrast, by way of showing how we know that the requirement to separate the priest from his household applies only to the Day of Atonement and to no other cultic occasion. The opening statement works out the problem of analogy, and the subsequent ones then introduce further problems of analogy, now out of distinct areas of the law of the cult for festival occasions. The movement of argument carries us forward at Nos. 6-8+9-11, and then we develop a new analogical argument at No. 12. This argument then is extended at No. 13, with secondary amplification through other disputes that are supposed to run parallel to the present one at No. 14. No. 19 then reverts to No. 12 and continues the argument commencing there. By specifying the subterranean issue the framer is able to transcend the limits of the case, so Nos. 20-23. The rest forms an appendix.

II. PROPORTIONS

The single dialectical composite takes a considerable place in the chapter in which it occurs:

$$43911/191424 = 22.9\%$$

I cannot identify a counterpart in any other chapter, and that yields the following:

$$43911/954390 = 4.6\%$$

VII

Bavli Tractate Sukkah

I find no dialectical arguments in this tractate.

VIII

Bavli Tractate Besah

I. An Analytical-Dialectical Argument at M. Bes. 2:2-3

The following composition pursues a single problem over a variety of types of law, namely, do we indeed enact a preventative measure[so as to protect a law that is itself simply a preventative measure? The discussion is more systematic than searching, since we bring the same question to each type of law; but the movement from topic to topic qualifies the composite as dialectical, if not marking it as brilliant in the depth of argument.

I.1   A.   **[If the festival day coincided with the day after the Sabbath, [that is, Sunday], the House of Shammai say, "They immerse everything before the Sabbath, [so as not to perform a purification rite on a holy day]. And the House of Hillel say, "Utensils [re to be immersed before the Sabbath:"]** *Now, all concur that, on the Sabbath, a utensil may not [be immersed so as to be purified]. What is the reason [that such purification is forbidden on the Sabbath]?*

       B.   Said Rabbah, "It is a preventative measure, [18A] lest someone takes [an unclean utensil] and, [to bring it to an immersion pool], carries it four cubits in public domain, [which is forbidden on the Sabbath]."

       C.   Said to him Abbayye, "[If] he has a pit [used as an immersion pool] in his courtyard, *what can you say?" [In this case, carrying in the public domain is not a concern.]*

       D.   [Rabbah] said to him, "[Prohibiting him from using] a pit in his courtyard is a preventative measure on account of [the possibility that one will come to err and will make use of] a pit in public domain."

       E.   *[Rabbah's explanation is] well and good with respect to the Sabbath, [on which carrying in public domain is prohibited].*

F. *[But] with respect to a festival day, [on which carrying is permitted], what can you say [to explain why it is prohibited to purify a utensil on it]?*

G. [The answer is that] they instituted a preventative measure [prohibiting purification on] the festival day on account of the [prohibition against purifying utensils on the] Sabbath.

H. *But do we [indeed] enact a preventative measure [so as to protect a law that is itself simply a preventative measure]?*

I. [Five attempts now are made to prove I's contention, that we do not enact such preventative measures. Each attempt fails.] [As proof that we do not enact such measures], *surely we have learned in the Mishnah* **[M. Bes. 2:3A-B]:**

J. **And they concur that they effect surface contact between water [that is unclean], contained in a stone utensil, [which is insusceptible to uncleanness, with water in an immersion pool] in order to render [the unclean water] clean.**

K. **But they do not immerse [unclean water in an unclean utensil that contains it].**

L. *Now if this is so, [as H suggests, that we commonly institute preventative measures], let us enact a preventative measure against effecting surface contact, [as at K], on account of [the possibility that someone will come to transgress by] immersing [unclean water in an unclean utensil, as at L]!*

M. [The Talmud explains why, in the specific case of K, a preventative measure was not enacted.] *Is it logical, [to expect a preventative measure to be enacted in the case at hand]?*

N. *If he has [much] good water [for drinking], why effect surface contact so as [to purify] this [small amount of water that has become unclean]?*

O. *Rather, [M. Bes. 2:3 must refer to a case in which] he does not have [much clean water at all], and since he does not have [much clean water], he is very careful with [that which he does have].* [For the reason given at P, an individual rarely needs to purify drinking water. It is unlikely that occasional immersion of unclean water will lead people to err and perform other, prohibited, acts of purification Contrary to J, the fact that no preventative measure is enacted in this case therefore does not prove that such preventative measures are not, where needed, employed. The conclusion of H stands.]

Chapter Eight. Besah

P. [A second attempt is made to substantiate I's challenge to H.] *[Abbayye] objected [to H]:*

Q. "[On a festival day] they may draw water in an unclean bucket, and [as a result the bucket] is [rendered] clean. [This is permitted because the individual's purpose is drawing water, not purifying the bucket. In this case we do not take account of the secondary effect of his actions.]

R. *"Now if it is so, [as H claims, that we commonly enact preventative measures], let us enact a preventative measure [against immersing the bucket while one fills it], lest one winds up [on a different occasion] immersing [the unclean bucket] by itself, [without intending to fill it at all]!"*

S. [S is unacceptable.] *That case [at R] is different [from the one at H and, contrary to S, can lead to no wrong action].*

T. *Since they permitted him only [to purify the bucket] through the act of drawing water, he will remember [that, on the festival day, it is forbidden to immerse the bucket simply for purposes of purification].* [For this reason, no preventative measure is needed in this *particular* case. But I's supposition, that such measures never are enacted, remains unproven. H stands.]

U. The following again attempts to support I's challenge to H.] *[Abbayye] objected:*

V. "[As for] a utensil that was rendered unclean before the eve of the festival, they do not immerse it on the festival day itself.

W. "[If it became unclean] on the festival day, they do immerse it on that [same] festival day.

X. *"Now if it is the case [as H claims, that we enact preventative measures so as to protect a different law], let us enact a prohibition [against immersing the utensil that become unclean] on the festival itself on account of [the possibility that someone may come to believe that it even is permitted to immerse a utensil that become unclean] prior to the eve of the festival!"*

Y. *[The flaw in Y's reasoning is exposed.] [A utensil's] becoming unclean on a festival day is not a common occurrence,*

Z. *and rabbis did not enact preventative measures in cases of occurrences that are not common.*

AA. *[Offering a different case in support of I, Abbayye] objected* **[see T. Y.T. 2:9]:**

BB. **"A utensil made unclean by a Father of Uncleanness — they do not immerse it on a festival day** [see M. Bes. 2:3B-C].

CC. **"[If it was made unclean] by an Offspring of Uncleanness, they do immerse it on the festival day.**

DD. *"Now if it is the case [as H claims, that preventative measures are enacted to protect different laws], then let us enact a preventative measure prohibiting this [act of immersing utensils rendered unclean by an Offspring of Uncleanness] on account of [the possibility that someone will come to disregard] this [other prohibition, against immersing that which was rendered unclean by a Father of Uncleanness]!"*

EE. *[As for utensils rendered unclean] by an Offspring of Uncleanness — in what circumstance are these found [to be a concern at all]?*

FF. *[They are a concern] only for priests. [Priests eat consecrated foods, which alone are made unclean by utensils rendered impure by an Offspring of Uncleanness. For common Israelites, such utensils are not a concern at all.]*

GG. [Yet] priests are careful [not to allow their utensils to be rendered unclean by an Offspring of Uncleanness]. [DD describes a rare occurrence. As AA explains, preventative measures are not enacted in the case of such rare occurrences. But, contrary to I, this does not prove that, in other cases, preventative measures are not used. H's conclusion therefore stands.]

HH. *[Another attempt to support I's challenge to H is made.]* Come and learn:

II. For said R. Hiyya b. Ashi said Rab, "A menstruating woman who [on a festival day] has no ritually clean clothes [to put on after her own immersion (permitted by the Hillelites, M. Bes. 2:3D)] may evade the law [against immersing clothing on the festival] by immersing [herself] while wearing her clothes."

JJ. *But if this is the case, [H, that we enact preventative measures], let us enact a preventative measure [prohibiting her from immersing in her clothing], lest she come to immerse [the clothes] by themselves!*

KK. *That case is different.*

LL. *Since she was permitted [to purify the clothes] only by wearing them [when she immerses herself], she will*

Chapter Eight. Besah

remember [that she may not immerse the clothes by themselves]. [No preventative measure is needed, since the woman does not become used to immersing her clothes alone on a festival day or Sabbath. This is different from the case of immersing a utensil. For being permitted to immerse a utensil on a festival day may well lead the individual to believe that he is permitted to perform exactly the same action on the Sabbath. This final challenge to H thus fails.]

I.2 A. [A new answer is given to the question of why, on a Sabbath or festival, immersing utensils — and clothing — is forbidden.] R. Joseph said, "It is a preventative measure on account of [the possibility that the one who has immersed the clothes will] wring [them]."

B. *Said to him Abbayye, "[That explanation] makes sense for the case of clothes, which can be wrung.*

C. *"But [as for] utensils, which cannot be wrung, what can you say [to explain why they may not be immersed on a Sabbath or festival]?"*

D. *[Joseph] said to him, "[The prohibition against immersing] these [utensils] is a preventative measure enacted to protect [the prohibition against immersing] these [items of clothing]."*

E. *[Abbayye] objected [to D's reasoning] using all of these objections [cited in the preceding unit].*

F. *But [Joseph] responded just as we responded [in the preceding unit].*

I.3 A. [Offering yet another explanation for why it is forbidden to immerse utensils on the Sabbath or festival day], R. Bibi said, "This is a preventative measure, lest [knowing that he can immerse the utensils on the festival] one waits [and does not do so early enough]." [By insisting that the individual immerse the utensils before the start of the Sabbath-festival sequence, the Houses, M. Bes. 2:2, assure that the individual will have clean dishes for the holy days.]

    B. *A Tannaite teaching accords with [the perspective of] R. Bibi:*

    C. [As for] a utensil that was rendered unclean before the eve of the festival —

    D. they do not [wait to] immerse it on the festival,

    E. [as a] preventative measure, lest the individual delays [and immerses it only after he has used it in its unclean state].

I.4 A. Raba said, "[One may not immerse utensils on a Sabbath or festival], because this looks like an act of repairing the utensil, [which is forbidden on the holy day]."

B. *If this is the reason, [it] likewise [should be forbidden for] a person [himself to immerse on a festival day, contrary to the Hillelites' position, M Bes 2:20]* [By immersing, people purify themselves so as to be permitted to eat consecrated food. This is an act of repair similar to that undergone by the utensil.]

C. *[The rule for people is different, since, in immersing], it looks like the person simply is cooling himself.*

D. *This [reasoning, C] is acceptable for the case of [a person immersing in] clean water, [in which one may indeed wish simply to bathe].*

E. *But [for the case of immersion in] dirty water, what can you say [to explain why one should be permitted to immerse in such water on a Sabbath or festival]?*

F. Said R. Nahman b. Isaac, "Sometimes a man comes [home] **[18B]** in very hot weather, and, [to cool off], he even bathes in [dirty] water, used for soaking [linen]." [No matter in what kind of water the individual immerses, it therefore looks as though he simply is cooling himself.]

G. *This [reasoning, F] is acceptable for the case of [immersion during] the summer, [when the person may indeed wish to cool off].*

H. *[But during] the rainy [winter] season, [when it is cold and people do not bathe to cool off], what can you say [to explain why the individual is permitted to immerse on a Sabbath or festival]?*

I. Said R. Nahman b. Isaac, "Sometimes a man returns from the field, filthy with mud and excrement, such that he bathes even during the rainy season." [Because the act of immersion looks simply like bathing, the individual is permitted to immerse on a Sabbath or festival.]

J. *This [reasoning, I] is acceptable for [the case of immersion on] the Sabbath, [when washing is permitted].*

K. *[But regarding] the Day of Atonement, [on which washing is forbidden], what can you say [to explain why it should be permitted to immerse on that day]?*

L. [Raba answers K's question by showing that, by analogy to the law for the Sabbath, ritual immersion is permitted on the Day of Atonement.] *Said Raba, "Is there any [action] which, on the Sabbath, is [not deemed to be in the category of work, such that it is] permitted, but which, on the Day of Atonement, is*

Chapter Eight. Besah

[considered work so as to be] forbidden? [No, there is not. That which is not work, so as to be permitted on the Sabbath, likewise is permitted on the Day of Atonement.]

M. "Since on the Sabbath [immersing] is permitted, [therefore] on the Day of Atonement it likewise is permitted."

N. *[But does Raba really accept [an argument phrased] "Since... [therefore]..."?*

　O. *But [to the contrary] we have learned in the Mishnah* [M. Shab. 14:4]:

　　P. **One who has a toothache may not, [on the Sabbath], suck vinegar through [his teeth, as a medication].**

　　Q. **But he may dip [his bread in vinegar and eat it] in his usual manner, and if [as a result] he is healed, he is healed, [but is not culpable for using a medication on the Sabbath].**

　R. *Now, we can point out a contradictory passage:*

　S. [On the Sabbath, one who has a toothache] may not suck [vinegar through his teeth] and [then] spit it out.

　T. But, [contrary to M. Shab. 14:4, cited at P], he may suck [vinegar through his teeth] and then swallow it.

　U. *[Solving the apparent contradiction] said Abbayye, "When we learned the Mishnaic passage [cited above at P], we learned it too to state [that, on the Sabbath, one may not] suck [vinegar through his teeth] and [then] spit it out, [but that one may suck the vinegar and then swallow it]."*

　V. *But [solving the contradiction in a different way], Raba said, "You may even state [that Mishnah's rule, P, is correctly phrased, forbidding one even to] suck [vinegar through his teeth] and swallow it.*

　W. *"But this is not contradictory [to the rule at V, which states that one may do so].*

　X. *"This [rule, V, which permits one to suck and then swallow vinegar, applies] before [one has] dipped [bread in the vinegar]. [In this case the individual is considered to drink the vinegar as the start of his meal, as an aperitif. This use of vinegar is permitted on the Sabbath, since it does not treat the vinegar as a medication.]*

　Y. *"[But] this [rule, P, which prohibits sucking and swallowing vinegar, applies] after one has dipped [his bread in the vinegar]." [The individual no longer would drink vinegar as part of his meal. He intends the vinegar only as a medication, a use prohibited on the Sabbath.]*

Z. [The point introduced by N now is made.] Now, if [Raba] really accepts [an argument phrased, "Since... therefore..."], we should state [in his name], "Since prior to dipping [his bread in vinegar] one is permitted [to suck vinegar and swallow it, therefore] after [he has] dipped [his bread in vinegar] he likewise is permitted [to suck vinegar and swallow, contrary to what M. Shab. 14:4 states]." [In the case at hand, Raba does not use a "Since... therefore..." argument. Accordingly we assume that Raba never uses such arguments. Contrary to L-M, therefore, he does not permit immersion on the Day of Atonement.]

AA. [Perhaps] Raba retracted this statement [cited in his name at V-Y]. [If Raba reverted to Abbayye's position, that according to both sources one always may suck and then swallow vinegar, the contention of Z would fall. For in this case it would appear that Raba does apply a "Since... therefore..." argument, so as to permit sucking and swallowing vinegar at all points in a meal. If this is the case, we also may assume that Raba applies such an argument for the case of immersion on the Day of Atonement.]

BB. [AA's resolution of the matter is not necessarily correct.] But how do we know that he retracted this [view, concerning the sucking and swallowing of vinegar]?

CC Perhaps he retracted this [other view, regarding immersion on the Day of Atonement]?

DD. [Final proof is offered that Raba indeed holds that one may immerse on the Day of Atonement.] Let this [possibility, raised at CC] not enter your mind!

EE. For it is taught on Tannaite authority:

FF. Anyone who requires immersion may immerse in the usual way,

GG. both on the ninth of Ab and the Day of Atonement. [The original contention of this unit thus stands, that the Hillelites permit people to immerse on holy days because doing so is like taking a bath. As Raba argues, this applies even on the Day of Atonement.]

The point at which exegetical shades over into dialectical discourse comes at D, which requires that we consider a variety of other types of law to investigate the question. To be sure, the movement is topical, rather than logical; but the upshot is an argument that does not stand still, and that, in testing a proposition, overspreads the limits of syllogistic argument. Nos. 2ff. then pursue the original question, but the framers find that, in order to do so, here again we have to cover a variety of topics of law, each of them bearing its own inner logic.

Chapter Eight. Besah

II. PROPORTIONS

The proportion of Chapter One contributed by the cited passage is as follows:

$$16422/235300 = 6.9\%$$

As to the proportion of the tractate as a whole, it is:

$$16422/716938 = 2.2\%$$

But the tractate overall is rich in complex analytical problems, though dialectics of a rhetorical, rather than a logical, character predominates.

IX

Bavli Tractate Rosh Hashanah

In this tractate I find no example of the dialectical argument.

X

Bavli Tractate Taanit

The form-analytical translation, which will make possible other analytical inquiries, is presently underway.

XI

Bavli Tractate Megillah

This tractate presents no examples of the dialectical argument.

XII

Bavli Tractate Moed Qatan

Chapter One has already dealt with what I called "a limited instance of the dialectical-analytical argument in Mishnah-Exegesis." In this tractate I find no other relevant composites.

XIII

Bavli Tractate Hagigah

In this tractate I find nothing relevant to our inquiry.

XIV

Bavli Tractate Yebamot

I. AN EXEGETICAL-DIALECTICAL AND ANALOGICAL-DIALECTICAL ARGUMENT AT M. YEB. 1:1-2

The following sizable composite pursues a dialectical argument concerning both legal and exegetical matters. We begin at the very beginning, though the part that moves outward from the exegetical project commences only at No. 6. Had we concluded with No. 5, our Mishnah-exegetical work would have been completed;

.5 A. *What is the scriptural basis of the rule of our Mishnah [that not only the forbidden class of woman, but also co-wives and co-wives of co-wives, also are exempt from having to enter levirate marriage and from having to perform the rite of removing the shoe]?*

B. *It is in line with that which our rabbis have taught on Tannaite authority:*

C. "And you shall not take a woman along with her sister, to be a co-wife to her, to uncover her nakedness, beside her in her lifetime" (Lev. 18:18) —

D. What is the point of the use of the words, "beside her"?

E. Since Scripture states, "Her husband's brother shall go in beside her" (Dt. 25:3), I might have supposed that Scripture here makes reference even to any of the forbidden relatives that are listed in the Torah [indicating that levirate marriage may take place, e.g., between a father and a daughter]! The use of the word "beside her" in both passages serves to establish a verbal analogy between the one and the other. Just as elsewhere it is only in the case of a religious duty that levirate marriage takes place, so here too it is only in the case of a religious duty in which the levirate marriage takes place. And yet did not the All-Merciful say explicitly, "You shall not take two sisters" (Lev. 18:18)? [The upshot is that levirate marriage is forbidden in the case of

153

F. So we are informed of the law governing the woman herself [who is in a consanguineous relationship]. How do we know the rule governing her co-wife [that the co-wife of such a woman also does not enter into any levirate connection at all]?

G. It derives from the language, "to be her co-wife" (Lev. 18:18).

H. Now we have the rule on the co-wife. How about the co-wife's co-wife?

I. That derives from the use by Scripture of the language, "to be a co-wife" rather than the language "to oppress" [Slotki: the former covers many co-wives, thus co-wife and the co-wife's co-wife].

J. So we have the rule governing the wife's sister. How do I know the rule governing all other consanguineous relationships?

K. Say: what distinguishes the case of the sister of the wife is that she stands in a consanguineous relationship, so that if one deliberately has sexual relations with her, he is liable to extirpation, and if it is inadvertent, he is liable to present a sin offering, and she is forbidden to enter into levirate marriage with his brother [should he die childless], so in the case of any woman who is in a consanguineous relationship with him, so that if he should have sexual relations with her deliberately, he is subject to extirpation, and if it was inadvertent, he would have to bring a sin offering, the woman would be forbidden to enter into levirate marriage with a surviving brother of such a man.

L. Now on the basis of Scripture, thus far, I know only that that is the case of that classification of women. How about their co-wives?

M. Say: what distinguishes the sister of the wife is that she stands in consanguineous relationship, and he is liable for deliberately having sexual relations with her to extirpation, and if it is inadvertent, to a sin offering, and she is forbidden to the levir and also her co-wife is forbidden to the levir. So any other classification of women who stands in a consanguineous relationship, and on account of which he is liable to extirpation for deliberately having sexual reactions with her, and to a sin offering if the act is inadvertent, and who is forbidden to the levir and whose co-wife is forbidden to the levir.

N. On the strength of this reasoning, sages have said: **Fifteen women [who are near of kin to their deceased, childless husband's brother] [because they cannot enter into levirate marriage with the deceased childless husband's brother also] exempt**

Chapter Fourteen. Yebamot

their co-wives, and the co-wives, from the rite of removing the shoe [halisah] and from levirate marriage, without limit.

O. Might I suppose that the co-wives of the further six consanguineous relations [**Six forbidden degrees are subject to a more strict rule than these, for they are validly married only to outsiders, not to one's paternal brother, and so their co-wives are permitted: (1) his mother, and (2) the wife of his father, and (3) the sister of his father, and (4) his sister from the same father, and (5) the wife of his father's brother, and (6) the wife of his brother from the same father**] of a still more weighty relationship also are forbidden [from entering into marriage with someone whom the forbidden relatives may not marry]?

P. Say: what distinguishes the sister of the wife is that she stands in consanguineous relationship, and he is liable for deliberately having sexual relations with her to extirpation, and if it is inadvertent, to a sin offering, and she is forbidden to the levir and also her co-wife is forbidden to the levir, so any other classification of women who stands in a consanguineous relationship, and on account of which he is liable to extirpation for deliberately having sexual relations with her, and to a sin offering if the act is inadvertent, and who is forbidden to the levir and whose co-wife is forbidden to the levir. That then excludes the case of the six forbidden relationships subject to a most weighty prohibition. Since these may never marry the other brothers, the co-wives are permitted, for the law of the co-wife applies only to the widows of a brother [Slotki: where one of the widows is a forbidden relative of one of the surviving brothers, and no forbidden relative of the deceased. As the relative is forbidden to marry the brother, her co-wife also is forbidden to him as his brother's wife. Where the relative however is married to a stranger, her co-wife is permitted to those to whom the relative herself is forbidden.]

Q. So we have derived the admonition in the stated cases. Whence the penalty?

R. Scripture has said, "For whoever shall do any of these abominations...shall be cut off from among their people" (Lev. 18:19).

.6 A. *The operative consideration, then, is that the All-Merciful has stated explicitly, "beside her." Then it is to be inferred that otherwise, levirate marriage may be contracted with the wife's sister. How come?*

B. *It is because we invoke the rule: let a positive religious duty come and set aside a negative religious duty.*
C. *Well, I could concede that we do say, it is because we invoke the rule: let a positive religious duty come and set aside a negative religious duty in a case in which the latter is merely a prohibition. But do we invoke that principle when the prohibition is one in which the penalty is extirpation? And, furthermore, how do we know the rule governing the negative commandment to begin with that it is superseded at all?*
[4A] *It is because it is written,* "You shall not wear mingled stuff" Dt. 22:11)..."you shall make you twisted cords" (Dt. 22:12), and in that connection said R. Eleazar, "How on the basis of Scripture do we know that the principle of the exegesis of passages based on juxtapositions derives from the Torah itself. As it is written, 'They are joined together forever and ever they are done in truth and uprightness' (Ps. 111:8)." And R. Sheshet said R. Eleazar b. Azariah, "How on the basis of Scripture do we know that the deceased childless brother's widow who is obligated to enter into levirate marriage with her late husband's surviving brother, in the case in which the latter is suffering with boils, is not to be muzzled [but may dissent from the marriage]? It is written, 'you shall not muzzle the ox in its ploughing' (Dt. 25:4), and, alongside, 'if brothers dwell together' (Dt. 25:5)."
D. *And said R. Joseph, "Even one who does not in general affirm the principle of the exegesis of passages based on juxtapositions, in the case of the book of Deuteronomy, he does interpret verses based on their juxtaposition. For lo, R. Judah in general does not in general affirm the principle of the exegesis of passages based on juxtapositions, but in the case of the book of Deuteronomy, he does interpret verses based on their juxtaposition."*
E. *How do we know that he in general does not in general affirm the principle of the exegesis of passages based on juxtapositions? As has been taught on Tannaite authority:*
F. Ben Azzai says, "It is stated, 'You shall not suffer a sorceress to live' (Ex. 22:17), and immediately beyond, 'Whosoever lies with a beast shall surely be put to death' (Ex. 22:18).

G. "The juxtaposition of the two topics is to indicate that, just as one who lies with a beast is put to death through stoning, so a sorceress also is put to death through stoning."

H. Said to him R. Judah, "And merely because one matter is juxtaposed to the next, shall we take this person out for execution through stoning?! [There must be better proof.]

I. "Rather, those who divine by a ghost or by a familiar spirit fall into the classification of of sorcery. Why were they singled out? It was so as to drawn an analogy to them, so as to tell you, 'Just as those who divine by a ghost or by a familiar spirit are put to death through stoning, so a sorceress who is to be executed is put to death through stoning.'"

J. *How do we know that in the case of the book of Deuteronomy, he does interpret verses based on their juxtaposition? As we have learned in the Mishnah:* **A man marries the woman raped by his father or seduced by his father, raped by his son or seduced by his son. R. Judah prohibits in the case of the one raped by his father or seduced by his father [M. Yeb. 11C-D].** *And said R. Giddal said Rab, "What is the scriptural basis for the position of R. Judah? As it is written, 'A man shall not take his father's wife and shall not uncover his father's skirt' (Dt. 23:1), meaning that he may not uncover a skirt which his father has seen. And how do we know that the text speaks of a woman whom his father has raped? It is written, 'Then the man that lay with her shall give to the father' (Dt. 22:29). And juxtaposed is: 'A man shall not take' (Dt. 23:1)."* [Simon, *Berakhot,* p. 129, n. 2: This shows that R. Judah derives lessons from juxtaposed texts in Deuteronomy.]"

K. *And rabbis?* [Slotki: how do they allow marriage of a woman outraged or seduced by one's father?]

L. *If the text really were juxtaposed, matters would be as you have said. But since the verses are not juxtaposed, "A man shall not take his father's wife" being written between them, the context speaks of a woman awaiting the decision of the levirate brother in law, and in marrying such a woman, a son [of the levir] transgressed two negative religious duties* [Slotki: one is that of marrying a woman who is nearly his father's wife, being subject to the levirate marriage; the other is that of marrying an aunt, the wife of his father's deceased brother].

.7 A. *And how come in the case of the book of Deuteronomy, he does interpret verses based on their juxtaposition?*
 B. *If you wish, I shall say that it is because there it is obvious [Slotki: from the proximity of the texts], and if you wish, I shall say, because in that context, there is a redundancy.*
 C. *If you wish, I shall say that it is because there it is obvious: for otherwise, the All-Merciful should have stated the prohibition in the passage in which Scripture deals with consanguineous relationships;*
 D. *and if you wish, I shall say, because in that context, there is a redundancy: for otherwise, the All-Merciful should have written, "A man shall not take his father's wife" (Dt. 23:1). Why add: "And shall not uncover his father's garment"?* **[4B]** *That proves that, in that context, there is a redundancy.*

.8 A. *So too in the case of show fringes [in which case one does violate the taboo against mixing species, though otherwise one does not do so], if you wish, I shall say that it is because there it is obvious [Slotki: from the proximity of the texts], and if you wish, I shall say, because in that context, there is a redundancy.*
 B. *If you wish, I shall say that it is because there it is obvious: for otherwise, the All-Merciful should have stated the religious duty in the section on show fringes, so what other purpose can there have been to present it here? [So the deduction must have been on the basis of juxtaposition.]*
 C. *and if you wish, I shall say, because in that context, there is a redundancy: for Scripture states, "Neither shall there come upon you a garment of two kinds of stuff mingled together" (Lev. 19:19). Why say, "You shall not wear a mingled stuff" (Dt. 22:11)? It must be that the purpose was to provide a redundant text.*

.9 A. *But these verses [Lev. 19:19, Dt. 22:11] surely are required, each for its own purpose. For had Scripture stated only,* "Neither shall there come upon you a garment of two kinds of stuff mingled together" (Lev. 19:19), *I might have supposed that anything that is put on is forbidden, including clothing that is carried by clothing dealers. So the All-Merciful stated,* "You shall not wear a mingled stuff" (Dt. 22:11), *showing that "putting on" must be comparable to wearing, that is to say, that there should be an aspect of personal enjoyment [which is not the case for the clothing dealer, who carries the garments only for sale]. And had Scripture stated only,* "You shall not wear a mingled stuff" (Dt. 22:11), *I might have supposed that it is in particular wearing that is forbidden, since the enjoyment is considerable, but merely putting on is not forbidden, so Scripture said,* "Neither shall there come upon you a garment of two kinds of stuff mingled together" (Lev. 19:19).

B. *If the verses were required for the stated purpose [and were not redundant], Scripture should have written only,* "You shall not wear mingled stuff." *Why add,* "wool and linen"? *[And if you propose that the purpose was to show that what is forbidden in context is wool and linen], it is written,* "Neither shall there come upon you a garment of two kinds of stuff mingled together," (Lev. 19:19), *in which connection a Tannaite authority of the household of R. Ishmael stated,* "Since Scripture commonly speaks of garments without further specification, and here Scripture has in one case [Lev. 13:47-8] specified wool and linen, all references must be understood as speaking of wool and linen. *Why then specify wool and linen here as well? It must be so as to provide a redundant text.*"

.10 A. *And still, the reference to wool and linen at Dt. 22:11 is required for an other purpose. For it might have entered your mind that the prohibition pertains to a case in which the benefit of the putting on is not all that great, but in regard to wearing the garment, where the benefit is great, any two species of fabrics are forbidden by the All-Merciful. So the All-Merciful has specified only* "wool and linen."

B. *If so, Scripture should have left out those items altogether, and we could have drawn a verbal analogy between the references to "mingled stuff" at Dt. 22:11 and Lev. 19:19.*

.11 A. *Now as to the Tannaite authority of the household of R. Ishmael, the operative consideration is that the All-Merciful has made explicit reference to wool and linen. Lo, if it were not for that fact, the use of mixed stuffs in show fringes would have been assumed to have been forbidden by the All-Merciful. And yet it is written,* "And they shall make them fringes in the corners of their garments" (Num. 15:38), *and a Tannaite authority of the household of R. Ishmael has taught,* "Wherever Scripture refers to 'garment,' it is one that is made of wool or flax, and yet the All-Merciful has said that 'purple' should be inserted into them and purple is wool! *And how do we know that purpose is wool? Because linen is flax, purple must be wool.* [Slotki: as the garment were either of wool or flax and linen flax was specified in the case of one, all the others must have been wool; now since it has been shown that purple is wool, it obviously follows that woolen show fringes are permissible in a garment of flax; what was the need then for a specific text to prove the permissibility of mingling wool and flax in show fringes?]

Chapter Fourteen. Yebamot

B. *The text nonetheless for necessary, for otherwise, one might have assumed that matters are to be read in accord with Raba. for Raba contrasted these verses: "It is written, 'The corner' [Cashdan: which implies that the fringes are to be of] the same kind of material as the corner; but it is also written, 'wool and linen.' How so? Woolen threads along with linen threads carry out the obligation of a garment to have show fringes whether these garments are made of the same material or material of some other kind; other kinds of threads serve to fulfill the requirement of show fringes in a garment of the same material, but not in a garment of some other material."*

C. *But lo, the Tannaite authority of the household of R. Ishmael does not concur with Raba [Slotki: for according to that authority, since garment denotes only such as is made of wool and linen, garments made of other materials require no show fringes. What need is there for the expression of wool and linen to differentiate these from other materials?]*

D. *The reference to wool and linen nonetheless is required. For otherwise one might have supposed that Raba's interpretation would yield the following: "the corner" implies that the fringes are to be made of the material of the corner, and that the sense of the All-Merciful is this: "Make wool fringes for wool garments, and linen ones for linen. Only when you make wool fringes for wool garments you must dye them, but you should not make wool fringes for linen or linen ones for wool. Hence, the All-Merciful specified wool and linen to show that even wool fringes may be made for linen garments, and linen fringes for wool ones.* [Slotki: mingled stuffs are permissible in the performance of the precept of show fringes.]

.12 A. **[5A]** *That poses no problem to the Tannaite authority of the household of R. Ishmael* [Slotki: that deduction from juxtaposed verses is such that a positive precept supersedes a negative one; since on the lines of his interpretation of the tet, wool and linen is superfluous, and free for the deduction that is mentioned]. *But as to rabbis [who do not interpret garment to be one of wool and flax], how do they know the same fact?*

B. *They derive it from the reference to "his head" (Lev. 14:9), for it has been taught on Tannaite authority:*

C. **[Sifra 151/Parashat Mesora Pereq 2/3:] "His head" (Lev. 14:9) — why does Scripture say so?**

D. **Because it is said, "A razor shall not pass across his [the Nazir's] head" (Num. 6:5),**

E. **might I think that this [prohibition] applies even though he is afflicted with plague?**

F. **Scripture says, "His head" (Lev. 14:9).**

G. *And the Tannaite authority at hand takes the position that rounding the whole of the head is classified as rounding.* [Slotki: such a rounding is generally forbidden but is permitted in the case of a leper, because Scripture explicitly stated 'shave all the hair of his head.' Thus it is proved that the positive precept of the shaving of the leper supersedes the prohibition of rounding off one's head. Similarly in the case of the levirate marriage, it might have been assumed that the positive precept of marrying the deceased brother's widow supersedes the prohibition of marrying a wife's sister; hence the necessity for a special text to prove that it does not.]

H. *One may raise this objection:* the distinctive trait that explains why the prohibition against rounding the head may be superseded is that it does not apply to everybody [women are not obligated].
I. Rather, the same point derives from the matter of "his beard" (Lev. 14:9), in line with that which has been taught on Tannaite authority:
J. **[Sifra 151/Parashat Mesora Pereq 2/4:] "And his beard" (Lev. 14:9):**
K. **Why does Scripture say so?**
L. **Because it is said, "The corner of their beard they [priests] shall not shave" (Lev. 12:5).**
M. **Might one think that this is the case even if he is afflicted with plague?**
N. **Scripture specifies, "His beard"(Lev. 14:9).**
O. Now since there is no point in applying it to a prohibition that does not apply to everybody [Slotki: that such a prohibition is superseded by a positive precept, having been deduced earlier from "his head,"] apply it to the matter of a negative commandment that does apply to everybody.
P. *Nonetheless, the reference to "his beard" still is needed [for a contextual purpose, so is not available for the present exercise at all]. For it might have entered your mind to suppose that rules governing priests are in a special case,* since the Scripture has assigned to them a great many additional religious duties that do not pertain to other castes, so even a prohibition that does not apply to all persons *would not be superseded in their case. Therefore it was necessary to use the cited language to show that it does supersede.*

Q. *The besought proposition derives in accord with the following Tannaite authority, as has been taught on Tannaite authority:*
R. "His head" (Lev. 14:9) — why does Scripture say so?
S. Because it is said, "A razor shall not pass across his [the Nazir's] head" (Num. 6:5),
T. might I think that this [prohibition] applies to a Nazirite who is afflicted with plague?
U. Scripture says, "His head" (Lev. 14:9). [Slotki: thus it is proved that a positive precept supersedes a prohibition.]
V. *One may raise this objection:* the distinctive trait that explains why the prohibition against rounding the head may be superseded is that the Nazirite is subject to gaining absolution [of a sage, who may release his vow [so he may not have to shave at all]. *And if you do not maintain that view, then lo, what about the established principle that* an affirmative commandment does not override a negative commandment and an affirmative commandment? *Why not prove the contrary from the case of the law governing the Nazirite suffering from the skin ailment?* [Slotki: the shaving of a Nazirite's head is forbidden by the precept that he must grow his hair long, and by the prohibition of allowing a razor to come upon his head]. *So the reason that no deduction may be made from the case of the Nazirite is that one may refute it on the basis of the fact that the Nazirite is subject to gaining absolution. Here too, one may raise the objection,* the distinctive trait that explains why the prohibition against rounding the head may be superseded is that the Nazirite is subject to gaining absolution.

W. *In point of fact* **[5B]** *the deduction derives from the original text [the use of mingled stuff in the case of the show fringes], namely: since Scripture could have used the expression,* "you shall make you fringes," [and not, "twisted cords" (Dt. 22:12)], *what need was there for the expression, "twisted cords"? One must conclude that it served the purpose of leaving the matter open for deduction.*

Y. *But that language serves the purpose of indicating the number of threads that are to be used in the show-fringes, as follows:* "Twisted thread" (Dt. 22:12) would involve two, but "Twisted cords" represents four, so one has to twist them into a cord; but from the middle they have to hang down as separate threads.

Z. If that were the intent of the framer of the passage, then Scripture could as well have said, "you shall not wear a mingled stuff, wool and linen" (Dt. 22:11). Why add, "together"? *One must conclude that it served the purpose of leaving the matter open for deduction.*

AA. *But the purpose of the text* ["together," Dt. 22:11] is to indicate that two stitches form a combination [of wool and flax materials] and one stitch does not [following Slotki].

BB. *If that were the case, the All-Merciful should have written,* "You shall not wear wool and linen together." Why say "mingled stuff"? *One must conclude that it served the purpose of leaving the matter open for deduction.*

CC. *But still, the cited language is required to make the point that* mingled stuff is forbidden only if it was hackled, spun, or twisted.

DD. *The fact is that all of these propositions derive from the reference to "mingled stuff."*

.13 A. *Thus far we have found that a positive commandment will come along and supersede a negative commandment standing on its own. But where do we find that a positive commandment supersedes a negative commandment, the punishment of which is extirpation, so that the language "beside her" should be required to forbid such an action in this special case?* [That is, to forbid the marriage of the levir and the widow of the deceased childless brother if she is a forbidden relative (Slotki)]? *And should you say that [the prohibition of marriage of the levir and the widow of the deceased childless brother if she is a forbidden relative] should be derived from the matter of circumcision* [Slotki: which must be performed on the eighth day of the child's birth, even though that day happens to coincide with the Sabbath, when such work is forbidden, and the penalty of extirpation is imposed], *there is a special consideration with regard to circumcision,* namely: thirteen covenants were made in connection with circumcision.
B. *So why not derive the principle from the case of the Passover lamb [which may be slaughtered even on the Sabbath, thus similar to the matter of circumcision]?*
C. *There is a special consideration with regard to offering the Passover lamb on the Sabbath,* namely: it involves extirpation. [Slotki: so it may also supersede the Sabbath; but it supplies no proof that a positive precept which is not so stringent, such as the marriage with the levir, also supersedes a prohibition involving extirpation.]
D. *So why not derive the principle from the case of the daily whole offering [which may be slaughtered even on the Sabbath, thus similar to the matter of circumcision]?*
E. *There is a special consideration with regard to offering the Passover lamb on the Sabbath,* namely: it is regular [and that is why it overrides the Sabbath; the issue at hand is therefore not resolved.]
F. *So it cannot be derived from a single case, but let it be derived from two of them!*
G. *Well, which two? Should it be the cases of circumcision and the Passover? But the distinctive trait tin both is that the penalty of extirpation applies [and that is why these supersede the Sabbath]. Should it derive from the Passover and the daily whole offering? But these represent requirements of the Most High. Should it derive from*

circumcision and the daily whole offering? But these are religious duties that pertained prior to the giving of the Torah, at least in accord with the opinion of him who maintains that the burnt offering that the Israelites offered in the wilderness was the daily whole offering. And, as a matter of fact, all three cannot yield the besought principle, since all of them pertained before the giving of the Torah [but that is not the case for the prohibition at hand].

H. Rather, this is the reason that a special text is required [namely, "beside her," Lev. 18:18, to indicate that the levirate marriage is forbidden if the widow is a forbidden relative of the surviving brother (Slotki)]:

I. [In the absence of Lev. 18:18,] *you might otherwise have supposed that* [the proposition that a positive religious duty supersedes a negative one that involves extirpation, so that a levir may marry his deceased childless brother's widow even if she is a forbidden relative (Slotki)] *derives from the case of the honor that is owing to the father and mother, in line with that which has been taught on Tannaite authority:*

J. Might one suppose that the honor owing to father and mother supersedes the Sabbath? It is stated to the contrary, "You will fear, every person his mother and his father, but you shall also keep my Sabbaths" (Lev. 19:3) — all of them are liable to carry out the honor that is owing to me.

K. *So if the father had said to him,* "Slaughter an animal for me," "Cook for me," *[on the Sabbath he must not do so]. Now the operative consideration is that Scripture has said,* "You will fear, every person his mother and his father, but you shall also keep my Sabbaths" (Lev. 19:3). *Then if Scripture had not made that statement, the honor owing to the parents would indeed have overridden the restrictions of the Sabbath!*

L. Not at all. **[6A]** *It is a case of a negative commandment comparable to the case of the ass driver* [Slotki: where a father ordered the son to violate the Sabbath by driving an ass; it is a prohibition that does not involve extirpation, unlike the act of slaughter or cooking, which does].

M. *But it is an established principle that a positive religious duty does override a negative one. Then would this case not provide the inference that it does not supersede a negative one [even a mere prohibition that does not involve the penalty of extirpation]? And should you say that the prohibitions* concerning the Sabbath present a special because, being more strict, the Tannaite authority in the following case speaks of prohibitions in general, and no one objects, as has been taught on Tannaite authority: How do we know that, **if his father said to him, "Contract corpse uncleanness," or if [under normal circumstances] he said to him, "Don't return it," he should not obey him.** one should not obey him? As it is said, "You shall fear every man his mother and his father and keep my Sabbaths: I am the Lord your God" (Lev. 19:3) — you all are obligated to honor me.

N. *Rather, the operative consideration is that one may pose the following objection: the distinguishing trait of these [cases, where the father orders the son to kill an animal or cook on the Sabbath] is that they represent acts that are essential in carrying out the religious duty [of honoring the father].* [Slotki: honoring the parents is entirely depending on its superseding the prohibition, e.g., cooking on the Sabbath. That is why it was necessary to have an explicit text to indicate that, even in such a case, a positive precept does not supersede a prohibition. In the case of the levirate marriage, however, the infringement of the prohibition is not absolutely essential to the fulfillment of the precept, since, instead of the marriage, the rite of removing the show may be arranged, and the question remains: what need is there of the verse "beside her"?]

O. *Rather, the reason [that the language "beside her is required] is that it might have entered your mind to suppose that* [the proposition that a positive commandment supersedes a negative commandment involving extirpation, so that the levirate marriage might take place even in such a case (Slotki)] *the building of the house of the sanctuary could have proven otherwise, as has been taught on Tannaite authority:*

P. Might one have supposed that the building of the house of the sanctuary should override the precepts of the Sabbath? Scripture states, "You shall keep my Sabbaths and fever my sanctuary" (Lev. 19:30) — all of them are obligated to pay me appropriate honor.

Q. *Now is it not a case in which one's father has told the son to build or to destroy, and the reason that that action does not supersede the Sabbath is that the All-Merciful has explicitly stated,* "You shall keep my Sabbaths and fever my sanctuary" (Lev. 19:30)? *Then if Scripture had not so stated, the action would have superseded the Sabbath* [Slotki: thus it follows that a positive precept does supersede a prohibition even though the latter involves extirpation].

R. *Not at all. It is a case of a negative commandment comparable to the case of the ass driver* [Slotki: where a father ordered the son to violate the Sabbath by driving an ass; it is a prohibition that does not involve extirpation, unlike the act of slaughter or cooking, which does].

S. *But it is an established principle that a positive religious duty does override a negative one. Then would this case not provide the inference that it does not supersede a negative one [even a mere prohibition that does not involve the penalty of extirpation]? And should you say that the prohibitions concerning the Sabbath present a special because, being more strict, the Tannaite authority in the following case speaks of prohibitions in general, and no one objects, as has been taught on Tannaite authority:* How do we know that, **if his father said to him, "Contract corpse uncleanness," or if [under normal circumstances] he said to him, "Don't return it," he should not obey him.** one should not obey him? As it is said, "You shall fear every man his mother and his father and keep my Sabbaths: I am the Lord your God" (Lev. 19:3) — you all are obligated to honor me.

T. *Rather, the operative consideration is that one may pose the following objection: the distinguishing trait of these [cases, where the father orders the son to kill an animal or cook on the Sabbath] is that they represent acts that are essential in carrying out the religious duty [of honoring the father].* [Slotki: honoring the parents is entirely depending on its superseding the prohibition, e.g., cooking on the Sabbath. That is why it was necessary to have an explicit text to indicate that, even in such a case, a positive precept does not supersede a prohibition. In the case of the levirate marriage, however, the infringement of the prohibition is not absolutely essential to the fulfillment of the precept, since, instead of the marriage, the rite of removing the show may be arranged, and the question remains: what need is there of the verse "beside her"?]

U. *Rather, the operative consideration is that one may pose the following objection: the distinguishing trait of these [cases, where the father orders the son to kill an animal or cook on the Sabbath] is that they represent acts that are essential in carrying out the religious duty [of honoring the father].* [Slotki: honoring the parents is entirely depending on its superseding the prohibition, e.g., cooking on the Sabbath. That is why it was necessary to have an explicit text to indicate that, even in such a case, a positive precept does not supersede a prohibition. In the case of the levirate marriage, however, the infringement of the prohibition is not absolutely essential to the fulfillment of the precept, since, instead of the marriage, the rite of removing the show may be arranged, and the question remains: what need is there of the verse "beside her"?]

V. *But the law concerning what is essential to carrying out the religious duty can have derived from the cited text [Lev. 19:30]!*

W. *True enough. Then what's the point of, "You shall keep my Sabbaths and have reverence for my sanctuary" (Lev. 19:30)?*

X. *It is required in line with that which has been taught on Tannaite authority:*

Y. *Might one suppose that one should revere the sanctuary? Scripture says, "You shall keep my Sabbaths and revere my sanctuary" (Lev. 19:30), meaning, "keep" is used in regard to the Sabbath and "revere" in regard to the sanctuary, to yield the comparison that follows: just as keeping is used in respect to the Sabbath* **[6B]**, *in the sense that one does not revere the Sabbath but the One who commanded the observance of the Sabbath, so in the matter of reverence used in regard to the sanctuary, one is to revere not the sanctuary but the One who gave the commandment concerning the sanctuary.*

.14 A. What is the reverence that is owing to the sanctuary?

B. **One should not enter the Temple mount with his walking stick, his overshoes, his money bag, or with dust on his feet. And one should not use [the Temple mount] for a shortcut. And spitting [there likewise is forbidden, as is proven by an argument] a minori ad majus [if you may not use it for a shortcut, you obviously may not spit there] [M. Ber. 9:5H-J].**

Chapter Fourteen. Yebamot

C. I know that that is so at the time that the house of the sanctuary is standing. How do I know that that is the case even when the house of the sanctuary is not standing?

D. Scripture states, "You shall keep my Sabbaths and revere my sanctuary" (Lev. 19:30) — just as when "keeping" pertains to the Sabbath, it is for all time, so when reverence refers to the sanctuary, it is for all time.

.15 A. *Rather, the reason [that the language "beside her is required] is that it might have entered your mind to suppose that the proposition might be derived from the prohibition of kindling a fire on the Sabbath.*

B. *For a Tannaite authority of the house of R. Ishmael [said], "You shall not kindle a fire [on the Sabbath]' (Ex. 35:3). What is the purpose of this statement?"*

C. *What is the purpose of this statement?! [We all know the answer]. If we speak from the viewpoint of R. Yosé, [that one should not kindle a flame] is singled out so as to indicate that [kindling a flame] is simply a negative commandment [violation of which is punished by flogging. Other violations of the Sabbath are punished by execution through stoning.]*

D. *If we speak from the viewpoint of R. Nathan, it is singled out in order to indicate that we treat a singular and punishable act each distinct violation of Sabbath-law [not grouping all of them and penalizing the whole].*

E. *For it has been taught on Tannaite authority:*

F. "Specification of kindling a flame [as a prohibited act] serves to place such an act in the category of a negative commandment," the words of R. Yosé.

G. R. Nathan says, "It serves to treat as a distinct act [punished by itself] that deed [or any other deed in violation of the Sabbath]."

H. *Rather, said Raba, "What posed a problem to the Tannaite authority was the word 'habitations' [at Ex. 35:3, not to kindle a flame 'in all of Israel's habitations']. Why is that word included?*

I. "[Here is what troubled the Tannaite authority at hand:] Since the Sabbath is an obligation that pertains to the person, and since an obligation pertaining to the person applies both in the Land and outside of the Land, why did the All-Merciful include the word 'habitations' [which speaks of the Land of Israel in particular]?"

J. In the name of R. Ishmael a disciple said, "It is because it is written, 'And if a man has committed a sin worthy of death and he be put to death' (Deut. 21:22). I might then take the view that that may be done whether on a weekday or on the Sabbath. In that case how shall I carry out the verse, 'Those who profane [the Sabbath] shall certainly be put to death' (Ex. 31:14)? It would refer to other forms of labor prohibited on the Sabbath, but not carrying out the death penalty imposed by a court. Or perhaps that statement encompasses also the execution of criminals convicted by a court. In that case how shall I interpret 'And he shall be put to death' (Deut. 21:22)? It would speak of weekdays, and not the Sabbath. Or perhaps it means that the execution is carried out even on the Sabbath? Scripture states, 'You shall not kindle a fire throughout your habitations' (Ex. 35:3), and elsewhere it is written, "And these things shall be for a statute of judgment for you throughout your generations in all your habitations' (Num. 35:29). Just as 'habitations' in that context speaks of matters pertaining to courts, so 'habitations' here speaks of matters pertaining to courts. Now when the All-Merciful has said, 'You shall not kindle a fire in all your habitations' (Ex. 35:3) [that must encompass not imposing the death penalty for the Sabbath, since one form of the death penalty is through 'burning.' So one cannot inflict the death penalty on the Sabbath, despite the argument a fortiori given above. And it further follows that one may not bury a neglected corpse on the Sabbath either.]"

K. *Now shall we not take for granted this accords with the position of R. Nathan, who maintains that the purpose is to show that even a single violation of the law imposes upon the offender the prescribed penalty, with the operative consideration being that the All-Merciful has written, "You shall kindle no fire" [meaning, not carry out the death penalty of burning on the Sabbath]. Then if Scripture had not made that statement, the upshot would have been that the execution would have superseded the Sabbath* [Slotki: though the penalties involved include that of extirpation; thus it follows that a positive precept may supersede even such a prohibition; so also in the case of the levirate marriage it might have been assumed that the precept of marrying one's deceased childless brother's widow supersedes the prohibition of marrying a consanguineous relative, despite the fact that such a transgression involves elsewhere the penalty of extirpation; hence it was necessary for Scripture to add, "beside her" (Lev. 18:18), to indicate that even a levirate marriage in such a case is forbidden].

L. *Not at all, this may accord with R. Yosé.*

M. *Well, even if it is in accord with R. Yosé, perhaps R. Yosé takes the view that not kindling a fire on the Sabbath is mentioned in its own terms in order to show that it is a mere prohibition of burning ordinarily; but the burning by the court would involve boiling a metal bar for the purpose of inflicting the death penalty, and* R. Sheshet said in that connection that there is no real difference between boiling a metal bar and boiling of dyes? [Slotki: the dyes were boiled in connection with construction of the tabernacle made by Moses, and labor that was done there defines the thirty-nine generative categories of labor that are forbidden on the Sabbath and involve extirpation].

N. *Said R. Shimi bar Ashi, "The Tannaite authority* [Slotki: who deduced from scriptural texts that a judicial death sentence may not be executed on the Sabbath] *requires the verses to support his position not because, ordinarily, he takes the view that a positive religious duty supersedes a negative one, but because in the present case,* [the assumption that the execution of a judicial death sentence might supersede the Sabbath (Slotki)] *might have been proven merely by an argument a fortiori, and this is the gist of his position:* How am I to interpret the verse, "Every one that profanes it shall surely be put to death" (Ex. 31:14)? This would pertain to all other types of work, excluding the labor of a court's inflicting the death penalty. But the execution of the death penalty by a court overrides the restrictions of the Sabbath, on the strength of the following argument a fortiori: **[7A]** if the act of service in the Temple, which is a most stringent matter and overrides the Sabbath, is itself superseded by a death sentence for murder, "And you shall take him from my altar that he may die" (Ex. 21:14), how much the more so should the Sabbath, which is overridden by the Temple service, also be overridden by an execution for murder on the Sabbath?

O. *Well, then, what is the sense of his statement, "Or it might rather..."?*

P. *This is the sense of his statement:* Burial of a neglected corpse might prove the contrary, since it overrides the Temple service but does not supersede the Sabbath." In that context, he argued, "There is an argument a fortiori that burying a neglected corpse should override the restrictions of the Sabbath. If the Temple service, which overrides the Sabbath, is overridden by the burial of a neglected corpse, by deduction from 'or for his sister' (Num. 6:7), how much the more should the Sabbath, which is overridden by the Temple service, be superseded by the burial of a neglected corpse. That is why it was necessary explicitly to state, "You shall kindle no fire" (Ex. 35:3).

Q. *Now in line with what we have taken for granted to begin with, that an affirmative religious duty comes along and overrides a negative religious duty, what is the sense of "or it might rather be..."?*

R. *This is the sense of the statement:* how am I to interpret the phrase, "Every one that profanes it shall surely be put to death" (Ex. 31:14)? This refers to other acts of labor, except for the court's inflicting the death penalty. But that would override the prohibitions of the Sabbath, since a positive religious duty [executing the criminal] overrides the negative religious duty. *But then he reversed himself and argued, one might suppose that a positive religious duty overrides a negative one when there is a mere negative religious duty standing on its own. But will it supersede a negative religious duty that involves extirpation? And then he concluded, even where a positive religious duty overrides a negative one, the negative one still is surely more weighty than the positive one [since a violation of a negative religious duty involves a flogging, while not doing a religious duty that is an affirmative commandment is not*

Chapter Fourteen. Yebamot   175

punished]. Nonetheless, the positive religious duty comes along and overrides the negative one. Then why in the world should one distinguish a minor from a major prohibition? Hence it was necessary for Scripture to state, "You shall kindle no fire."

.16 A. [Slotki: now that it is concluded that the need of the scriptural text prohibiting the execution of a death sentence on the Sabbath is because otherwise permissibility thereof might have been argued a minori and not on the ground of the principle that a positive command supersedes a prohibition, there is no proof available for the assumption that a positive precept supersedes a prohibition that involves extirpation, and thus the original question again arises: what need was there for the specific text of Lev. 18:18, "besides her," to indicate the obvious, that the positive precept of the levirate marriage does not supersede the prohibition of marrying a consanguineous relative?] *Still, it was necessary to invoke a specific text. For otherwise, it might have entered your mind to suppose that* this wife of the deceased brother should be classified as something that was covered by an encompassing rule and was singled out from the classification of things covered by the encompassing rule to teach a lesson, and not to teach a lesson concerning that classification itself, but rather, to teach a lesson concerning the encompassing rule in its entirety. *For so it has been taught on Tannaite authority:*

  B. In the case of any matter that was covered by an encompassing principle but that was singled out from within that encompassing principle for the specification of a given rule, what is specified pertains to not only that particular item but to the entire class of items of which it is a part. How so? "But the person who eats of the flesh of the sacrifice of the Lord's peace offerings while an uncleanness is on him — that person shall be cut off from his people" (Lev. 7:20): now were not peace-offerings encompassed within the governing principle of all Holy Things? And why has that class of Holy Things been singled out? It is to draw an analogy from them to all other items of its class, in this manner: just as peace offerings are Holy Things assigned to the altar, and on their account people bear liability to extirpation, so on account of everything that is in the category of Holy Things assigned to the altar, people will bear liability to extirpation. This then excludes that which has been assigned to the upkeep of the Temple house [and not for use on the altar]. [Porusch, to *Keritot* 2B: and here likewise all cases of incestuous relationships ought to be derived from the reference to "his sister"].

C. *Now here likewise, the wife of the brother was covered* among all of the consanguineous relationships, and why was she singled out? To form a comparison between her and others and to tell you that, just as the brother's wife is permitted [to marry the levir if the brother dies childless], so all the other consanguineous relations likewise are permitted. [Slotki: a text was consequently needed to intimate that the law is not so.]

D. *But are they really similar? There, in the case of sanctified objects, the encompassing generalization pertained to what is prohibited, and the particularization thereof likewise pertained to what is prohibited. But here, by contrast, in the case of levirate marriage and the consanguineous relations, the encompassing rule pertains to what is prohibited, but the particularization thereof deals with what is permitted [so the two are not comparable at all]!*

E. Rather, the comparison is to be drawn to something that was covered by an encompassing rule and then was singled out in order to be made the subject of a fresh rule altogether, in which case you cannot restore it to the governance of the encompassing rule unless Scripture itself explicitly does so. *That is in line with what has been taught on Tannaite authority:*

F. If a matter was covered by an encompassing rule but then was singled out for some innovative purpose, you have not got the right to restore the matter to the rubric of the encompassing rule unless Scripture itself explicitly does so.

G. How so?

H. "And he shall kill the lamb in the place where they kill the sin offering and the burnt offering, in the holy place; for the guilt offering, like the sin offering, belongs to the priest; it is most holy" (Lev. 14:13) —

I. Now what need does Scripture have to state, "for the guilt offering, like the sin offering"? [Freedman: for if it is to teach that it is slaughtered in the north, that follows from the first half of the verse; if it teaches that sprinkling of the blood and eating the meat follow the rules of the sin offering, that is superfluous, since it is covered by the general regulations on s=guilt offerings given at Lev. 7:1-10]. And why does Scripture state, "for the guilt offering, like the sin offering"?

J. The reason is that the guilt offering presented by the person healed of the skin ailment was singled out for the innovative purpose of indicating the following:

K. in regard to the thumb of the hand, big toe of the foot, and right ear, you might have thought that the rite does not require the presentation of the blood of the offering and the parts to be burned up on the altar. **[7B]** Scripture therefore states, "for the guilt offering, like the sin offering," to show that just as the sin offering's blood and sacrificial parts have to be presented on the altar, so the blood and sacrificial parts of the guilt offering presented by the person healed of the skin ailment have to be presented on the altar.

L. *Now had Scripture itself not restored it* [to line the leper's guilt offering up with the other guilt offerings (Slotki)], *I might have supposed that it was singled out only in regard to what was explicitly specified but not for any other purpose. Here too, in the case of the levirate marriage, I might have supposed that only the brother's wife, who is explicitly mentioned, is permitted, but not any of the other forbidden relatives.* [Slotki: the question consequently rises again: what need was there for "beside her" at Lev. 18:18?]

.17 A. [The reason that the superfluous text was needed] was that you might have argued that the law of the wife's sister should derive from what pertains in the case of the brother's wife: just as a levir may marry the brother's wife, so he may marry the wife's sister [and the superfluous text, "beside her" serves to eliminate that possibility].

B. *But are the cases parallel? There, in the case of the brother's wife, there is only one grounds for prohibition; here, in the case of the wife's sister, there are grounds for prohibition on two counts* [brother's wife, and wife's sister, hence how could the one be deduced from the other (Slotki)]? *What might you have said? Since the brother's wife [who is also the wife's sister, and whose husband died childless] was permitted in regard to one prohibition [that of marrying the brother's wife in a levirate marriage], she was also permitted in the case* of the other the prohibition of marrying one's wife's sister]. [So we are informed that that is not the case, by the superfluous language under discussion.]

C. And on what basis do you maintain that we invoke the principle, since something is permitted in one regard, it is permitted in some other? It derives from that which has been taught on Tannaite authority:

D. If the eighth day of the purification period of a person afflicted with the skin ailment [of Leviticus 13-14] coincided with the eve of the Passover, and who had an emission on that day [before offering his sacrifices in completion of the purification rite], and who immersed himself [although he had immersed on the previous day on account of his leprosy, doing so again by reason of his emission] — sages said, "Even though any other person in the status of one who has immersed but awaits sunset for the completion of his purification may not enter the Temple, this one may enter the Temple [for his purification rite]. It is better that fulfilling an affirmative religious duty that bears the penalty of extirpation [the Passover offering, and completing the purification rite allows the man to eat the Passover offering that night, and that is an affirmative religious duty] should come along and set aside an affirmative religious duty that does not carry with it the penalty of extirpation [that is, the one who has immersed and awaits sunset is not to come into the Levitical camp, but if he does so, he does not incur the penalty of extirpation]."

E. And R. Yohanan said, "Even an affirmative action is not connected with that matter, so far as the law of the Torah is concerned. For it is said, 'And Jehoshaphat stood in the congregation of Judah and Jerusalem in the house of the Lord before the new court' (2 Chr. 20:5)."

F. And what is the meaning of 'the new court'?

G. Said R. Yohanan, "They innovated there and ruled, 'A person who has immersed and awaits for sunset to complete his purification must not enter the Levitical camp.'"

H. And said Ulla, "What is the operative consideration [that the leper was permitted to extend his hands into the

Chapter Fourteen. Yebamot

sanctuary, while in Ulla's view, an unclean person cannot project therein even part of his body? (Slotki)] Since he was permitted in regard to his leprosy, he also was permitted in regard to his unclean semen." [Slotki: thus it is proved that since something was permitted in one respect, the permission remains in force even when another prohibition may be involved in another respect. The same argument might have also applied to a wife's sister or widow of a deceased brother, hence the need of the next, "beside her."]

I. **[8A]** *That comparison serves where the deceased brother married first [a brother's wife who is also the sister of his wife] and the surviving married his brother's wife's sister afterward [thus adding to the one prohibition]. In such a case, since the prohibition of the brother's wife was removed [through the requirement of entering into levirate marriage], that of the wife's sister also is removed. But if the surviving brother had married first, and then the deceased brother married later on, the prohibition of the wife's sister was in force first* [Slotki: and could not consequently be removed by the removal of a prohibition that took effect subsequent to it].

J. *Furthermore, even if the deceased had married first, the comparison would work in a case in which the deceased had married and died, and then the surviving brother married, so the widow was eligible in the interval* [Slotki: between the death of her husband and the marriage of her sister by his surviving brother; this case would be analogous to that of the leper who was eligible to bring his sacrifices on the eighth day of his purification during the interval between the beginning of the day and the hour on that day that he contracted the new uncleanness by his discharge.] *But if the deceased had married, and before he died the wife's sister was married by the surviving brother, the widow was never for a moment eligible for his brother. Doesn't Ulla admit that,* if the leper observed semen on the night prior to the eighth day of the purification process, he must not poke his hand into the sanctuary on account of the thumb, because, at the time he was eligible to bring the sacrifice [as a leper who had been rendered clear, on the eighth day of the purification], he was not free of uncleanness [Slotki: owing to the discharge of the semen which occurred in the night. As a sacrifice must be brought in the day time only, there was not a single moment during which he was eligible to bring the sacrifices as someone clean in all respects. The prohibition therefore remains in force. So also in the case of a wife's sister as regards the levirate marriage. The question therefore arises again, what need was there for the superfluous text of Lev. 18:18?].

K. *Rather, [the reason that the superfluous text was needed] was to deal with a case in which the deceased brother married first and then died, and the surviving brother married the widow's sister thereafter* [Slotki: so that there was an interval during which he was permitted to marry the widow].

L. *Or, if you prefer, I shall say, it might have been deduced by means of the analogy of R. Jonah. For* R. Jonah — others say, R. Huna b. R. Joshua — said, "Said Scripture, 'For whosoever shall do any of these abominations shall be cut off' (Lev. 18:29) — all forbidden relatives thus are treated as comparable to the wife of the brother [and form a single group]." Here too, as a brother's wife is permitted [to the levir], so all the other forbidden relatives are permitted. Scripture thus had to say 'besides her' (Lev. 18:18) [to intimate they are not permitted (Slotki)].

.18 A. *Said R. Aha of Difti to Rabina, "Well, now, since all of the other forbidden consanguineous relationships may be compared to the generative analogy of the wife of the brother, or may also be compared to the generative analogy of the sister of the wife, how come you seize upon the analogy of the sister of the wife. Rather, invoke the analogy of the wife of the brother"* [Slotki: and levirate marriage with all of them would thus be permitted].

B. *"If you wish, I shall say that when one may draw an analogy that will yield a lenient ruling and a strict ruling, then one invokes the analogy that yields strict rules, and if you prefer, I shall say, in the former cases [in that of the wife's sister, and all the other forbidden relatives other than the brother's wife] we deal with* two prohibitions, and there we deal with two as well [forbidden relatives and brother's wife], and two prohibitions may be inferred from two others; in the latter case, on the other hand, [if the brother's wife is not a consanguineous relative] there is only a single basis for prohibiting the marriage [that is, the brother's life], and a double prohibition may not be derived from the analogy of a single one."

.19 A. Raba said, "The prohibition of the levir's marrying a consanguineous relative does not require scriptural proof anyhow, since an affirmative commandment [that the levir marry the widow of the deceased childless brother] does not override a negative commandment, violation of which is penalized by extirpation. Where there is a requirement of scriptural proof, it concerns it is to prohibit the levir from marrying the co-wife."

B. But is it the fact that there is no need for a proof on the basis of Scripture that the woman standing in consanguineous relationship to the levir may not marry the widow? But lo, it has been taught on Tannaite authority: ["And you shall not take a woman along with her sister, to be a co-wife to her, to uncover her nakedness, beside her in her lifetime" (Lev. 18:18) — what is the point of the use of the words, "beside her"? Since Scripture states, "Her husband's brother shall go in beside her" (Dt. 25:3), I might have supposed that Scripture here makes reference even to any of the forbidden relatives that are listed in the Torah [indicating that levirate marriage may take place, e.g., between a father and a daughter]! The use of the word "beside her" in both passages serves to establish a verbal analogy between the one and the other. Just as elsewhere it is only in the case of a religious duty that levirate marriage takes place, so here too it is only in the case of a religious duty in which the levirate marriage takes place. And yet did not the All-Merciful say explicitly, "You shall not take two sisters" (Lev. 18:18)? (The upshot is that levirate marriage is forbidden in the case of consanguineous relationships, just as our

Mishnah-passage has indicated)]. So we are informed of the law governing the woman herself...

C. *That proof was required to cover the case of the co-wives [and the proof covering the woman herself was merely a prologue to the main event].*

D. But lo, it is explicitly set forth as the Tannaite formulation: So we are informed of the law governing the woman herself [who is in a consanguineous relationship]. How do we know the rule governing her co-wife [that the co-wife of such a woman also does not enter into any levirate connection at all]?

E. *That is on account of their co-wives [and the whole antecedent discussion was simply to prepare the way for the discussion of proof on the basis of Scripture for the rule governing the co-wives of the co-wives].*

F. *Come and take note:* Rabbi says, "Instead of saying, 'and take...,' Scripture states, 'and take her,' so too, instead of saying 'and perform the duty of a husband's brother,' Scripture states, 'and perform the duty of a husband's brother unto her' (Dt. 25:5). The purpose of these formulations is to prohibit levirate marriage with forbidden relatives and their co-wives." [Slotki: this shows that a scriptural text is required even in the case of forbidden relatives themselves, to prove that levirate marriage is prohibited.]

G. *Read:* to prohibit the levitical marriage of co-wives of forbidden consanguineous relatives.

H. *But lo, two references to Scripture have been given [covering two, not one, category]! Is that not to provide one for the consanguineous relation and the other for the co-wife of that relation?*

I. *No. Both this and that refer to the co-wife, and one serves to prohibit the co-wife when there is a religious duty involved, the other to permit the co-wife when there is no religious duty involved* [Slotki: as in the instance of a co-wife of a forbidden relative who married a stranger].

J. *Then what is the scriptural foundation for the stated conception?*

K. "Instead of saying, 'and take...,' Scripture states, 'and take her,' *meaning, only where levirate marriage may take place is the co-wife forbidden, but where there is no consideration of levirate marriage, the co-wife is permitted [Slotki: to be married by the man to whom the relative herself is forbidden].*
L. *Said R. Ashi, "A close reading of our Mishnah-paragraph yields the same result:* **Fifteen women exempt their co-wives, and the co-wives, from the rite of removing the shoe [halisah] and from levirate marriage, without limit.** *But it is not stated,* both are exempt and also exempt their co-wives."
M. That is decisive proof.

.20 A. *And what explains the difference between the consanguineous relative, who requires no proof-text for the stated proposition, and the other class of wife? It is because an affirmative commandment [that the levir marry the widow of the deceased childless brother] does not override a negative commandment, violation of which is penalized by extirpation.*
B. *But then the case of the co-wife also should require no proof from Scripture, since the same principle applies, namely, an affirmative commandment [that the levir marry the widow of the deceased childless brother] does not override a negative commandment, violation of which is penalized by extirpation.*
C. *Said R. Aha bar Bibi Mar to Rabina, "This is what has been said in the name of Raba: 'The case of the co-wife also requires no proof from Scripture. Where a verse of Scripture is required,* **[8B]** *it is to permit the co-wife in a case in which the religious requirement of levirate marriage does not pertain at all."*
D. *And what is the scriptural proof for that proposition?*
E. Scripture states, "besides her," to indicate, only in a case in which "unto her" *pertains is she forbidden, but where the other may*

not enter levirate marriage, she is permitted.

.21 A. Said Rammi bar Hama to Raba, "Might I not say that the consanguineous relative herself [that is, the wife's sister] would be permitted to marry the levir in a case in which the religious duty of levirate marriage is not applicable?"

B. *But is not that proposition contrary to the result of an argument a fortiori, namely: if she is forbidden to marry in a case in which the religious duty of levirate marriage does apply, is she going to be permitted in a case in which the religious duty does not apply?*

C. *He said to him, "To the contrary, the case of the co-wife will prove the contrary, for in a case in which there is the religious duty of levirate marriage she is forbidden to marry the levir, but in a situation in which there is no such religious duty, she is permitted [as we have already established]!"*

D. He said to him, "That is because Scripture has said, 'besides her in her lifetime' (Lev. 18:18), meaning, so long as she lives." [So long as the wife is alive, her sister may not marry the husband, and the other relations derive from the case of the wife's sister.]"

E. *But is not the language,* "besides her in her lifetime" (Lev. 18:18), *required to eliminate the prohibition of marriage after the wife has died?* [That is, the wife's sister may not be married by the levir only when the wife herself is still alive; once she has died, the levir may take the wife's sister as his levirate wife.]

F. *That derives from the text,* "And a woman to her sister" (Lev. 18:18).

G. *If that rule actually derives only from the text,* "And a woman to her sister" (Lev. 18:18), *one might have supposed that, if the wife were divorced, the sister would be permitted to the levir; so it is said in so many words,* "in her lifetime," *meaning, so long as she is alive, even* though divorced, the sister must not marry the levir.

H. *Rather, said R. Huna bar Tahalipa in the name of Raba, "There are two verses of Scripture:* 'you shall not take a woman to her sister to be a co-wife to her' (Lev. 18:18) [implying that both the wife's sister and her co-wife are forbidden to marry the levir]; an, further, 'to uncover her nakedness' (Lev. 18:18), *which speaks of only a single relationship when it refers to 'her, not their.'* How so? Where the religious duty of levirate marriage pertains, both are forbidden, but where it does not pertain, while the forbidden relative is forbidden, her co-wife would be permitted."

I. To the contrary! Where the religious duty of levirate marriage pertains, while the forbidden relative may not marry the levir, the co-wife may do so, but where it does not pertain, both would be forbidden!

J. If so, Scripture should not have said, "beside her."

.22 A. *Said R. Ashi to R. Kahana, "How come this expression, 'beside her,' bears the implication of prohibition? Maybe it bears the sense of 'permission,' and this is what the All-Merciful had in mind:* 'You shall not take a woman to her sister to be a co-wife to her' (Lev. 18:18) — neither herself nor her co-wife where 'to her' does not apply [Slotki: where the law of levirate marriage does not apply], but where 'unto her' does apply [that is, when there is a levirate marriage], both would be permitted."

B. *"If so, when how would we find a case in which the reference* 'uncovering the nakedness' would pertain to only one and not two [Lev. 18:18 speaks of the prohibition of a single class of relationship, as we have already said], since, if it were a case in which the religious duty of levirate marriage pertained, both by this reasoning would be permitted, and if not, then both would be forbidden."

.23 A. *Reverting to a detail of the foregoing:* Rabbi says, "Instead of saying, 'and take...,' Scripture states, 'and take her,' so too, instead of saying 'and perform the duty of a husband's brother,' Scripture states, 'and perform the duty of a husband's brother unto her' (Dt. 25:5). The purpose of these formulations is to prohibit levirate marriage with forbidden relatives and their co-wives:" *But is there any reference here at all to co-wives? And furthermore, the law governing co-wives derives from the language,* "to be her co-wife" (Lev. 18:18). [Slotki: how then could it be said to be derived from a difference verse?]

B. *Rabbi makes use of the language "to be her co-wife" in the setting of R. Simeon's deduction [to be given below, folio 28B].*

C. *And where do we find reference to the co-wife [at Dt. 25:5, which is the verse to which Rabbi makes reference]?*

D. *This is the sense of his statement:* "If so, Scripture should have said, 'and take.' Why say, 'and he shall take her'? *In any case in which there is the possibility of two marriages, if he has a choice in the matter, he may marry whichever one he prefers and both are permitted; but if not, then both are forbidden.* 'And perform the duty of a husband's brother to her' *then shows that where there is the requirement of levirate marriage, the co-wife is forbidden, but where there is no requirement of levirate marriage, the co-wife is permitted."*

E. *And what about rabbis [who reject Rabbi's choice of a proof-text]? How do they read the verse,* "And he shall take her"?

F. *They require it in line with the position of R. Yosé bar Hanina, for* said R. Yosé bar Hanina, "'...and he shall take her...' teaches that the levir may divorce her with a writ of divorce [after marrying her, and not go through the rite of removing the shoe] and then may remarry her. 'And he shall perform the duty of a husband's brother to her' even over her protest." [Slotki: 'and he takes her to him to wife' means, as soon as he has taken her, she is regarded henceforth in all respects as his wife, as if she had never been forbidden to him as a brother's wife].

G. *And Rabbi?*

H. *He derives the proposition of R. Yosé bar Hanina from the language,* "to a wife," *and that the levirate marriage may take place even over her protest from,* "her husband's brother shall go in unto her" (Dt. 25:5).

I. *And how does Rabbi interpret the language,* "beside her"?

J. *He requires it in line with that which we have learned in the Mishnah:* **The court is liable only if they will give an erroneous decision in a matter, the deliberate commission of which is punishable by extirpation, and the inadvertent commission of which is punishable by a sin offering, and so in the case of the anointed [high priest], [9A] and [they are] not [liable] in the case of idolatry, except in the case in which they gave instruction in a matter the deliberate commission of which is punishable by extirpation, and the inadvertent commission of which is punishable by a sin offering [M. Hor. 2:3D-F].** *And we have further learned in the Mishnah:* **In the case of all the commandments in the Torah, on** account of which they are liable for deliberate violation to extirpation, and on account of inadvertent violation to a sin offering, an individual brings a female lamb or a female goat [Lev. 4:28, 32], a ruler brings a male goat [Lev. 4:23], and an anointed [high priest] and a court bring a bullock [M. 1:5, 2:1]. But in the case of idolatry, the individual, ruler, and anointed [high priest] bring a female goat [Num. 15:27]. And the court brings a bullock and a goat [M. 1:5], a bullock for a whole offering and a goat for a sin offering [M. Hor. 2:6]. *Now what is the scriptural basis for these rulings? It is in line with that which our rabbis have taught on Tannaite authority:* "When the sin wherein they have sinned is known" (Lev. 4:14) — Rabbi says, "Here [in the context of a court's erroneous ruling] we find a reference to beside the other', and in the context of the marriage to two sisters, we find the same usage. Just as, in that other case, if the sin is done deliberately, the penalty is extirpation, and if it is done unwittingly, a sin-offering, so here too, if the sin was done deliberately, extirpation is involved, but if it was unwitting, then a sin offering."

K. *So we have found the scriptural source for the rule governing the community. Whence the rule for the anointed priest?*

L. In the case of the anointed priest, it is written, "So as to bring guilt upon the people" (Lev. 4:3) — lo, the anointed priest is in the same classification as the community.

M. The rule governing the individual and the ruler derives from the verbal analogy formed by the occurrence of the word "things" in both contexts [Lev. 4:22, Lev. 4:13].

N. **and [they are] not [liable] in the case of idolatry, except in the case in which they gave instruction in a matter the deliberate commission of which is punishable by extirpation, and the inadvertent commission of which is punishable by a sin offering:** with respect to the congregation in the matter of idolatry, the rule derives from the analogy formed by the common appearance of the language, "from the sight" (Lev. 4:13). The rule pertaining to the individual, the ruler, and the anointed priest, from "and if one soul..." (Num. 15:27), implying that there is no distinguishing between an individual, a ruler, and an anointed high priest; and the use of the conjunctive, "and" joins them to the prior subject, so the the case of the individual, ruler, and high priest may be deduced from the case of the congregation.

O. *And how do rabbis drive this same inference [* **[they are not liable ...except in the case in which they gave instruction in a matter the deliberate commission of which is punishable by extirpation, and the inadvertent commission of which is punishable by a sin offering***]?*

P. *They derive it on the basis of the way in which R. Joshua b. Levi interpreted Scripture to his son:* "'You shall have one torah for him who does anything in error, but the soul that does anything deliberately...' (Num. 15:29-30) — the entirety of the Torah in this way is treated as analogous to the prohibition of idolatry. Just as, in respect to idolatry, [they are] not [liable] in the case of idolatry, except in the case in which they gave instruction in a matter the deliberate commission of which is punishable by extirpation, and the inadvertent commission of which is punishable by a sin offering, so in the case of all other transgressions, the same rule applies, namely, it must be a matter the deliberate commission of which is punishable by extirpation, and the inadvertent commission of which is punishable by a sin offering."

Q. So we have found proof for the rule governing the individual, the ruler, and the anointed high priest, in respect to idolatry and also all other commandments. How do we know that the same rule applies to the congregation in the case of idolatry?

R. Said Scripture, "And if one soul" (Num. 15:27) — and what has been said already then imposes its meaning on what occurs now, with the result that what applies to the congregation applies to the individual.

S. And what about the congregation in the case of all other commandments?

T. It derives from the verbal analogy imposed by the use, in both contexts, of "from the eyes."

U. *And how does Rabbi interpret the verse, "You shall have one torah for him who does anything in error, but the soul that does anything deliberately..." (Num. 15:29-30)?*

V. *He requires it in line with that which has been taught on Tannaite authority:* Since we find that Scripture has distinguished individuals from the group [in the case of the inhabitants of a town condemned for idolatry, Dt. 13:13ff.], subjecting individuals to death through stoning but sparing their property, while the group is put to death by the sword and their property destroyed, we might also assume that such a distinction should be made between the sacrifices of the one and those

Chapter Fourteen. Yebamot

of the other. But, to the contrary, Scripture instructs us, "You shall have one torah for him who does anything in error, but the soul that does anything deliberately..." (Num. 15:29-30).

W. *Objected R. Hilqiah of Hagronayya, "Is then the operative consideration that Scripture has stated, 'You shall have one torah for him who does anything in error, but the soul that does anything deliberately'? If it were not for that fact, should I have supposed that such a distinction, among the sacrifices brought by each party, should be drawn? Then what could they present as their offering? Should they present a bullock? The congregation [a majority of the tribes] presents a bullock for the transgression of any one of all the other commandments [and what distinction would there be between the sin offerings of the condemned city and those of the congregation? (Slotki)]. Should they bring a lamb? But an individual presents a lamb if he transgresses any of the other commandments. Should it be a he-goat? A ruler brings one in the cases of violating any of the other commandments. Should it be a bullock for a burnt offering and a goat for a sin offering? These are presented by the congregation in the case of idolatry? Should it be a she goat? This is the sin offering of the private party.* [So no distinction among the sacrifices could be made, and what need is there for the cited text, Num. 15:29 (Slotki)?]"

X. *The cited verse really is required. For it might have entered your mind to suppose that, since the congregation in the case of an erroneous ruling presents a bullock for a burnt offering and a he-goat for a sin offering, these should present the*

> *same, but in reverse order* [Slotki: a bullock for a sin offering and a he goat for a burnt offering]. *Or perhaps it might have been necessary for the people of the condemned city to bring a special sin offering but there might be none for their particular situation. So it was necessary to tell us explicitly that the sacrifices are the same throughout.*

No. 6 takes leave of the initial, Mishnah-exegetical task because it asks to generalize, and once generalization commences, the dialectical dynamic comes into play, and that is made explicit at 6.B, let a positive religious duty come and set aside a negative religious duty. This takes over and directs attention to a variety of legal topics. We are then moved into another range of generalizations, having to do with generalizations of exegetical rules in the reading of Scripture. No. 7 then complements the foregoing, and No. 8 broadens the focus once more. No. 9 then challenges the result of No. 8, and No. 10 continues the same challenge. No. 12 once more generalizes, again as to governing exegetical principles in the reading of Scripture. Then, building on the result, No. 13 reverts to our original, generalizing question: Thus far we have found that a positive commandment will come along and supersede a negative commandment standing on its own. But where do we find that a positive commandment supersedes a negative commandment, the punishment of which is extirpation...? The secondary amplification, Nos. 14, 15, gives way at No. 17 to the original question. Nos. 18, 19 take up the exegetical problem once more. Here we see one of the marks of the dialectical argument, the possibility of breaking off at a variety of points without a loss to the meaning of what is already set forth and established. But a special trait of this composition is still more interesting, the fact that the argument moves on two distinct tracts, the one exegetical, the other analytical (the analysis of analogies).

II. AN ANALYTICAL-DIALECTICAL ARGUMENT AT M. YEB. 3:9I-L

We take up the analysis of a proposed principle of law, concerning the question of whether or not a prohibition may apply to that which is already subject to a prohibition, that is, can a prohibition can apply to something that is forbidden already by reason of another injunction? Nos. 2-3 set the stage, and the dialectical argument begins with No. 4:

.2   A.   *Our rabbis have taught on Tannaite authority:*
       B.   **"If the levir had sexual relations with the widow [while his wife was still alive], he is liable on her account on the count of having sexual relations with the wife of his brother and also on the count of his wife's sister," the words of R. Yosé.**
       C.   R. Simeon says, "He is liable only on the count of his brother's wife alone" [cf. T. Yeb. 5:8E-H].

Chapter Fourteen. Yebamot 193

.3   A.   *But lo, it has been taught on Tannaite authority:* R. Simeon says, "He is liable only on the count of his wife's sister alone"!

     B.   *There is no contradiction. The one speaks of a case in which the surviving brother married first, then the now-deceased one married afterwards.* [The prohibition of the wife's sister came into force first, then the prohibition of the other sister, and the added prohibition on the count of the brother's wife could not take effect where one prohibition was in force (Slotki).] *The other speaks of a case in which the now-deceased brother got married first, and then the now-surviving brother got married.*

     C.   *And as to the position of R. Simeon, in a case in which the now deceased brother got married and then the now-surviving brother did, since the prohibition on the count of the sister's wife does not apply, let her actually enter into levirate marriage?*

     D.   *Said R. Ashi, "The prohibition on the count of the wife's sister is suspended, and when the prohibition on the count of the brother's wife is removed, that prohibition comes into force, so it cannot be treated as though it were not present at all."*

.4   A.   *And does R. Yosé take the view that a prohibition may apply to that which is already subject to a prohibition* [a prohibition can apply to something that is forbidden already by reason of another injunction]?

     B.   *And have we not learned in the Mishnah,* **He who is declared liable to be put to death through two different modes of execution at the hands of a court is judged to be executed by the more severe. If he committed a transgression which is subject to the death penalty on two separate counts, he is judged on account of the more severe. R. Yosé says, "He is judged by the penalty that first applies to what he has done"** [M. San. 9:4A-C]. *And it has been taught on Tannaite authority:* How is this done? Said R. Yosé, "**He is judged by the penalty that first applies to what he has done.** If he had sexual relations with his mother-in-law, who was then married, he is judged on the count of having had sexual relations with his mother-in-law. If it was simply a married woman but she then became his mother-in-law, he is judged on the count of her having been a married woman."

C. **[32B]** Said R. Abbahu, "R. Yosé concedes that when the new prohibition is more encompassing, [then we do judge the case on that count]."

D. *That poses no problem in a case in which the now-surviving brother had married one of the sisters first, and the now-deceased brother had married the other sister afterward since the prohibition had been broadened to the brothers, the prohibition was broadened to him as well.* [Slotki: Yosé admits the imposition of the prohibition of 'brother's wife" upon that of "wife's sister," even where the latter prohibition was already in force, because the former, unlike the latter, is applicable not only to him alone but to the other brothers also. In the case of a married woman who became his mother-in-law where the first prohibition was of a wider range, the woman being forbidden to all men except her husband, and the later one, forbidden to him only, of a restricted range, the second prohibition cannot be imposed upon the first.] *But where is the augmentation of the prohibition in a case in which the now-deceased brother married* [Slotki: bringing into force the prohibition of brother's wife, which is applicable to all brothers] *and then the now-surviving brother married? And should you say, because [by marrying the other sister] he is forbidden to marry all the sisters, in fact, that is merely an encompassing prohibition* [but does not place any further restriction so far as the widow herself is concerned upon any other men (Slotki)].

E. Rather, said Raba, "[In interpreting Yosé's position,] I regard him as though he had carried out two violations, but he is liable on only one count [since, as a matter of fact, Yosé does not take the view that a prohibition may apply to that which is already subject to a prohibition]."

F. *And so when Rabin came,* he said R. Yohanan [said], "[In interpreting Yosé's position,] I regard him as though he had carried out two violations, but he is liable on only one count [since, as a matter of fact, Yosé does not take the view that a prohibition may apply to that which is already subject to a prohibition]."

G. *So what difference does it make [that he is in fact guilty on two counts]?*

H. He is to be buried among those who are totally wicked people.

Chapter Fourteen. Yebamot

.5 A. *And the same matter is subject to dispute in that which has been stated:*
B. A non-priest who performed an act of Temple service on the Sabbath —
C. R. Hiyya says, "He is liable on two counts" [violating the Sabbath, performing an act of service even though he is not a priest].
D. Bar Qappara says, "He is liable only on one count."
E. R. Hiyya leaped forward and swore, "By the Temple! Thus have I heard from Rabbi: 'two counts'!"
F. Bar Qappara leaped forward and swore, "By the Temple! Thus have I heard from Rabbi: 'one count'!"
G. R. Hiyya commenced laying out his arguments: "The Sabbath is forbidden for all. When labor on it was permitted in the sanctuary, it was for priests that acts of labor were permitted: priests, not non-priests. So there is here violation on the count of a non-priest's performing an act of service, and also on the count of the Sabbath."
H. Bar Qappara commenced laying out his arguments: "The Sabbath is forbidden for all. When labor on it was permitted in the sanctuary, it was for acts of labor having to do with the sanctuary; so the only count on which guilt has been incurred is violation on the count of a non-priest's performing an act of service."

.6 A. A blemished priest who performed an act of Temple service while in a condition of uncleanness —
B. R. Hiyya says, "He is liable on two counts" [violating the Sabbath, performing an act of service even though he is not a priest].
C. Bar Qappara says, "He is liable only on one count."
D. R. Hiyya leaped forward and swore, "By the Temple! Thus have I heard from Rabbi: 'two counts'!"
E. Bar Qappara leaped forward and swore, "By the Temple! Thus have I heard from Rabbi: 'one count'!"
F. R. Hiyya commenced laying out his arguments: "Performing an act of Temple service while in a condition of uncleanness was forbidden to all persons, but when it was permitted in the sanctuary [e.g., for an offering in behalf of the community], it was permitted only for unblemished priests, not for blemished ones. So there is a violation here on the count of an act of

Temple service performed by a blemished priest, and in addition on the count of uncleanness."

G. Bar Qappara commenced laying out his arguments: "Performing an act of Temple service while in a condition of uncleanness was forbidden to all persons, but when it was permitted, it was permitted in the sanctuary. So there is present only violation on account of the act of service's being done by a blemished priest."

.8 A. A non-priest who ate the meat of a bird whose head was pinched off [as is done in the rite of killing the bird for a sacrifice in the Temple —
B. R. Hiyya says, "He is liable on two counts."
C. Bar Qappara says, "He is liable only on one count."
D. R. Hiyya leaped forward and swore, "By the Temple! Thus have I heard from Rabbi: 'two counts'!"
E. Bar Qappara leaped forward and swore, "By the Temple! Thus have I heard from Rabbi: 'one count'!"
F. R. Hiyya commenced laying out his arguments: "Eating carrion was forbidden to all, and, when it was permitted in the sanctuary, it was permitted to the priests. So it was permitted only to the priests, not to non-priests. Hence the violation is on the count of the eating of holy food by a non-priest and the count of eating bird-meat that has been slaughtered through pinching off the head [rather than in the normal manner for the slaughter of ordinary birds outside of the cult]."
G. Bar Qappara commenced laying out his arguments: "Eating carrion was forbidden to all, and, when it was permitted in the sanctuary, it was permitted in the sanctuary. There is in this case, therefore, violation only on the count of the eating of holy food by a non-priest."

.9 A. *[33A] What is at stake in the dispute?*
B. *At issue is the status of an encompassing prohibition in the opinion of R. Yosé. R. Hiyya takes the position that R. Yosé imposes guilt on two counts in the case of an encompassing prohibition. Bar Qappara maintains that he imposes liability on only one count.*
C. *So what an encompassing prohibition is present here? Now, to be sure, in the case of a non-priest [who performed an act of Temple service on the*

Sabbath], there is no problem, since to begin with [prior to the Sabbath] he was permitted to do common labor but forbidden to do an act of service on the Sabbath, and when the Sabbath took effect, just as he was now forbidden to do any other common labor, so he also was forbidden to perform an act of service in the Temple. [Slotki: the prohibition being comprehensive in that it included both ordinary work and Temple service; but it is not a prohibition of a wider range, since the prohibition of the Temple service itself was in no way extended.] *So too, the blemished priest to begin with was permitted to eat holy food but forbidden to perform an act of Temple service; when he became unclean, since he was forbidden to eat holy meat, he also is forbidden to carry out an act of Temple service.* [Slotki: the prohibition comprehending the Temple service as well as the consumption of sacrificial meat.] *But as to the matter of meat from a bird killed by pinching the neck, at one and the same moment the prohibitions took effect [Slotki: before the head was pinched, there was only the prohibition on the count of sacrilege, which included the priests; the two prohibitions, of carrion and to non-priests of the meat of fowl killed by pinching the head set in simultaneously], so what we have in hand is prohibitions that come about simultaneously, but not those that are further encompassing* [Slotki: so how could the dispute in this case be dependent on the principle of the encompassing prohibition]?

D. *Rather, what is at issue between them is the status of prohibitions that take effect simultaneously in regard to the position of R. Yosé. R. Hiyya takes the view that R. Yosé imposes liability on two counts in a case in which prohibitions take effect simultaneously, and Bar Qappara maintains that he imposes liability on only one count alone.*

E. *And here, what sort of prohibitions that take effect simultaneously are involved? In the instance of the non-priest who carried out on the Sabbath an act of Temple service, it would involve a case in* which he had been a minor but on the Sabbath produced puberty-signs in the form of two pubic hairs, in which case, at that single moment, he became liable on the counts of being a non-priest and violating the Sabbath. In the case of the blemished priest too, it would involve a case in which he had been a minor but produced two pubic hairs while unclean, so that liability as an adult priest with a blemish and an unclean priest took place at one and the same moment. Or someone cut his finger with an unclean knife [simultaneously being blemished and contracting uncleanness].

F. *Now [to reconcile the opposing opinions in Rabbi's name,] with reference to the position of R. Hiyya, when [Hiyya] presented his view, he was taught [by Rabbi] in accord with the position of R. Yosé, and Bar Qappara was taught in accord with the position of R. Simeon [who claims that Rabbi recognizes one count of guilt only within the position of Yosé]. But from the perspective of Bar Qappara, R. Hiyya has to be regarded as a mere liar. [Since this is unthinkable,] what must be at stake in the dispute is the rule governing prohibitions that take effect simultaneously, within the position of R. Simeon.* [Slotki: Hiyya maintains that Simeon subjected the transgression to one offence only in the case of an encompassing prohibition, but in the case of simultaneous prohibitions he concurs with Yosé that there is liability on two counts; Bar Qappara holds that Simeon disagrees with Yosé even in regard to simultaneous prohibitions.]

.10 A. *When R. Hiyya took an oath, it was to remove R. Simeon's view from its presumptive standing* [affirming that Simeon favors the lenient position only in the case of the encompassing prohibition but not of simultaneous prohibitions (Slotki)]. *But why in the world did Bar Qappara have to take an oath?*

B. *That is a problem.*

C. *Within the position of Bar Qappara, there is no problem in explaining the contradictory statements by maintaining that, when Rabbi formulated the Tannaite rule for him, it was within the position of R. Simeon that he did so, and when he formulated the Tannaite rule for R. Hiyya, he set forth the position of R. Yosé* [Slotki: and Hiyya mistook him to be reporting Simeon's view and thus the discrepancy arose]. *But from R. Hiyya's position, Bar Qappara must be be regarded as a mere liar. [Since this is unthinkable,] R. Hiyya will say to you, "When Rabbi set forth the Tannaite formulation for him, he presented only two cases [the non-priest performing the Temple rite on the Sabbath, the blemished priest who performed an act of service when unclean] in which the transgressor is exempt [on one of the two counts].* **[33B]** *Thus he taught him as a Tannaite position the rule governing the encompassing prohibition as R. Simeon set forth that rule. But Bar Qappara understood the case of the non-priest who ate the meat of a bird killed by pinching the bird, and, since it looked like the others, he disposed of it like the others. Then, when he looked into the matter and found that the case was possible only as one in which prohibitions took effect simultaneously, he supposed that, as this one involved simultaneous prohibitions, so the others did too, and, since in the other cases, the violator is exempt on one count, so he assumed the same in this case.*

D. *An objection was raised:* **"A non-priest who carried out on the Sabbath an act of Temple service, or a blemished priest who performed an act of Temple service while unclean — the counts of liability are present deriving from an act of service by a non-priest, desecration of the Sabbath, an act of service by a blemished priest, and an act of service in a state of uncleanness,"** the words of R. Yosé. R. Simeon says, **"He is liable only on the counts of being a non-**

priest in the Temple cult and a blemished priest alone" [T. Yeb. 5:8G-H]. *But the matter of the meat of a bird killed by pinching the neck has been omitted in this version [so the two parties concur here]! Now on whose account has it been omitted? If we propose that it is on account of R. Yosé, then, if R. Yosé imposes liability on two counts where the prohibition is encompassing, how much the more so will he do so when the prohibitions are simultaneous. So it must be on account of R. Simeon [Slotki: who despite his opinion that in the two cases mentioned only one penalty is involved agrees with Yosé that in the case of the fowl killed in accord with the Temple rite, two penalties are involved], who thus exempts one from double liability only where the prohibition is encompassing, but would impose liability on two counts when the prohibitions take place simultaneously. This then refutes Bar Qappara's explanation of matters.*

E. Sure does.

As noted, Nos. 2-3 may reach closure without investigating what forms the center of what follows, whether a prohibition can apply to something that is forbidden already by reason of another injunction. As soon as that general question is introduced, we turn to another area of law (wholly within the framework of Yosé's position). Then yet another topic takes its place, at Nos. 5-8. The issue then is explicitly reconsidered at No. 9.

III. PROPORTIONS

The large composites we have examined take a considerable position in their chapters but do not much affect the character of the tractate overall: AN EXEGETICAL-DIALECTICAL AND ANALOGICAL-DIALECTICAL ARGUMENT

AT M. YEB. 1:1-2 $78145/187129 = 4.1\%$

AN ANALYTICAL-DIALECTICAL ARGUMENT

AT M. YEB. 3:9I-L $15923/119290 = 13.3\%$

When we consider the tractate as a whole, these are the proportions that emerge:
$$94058/1586022 = 5.9\%$$

XV

Bavli Tractate Ketubot

This tractate provides no instances of dialectical-analytical composites. That is a surprising result, since the tractate takes its place among the more penetrating and interesting ones. In my *The Talmud of Babylonia. A Complete Outline.* Atlanta, 1995: Scholars Press for *USF Academic Commentary Series.* II. *The Division of Women,* on this tractate, I am able to demonstrate that all but two composites of an other-than-Mishnah-exegetical character in fact amplify the Mishnah's own topics. Where a composite has no bearing upon the Mishnah's statement but at the same time may claim to make a coherent and intelligible statement in the Talmud's context if not the Mishnah's, the point that is made concerns two matters: sages special, supernatural situation and the age to come and the advent of the Messiah. This latter topic, for the present tractate, falls within the natural range of the Mishnah's interest; that is, once we speak of the priority of residence in the Holy Land, the reversion of all Israel to the Holy Land in the world to come or the Messiah's day represents a natural next step. The only significant composites that impart a dimension on a topic introduced by the Mishnah but not required thereby then add sages' perspective on matters. The upshot is that this tractate's treatment of the Mishnah-counterpart is Mishnah-exegetical, only a negligible proportion of the composites attempting to accomplish any other purpose.

XVI

Bavli Tractate Nedarim

This tractate is comprised of Mishnah-exegetical and topical composites, with no analytical-dialectical or exegetical-dialectical entries at all.

XVII

Bavli Tractate Nazir

When the form-analytical translation of this tractate is complete, we shall have a basis for further exercises, such as the one underway in this monograph.

XVIII

Bavli Tractate Sotah

Mishnah-tractate Sotah presents a vast amount of information but few generative principles, and the Talmud-tractate follows suit; naturally, no dialectical-analytical compositions find a place therein.

XIX

Bavli Tractate Gittin

I. AN ANALYTICAL-DIALECTICAL ARGUMENT AT M. GIT. 5:4G-I

The most effective dialectical arguments take up an abstract principle and work through diverse cases to examine the workings of that principle. In the following instance, we deal with the distinction between deliberate and inadvertent damages of an impalpable character. One party treats them as the same, both being liable; the other, as the same, both being exempt.

I.2   A.   Said Hezekiah, "By the law of the Torah, all the same are the one who does such a thing inadvertently and the one who does it deliberately: Each is liable. *How come? This falls into the category of damage that is not readily discernible, and damage that is not readily discernible is classified as actionable.* So how come they have said that if it is done inadvertently, one is exempt from having to pay compensation? It is so that in such cases people will inform the owner."

    B.   *If that is the operative consideration, then even if it is done deliberately, the same rule should apply!*

    C.   *Well now, since the person has deliberately intended to do damage to the other, do you think that he isn't going to go and tell him? [Of course he will, so we don't have to encourage him to do so anyhow.]*

  D.   And R. Yohanan said, "By the law of the Torah, all the same are the one who does such a thing inadvertently and the one who does it deliberately: Each is exempt from liability. *How come? This falls into the category of damage that is not readily discernible, and damage that is not readily discernible is classified as not actionable.* So how come they have said that if it is done deliberately, one is liable to having to pay compensation? So that people won't run around and impart uncleanness to the foods belonging to others that require

209

preservation in a state of cultic cleanness, thinking, 'I'm exempt anyhow.'"

E. *We have learned in the Mishnah:* **Priests who deliberately imparted the status of refuse to a sacrifice in the sanctuary are liable [M. 5:4J].** *And in that connection it is taught as a Tannaite statement:* **It is on account of the good order of the world.** *Now, if you maintain that damage that is not readily discernible is classified as actionable, then those who do so inadvertently obviously are exempt from all penalty, so why is it necessary to specify that this is* **on account of the good order of the world***?*

F. *But that is precisely the intent of the statement, namely,* **priests who deliberately imparted the status of refuse to a sacrifice in the sanctuary are liable** — lo, if they did it inadvertently, they are exempt **on account of the good order of the world.**

G. *Objected R. Eleazar,* "He who performs an act of labor with water set aside for the preparation of purification water or with a red cow that has been designated for the purification-offering is exempt under the laws of humanity but liable under the laws of Heaven. *Now if you maintain that damage that is not readily discernible is classified as actionable, then he should be liable also under the laws of humanity.*"

H. *He raised the objection, but he also resolved it:* "The act of labor under discussion is one in which he brought it into a stall planning to let it give suck and threshing with it [there was no work things for which a court could punish him, but he is punished by Heaven for his intention (Simon)]; in the case of the water, the work that he did was to balance weights against its weight."

I. But didn't Raba say, "Purification water **[53B]** that one used for balancing against weights remains valid"?

J. *No problem, the one refers to weighing against the water, the other, weighing in it.*

K. *But when he weighs in it, he is performing an act of labor with it, and if damage that is not discernible is classified as actionable, then he should be liable also at the hands of an earthly court! Rather, both rules refer to doing so by weighing against the water, but there still is no problem, and [Eleazar] speaks of a case where he momentarily lost sight of the fact that it was purification water [in which case the water is*

Chapter Nineteen. Gittin

disqualified, but he is not liable], and the other speaks of a case in which he was well aware of what it was.

L. Objected R. Pappa, "**[If he stole] (1) a coin, and it was declared invalid, (2) heave-offering, and it became unclean, (3) leaven, and the festival of Passover passed [making it no longer available for Israelite use], (4) a beast, and a transgression was committed upon it, or (5) [a beast] which was invalidated for use on the altar, or (6) which was going forth to be stoned, [the robber] says to him, 'Here is what is yours right in front of you!'** [M. B.Q. 9:2I-J]. *Now if you take the position that damage that is not readily discernible is classified as actionable, then this party is nothing other than a robber and has to pay back good money!*"

M. *That is a valid refutation.*

I.3 A. *May we say that the same issue is what is at stake in the following Tannaite conflict:*

B. "**He who imparted uncleanness [to the clean food of someone else], and he who mixed heave-offering into the produce of someone else, and he who mixed another's wine with libation wine** — all the same is he who did so inadvertently and he who did it deliberately, he is liable," the words of R. Meir.

C. R. Judah says, "If he did so inadvertently, he is exempt; if he did so deliberately, he is liable."

D. *Is this not what is at issue between them, namely, the one authority takes the view that damage that is not discernible is actionable, and the other holds that it is not actionable?*

E. Said R. Nahman bar Isaac, "*All parties concur that damage that is not discernible is not actionable, but here what is at issue is whether or not we impose an indemnity upon one who acts inadvertently on account of the indemnity that is imposed on one who acts deliberately. For the one authority takes the view that sages have imposed an indemnity on one who acts inadvertently on account of one who does so deliberately, and the other authority maintains that sages have not imposed an indemnity on one who acts inadvertently on account of one who does so deliberately.*"

F. *Then one must contrast what R. Meir has said with another statement of R. Meir, and one must further contrast a statement of R. Judah's with another statement that R. Judah has made, for it has been taught on Tannaite authority:* "**One who tithes [his produce], or who cooks on the Sabbath — [if he does so] unintentionally, he may eat [the food he has prepared]; [but if he does so] intentionally, he may not eat [the food] [M. Ter. 2:3D-F],**" the words of R. Meir. R. Judah says, "If he did so inadvertently, he may eat the food at the end of the Sabbath, if it was done deliberately, he may never eat it." R. Yohanan the Sandal Maker says, "If he did so inadvertently, at the end of the Sabbath he may give to others to eat, but not to himself; if he did so deliberately, it may never be eaten either by him or by others." *So one must contrast what R. Meir has said with another statement of R. Meir, and one must further contrast a statement of R. Judah's with another statement that R. Judah has made.*

G. *There is no conflict between what R. Meir has said and another statement of R. Meir, for when rabbis imposed such an extrajudicial indemnity, it involved a ruling of rabbis, but as to a ruling of the Torah, they imposed no such indemnity.*

H. *Yes, but the prohibition against making libations derives from the Torah, and there an indemnity has been imposed!*

I. *That is because of the strict enforcement that is generally imposed upon the laws against idolatry.*

J. *There is no conflict between a statement of R. Judah's and another statement that R. Judah has made, for when rabbis imposed such an extrajudicial indemnity, it involved a ruling of the Torah, but as to a ruling of the rabbis, they imposed no such indemnity.*

K. *But lo, the prohibition against making a libation derives from the Torah, and they imposed no such indemnity!*

L. *Because of the stringent character of the prohibition against idolatry, people themselves avoid doing such things [and no further stringency is needed].*

M. *There is a contrast to be drawn between two teachings of R. Meir with respect to the enforcement of the rules of the Torah, for it has been taught on Tannaite* authority: "**One who plants [a tree] on the Sabbath — [if he does so] unintentionally, he may leave it [to grow]; [but if he does so] intentionally, he must uproot [it]. But in the Seventh Year [of the sabbatical cycle], whether [he has planted the tree] unintentionally or intentionally, he must uproot it,**" [M. Ter. 2:3Gff.] the words of R. Meir. R. Judah says, "In the Seventh Year, if he planted it inadvertently, he may let it grow, but if he did so deliberately, he must uproot it; if he did so on the Sabbath, whether it was inadvertent or deliberately, he must uproot it."

N. *Well, according to your reasoning, the passage itself should present problems to you, for both categories — the Sabbatical Year, the Sabbath — derive from the Torah, so what's the difference between the Sabbath and the Sabbatical Year? But, in point of fact, in that very context, R. Meir explains the operative consideration behind his ruling, namely,* said R. Meir, "How come I maintain, **One who plants [a tree] on the Sabbath — [if he does so] unintentionally, he may leave it [to grow]; [but if he does so] intentionally, he must uproot [it]. But in the Seventh Year [of the sabbatical cycle], whether [he has planted the tree] unintentionally or intentionally, he must uproot it**? Because the Israelites reckon from the Sabbatical Year [Simon: they will remember if a tree was planted in the Sabbatical Year, and if it is allowed to remain, they may take it as a precedent, so it was necessary to impose an indemnity in this case], **[54A]** but they don't reckon from the Sabbath. Another matter: The Israelites are suspect of neglecting the Sabbatical Year but they are not suspect of neglecting the Sabbath."

O. *What's the point of "another matter"?*

P. *This is the sense of his statement: Should you say that, in regard to the Sabbath, too, sometimes the thirtieth day prior to the New Year at the commencement of the Sabbatical Year coincides with the Sabbath, so if he plants a tree on that day, he will have a year before the next New Year, but otherwise, not, then I shall give you the alternative consideration, namely,* the Israelites are suspect of neglecting the Sabbatical Year but they are not suspect of neglecting the Sabbath.

Q. *The two statements of R. Judah don't conflict, for where R. Judah lived, the Seventh Year was taken very seriously, for someone would say to another by way of insult, "Stranger son of a woman who is a stranger," to which the other would retort, "Well, for my part, I don't eat produce of the Seventh Year the way you do."*

I.4 A. *Come and take note:* If unwittingly someone ate unclean priestly rations, he pays back unconsecrated food that is cultically clean. If he paid back unconsecrated food that was cultically unclean, Sumekhos says in the name of R. Meir, "If he did so inadvertently, his restitution is valid. If he did so deliberately, his restitution is not valid." Sages say, "All the same one way or the other, his act of restitution is valid, but he has to go and pay in addition unconsecrated food that is cultically clean." *And we reflected on this matter: If he made restitution deliberately why should it not be valid? He should be blessed. For he has eaten something of the priestly ration which a priest cannot eat when he is unclean but paid him back with something that the priest may eat when he is clean! And said Raba, and some say, Kadi, "The formulation is flawed, and this is how it should read:* If unwittingly someone ate unclean priestly rations, he pays back anything at all. If he ate priestly rations that was cultically clean, he must pay back unconsecrated food that is cultically clean. If he paid back unconsecrated food that was cultically unclean, Sumekhos says in the name of R. Meir, 'If he did so inadvertently, his restitution is valid. If he did so deliberately, his restitution is not valid.' Sages say, 'All the same one way or the other, his act of restitution is valid, but he has to go and pay in addition unconsecrated food that is cultically clean.'" *And said R. Aha b. R. Iqa, "Whether or not they have imposed an extrajudicial penalty on the basis of doing so inadvertently on account of the case of doing so deliberately is at issue between them."*

B. *But how are the cases parallel? There, the man has every intent of paying back what he has done, so should we go and impose an indemnity on him?*

Chapter Nineteen. Gittin

C. *Come and take note:* If the blood of an offering was made unclean and inadvertently was sprinkled, it is acceptable; if this was done deliberately, it is not accepted.

D. *R. Meir will say to you, "But how are the cases parallel? There, the man has every intention of effecting atonement. Now should we go and impose an indemnity on him?"*

E. *Come and take note:* **One who tithes [his produce], or who cooks on the Sabbath — [if he does so] unintentionally, he may eat [the food he has prepared]; [but if he does so] intentionally, he may not eat [the food] [M. Ter. 2:3D-F].**

F. *But how are the cases parallel? There, the man has every intention of properly preparing his food. Now should we go and impose an indemnity on him?*

G. *Come and take note:* **One who immerses [unclean] utensils on the Sabbath — [if he does so] unintentionally, he may use them; [but if he does so] intentionally, he may not use them [M. Ter. 2:3A-C].**

H. *But how are the cases parallel? There, the man has every intention of purifying his utensils. Now should we go and impose an indemnity on him?*

I.5 A. *In respect to rulings that derive from the authority of rabbis, a contrast should be drawn between one teaching of R. Judah and another such teaching, for it has been taught on Tannaite authority:* **[54B] [If] (1) the nuts were split [M. Orl. 3:8],** (2) the pomegranates cut open, (3) the jars [of wine] opened, (4) the gourds cut into, or (5) the loaves broken into, all the same if this happened inadvertently or deliberately, they are not neutralized in [a ratio of] one [part of forbidden produce] to two hundred [parts of permitted produce]," the words of R. Meir. R. Judah, R. Yosé, and R. Simeon say, "If this happened inadvertently, they are neutralized; if it happened deliberately, they are not neutralized." *Now here is a case in which the prohibition derives from the Torah, which maintains that what is forbidden is neutralized in a proportion of one to two, and rabbis decreed that* the proportion must be less than one to two hundred, and yet R. Judah imposes an indemnity in the case of one's doing the deed inadvertently!

B. *Well, in that case R. Meir has a special consideration in mind, namely, without such an indemnity, someone may act with deceit.*

I.6 A. *Now there is a conflict among teachings assigned to R. Yosé, for we have learned in the Mishnah:* [As for] a sapling [subject to the restriction] of orlah, or [a sapling prohibited under the laws] of diverse kinds in a vineyard, which was mixed together with [permitted] saplings — behold, this one may not pick [fruit from any of the trees]. If he picked, [the forbidden produce] is neutralized in [a ratio of] one [part of forbidden fruit] to two hundred [parts of permitted fruit]. And this is so provided that he does not purposely [pick the produce in order to have it neutralized]. R. Yosé says, "Even [if] he purposely picks [the produce], it is neutralized in two hundred and one" [M. Orl. 1:6].

B. *Lo, in this connection it has been stated,* said Raba, "It is taken for granted that someone will not invoke a prohibition for his entire vineyard by reason of a single sapling."

C. *And so, too, when Rabin came,* he said R. Yohanan [said], "It is taken for granted that someone will not invoke a prohibition for his entire vineyard by reason of a single sapling."

The argument is set forth at A-D. Then we move on to cases that are deemed to run parallel to the issue at hand, E-G. This leads to yet another case, G, and still another at L. As is common in the dialectical-analytical procedure initiated at the Amoraic level, we then move on to what are held to be parallel disputes among Tannaite authorities, and I.3 does just that. We articulate why we maintain the matters to run along the same lines, D, and then, E, propose to iron out the disagreement so that the issue is not the same at all. And — an absolutely emblematic trait of a dialectical argument, we move forthwith into new territory, this time asking how, in light of the proposed theory, we deal with a consequent conflict between opinions of the cited authority, which turn out to contradict one another. That exercise, at F, permits us to revert to our basic dispute in principle. At I.3M, we repeat the procedure, moving once more into adjacent but untouched territory. I.4 goes on along the same path, as do I.5,6. I cannot point to a more perfect example of Talmudic dialectics at their most productive.

Chapter Nineteen. Gittin *217*

II. PROPORTIONS

The one item we do have takes up the following proportion of the chapter in which it occurs:

$$15634/160438 = 9.7\%$$

In the tractate as a whole, matters are as follows:

$$15634/929331 = 1.6\%$$

XX

Bavli Tractate Qiddushin

The composites of this tractate, with only a few exceptions, are devoted to Mishnah-exegesis and amplification. To show in a graphic way the simple meaning of that statement, I reproduce my outline of the entire tractate. In it, not a single composition, let alone a composite, attempts anything like an analytical-dialectical argument or an exegetical-dialectical one. A negligible part of the whole is devoted to a free-standing topical appendix; to show that fact I underline the composites that undertake other than Mishnah-exegesis or amplification.

I. MISHNAH-TRACTATE QIDDUSHIN 1:1
   A. A WOMAN IS ACQUIRED AS A WIFE IN THREE WAYS, AND ACQUIRES FREEDOM FOR HERSELF TO BE A FREE AGENT IN TWO WAYS:
   1. I:1: What differentiates the present passage, in which case the Tannaite formula commences, A woman is acquired as a wife, from the passage to come, in which case the Tannaite formula uses the language, A man effects betrothal lit.: consecrates on his own or through his agent (M. 2:1A)? Why not say, a woman is betrothed, rather than, is acquired?
   2. I:2: And how come the Tannaite framer of the passage uses the feminine form of the word three, rather than the masculine form?
      a. I:3: Secondary development of the foregoing.
         i. I:4: As above.
   3. I:5: What exclusionary purpose – three, no more – is served by specifying the number at the opening clause and at the consequent one?
   4. I:6: The exclusionary purpose of specifying the number at the concluding clause serves to eliminate the rite of removing the shoe. For it might have entered your mind to suppose that the possibility of the rite of removing the shoe should derive by an argument a fortiori from the case of the levirate

219

wife. If a levirate wife, who is not freed by a divorce, is freed by the rite of removing the shoe, then this one the levirate wife who is freed by divorce surely should be freed by a rite of removing the shoe. Thus we are informed that that is not the case.

B. SHE IS ACQUIRED THROUGH MONEY:
1. II:1: What is the scriptural source of this rule?
   a. II:2: But does the verse serve the present purpose? Surely it is required in line with that which is taught on Tannaite authority...
      i. II:3: And it was necessary to provide a verse of Scripture to indicate that the minor daughter's token of betrothal is assigned to her father, and it also was necessary to find a verse of Scripture to indicate that her wages are assigned to her father...So both proofs were required.
      ii. II:4: Gloss of a detail of II:2.
2. II:5: That she is acquired through money is derived by the following Tannaite authority on a different basis, as has been taught on Tannaite authority: "When a man takes a wife and has sexual relations with her, then it shall be, if she find no favor in his eyes, because he has found some unseemly thing in her" (Deut. 24:1) – the sense of "take" refers only to acquisition through a payment of money, in line with the verse, "I will give the money for the field; take it from me" (Gen. 23:13). But cannot the same be proven by an argument a fortiori: If a Hebrew slave girl, who cannot be acquired by an act of sexual relations, can be acquired by money, a wife, who may be acquired in marriage by an act of sexual relations, surely can be acquired by money! A levirate wife proves the contrary, since she may be acquired by sexual relations but not by a money payment. But what distinguishes the levirate wife is that she cannot be acquired by a deed, and can you say the same of an ordinary wife, who can be acquired by a deed? So it is necessary for Scripture to teach, "When a man takes a wife and has sexual relations with her, then it shall be, if she find no favor in his eyes, because he has found some unseemly thing in her" (Deut. 24:1) – the sense of "take" refers only to acquisition through a payment of money, in line with the verse, "I will give the money for the field; take it from me" (Gen. 23:13) (Sifré Deut. CCLXVIII.I.1).

Chapter Twenty. Qiddushin

a. II:6: Continuation of the passage of Sifré Dt. cited above. "...And possesses her has sexual relations with her": This teaches that a woman is acquired through an act of sexual relations. One might have reasoned as follows: If a deceased childless brother's widow, who may not be acquired through a money payment, may be acquired through an act of sexual relations, a woman, who may be acquired through a money payment, logically should be available for acquisition through an act of sexual relations. But a Hebrew slave girl will prove the contrary, for she may be acquired through a money payment, but she is not acquired through an act of sexual relations. On that account, you should not find it surprising for an ordinary woman, who, even though she may be acquired through a money payment, may not be acquired through an act of sexual relations (Sifré Deut. CCLXVIII.I.2).

C. A WRIT:

1. III:1: A writ: And how on the basis of Scripture do we know that a woman may be acquired by a deed? It is a matter of logic. If a payment of money, which does not serve to remove a woman from a man's domain as does a writ of divorce, lo, it has the power of effecting acquisition, a deed namely, a writ of marriage or a marriage contract, which does in the form of a writ of divorce have the power to remove a woman from the domain of a man, surely should have the power of effecting acquisition. No, if you have made that statement concerning the payment of money, which does have the power of effecting acquisition of things that have been designated as Holy and of produce in the status of second tithe there being an exchange of money for such objects, by which the objects become secular and the money becomes consecrated, will you make the same statement concerning a writ, which does not have the power of effecting acquisitions of Holy Things and produce in the status of second tithe, for it is written, "And if he who sanctifies the field will in any manner redeem it, then he shall add the fifth part of the money of your estimation, and it shall be assigned to him" (Lev. 27:19)? Scripture says, "and he writes her a bill of divorcement, hands it to her, and sends her away from his house; she leaves his household and becomes the wife of another man." Her relationship to the latter is

comparable to her leaving the former. Just as her leaving the former is effected through a writ, so her becoming wife to the latter may be effected through a writ (Sifré Deut. CCLXVIII.I.3).

2. III:2: Raba said, "Said Scripture, 'And he shall write for her' (Deut. 24:1) – through what is in writing a woman is divorced, and she is not divorced through a money payment."

   a. III:3: While it is not possible to derive the rule governing one mode of acquisition from another the various arguments having failed, maybe it's possible to infer one from two others so that if we can show that it is possible to effect acquisition through two modes that work elsewhere and also that work in respect to a betrothal, then a third, that works elsewhere, can work in this case too?

   b. III:4: Said R. Huna, "The marriage canopy effects acquisition of title to the woman, on the strength of an argument a fortiori: If a money payment, which on its own does not confer the right to eat priestly rations, effects transfer of title to the husband over the woman, the marriage canopy, which does confer the right to eat priestly rations, surely should effect the transfer of title."

      I. III:5: As to Huna's statement, said Rabbah, "There are two refutations of what he has said: First, we learn in the Mishnah the language, three, not four; and furthermore, isn't it the simple fact that the marriage canopy completes the relationship only in consequence of an act of betrothal? But can the marriage canopy complete the relationship not in the aftermath of an act of betrothal, so that we may deduce that, when it is not in consequence of an act of betrothal, there is the same result as the marriage canopy following such an act?"

3. III:6: Our rabbis have taught on Tannaite authority: With money, how so? If he gave her money or what is worth money and said to her, "Lo, you are consecrated to me," "Lo, you are betrothed to me," "Lo, you are for me as a wife," lo, this one is consecrated. But if she gave it to him and said to him, "Lo, I am consecrated to you," "Lo, I am betrothed to you," "Lo, I am yours as a wife," she is not consecrated T. Qid. 1:1B-D.

Chapter Twenty. Qiddushin

    a.   III:7: Objected R. Pappa, "So is the operative consideration only that he gave the money and he made the statement? Then if he gave the money and she made the statement, she is not betrothed? Then note what follows: But if she gave it to him and said to him, "Lo, I am consecrated to you," "Lo, I am betrothed to you," "Lo, I am yours as a wife," she is not consecrated! So the operative consideration is that she gave the money and she made the statement. Lo, if he gave the money and she made the statement, there would be a valid betrothal!"

4.   III:8: Said Samuel, "In the matter of a betrothal, if he gave her money or what is worth money and said to her, 'Lo, you are sanctified,' 'Lo you are betrothed,' 'Lo, you are a wife to me,' lo, this woman is consecrated. 'Lo, I am your man,' 'Lo, I am your husband,' 'Lo, I am your betrothed,' there is no basis for taking account of the possibility that a betrothal has taken place. And so as to a writ of divorce: If he gave her the document and said to her, 'Lo, you are sent forth,' 'Lo, you are divorced,' 'Lo, you are permitted to any man,' lo, this woman is divorced. 'I am not your man,' 'I am not your husband,' 'I am not your betrothed,' there is no basis for taking account of the possibility that a divorce has taken place."

5.   III:9: Our rabbis have taught on Tannaite authority: "Lo, you are my wife," "Lo, you are my betrothed," "Lo, you are acquired by me," she is consecrated. "Lo, you are mine," "Lo, you are in my domain," "Lo, you are subject to me," she is betrothed.

    a.   III:10: So why not form them all into a single Tannaite statement?

6.   III:11: The question was raised: "If he used the language, 'Singled out for me,' '...designated for me,' '...my helpmate,' 'you are suitable for me, ' 'you are gathered in to me,' 'you are my rib,' 'you are closed in to me,' 'you are my replacement, ' 'you are seized to me,' 'you are taken by me,' what is the consequence?"

7.   III:12: The question was raised, "If he said, 'You are my betrothed bondmaid,' what is the law?"

    a.   III:13: Secondary clarification. With what situation do we deal in the interpretation of the language just now cited as effective? Should I say that it is a situation in which he is not talking with her about business having to do with her writ of divorce or her betrothal? Then how in the world should she know what he is talking about with her?! But rather, it is a case in which he is talking with her about business having to do with her writ of divorce or her betrothal. Then, even if he said nothing at all, but merely gave her money, she is still betrothed, for we have learned in the Mishnah: If he was speaking to his wife about matters relevant to her divorce contract or her bride price and did not make it explicit – R. Yosé says, "It is sufficient for him simply to give her the contract or bride price without a declaration." R. Judah says, "He must make it explicit" (M. M.S. 4:7). And said R. Huna said Samuel, "The decided law accords with R. Yosé."

    I. III:14: Analysis of a subordinate proof of the foregoing.
       A. III:15: Secondary analysis of the foregoing.
       B. III:16: Gloss of the matter.

8. III:17: And so as to a writ of divorce: If he gave her the document and said to her, "Lo, you are sent forth," "Lo, you are divorced," "Lo, you are permitted to any man," lo, this woman is divorced. It is obvious that if he gave her her writ of divorce and said to his wife, "Lo, you are a free woman," he has not said anything effective. If he said to his female slave, "Lo, you are permitted to any man," he has not said anything effective. If he said to his wife, "Lo, you are your own property," what is the law? Do we say that he made that statement with respect to work? Or perhaps, he meant it to cover the entirety of the relationship?

9. III:18: Said Rabina to R. Ashi, "If he said to his slave, 'I have no business in you,' what is the upshot? Do we say that the sense is, I have no business in you in any way whatsoever? Or perhaps he made that statement with respect to work?"

10. III:19: Said Abbayye, "If someone effects a betrothal with a loan, the woman is not betrothed. If it is with the benefit of a debt, she is betrothed, but this is not to be done, because it constitutes usury accomplished through subterfuge."

11. III:20: Said Raba, "If someone said, 'Take this maneh on the stipulation that you return it to me,' in regard to a purchase, he does not acquire title for example, real estate

would not be acquired if the money has to be returned; in the case of a woman, she is not betrothed; in the case of redeeming the firstborn, the firstborn is not redeemed; in the case of priestly rations, he has carried out the duty of handing it over, but it is not permitted to do it that way, since it appears to be the case of a priest who assists in the threshing floor in order to get the priestly rations, and that is not permitted because of the indignity."

12. III:21: Said Raba, "If a woman said, 'Give a maneh to Mr. So-and-so and I shall be betrothed to you,' she is betrothed under the law of surety, namely: Even though a surety does not derive benefit from the loan, he obligates himself to repay it; so this woman too, though she derives no benefit from the money, still obligates and cedes herself as betrothed. If someone said, 'Here is a maneh, and be betrothed to Mr. So-and-so' – she is betrothed under the law governing a Canaanite slave, namely: In the case of a Canaanite slave, even though he himself loses nothing when someone else gives his master money to free him, he nonetheless acquires ownership to himself, so even though this man personally loses nothing, he acquires the woman.

13. III:22: Raba raised this question: "'Here is a maneh and I'll become betrothed to you' and the man accepted it saying, 'Be betrothed to me with it', what is the law?"Raba raised this question: "'Here is a maneh and I'll become betrothed to you' and the man accepted it saying, 'Be betrothed to me with it', what is the law?"

14. III:23: Said Raba, "If a man said, 'Be betrothed to half of me,' she is betrothed; 'half of you be betrothed to me,' she is not betrothed."

15. III:24: Raba raised the question, "If one said, 'Half of you is betrothed with half of this penny, and half of you is betrothed with the other half,' what is the law? Once he said to her, 'a half penny,' he has divided the money and there is no valid betrothal, or maybe what he was doing was just counting out the matter betrothing her for the penny, half for half? If, then, you should maintain that he was just counting the matter out, what if he said, 'half of you for a penny, and half of you for a penny,' what is the law? Since he has said, 'for a penny,' and 'for a penny,' he has divided his statement and it is null, or maybe, if the procedure was on a single day, what he was doing was counting out the

matter? And if you say that, if it was on the same day, he was counting out the matter, then what if he said, 'half of you for a penny today, and the other half of you for a penny tomorrow'? Since he said, 'tomorrow,' he has divided it up and the transaction is null, or perhaps this is what he meant: The betrothal starts right away but won't be finished until tomorrow? And if he said, 'both halves of you for a penny,' here he certainly has made the entire proposition all together, or maybe a woman can't be betrothed by halves?"

16. III:25: Raba raised the question, "What if a man said, 'Your two daughters are betrothed to my two sons for a penny'? Do we invoke as the operative criterion the one who gives and the one who receives, so there is a valid monetary transaction one person gives and one person receives the penny, there is no transaction under that sum? Or perhaps we invoke the criterion of the one who betroths and the one who is betrothed, so there is no monetary transaction here?"

17. III:26: R. Pappa raised the question, "What if a man said, 'Your daughter and your cow are mine for a penny'? Do we interpret the language to mean, 'your daughter for a half-penny and your cow for a half-penny,' or perhaps 'your daughter for a penny,' and ownership of title to your cow by the act of drawing it?"

18. III:27: R. Ashi raised the question, "What if a man said, 'Your daughter and your real estate are mine for a penny'? Do we interpret the language to mean, 'your daughter for a half-penny and your property for a half-penny,' or perhaps 'your daughter for a penny, and ownership of title to your property through usucaption'?"

    a. III:28: Case. There was a man who betrothed a woman with a token of silk. Said Rabbah, "It is not necessary to perform an act of valuation in advance to inform the woman of its value." R. Joseph said, "It is necessary to perform an act of valuation in advance to inform the woman of its value."

        I. III:29: Gloss: Said R. Joseph, "How do I know it? Because it has been taught on Tannaite authority...."

19. III:30: Said R. Eleazar, "If the man said, 'Be betrothed to me for a maneh,' but he gave her a denar, lo, this woman is betrothed, and he has to make up the full amount that he has promised. Why is that the rule? Since he referred to a maneh but gave her only a denar, it is as though he had said to her, '...on the

stipulation...,' and said R. Huna said Rab, 'Whoever uses the language, "on the stipulation that...," is as though he says, "...as of now."'" Thus it is as though he said, "Be betrothed to me immediately for a denar, on condition that I gave you a maneh later."
   a. III:31: Gloss.
   b. III:32: Gloss.
20. III:33: Said R. Nahman, "If he said to her, 'Be betrothed to me with a maneh,' and he gave her a pledge for it, she is not betrothed. There is no maneh here, there is no pledge here." She neither received the maneh nor did he actually give her a pledge, since that has to be returned.
   a. III:34: Case.
21. III:35: Our rabbis have taught on Tannaite authority: "Be betrothed to me with a maneh," and she took it and threw it into the sea or fire or anywhere where it is lost – she is not betrothed (T. Qid. 2:8A-C).
   a. III:36: Gloss.
22. III:37: Our rabbis have taught on Tannaite authority: "Be betrothed to me with this maneh" – "Give it to my father or your father" – she is not betrothed. "...On condition that they accept it for me" – she is betrothed (T. Qid. 2:8D-E).
   a. III:38: Gloss.
23. III:39: "Be betrothed to me with a maneh" – "Give them to Mr. So-and-so." She is not betrothed. "...On condition that Mr. So-and-so accept the money for me," she is betrothed (T. Qid. 2:8D-G).
   a. III:40: Gloss.
24. III:41: Our rabbis have taught on Tannaite authority: "Be betrothed to me for this maneh" – "Put it on a rock" – she is not betrothed. But if the rock belonged to her, she is betrothed.
   a. III:42: R. Bibi raised this question: "If the rock belonged to the two of them, what is the law?"
25. III:43: "Be betrothed for this loaf of bread" – "Give it to a dog" – she is not betrothed. But if the dog belonged to her, she is betrothed.
   a. III:44: R. Mari raised this question: "If the dog was running after her, what is the law? In exchange for the benefit that she gets in being saved from the dog, she has determined to assign to him title over herself? Or perhaps she has the power to say, 'By the law of the Torah, you were obligated to save us?'"

26. III:45: "Be betrothed to me for this loaf of bread" – "Give it to that poor man" – she is not betrothed, even if it was a poor man who depended on her.
    a. III:46: How come?
        I. III:47: Case.
        II. III:48: Case
        III. III:49: Case.
27. III:50: The question was raised: "What if she said, 'give me,' 'let me drink,' or 'throw them down'?"
28. III:51: A writ: Our rabbis have taught on Tannaite authority: A writ: How so? If one wrote on a parchment or on a potsherd, even though they themselves were of no intrinsic value, "Lo, your daughter is betrothed to me," "Your daughter is engaged to me," "Your daughter is a wife for me" – lo, this woman is betrothed.
29. III:52: Said Raba said R. Nahman, "If one wrote on a piece of paper or a sherd, even though these were not worth a penny, 'Your daughter is consecrated to me,' 'Your daughter is betrothed to me,' 'Your daughter is mine as a wife,' whether this is effected through her father or through herself, she is betrothed by the father's consent. That is the case if she had not reached maturity. If one wrote for her on a piece of paper or a sherd, even though these were not worth a penny, 'You are consecrated to me,' 'You are betrothed to me,' 'You are mine as a wife,' whether this is effected through her father or through herself, she is betrothed by her own consent."
30. III:53: R. Simeon b. Laqish raised the question, "As to a deed of betrothal that was not written for the purpose of betrothing this particular woman, what is the law? Do we treat as comparable the formation of a marriage and its dissolution, so that, just as in the case of its dissolution, we require that the writ of divorce be written for the particular purpose of divorcing this woman, so in the case of the formation of the marriage, we require the writ of betrothal to be written for the particular purpose of betrothing this woman? Or do we treat as comparable the several modes for effecting a betrothal: Just as the betrothal by a monetary token need not be accomplished by a token prepared for her sake in particular, so betrothal by a deed does not have to be through a deed prepared for this particular woman?"

Chapter Twenty. Qiddushin

31. III:54: It has been stated: If someone wrote a deed of betrothal in her name but without her knowledge and consent – Rabbah and Rabina say, "She is betrothed." R. Pappa and R. Sherabayya say, "She is not betrothed."

D. OR SEXUAL INTERCOURSE.
1. IV:1: What is the scriptural source of this rule?
2. IV:2: The question was raised: Is it the beginning of the act of intercourse that effects the acquisition of the woman, or the end of the act of sexual relations that does? The practical difference would derive from a case in which he performed the initial stage of sexual relations, then she put out her hand and accepted a token of betrothal from someone else; or the case of whether a high priest may acquire a virgin through an act of sexual relations. What is the rule?
3. IV:3: The question was raised: Do sexual relations effect a consummated marriage or merely a betrothal? The practical difference would pertain to the question of whether he inherits her estate, contracts uncleanness to bury her if he is a priest, and abrogates her vows. If you maintain that sexual relations effect a consummated marriage, then he inherits her estate, contracts uncleanness to bury her if he is a priest, and abrogates her vows. If you maintain that sexual relations effect only betrothal, then he does not inherit her estate, contract uncleanness to bury her if he is a priest, and abrogate her vows. What is the rule?

E. THROUGH MONEY: THE HOUSE OF SHAMMAI SAY, "FOR A DENAR OR WHAT IS WORTH A DENAR."
1. V:1: What is the operative consideration in the mind of the House of Shammai? Said R. Zira, "For a woman is particular about herself and is not going to allow herself to become betrothed for less than a denar."
   a. V:2: Gloss of a detail of the foregoing.
2. V:3: R. Simeon b. Laqish says, "The operative consideration behind the ruling of the House of Shammai is in accord with Hezekiah, for said Hezekiah, 'Said Scripture, "then shall he let her be redeemed" (Ex. 21:8) – this teaches that she deducts from her redemption money and goes out free.' Now if you maintain that the master gives her a denar when he buys her, which would be the counterpart to the token of betrothal, then there is no problem; but if you say it was a mere penny, then what deduction can be made from a penny?"

3. V:4: Raba said, "This is the operative consideration for the position of the House of Shammai: So that Israelite women won't be treated as ownerless property."

F. AND THE HOUSE OF HILLEL SAY, "FOR A PERUTAH OR WHAT IS WORTH A PERUTAH." AND HOW MUCH IS A PERUTAH? ONE EIGHTH OF AN ITALIAN ISSAR.

1. VI:1: R. Joseph considered ruling, "A penny, of any sort however debased."
    a. VI:2: Gloss of a detail of the foregoing.
2. VI:3: Said Samuel, "If one betrothed a woman with a date, even if a kor of dates were at a denar, she is deemed betrothed, for we take account of the possibility that in Media it may be worth a penny."
    a. VI:4: Case.
    b. VI:5: Case.
    c. VI:6: Case.
    d. VI:7: Case.
    e. VI:8: Case.
3. VI:9: When R. Assi died, rabbis assembled to collect his traditions. Said one of the rabbis, R. Jacob by name, "This is what R. Assi said R. Mani said, 'Just as a woman may not be acquired with less than a penny, so real estate cannot be acquired for less than a penny.'"
    a. VI:10: Same attributive framework, different ruling: Further, in session they said, "Lo, in regard to what R. Judah said Samuel said, 'Whoever doesn't know the essentials of writs of divorce and betrothals should not get involved in them,' said R. Assi said R. Yohanan, 'And such folk are more of a problem to the world than the generation of the flood, for it has been stated, "By swearing, lying, killing, stealing, and committing adultery, they spread forth and blood touches blood"' (Hos. 4:2)."
    b. VI:11: Same attributive framework, different ruling: Further, in session they said, "Lo, in regard to what we have learned in the Mishnah, the woman who brought her sin-offering, and died – let the heirs bring her burnt-offering. If she brought her burnt-offering and died, the heirs do not bring her sin-offering (M. Qin. 2:5O-Q), and, in which regard, said R. Judah said Samuel, 'That rule applies to a case in which she had designated the offering while she was yet alive, but not otherwise,'

therefore taking the view that the obligation incurred by a debt is not based on the law of the Torah. Thus, if a man borrows money, we do not say that his property is automatically mortgaged for its repayment, so that in the event of his death, his heirs are liable on the law of the Torah, since they inherit mortgaged property unless the debtor explicitly mortgages his goods in a bond; here too, the woman is under an obligation to God to bring a sacrifice, yet, since she did not designate an animal for it, no obligation lies on the heirs – said R. Assi said R. Yohanan, 'That rule applies even though she had not designated the offering while she was yet alive, but not otherwise,' therefore taking the view that the obligation incurred by a debt is based on the law of the Torah – in that context, lo, the dispute was set forth in another connection and hardly required repetition.

G. AND SHE ACQUIRES HERSELF THROUGH A WRIT OF DIVORCE OR THROUGH THE HUSBAND'S DEATH:
   1. VII:1: Well, there is no problem identifying the source for the rule concerning divorce, since it is written, "And he shall write for her a writ of divorce" (Deut. 24:1). But as to the husband's death, how do we know it?

H. THE DECEASED CHILDLESS BROTHER'S WIDOW IS ACQUIRED THROUGH AN ACT OF SEXUAL RELATIONS.
   1. VIII:1: How on the basis of Scripture do we know that she is acquired by an act of sexual relations?

I. AND ACQUIRES FREEDOM FOR HERSELF THROUGH A RITE OF REMOVING THE SHOE:
   1. IX:1: How on the basis of Scripture do we know it?

J. ...OR THROUGH THE LEVIR'S DEATH:
   1. X:1: How do we know it? It derives from an argument a fortiori: If a married woman, who, if she commits adultery, is put to death through strangulation, is released by the death of the husband, a levirate widow, who is forbidden merely by a negative commandment from marrying someone else all the more so should be freed by the death of the levir!
      a. X:2: A married woman also should be freed through the rite of removing the shoe, by reason of an argument a fortiori based on the levirate widow, namely: If a levirate wife, who is not freed by a divorce, is freed by the rite of removing the shoe, then this one the levirate wife who is freed by divorce surely should be freed by

a rite of removing the shoe. Thus we are informed that that is not the case. Said Scripture, "Then he shall writ her a writ of divorce" (Deut. 24:1) – through a writ he divorces her, but he doesn't divorce her in any other way.

II. MISHNAH-TRACTATE QIDDUSHIN 1:2
   A. A HEBREW SLAVE IS ACQUIRED THROUGH MONEY:
      1. I:1: How on the basis of Scripture do we know this?
         a. I:2: Supplement to the exegetical process of the foregoing.
            A. I:3: Complement to the foregoing.
            B. I:4: As above.
            C. I:5: As above.
            D. I:6: As above.
              1. I:7: Gloss of the foregoing.
            E. I:8: Continuation of the exposition of I:6.
            F. I:9: Continuation of I:8's expansion of the foregoing analysis of exegetical principles.
              1. I:10: Gloss of the foregoing.
   B. ...AND A WRIT:
      1. II:1: How on the basis of Scripture do we know that fact?
   C. AND HE ACQUIRES HIMSELF THROUGH THE PASSAGE OF YEARS:
      1. III:1: For it is written, "Six years he shall serve, and in the seventh he shall go free for nothing" (Ex. 21:2).
   D. ...BY THE JUBILEE YEAR:
      1. IV:1: For it is written, "He shall serve with you into the year of Jubilee" (Lev. 25:40).
   E. AND BY DEDUCTION FROM THE PURCHASE PRICE REDEEMING HIMSELF AT THIS OUTSTANDING VALUE (LEV. 25:50-51).
      1. V:1: Said Hezekiah, "For said Scripture, 'Then shall he let her be redeemed' (Ex. 21:8) – this teaches that she makes a deduction from her redemption money and goes out free."
      2. V:2: A Tannaite statement: And he acquires title to himself through money or a cash equivalent or through a writ.
   F. THE HEBREW SLAVE GIRL HAS AN ADVANTAGE OVER HIM. FOR SHE ACQUIRES HERSELF IN ADDITION THROUGH THE APPEARANCE OF TOKENS OF PUBERTY:
      1. VI:1: Said R. Simeon b. Laqish, "A Hebrew slave girl has acquired from the domain of her master possession of herself as a free woman upon the death of her father. That is the result of an argument a fortiori: If the appearance of puberty

Chapter Twenty. Qiddushin 233

signs, which do not free her from her father's authority, free her from the authority of her master, then death, which does free her from her father's authority the father's heirs have no claim on her, surely should free her from her master's authority whose heirs should not inherit her!"

G. TOPICAL APPENDIX CONCERNING SEVERANCE PAY.

  a. VI:2: One Tannaite version states, The severance pay the gifts given at the end of six years of a Hebrew slave boy belongs to himself and that of a Hebrew slave girl belongs to herself. Another Tannaite version states, The severance pay the gifts given at the end of six years of a Hebrew slave girl and things that she finds belong to her father, and her master has a claim only to a fee for loss of time taken up by finding the lost object. Is it not the case that the one speaks of a girl who goes forth by reason of the advent of puberty signs in which case the severance pay goes to the father, the other liberated at the death of the father?

  b. VI:3: Gloss of a detail of VI:1. And these are the ones that get severance pay: Slaves freed by the passage of six years of service, the Jubilee, the master's death, and the Hebrew slave girl freed by the advent of puberty signs. But one who runs away or who is freed by deduction from the purchase price don't get severance pay. R. Meir says, "A runaway doesn't get severance pay, but he who is freed by deduction from the purchase price does get severance pay." R. Simeon says, "Four are given severance pay, three in the case of males, three in the case of females. And you cannot say there are four in the case of the male, because puberty signs are not effective in the case of a male, and you cannot say there is boring of the ear in the case of the female."

    I. VI:4: Gloss of a detail of the foregoing.
    A. VI:5: As above.

  1. VI:6: Our rabbis have taught on Tannaite authority: How much do they give in severance pay? "Five selas worth of each kind mentioned in Scripture Deut. 15:14: 'Out of your flock and out of your threshing floor and out of your wine press', that is, fifteen in all," the words of R. Meir. R. Judah says, "Thirty, as in the thirty paid for a gentile slave" (Ex. 21:32). R. Simeon says, "Fifty, as in the fifty for valuations" (Lev. 27:3).

a. VI:7: Gloss of the foregoing. What is the scriptural basis for R. Meir's conclusion?
b. VI:8: As above. What is the scriptural basis for the position of R. Judah?
c. VI:9: As above. What is the scriptural basis for the position of R. Simeon?
   I. VI:10: Secondary analysis of the dispute. Well, now, from R. Meir's perspective, we can understand why Scripture states, "out of your flock and out of your threshing floor and out of your wine press" (Deut. 15:14). But from R. Judah's and R. Simeon's viewpoint, why are these items – flock and threshing floor and wine press – required?
   II. VI:11: As above.
      A. VI:12: Tertiary observation on the composite. And it was necessary for all of these items to be made articulate. For if the All-Merciful had made reference to the flock, I might have thought that the law applies to animate creatures but not to what grows from the soil. So the All-Merciful has written, "threshing floor." And if the Scripture had made reference only to threshing floor, I might have thought that the gift may be what grows from the soil but not animate creatures. So Scripture wrote, "flock."
2. VI:13: Our rabbis have taught on Tannaite authority: "Furnishing him, you shall furnish him liberally" (Deut.15:14): I know only that if the household of the master has been blessed on account of the slave, that one must give a present. How do I know that even if the household of the master was not blessed on account of the slave, a gift must be given? Scripture says, "Furnishing him, you shall furnish him liberally" (Deut.15:14) – under all circumstances. R. Eleazar b. Azariah says, "If the household has been blessed for the sake of the slave, a present must be given, but if not, then the present need not be made" (Sifré Deut. CXIX:III.1).
3. VI:14: Our rabbis have taught on Tannaite authority: The Hebrew slave boy serves the son but doesn't serve the daughter. The Hebrew slave girl serves neither the son nor the daughter. The slave whose ear has been bored and the slave that is sold to a gentile serves neither the son nor the daughter.

Chapter Twenty. Qiddushin 235

      a. VI:15: What is the source for that ruling?
      b. VI:16: As above.
      c. VI:17: As above.
          I. VI:18: Expansion on a detail introduced in VI:17.

H. REVERSION TO THE EXPOSITION OF THE MISHNAH'S COMPARISON OF THE MALE AND FEMALE SLAVE

1. VI:19: "…A fellow Hebrew, man or woman": Rules pertain to the Hebrew male that do not pertain to the Hebrew female, and rules pertain to the Hebrew female that do not pertain to the Hebrew male: Rules pertain to the Hebrew male: For a Hebrew male goes forth through the passage of years and at the Jubilee and through the deduction of the years yet to be served by the payment of money and through the death of the master, none of which applies to the Hebrew female slave. A Hebrew female slave goes forth when she produces puberty signs, she may not be sold to third parties, she may be redeemed even against her wishes, none of which applies to the Hebrew male slave. Lo, since it is the fact, therefore, that rules pertain to the Hebrew male that do not pertain to the Hebrew female, and rules pertain to the Hebrew female that do not pertain to the Hebrew male, it is necessary to make explicit both the Hebrew man and the Hebrew woman (Sifré Deut. CXVIII:III.2).

    a. VI:20: Gloss of the foregoing.
    b. VI:21: Gloss of the foregoing.
        I. VI:22: Gloss of the gloss.
            A. VI:23: Gloss of the gloss of the gloss.
    c. VI:24: Continuation of the gloss of VI:19.
        I. VI:25: As above: Rabbah bar Abbuha raised this question: "Does designating the slave girl for marriage effect the status of a fully consummated marriage or does it bring about the status of betrothal? The upshot is the familiar issue of whether or not he inherits her estate, contracts uncleanness to bury her if he is a priest and she dies, and abrogates her vows. What is the law?"
        II. VI:26: R. Simeon b. Laqish raised this question: "What is the law on designating the slave girl for his minor son? 'His son' (Ex. 21:9) is what Scripture has said, meaning, his son of any classification? Or perhaps, 'his son' comparable to him, meaning, just as he is an adult, so his son must be an adult?"

> A. VI:27: Secondary inquiry pertinent to a detail of the foregoing.
>> 1. VI:28: Tertiary development of a point in the foregoing.
>> 2. VI:29: Continuation of the foregoing.
> 2. VI:30: Our rabbis have taught on Tannaite authority: How is the religious duty of designating the slave girl carried out? The master says to her in the presence of two valid witnesses, "Lo, you are consecrated to me," "Lo, you are betrothed to me," – even at the end of six years, even near sunset at the end of that time. And he then deals with her in the custom of a matrimonial bond and he does not deal with her in the custom of servitude. R. Yosé b. R. Judah says, "If there is enough time left on that last day for her to work for him to the value of a penny, she is betrothed, and if not, she is not betrothed." This matter may be compared to one who says to a woman, "Be betrothed to me as from now, after thirty days have gone by," and someone else comes along and betroths her within the thirty days. So far as the law of designation is concerned, she is betrothed to the first party.
>> a. VI:31: Now whose position is served by this parable? Should we say the parable pertains to the position of R. Yosé b. R. Judah? Lo, if there is enough time left on that last day for her to work for him to the value of a penny, she is betrothed, and if not, she is not betrothed!
> 3. VI:32: It has further been taught on Tannaite authority: "He who sells his daughter and went and accepted betrothal for her with a second party has treated the master shabbily, and she is betrothed to the second party," the words of R. Yosé b. R. Judah. But sages say, "If he wants to designate her as a wife for himself or for a daughter, he may do so." This matter may be compared to one who says to a woman, "Be betrothed to me after thirty days have gone by," and someone else comes along and betroths her within the thirty days. So far as the law of designation is concerned, she is betrothed to the second party.
>> a. VI:33: Now whose position is served by this parable? Should we say the parable serves the position of rabbis? Lo, rabbis maintain, "If he wants to designate her as a wife for himself or for a daughter, he may do so."
> 4. VI:34: It has further been taught on Tannaite authority: "He who sells his daughter and agreed that it was on condition

that her master not designate her as a wife for himself or his son, the stipulation is valid," the words of R. Meir. And sages say, "If he wanted to designate her as a wife for himself or his son, he may do so, since he has made a stipulation contrary to what is written in the Torah, and any stipulation in violation of what is written in the Torah is null."
- a. VI:35: Well, then, from R. Meir's perspective, is his stipulation valid? And hasn't it been taught on Tannaite authority....
  - I. VI:36: Secondary development of a subordinate point in the foregoing.
5. VI:37: Our rabbis have taught on Tannaite authority: "If he came in by himself, he shall go out by himself" (Ex. 21:3) – he comes in with his body whole and undamaged, and he goes out in the same condition. R. Eliezer b. Jacob says, "He comes in single, he goes out single."
   - a. VI:38: Gloss.
   - b. VI:39: Gloss.
6. VI:40: Our rabbis have taught on Tannaite authority: If a person was sold as a slave for a maneh and increased in value so that he was then worth two hundred zuz, how do we know that they reckon with his value only at the rate of a maneh? As it is said, "He shall give back the price of his redemption out of the money that he was bought for" (Lev. 25:51). If he was sold for two hundred zuz and lost value and was priced at a maneh, how do we know that we reckon his worth only at a maneh? As it is said, "According to his years shall he give back the price of his redemption" (Lev. 25:52). Now I know thus far that that is the rule for a Hebrew slave who is sold to an idolator, and who is redeemed by his family, for his hand is on the top. How do I know that the same rule applies to an Israelite who owns a Hebrew slave who is up for redemption? Scripture states, "A hired servant" in two different contexts Lev. 25:40, a slave sold to an Israelite, and Lev. 25:50, a slave sold to an idolator, serving therefore to establish an analogy between them and to invoke for the one the rules that govern the case of the other. The lenient ruling for the slave governs the redemption of the field.
   - a. VI:41: There is the possibility of interpreting the verses referring to the redemption of the Hebrew slave in a lenient way favoring the redemption and making it easy

and in a strict way. Why do you choose to do so in a lenient way? I might propose that they should be interpreted in a strict way.

7. VI:42: R. Huna bar Hinena asked R. Sheshet, "A Hebrew slave sold to a gentile – may he be redeemed by halves or may he not be redeemed by halves? Do we derive the meaning of 'his redemption' by analogy to the rule governing redeeming a field of possession, namely, just as a field of possession cannot be redeemed by halves, so he cannot be redeemed by halves? Or maybe we invoke that analogy to produce a lenient rule but not to produce a strict rule?"

8. VI:43: R. Huna bar Hinena asked R. Sheshet, "He who sells a house in a walled city – is the house redeemed by halves or is it not redeemed by halves? Do we derive the meaning of 'his redemption' by analogy to the rule governing redeeming a field of possession, namely, just as a field of possession cannot be redeemed by halves, so he cannot be redeemed by halves? Or maybe where Scripture made that point explicit, it stands, but where not, it is not made explicit and so is null?" He said to him, "We derive the answer from the exegesis of R. Simeon that one may borrow and redeem and redeem by halves. For it has been taught on Tannaite authority: '"And if a man shall sanctify to the Lord part of the field of his possession, and if he that sanctified the field will indeed redeem it" (Lev. 25:52) – this teaches that one may borrow and redeem and redeem by halves. Said R. Simeon, "What is the reason? The reason is that we find in the case of one who sells a field of possession that he enjoys certain advantages. That is, if the Jubilee Year comes and the field has not been redeemed, it automatically reverts to the owner at the Jubilee Year. On the other hand, for that very reason, he suffers the disadvantages that he may not borrow to redeem the field and he may not redeem the field in halves. But the opposite considerations apply to one who sanctifies a field of possession. For, on the one side, he suffers a disadvantage in that, if the Jubilee Year comes and the field has not been redeemed, it automatically goes forth to the ownership of the priests. So, by contrast, he is given an advantage, in that he may borrow in order to redeem the field and he may redeem it in halves.'" Lo, one who sells a house in a walled city, too – since he suffers the disadvantage in that, if a complete year goes by and the field is not

redeemed, it is permanently alienated; but he gains the advantage that he can borrow and redeem and redeem by halves."
   a. VI:44: Development of the foregoing analytical argument.
   b. VI:45: Another question on the same topic bearing the same attribution.
      I. VI:46: Gloss of a subordinated detail of the foregoing.
I. THE SLAVE WHOSE EAR IS PIERCED IS ACQUIRED THROUGH AN ACT OF PIERCING THE EAR (EX. 21:5).
   1. VII:1: For it is written, "Then his master shall bore his ear through with an awl" (Ex. 21:6).
J. AND HE ACQUIRES HIMSELF BY THE JUBILEE AND BY THE DEATH OF THE MASTER.
   1. VIII:1: For it is written, "and he shall serve him" but not his son or daughter; "forever" – until the "forever" of the Jubilee.
   2. VIII:2: Our rabbis have taught on Tannaite authority: "'An awl' (Deut. 15:17): I know only that an awl is sufficient for boring the ear of the slave. How do I know that sufficient also would be a prick, thorn, borer, or stylus? Scripture states, 'Then you shall take' (Deut. 15:12) – including everything that can be taken in hand," the words of R. Yosé b. R. Judah. Rabbi says, "Since the verse says, 'an awl,' we draw the conclusion that the awl is made only of metal, and so anything that is used must be metal. Another matter: 'You shall take an awl' – teaches that a big awl is meant." Said R. Eleazar, "R. Yudan b. Rabbi would expound as follows: 'When they pierce the ear, they do it only through the earlobe.' Sages say, 'A Hebrew slave of the priestly caste is not subjected to the boring of the ear, because that thereby blemishes him.'"
   a. VIII:3: What is at issue here?
   b. VIII:4: Further gloss of VIII:2.
   c. VIII:5: Said R. Eleazar, "R. Yudan b. Rabbi would expound as follows: 'When they pierce the ear, they do it only through the earlobe.' Sages say, 'A Hebrew slave of the priestly caste is not subjected to the boring of the ear, because that thereby blemishes him'":
   3. VIII:6: The question was raised: "A Hebrew slave who is a priest – what is the law as to his master's giving him a Canaanite slave girl? Is this an anomaly, in which case there

is no distinguishing priests from Israelites? Or perhaps priests are exceptional, since Scripture imposes additional religious duties on them?" Rab said, "It is permitted." And Samuel said, "It is forbidden."

K. TOPICAL APPENDIX ON THE MARRIAGE TO THE CAPTIVE WOMAN OF GOODLY FORM
   1. VIII:7: Joined for formal reasons, namely, same form, same attributions of disputing opinions. The question was raised: "A priest – what is the law as to his taking 'a woman of goodly form' (Deut. 21:11)? Is this an anomaly, in which case there is no distinguishing priests from Israelites? Or perhaps priests are exceptional, since Scripture imposes additional religious duties on them?" Rab said, "It is permitted." And Samuel said, "It is forbidden."
   2. VIII:8: Our rabbis have taught on Tannaite authority: "When you take the field against your enemies, and the Lord your God delivers them into your power, and you take some of them captive, and you see among the captives a beautiful woman and you desire her and would take her to wife, you shall bring her into your house, and she shall trim her hair, pare her nails, and discard her captive's garb. She shall spend a month's time in your house lamenting her father and mother. After that you may come to her and possess her, and she shall be your wife. Then, should you no longer want her, you must release her outright. You must not sell her for money; since you had your will of her, you must not enslave her" (Deut. 21:10-14). "...And you see among the captives": At the time of the taking of the captives. "...A beautiful woman": Even a married woman (Sifré Deut. CCXI:II.1-2).

L. REVERSION TO THE EXPOSITION OF THE LAW CONCERNING SLAVE WHO WISHES TO REMAIN WITH HIS MASTER
   1. VIII:9: Our rabbis have taught on Tannaite authority: "But should he say to you, 'I do not want to leave you,' for he loves you and your household and is happy with you, you shall take an awl and put it through his ear into the door, and he shall become your slave in perpetuity. Do the same with your female slave. When you do set him free, do not feel aggrieved, for in the six years he has given you double the service of a hired man. Moreover, the Lord your God will bless you in all you do" (Deut. 15:12-17): Is it possible to suppose that this may take place one time only? Scripture

says, "But should he say to you, 'I do not want to leave you,'" – unless he says so and repeats it. If he said so during the six years, but did not say so at the end of the six years, lo, this one does not have his ear pierced to the doorpost, for it is said, "I do not want to leave you" – which applies only if said at the time of his leaving. If he said so at the end of the six years, but did not say so during the six years, lo, this one does not have his ear pierced to the doorpost, for it is said, "But if the slave should say to you...," that is, while he is yet a slave (Sifré Deut. CXXI.I.1-3).

   a. VIII:10: Gloss of the foregoing.

2. VIII:11: Our rabbis have taught on Tannaite authority: If he has a wife and children, and his master does not have a wife and children, lo, this one does not have his ear pierced to the doorpost, as it is said, "...for he loves you and your household and is happy with you." (Sifré Deut. CXXI:II.2).

   a. VIII:12: Gloss.

3. VIII:13: Our rabbis have taught on Tannaite authority: "Because he fares well with you" (Deut. 15:16). He must be with you and at your status in food and in drink, so that you may not eat a piece of fine bread while he eats a piece of coarse bread, you may not drink vintage wine while he drinks new wine, you may not sleep on a soft bed while he sleeps on the ground. On this basis it is said that he who buys a Hebrew slave is like one who buys a master for himself.

4. VIII:14: Our rabbis have taught on Tannaite authority: "Then he shall go out from you, he and his children with him" (Lev. 25:41): Said R. Simeon, "If he was sold, were his sons and daughters sold? But on the basis of this verse, it is the fact that his master is obligated for food for his children."

   a. VIII:15: Gloss.

5. VIII:16: Our rabbis have taught on Tannaite authority: If Scripture had said, "...his ear on the door," I might have thought, then let a hole be bored against his ear through the door. So it is only the door, but not his ear. "Not his ear"?! But it's written, "and his master shall bore his ear through with an awl" (Ex. 21:6). Rather, I might have said, the ear is bored outside and then placed on the door, and a hole bored through the door opposite his ear. Therefore it is said, "and you shall thrust it through his ear into the door." How? The boring goes on until the door is reached.

6. VIII:17: "The door": May I then infer that that is so whether it is removed from the hinges or not? Scripture states, "unto the door or unto the doorpost" (Ex. 21:6): Just as the doorpost must be standing in place, so the door must be standing in place.
7. VIII:18: Rabban Yohanan ben Zakkai would expound this verse in the manner of a homer exegesis: "How come the ear was singled out of all the limbs of the body? Said the Holy One, blessed be He, 'The ear, which heard my voice at Mount Sinai at the moment that I said, "For to me the children of Israel are slaves, they are my slaves" (Lev. 25:55), nonetheless went and acquired a master for itself. So let it be pierced.'"

III. MISHNAH-TRACTATE QIDDUSHIN 1:3
   A. A CANAANITE SLAVE IS ACQUIRED THROUGH MONEY, THROUGH A WRIT, OR THROUGH USUCAPTION.
      1. I:1: How on the basis of Scripture do we know this fact?
      2. I:2: A Tannaite statement: Also through barter.
      3. I:3: Said Samuel, "A Canaanite slave is acquired also through drawing. How so? If the purchaser grabs the slave and he goes with him, he acquires title to him; if he calls him and he goes to him, he does not acquire title to him."
         a. I:4: Gloss of I:3:
      4. I:5: Our rabbis have taught on Tannaite authority: How is a slave acquired through an act of usucaption? If the slave fastened the shoe of the man or untied it or if he carried his clothing after him to the bathhouse, or if he undressed him or washed him or anointed him or scraped him or dressed him or put on his shoes or lifted him up, the man acquires title to the slave. Said R. Simeon, "An act of usucaption of this kind should not be greater than an act of raising up, since raising up an object confers title under all circumstances."
         a. I:6: What is the meaning of this statement?
         b. I:7: Now that you have said, if the slave lifted up his master, the master acquires title, then what about the following: A Canaanite slave girl should be acquired through an act of sexual relations since in that situation she lifts up the master?
            I. I:8: Case.

Chapter Twenty. Qiddushin   243

B. "AND HE ACQUIRES HIMSELF THROUGH MONEY PAID BY OTHERS OR THROUGH A WRIT OF INDEBTEDNESS TAKEN ON BY HIMSELF," THE WORDS OF R. MEIR.

1. II:1: "And he acquires himself through money paid by others or through a writ of indebtedness taken on by himself," the words of R. Meir: Through money paid by others – but not by money paid by the slave himself? With what situation do we deal? Should we say, without his knowledge and consent? Then note: We have heard that R. Meir holds, it is a disadvantage for the slave to go forth from the possession of his master to freedom, and we have learned as a Tannaite statement in the Mishnah, For they act to the advantage of another person not in his presence, but they act to his disadvantage only in his presence (M. Git. 1:6F). So it is obvious that it is with the slave's knowledge and consent, and so we are informed that it may be done through money paid by others – but not by money paid by the slave himself. Then it follows that there is no possibility for a slave to acquire title to anything without his owner's participation. But then note what follows: Through a writ of indebtedness taken on by himself! So if it is taken on by himself, it is a valid medium of emancipation, but if it is taken on by others, it is not! Now if it is with his own knowledge and consent, then why can it not be validly done by third parties? And should you say, what is the meaning of, through a writ of indebtedness taken on by himself? It means, even through a writ of indebtedness taken on by himself, and so we are informed that the advent of his writ of emancipation and his right to form a domain unto himself come about simultaneously, lo, that is not how it has been taught as a Tannaite statement, for lo, it has been taught on Tannaite authority: "...By a writ undertaken on his own account, but not one undertaken by others," the words of R. Meir (T. Qid. 1:6F).

C. AND SAGES SAY, "BY MONEY PAID BY HIMSELF OR BY A WRIT TAKEN ON BY OTHERS:"

1. III:1: If the money is paid by himself, it liberates him, but if it is paid by others, it doesn't? Now why should this be the case? Granting that this is without his knowledge and consent, in any event notice: We know that rabbis take the position that it is to the slave's advantage to leave the master's domain for freedom, and we have learned in the Mishnah,

For they act to the advantage of another person not in his presence, but they act to his disadvantage only in his presence (M. Git. 1:6F). And should you say, what is the meaning of paid by himself? Also money paid by himself, and so we are informed that here is every possibility for a slave to acquire title to anything without his owner's participation, if so, note what follows: By a writ taken on by others – not undertaken by him himself! And yet it is an established fact for us that the advent of his writ of emancipation and his right to form a domain unto himself come about simultaneously. And should you say, what is the meaning of by a writ taken on by others? Also by a writ taken on by others, and so we are informed that it is to the slave's advantage to leave the master's domain for freedom, if so, then why not blend the whole and repeat the entire matter in a single statement, namely: With money and with a writ, whether taken on by others or taken on by himself?

    a. III:2: Rabbah asked, "From the perspective of R. Simeon b. Eleazar, what is the law on a Canaanite slave's appointing a messenger to receive his writ of emancipation from the hand of his master? Since we derive a verbal analogy on the basis of the word 'to her' that appears both in his context and in that of a woman, he is in the status of a woman, or perhaps, as to a woman, since she has the power to receive her writ of divorce, an agent also can do so, but a slave, who has not got the power to receive his writ of emancipation, also has not got the power to appoint an agent?"

D. "...ON CONDITION THAT THE MONEY BELONGS TO OTHERS:"

    1. IV:1: May we then say that this is what is at issue between sages and R. Meir: R. Meir takes the position that the slave has no right of effecting title without his master's participation, and a woman has no right of effecting title without her husband's participation, while rabbis maintain that the slave has the right of effecting title without his master's participation, and a woman has the right of effecting title without her husband's participation?

    2. IV:2: A Tannaite statement: A gentile slave goes free through the loss of his eye, tooth, or major limbs that do not grow back in line with Ex. 21:26-27. Now there is no problem understanding why that is so for the eye and tooth, since they are made explicit in Scripture, but on what basis do we know that that is the fact for the loss of the major limbs?

3. IV:3: Our rabbis have taught on Tannaite authority: "In all these cases, a slave goes forth to freedom, but he requires a writ of emancipation from his master," the words of R. Simeon. R. Meir says, "He doesn't require one." R. Eliezer says, "He requires one." R. Tarfon says, "He doesn't require one." R. Aqiba says, "He requires one."
   a. IV:4: What is the scriptural basis for the position of R. Simeon? of R. Meir?
4. IV:5: Our rabbis have taught on Tannaite authority: If the master hit the slave on his eye and blinded him, on his ear and deafened him, the slave goes forth by that reason to freedom. If he hit an object that was opposite the slave's eye, and the slave cannot see, or opposite his ear, so that he cannot hear, the slave does not go forth on that account to freedom.
   a. IV:6: Said R. Shemen to R. Ashi, "Does that bear the implication that noise is nothing? But didn't R. Ammi bar Ezekiel teach as a Tannaite statement: A chicken that put its head into an empty glass jar and crowed and broke the jar – the owner pays full damages? And said R. Joseph, 'They say in the household of the master: A horse that neighed or an ass that brayed and broke utensils – the owner pays half-damages'!"
5. IV:7: Our rabbis have taught on Tannaite authority: If he hit his eye and impaired his eyesight, his tooth and loosened it, but he still can use them at this time, the slave does not go forth on their account to freedom, but if not, the slave does go forth on their account to freedom. It has further been taught on Tannaite authority: If the slave had poor eyesight but the master totally blinded him, or if his tooth was loose and the master knocked it out, then, if he could use them before-times, the slave goes free on their account, but if not, the slave does not go free on their account.
   a. IV:8: And it was necessary to state both rules.
6. IV:9: Our rabbis have taught on Tannaite authority: Lo, if his master was a physician, and the slave told him to paint his eye with an ointment, and the master blinded him, or to drill his tooth and he knocked it out, the slave just grins at his master and walks out free. Rabban Simeon b. Gamaliel says, "'...and he destroy it' (Ex. 21:26) – only if he intends to destroy it."

a. IV:10: So how do rabbis deal with the clause, "...and he destroy it" (Ex. 21:26)?
7. IV:11: Said R. Sheshet, "If the slave's eye was blind and the master removed it, the slave goes forth to freedom on that account. How come? Because he now lacks a limb."
8. IV:12: Said R. Hiyya bar Ashi said Rab, "If the slave had an extra finger and the master cut it off, the slave goes out free."
9. IV:13: A slave whose master castrated him, what is the law on classifying this blemish? Is it tantamount to one that is visible to the eye or is it not?
a. IV:14: Expansion of a detail of the foregoing.
b. IV:15: Expansion of a detail of the foregoing.

IV. MISHNAH-TRACTATE QIDDUSHIN 1:4
A. "LARGE CATTLE ARE ACQUIRED THROUGH DELIVERY, AND SMALL CATTLE THROUGH LIFTING UP," THE WORDS OF R. MEIR AND R. ELEAZAR. AND SAGES SAY, "SMALL CATTLE ARE ACQUIRED THROUGH AN ACT OF DRAWING."
1. I:1: Rab expounded in Qimhunayya, "Large cattle are acquired through drawing the beast."

V. MISHNAH-TRACTATE QIDDUSHIN 1:5
A. PROPERTY FOR WHICH THERE IS SECURITY IS ACQUIRED THROUGH MONEY:
1. I:1: How on the basis of Scripture do we know that fact?
2. I:2: Rab, "This rule was repeated only in reference to a place in which they do not write out a deed, but in a place where they did write out a deed, money by itself does not effect transfer of title."
B. WRIT:
1. II:1: How on the basis of Scripture do we know that fact?
2. II:2: Said Samuel, "This rule was repeated only in reference to a deed of gift, but as to a deed of sale, the transfer of title takes place only when the purchaser gives him the cash."
C. AND USUCAPTION:
1. III:1: How on the basis of Scripture do we know that fact?
D. AND THAT FOR WHICH THERE IS NO SECURITY IS ACQUIRED ONLY BY AN ACT OF DRAWING FROM ONE PLACE TO ANOTHER:
1. IV:1: How on the basis of Scripture do we know that fact?
E. PROPERTY FOR WHICH THERE IS NO SECURITY IS ACQUIRED ALONG WITH PROPERTY FOR WHICH THERE IS SECURITY THROUGH MONEY, WRIT, AND USUCAPTION:

1. V:1: How on the basis of Scripture do we know that fact?
2. V:2: The question was raised: "Do the movables have to be heaped upon the land to be transferred, or is that not the case?"
3. V:3: The question was raised: "Do we require the explicit statement that the movables are acquired by virtue of the acquisition of the land, or do we not require such an explicit statement?"
4. V:4: The question was raised: "What if the field is transferred through sale, but the movables are transferred as a gift?" Are the movables then transferred along with the real estate?
5. V:5: The question was raised: If the field went to one party and the movables to another, what is the rule?
6. V:6: Said Raba, "The rule that movables are acquired along with land applies only if the purchaser had paid money for all of the movables. But if he had not paid money for them all, he acquires only the movables that are covered by his money."
    a. V:7: That supports the position of Samuel, for said Samuel, "If one has sold to the other ten fields in ten provinces, so that, once the purchaser has acquired one of them by usucaption, he has acquired all of them."

F. AND PROPERTY FOR WHICH THERE IS NO SECURITY IMPOSES THE NEED FOR AN OATH ON PROPERTY FOR WHICH THERE IS SECURITY.
1. VI:1: Said Ulla, "How on the basis of the Torah do we derive the rule of the superimposed oath by which, if one is required to take an oath on one count, he may be forced to extend the oath to other counts? As it is said, 'And the woman shall say, Amen, Amen,' and we have learned in the Mishnah: To what does she say, Amen, Amen?...'Amen that I have not gone aside while betrothed, married, awaiting levirate marriage, or wholly taken in Levirate marriage' (M. Sot. 2:5A-D). Now as this reference to her having been betrothed, what can it possibly mean? If we say that he expressed his warning of jealousy to her when she was betrothed, and then she went aside with the alleged lover, and is now made to drink the bitter water while still betrothed, then is a woman who has been merely betrothed required to undergo the ordeal of drinking the bitter water as a woman accused of adultery? Lo, we have learned in the Mishnah: A betrothed girl and a deceased childless brother's widow awaiting levirate marriage neither undergo the ordeal of drinking the

bitter water nor receive a marriage contract, since it is written, 'When a wife, being subject to her husband, goes astray' (Num. 5:29) – excluding the betrothed girl and the deceased childless brother's widow awaiting levirate marriage (M. Sot. 4:1A-C). And if it is proposed that she was warned when betrothed, then went aside with the alleged lover, and now has to drink that she has been married, do the waters test her under these conditions? Has it not been taught on Tannaite authority: 'And the man shall be free from iniquity, and the woman shall bear her iniquity' (Num. 5:31). The sense of the foregoing verse of Scripture is that when the man is free of transgression, the water puts his wife to the test, and if the man is not free of transgression, the water does not put his wife to the test? Rather, the oath can be imposed to cover the specified matter only because it is superimposed."

2. VI:2: Then to what extent is a superimposed oath carried?

VI. MISHNAH-TRACTATE QIDDUSHIN 1:6A-F

A. WHATEVER IS USED AS PAYMENT FOR SOMETHING ELSE – ONCE THIS ONE HAS EFFECTED ACQUISITION THEREOF THE OTHER HAS BECOME LIABLE FOR WHAT IS GIVEN IN EXCHANGE. HOW SO? IF ONE EXCHANGED AN OX FOR A COW, OR AN ASS FOR AN OX, ONCE THIS ONE HAS EFFECTED ACQUISITION, THE OTHER HAS BECOME LIABLE FOR WHAT IS GIVEN IN EXCHANGE.

1. I:1: Whatever is used as payment for something else: What is subject to barter? Money. It is assumed that the language, Whatever is used as payment for something else includes money. Hence the point is: If A exchanges a cow for B's money, the money not being given as payment but as barter, just as an ox might be given, then as soon as A gets the money, B accepts liability for whatever happens to the cow, which is now subject to his title; that is the case even though if the money had been given as payment, the receipt of the money by A would not have transferred title of the cow to B. That then proves money may be treated as an object of barter.

VII. MISHNAH-TRACTATE QIDDUSHIN 1:6G-H

A. THE RIGHT OF THE MOST HIGH IS EFFECTED THROUGH MONEY, AND THE RIGHT OF ORDINARY FOLK THROUGH USUCAPTION. ONE'S WORD OF MOUTH DEDICATION OF AN OBJECT TO THE MOST HIGH IS EQUIVALENT TO ONE'S ACT OF DELIVERY TO AN ORDINARY PERSON.

1. I:1: Our rabbis have taught on Tannaite authority: How is the right of the Most High...effected through money? If the Temple treasurer handed over money for a beast, even if the animal is located on the other side of the world, he acquires title to it, but an ordinary person acquires title only by performing the act of drawing the beast. How is it so that one's word of mouth dedication of an object to the Most High is equivalent to one's act of delivery to an ordinary person? He who says, "This ox is a burnt-offering," "This house is sanctified," even if they are at the other side of the world, the sanctuary acquires title. In the case of an ordinary person, he acquires title only by performing an act of drawing or usucaption. If a common person performed the act of drawing when the beast was worth a maneh but did not suffice to redeem the beast, paying the money, until the price rose to two hundred zuz, he must pay the two hundred. How come? Scripture says, "And he will pay the money and depart," meaning, if he has given the money, lo, these belong to him, but if not, they do not belong to him. If he performed the act of drawing when it was worth two hundred zuz but did not suffice to redeem it before the price fell to a maneh, he still has to pay two hundred zuz. How come? So that the rights of a common person should not be stronger than those of the sanctuary. If he redeemed it when it was worth two hundred but did not suffice to draw the beast before the price went down to a maneh, he has to pay the two hundred zuz. How come? Scripture says, "And he will pay the money and depart." If he redeems it at a maneh and did not suffice to perform the act of drawing before it went up to two hundred zuz, what he has redeemed is redeemed, and he pays only a maneh (T. Ar. 4:4A-G).

VIII. MISHNAH-TRACTATE QIDDUSHIN 1:7
   A. FOR EVERY COMMANDMENT CONCERNING THE SON TO WHICH THE FATHER IS SUBJECT – MEN ARE LIABLE, AND WOMEN ARE EXEMPT:
      1. I:1: What is the meaning of For every commandment concerning the son to which the father is subject...? Should we say, from every religious duty that the son is required to do for the father, women are exempt? But hasn't it been taught on Tannaite authority: "Every man his mother and his father you shall fear" (Lev. 19:27) – I know only that that applies to the man. How do I know that it applies to the

woman? When Scripture says, "his mother and his father you shall fear," lo, both of them are included?

2. I:2: Thus we learn as a Tannaite statement here that which our rabbis have taught on Tannaite authority: The father is responsible with respect to his son to circumcise him, to redeem him, to teach him Torah, to marry him off to a woman, and to teach him a trade. And there are those who say, also to teach him to swim. R. Judah says, "Anyone who does not teach his son a trade is as though he trains him to be a gangster" (T. Qid. 1:11F-H).

   a. I:3: Secondary gloss of the foregoing. How on the basis of Scripture do we know that he must do so?
   b. I:4: Secondary gloss of the foregoing. How on the basis of Scripture do we know that he must do so?
      I. I:5: Our rabbis have taught on Tannaite authority: M. Bekh. 8:6M-P: If a man who was firstborn son had a firstborn son and was told that he had not been redeemed so that he is to redeem himself and he is to redeem his son, he comes before his son. R. Judah says, "His son comes before him. For the requirement of redeeming him the father falls upon his father, while the requirement of redeeming his son falls on him." If he was to be redeemed and his son was to be redeemed, he takes precedence over his son. R. Judah says, "His son takes precedence over him, for the religious duty pertains to his father, and the religious duty involving the son pertains to the father."
      II. I:6: Our rabbis have taught on Tannaite authority: If a man was obligated to redeem his son and to make a pilgrimage for the festival, he first redeems his son and then makes the pilgrimage for the festival. R. Judah says, "He makes the pilgrimage for the festival and then he redeems his son, for the former is a religious duty that will pass with the passage of time, but the other is a religious duty that will not pass with the passage of time" (T. Bekh. 6:10A-C).
      III. I:7: Our rabbis have taught on Tannaite authority: How do we know that if a man had five firstborn sons by five wives, he is required to redeem all of them? Scripture states, "All the firstborn of your sons shall you redeem" (Ex. 34:20).

c. I:8: Further gloss of I:2. To teach him Torah: How on the basis of Scripture do we know that fact?

   I. I:9: Our rabbis have taught on Tannaite authority: If he had to study Torah and his son likewise, he takes precedence over his son. R. Judah says, "If his son was an eager student, gifted and retentive, his son takes precedence over him" (T. Bekh. 6:10F-H).

   A. I:10: That is in line with the case of R. Jacob b. R. Aha bar Jacob, whose father sent him to Abbayye. When he came home, his father observed that his traditions were not very sharp. He said to him, "I'm better than you are. So you stay here, and I'll go."

   II. I:11: Our rabbis have taught on Tannaite authority: If someone had to study the Torah and get married, let him study the Torah and then get married. But if he can't live without a wife, let him get married and then study the Torah (T. Bekh. 6:10D-E).

   A. I:12: Said R. Judah said Samuel, "The law is: One marries a wife and then studies Torah."

      1. I:13: Secondary discussion of the same issue as I:11.
      2. I:14: Secondary discussion of the same issue as I:11.
      3. I:15: Secondary discussion of the same issue as I:11.
      4. I:16: Secondary discussion of the same issue as I:11.
      5. I:17: Secondary discussion of the same issue as I:11.

   III. I:18: To what extent is a man obligated to teach his son Torah?

   A. I:19: Secondary expansion of the foregoing.

   IV. I:20: Said R. Safra said R. Joshua b. Hananiah, "What is the meaning of the verse, 'and you shall teach them diligently to your children' (Deut. 6:7)? Read the letters to yield not 'repeat' but rather 'divide into three,' so that a person should always divide years into three parts: a third for Scripture, a third for Mishnah, a third for talmud."

v. I:21: Therefore the early masters were called scribes those who numbered, because they would count up all the letters in the Torah. For they would say, "The W in the word belly (gahon) Lev. 11:42: "whatever goes on the belly" is the midpoint among all of the letters of a scroll of the Torah. The words 'diligently enquire' at Lev. 10:16 mark the midpoint among the words; the word 'he shall be shaven' (Lev. 13:33) marks half the verses; in the verse, 'the boar out of the wood does ravage it' (Ps. 80:14), the ayin of the word for forest marks the midpoint of the Psalms; 'but he, being full of compassion, forgives their iniquity' (Ps. 78:38) marks the midpoint of all of the verses of Psalms."

A. I:22: Secondary expansion of the foregoing.
B. I:23: Secondary expansion of the foregoing.
C. I:24: Secondary expansion of the foregoing.

vi. I:25: Our rabbis have taught on Tannaite authority: "And you shall teach them diligently to your children" (Deut. 6:7): "That is to say, 'Impress them upon your children': The meaning of "impressing," or "repeating," is that the teachings of the Torah should be so sharp in your mouth that when someone asks you something, you should not stammer. But you should give a reply forthwith. So Scripture says, "Say to wisdom, 'you are my sister,' and call understanding your kinswoman" (Prov. 7:4). "Bind them on your fingers, write them on the table of your heart" (Prov. 7:3). "Your arrows are sharp" (Ps. 45:6). "The peoples fall under you, they sink into the heart of the king's enemies" (Ps. 45:6). "As arrows in the hand of a mighty man, so are the children of one's youth" (Ps. 127:4). And concerning these children: "Happy is the man who has his quiver full of them, they shall not be put to shame when they speak with their enemies in the gate" (Ps. 127:5) (Sifré Deut. XXXIV:I.1-2).

vii. I:26: Our rabbis have taught on Tannaite authority: "Therefore impress these my words upon your very heart; bind them as a sign on your hand and let them serve as a symbol on your forehead; and teach them to your children, reciting them when you stay at home and when you are away, when you lie down and when you get up, and inscribe them on the doorposts of your house and on your gates, to the end that you and your children may endure in the land that the Lord swore to your fathers to assign to them, as long as there is a Heaven over the earth" (Deut. 11:18-21): This use of the word impress, which can be read to sound like "medicine, ointment" indicates that words of Torah are compared to a life-giving medicine. The matter may be compared to the case of a king who grew angry with his son and gave him a severe blow, but then put a salve on the wound and said to him, "My son, so long as this bandage is on the wound, eat whatever you like, drink whatever you like, and wash in either warm or cold water, and nothing will do you injury. But if you remove the bandage, the sore will immediately begin to produce ulcers." So the Holy One, blessed be He, said to Israel, "My children, I have created in you an impulse to do evil, than which nothing is more evil. 'Sin crouches at the door and to you is its desire' (Gen. 4:7). Keep yourselves occupied with teachings of the Torah, and sin will not control you. But if you leave off studying words of the Torah, lo, it will control you, as it is said, 'and to you is its desire' (Gen. 4:7). And not only so, but all of its undertakings concern you. But if you want, you will control it, as it is said, 'But you may rule over it' (Gen. 4:7)." And Scripture says, "And if your enemy is hungry, give him bread to eat, and if he is thirsty, give him water to drink, for you will heap coals of fire upon his head" (Prov. 25:21-22) (Sifré Deut. XLVI.I.2).

VIII. I:27: Our rabbis have taught on Tannaite authority: So formidable is the lust to do evil that even its creator has called it evil, as it is written, "For that the desire of man's heart is evil from his youth" (Gen. 8:21).

IX. I:28: A Tannaite statement of the household of R. Ishmael: "If that vile one meets you, drag it to the house of study. If it is a stone, it will dissolve. If it is iron, it will be pulverized. If it is a stone, it will dissolve," as it is written, "Lo, everyone who is thirsty, come to water" (Isa. 55:1). And it is written, "The water wears down stones" (Job 14:19). "If it is iron, it will be pulverized," as it is written, "Is not my word like fire, says the Lord, and like a hammer that breaks the rock into pieces" (Jer. 23:29).

  d. I:29: Further gloss of I:2. To marry him off to a woman: What is the source in Scripture?

  e. I:30: Further gloss of I:2. And to teach him a trade: What is the source in Scripture?

  f. I:31: Further gloss of I:2. And there are those who say, also to teach him to swim: How come?

  g. I:32: Further gloss of I:2. R. Judah says, "Anyone who does not teach his son a trade trains him to be a gangster": Can you imagine, to be a gangster?! Rather, is as though he trains him to be a gangster.

B. AND FOR EVERY COMMANDMENT CONCERNING THE FATHER TO WHICH THE SON IS SUBJECT, MEN AND WOMEN ARE EQUALLY LIABLE.

 1. II:1: What is the definition of for every commandment concerning the father to which the son is subject? Should we say, for all of the religious duties that a father is obligated to do for his son, women are obligated as well? But hasn't it been taught on Tannaite authority: The father is responsible with respect to his son to circumcise him, to redeem him – the father, not the mother.

C. MISCELLANY ON THE HONOR OF MOTHER AND FATHER

 1. II:2: Our rabbis have taught on Tannaite authority: It is said, "Honor your father and your mother" (Ex. 20:12), and it is further said, "Honor the Lord with your wealth" (Prov. 3:9). Scripture thereby establishes an analogy between the honor of father and mother and the honor of the Omnipresent. It is said, "He who curses his father or his mother will certainly die" (Prov. 20:20), and it is said, "Any person who curses his God will bear his sin" (Lev. 24:15). Scripture thereby establishes an analogy between cursing father and mother and cursing the Omnipresent. But it is not possible to refer to smiting Heaven in the way in which one is warned not to hit one's parents. And that is entirely reasonable, for all three of them are partners in a human being (Sifra Qedoshim CXCV:II.3).

 2. II:3: Our rabbis have taught on Tannaite authority: Three form a partnership in the creation of a human being, the

Chapter Twenty. Qiddushin

Holy One, blessed be He, one's father and one's mother. When someone honors father and mother, said the Holy One, blessed be He, "I credit it to them as though I had lived among them and they honored me."

3. II:4: It has been taught on Tannaite authority: Rabbi says, "It is perfectly self-evident to the One who spoke and brought the world into being that the son honors his mother more than his father, because she influences him with kind words. Therefore the Holy One, blessed be He, gave precedence to honoring the father over honoring the mother. But it also is perfectly self-evident before the One who spoke and brought the world into being that the son fears the father more than the mother, because he teaches him Torah. Therefore the Holy One, blessed be He, gave priority to fear of the mother over fear of the father."

4. II:5: A Tannaite authority repeated before R. Nahman: "When someone gives anguish to his father or his mother, said the Holy One, blessed be He, 'I did well in not living among them, for if I lived among them, they would have given me anguish, too.'
   a. II:6: Topical expansion on the anguish of God.
   b. II:7: Topical expansion on the anguish of God.

5. II:8: A widow's son asked R. Eliezer, "If father says, 'Give me a glass of water,' and mother says, 'Give me a glass of water,' to which of them do I give precedence?"

6. II:9: Ulla the elder gave this exposition at the gate of the patriarch: "What is the meaning of Scripture, 'All the kings of the earth shall praise you, Lord, for they have heard the words of your mouth' (Ps. 138:4)? What is stated is not, 'the word of your mouth,' but 'the words of your mouth.' So when the Holy One, blessed be He, said, 'I am the Lord your God' 'you shall have no other Gods before me,' (Ex. 20:2-3), said the nations of the world, 'All he wants is his own self-aggrandizement.' When he said, 'Honor your father and your mother' (Ex. 20:12), they retracted and confessed to the validity of the first statements as well."

7. II:10: They asked R. Ulla, "To what extent is one obligated to honor father and mother?"
   a. II:11: Gloss of a secondary detail of the foregoing.
   b. II:12:Further response to the issue of II:10: Illustrative story: When R. Dimi came, he said, "Once Dama was dressed in a gold embroidered silk coat, sitting among

the Roman nobles, and his mother came along and tore it from him and hit him on the head and spat in his face, but he did not in any way answer back to her."

c. II:13: Further response to the issue of II:10: A Tannaite statement of Abimi b. R. Abbahu: There is he who feeds his father pheasant to eat but this drives the son from the world, and there is he who binds his father up to the grinding wheel, and this brings the son into the world to come. Someone fed the father pheasants but when the father asked how he could afford them, said, "It's none of your business, chew and eat." By contrast, someone was grinding on a mill and the father was summoned for the corvée, so the son said to the father, "You grind for me and I'll go in your place."

d. II:14: Further response to the issue of II:10: Said R. Abbahu, "For instance, my son Abimi carried out in an exemplary manner the religious duty of honor of parents."

e. II:15: Further response to the issue of II:10: Said R. Jacob bar Abbuha to Abbayye, "How about someone like me? For when I come home from the household of the master, father pours a cup for me, and mother mixes – what am I supposed to do?"

f. II:16: Further response to the issue of II:10: R. Tarfon's mother – whenever she wanted to get into bed, he would bend down and let her climb up on his back, and when she wanted to get out, she would step down on him. He went and praised himself in the schoolhouse. They said to him, "So you still haven't got to half the honor that is owing: Has she thrown down a money bag in your presence into the sea, without your answering back to her?"

g. II:17: As above. R. Joseph – when he heard the sound of his mother's steps, he said, "Let me arise before the Presence of God, who approaches."

8. II:18: Said R. Yohanan, "Happy is he who never knew his parents since it is so hard properly to honor them."

9. II:19: R. Yohanan – when his mother was carrying him, his father died, and when his mother bore him, she died.

10. II:20: Free-standing story: R. Assi had an aged mother. She said to him, "I want some jewelry." So he made it for her.

D. REVERSION TO THE EXPOSITION OF THE PROPOSITION OF THE MISHNAH-RULE

Chapter Twenty. Qiddushin

1. II:21: Our rabbis have taught on Tannaite authority: The child must honor the parent in life and after death. In life: How so? If one is obeyed somewhere because of his father, he shouldn't say, "Let me go for my own sake," "Wish me Godspeed for my own sake," "Free me for my own sake," but only, "For my father's sake." And after death: How so? If one was saying something he had heard from his father's own mouth, he should not say, "This is what my father said," but rather, "This is what my father, my teacher, for whose resting place may I be an atonement, said."
2. II:22: Our rabbis have taught on Tannaite authority: A sage changes the name of his father and the name of his teacher, but the interpreter doesn't change the name of his father or the name of his teacher. The sage when using an interpreter to give a teaching he heard from his father does not refer to his father by name but by the formula, "my father and my teacher," but the interpreter doesn't do that.
3. II:23: Our rabbis have taught on Tannaite authority: What is the form of reverence that is owing? The son should not sit in his place, speak in his place, contradict him. What is the form of honor that is owing? The son should feed him, give him drink, dress him, cover him, bring him in and take him out (Sifra CXCIX.I.5).
    a. II:24: The question was raised: "At whose expense must he feed him and so on?"
    b. II:25: Story in illustration of the proposition, Lo, if one's father was violating the teachings of the Torah, he should not say to him, 'Father, you have violated the teachings of the Torah.' Rather, one should say to him, 'Father, this is what is written in the Torah.'"
4. II:26: Eleazar b. Matthias says, "If father says, 'Give me a drink of water,' and I have a religious duty to carry out, I ignore the honor owing to father and I carry out the religious duty, for both father and I are obligated to carry out religious duties."
5. II:27: Said R. Isaac b. Shila said R. Mattenah said R. Hisda, "If a father renounced the honor that is coming to him, the honor that is coming to him is validly renounced. If the master renounced the honor that is coming to him, the honor that is coming to him is not renounced."
6. II:28: Said R. Ashi, "Even from the perspective of him who has said, 'The master who has renounced the honor coming

to him – the honor coming to him is renounced,' nonetheless, the patriarch who has renounced the honor coming to him – the honor coming to him is not renounced."

7. II:29: Our rabbis have taught on Tannaite authority: "You shall rise up before the hoary head" (Lev. 19:32): Might one suppose that one is obligated to rise up even before a malefactor? Scripture says, "elder." An "elder" is only a sage, as it is said, "Collect for me seventy men of the elders of Israel" (Num. 11:16). R. Yosé the Galilean says, "An 'elder' is only one who has acquired wisdom, as it is said, 'The Lord created me at the beginning of his way' (Prov. 8:22)." Might one suppose that one should rise up before him only from a distance? Scripture says, "and honor the face of an elder." If then it is to "honor the face of an elder," might one suppose that one should honor him with money? Scripture says, "rise up...and honor...." Just as "rising up" does not involve an expenditure of money, so "honoring" does not involve an expenditure of money. Might one suppose that he has to rise up before him in the toilet or bathhouse? Scripture says, "You shall rise up and you shall honor": I have commanded you to rise up only in a place in which that confers honor. Might one suppose that if one saw him, one may close his eyes as though he had not seen him? Lo, the matter is handed over to the heart, for it is said, "You shall fear your God, I am the Lord" – in connection with anything that is handed over to the heart, the fear of God is invoked. R. Simeon b. Eleazar says, "How do we know that an elder should not make trouble for others? "Scripture says, 'an elder and you shall fear your God'" (Sifra CCIV:III.1).
   a. II:30: What R. Yosé the Galilean says is the same as what the first Tannaite authority says!
   b. II:31: Further gloss of II:29.
   c. II:32: Further gloss of II:29.
   d. II:33: Further gloss of II:29.
      I. II:34: Topical extension of the foregoing.
   e. II:35: Further gloss of II:29.
   f. II:36: Further gloss of II:29.

E. **TOPICAL COMPOSITE ON RISING BEFORE ONE'S MASTER**
   1. II:37: Said R. Aibu said R. Yannai, "A disciple of a sage is allowed to stand up before his master only morning and night, so that the honor accruing to the master is no more than the honor owing to Heaven."

Chapter Twenty. Qiddushin

2. II:38: Said R. Eleazar, "Any disciple who does not arise before his master is called wicked and will not live a long time, and his learning will be forbidden: 'But it shall not be well with the wicked, neither shall he prolong his days which are as a shadow, because he doesn't fear God' (Qoh. 8:13). Now I don't know the meaning of this 'fear,' but when Scripture says, 'you shall rise up before the hoary head...and fear your God' (Lev. 19:32), then 'fear' means 'rising.'"
3. II:39: The question was raised: If his son was also his master, what is the law about his standing before his father?
4. II:40: The question was raised: What if his son was his master, should his father stand before him?
5. II:41: The question was raised: Is riding equivalent to walking so the disciples stand when the master rides by, or is that not the case?
6. II:42: The question was raised: What is the law about rising before a scroll of the Torah?
7. II:43: "And when Moses went into the tent, all the people rose up and stood and looked after Moses until he was gone into the tent" (Ex. 33:8): R. Ammi and R. Isaac Nappaha – One said, "It was derogatory." The other said, "It was a compliment."

F. FOR EVERY POSITIVE COMMANDMENT DEPENDENT UPON THE TIME OF YEAR, MEN ARE LIABLE, AND WOMEN ARE EXEMPT.

1. III:1: Our rabbis have taught on Tannaite authority: What is the definition of a positive commandment dependent upon the time of day or year? Building a tabernacle at the festival of Tabernacles, carrying the palm branch on that festival, sounding the ram's horn, wearing shoe fringes, putting on phylacteries. And what is the definition of a positive commandment not dependent upon time? The fixing of an amulet to the doorpost, the erection of a parapet (Deut. 22:8), returning lost property, sending forth the dam from the nest (T. Qid. 1:10A-C).
    a. III:2: Is this an encompassing generalization here? But what about unleavened bread, rejoicing on the festivals, and assembly on the Festival of Sukkot in the Seventh Year (Deut. 31:12) which include women, but which depend on a particular time, and for which women are obligated! And furthermore: What about study of the Torah, procreation, and the redemption of the firstborn, which are not religious duties that depend on a particular time, and yet women are exempt from these?

3. III:3: For every positive commandment dependent upon the time of year, men are liable, and women are exempt: How do we know this rule?
4. III:4: What about the building of the tabernacle, which is a positive commandment dependent upon the time of year?
5. III:5: But what about the pilgrimage, which is a positive commandment dependent upon the time of year?

G. AND FOR EVERY POSITIVE COMMANDMENT NOT DEPENDENT UPON THE TIME, MEN AND WOMEN ARE EQUALLY LIABLE. FOR EVERY NEGATIVE COMMANDMENT, WHETHER DEPENDENT UPON THE TIME OR NOT DEPENDENT UPON THE TIME, MEN AND WOMEN ARE EQUALLY LIABLE:
1. IV:1: What is the scriptural basis for this rule?

H. ...EXCEPT FOR NOT MARRING THE CORNERS OF THE BEARD, NOT ROUNDING THE CORNERS OF THE HEAD (LEV. 19:27), AND NOT BECOMING UNCLEAN BECAUSE OF THE DEAD (LEV. 21:1).
1. V:1: There is no problem understanding the exception of defiling oneself to bury a corpse, since it is explicitly written that this applies only to males: "Speak to the priests, the sons of Aaron: No one shall defile himself for the dead among his people" (Lev. 21:1) – the sons of Aaron, not the daughters of Aaron. But how on the basis of Scripture do we know that the same pertains to not marring the corners of the beard, not rounding the corners of the head?
2. V:2: Isi taught as a Tannaite statement: "So, too, are women exempt from the prohibition of baldness" (Lev. 21:5).

IX. MISHNAH-TRACTATE QIDDUSHIN 1:8
A. THE CULTIC RITES OF LAYING ON OF HANDS:
1. I:1: For it is written, "Speak to the sons of Israel...and he shall lay his hand upon the head of the burnt-offering" (Lev. 7:29-30) – The sons of Israel, not the daughters of Israel do it.
B. WAVING:
1. II:1: For it is written, "Speak to the sons of Israel...the fat...may be waved" (Lev. 6:7). The sons of Israel, not the daughters of Israel do it.
C. DRAWING NEAR:
1. III:1: For it is written, "And this is the law of the meal-offering: The sons of Aaron shall offer it – The sons of Aaron, not the daughters of Aaron do it.
D. TAKING THE HANDFUL:

Chapter Twenty. Qiddushin   261

    1. IV:1: For it is written, "And he shall bring it to Aaron's sons, the priests, and he shall take out of it his handful of the fine flour" (Lev. 2:2) – The sons of Aaron, not the daughters of Aaron do it.

E. BURNING THE FAT:

    1. V:1: For it is written, "And Aaron's sons shall burn it" (Lev. 2:2). The sons of Aaron, not the daughters of Aaron do it.

F. BREAKING THE NECK OF A BIRD:

    1. VI:1: For it is written, "And he shall wring off his head and burn it on the altar" – Treating as comparable wringing the neck and burning the fat.

G. AND RECEIVING THE BLOOD APPLY TO MEN AND NOT TO WOMEN:

    1. VII:1: For it is written, "And the priests, the sons of Aaron," and a master has said, "'And they shall bring' refers to receiving the blood."

H. SPRINKLING:

    1. VIII:1: Sprinkling what? If it is the blood of the red cow, "Eleazar" the priest is written in that connection. And if it is the blood that is sprinkled in the inner sanctum of the Temple for example, on the veil and golden altar, then the anointed priest is required for that, for example, Lev. 4:5.

I. ...EXCEPT IN THE CASE OF A MEAL-OFFERING OF AN ACCUSED WIFE AND OF A NAZIRITE GIRL, WHICH THEY WAVE.

    1. IX:1: Said R. Eleazar to R. Josiah, his contemporary, "You may not take your seat until you explain the following matter: How do we know that the meal-offering of the accused wife had to be waved?" He replied, "How do we know indeed! It is written, 'And he shall wave' (Num. 5:25)!"

X. MISHNAH-TRACTATE QIDDUSHIN 1:9

    A. EVERY COMMANDMENT WHICH IS DEPENDENT UPON THE LAND APPLIES ONLY IN THE LAND, AND WHICH DOES NOT DEPEND UPON THE LAND APPLIES BOTH IN THE LAND AND OUTSIDE THE LAND:

        1. I:1: What is the meaning of, which is dependent upon, and what is the meaning of, which does not depend upon? If I say that the sense of which is dependent upon pertains where the language, "entering the Land" is used, and the sense of which does not depend upon pertains where the language, "entering the Land" is not used, then what about the matters of phylacteries and the disposition of the firstling of an ass, which pertain both in the Land of Israel and abroad, even though the language "entering the Land" is used in their connection?

2. I:2: What is the scriptural basis for that rule?

B. ...EXCEPT FOR ORLAH PRODUCE OF A FRUIT TREE IN THE FIRST THREE YEARS OF ITS GROWTH AND MIXED SEEDS. R. ELIEZER SAYS, "ALSO: EXCEPT FOR THE PROHIBITION AGAINST EATING NEW PRODUCE BEFORE THE OMER IS WAVED ON THE SIXTEENTH OF NISAN."

1. II:1: The question was raised: Is the dissenting opinion of R. Eliezer meant to yield a lenient ruling or a strict ruling? It is meant to yield a strict ruling, and this is the sense of the passage: The initial authority says, except for orlah and mixed seeds, these deriving from a traditional law; that is so, even though one might argue, to the contrary, these represent an obligation that is connected with the soil, but the consideration of the use of new produce only after the waving of the barley sheaf is practiced only in the Land but not overseas. How come? "Dwelling" means, after taking possession and settling down Lev. 23:14: It shall be a statute throughout your generations in all your dwellings," and that might mean, even outside of the Land; but even in the Land this rule came into force only after the Israelites had settled down, not while they were fighting for and dividing up the country. And then R. Eliezer comes along to say: Also the consideration of the use of new produce only after the waving of the barley sheaf is practiced in the Land but not overseas. How come? "Dwelling" means, anywhere where you dwell.

   a. II:2: Secondary development of the result of the foregoing.

      I. II:3: Now that you have taken the position, Every religious duty that is an obligation of the person applies whether in the Land or abroad, but if it is an obligation that is incumbent upon the soil, it applies only in the land, then what is the point of "dwelling" that the All-Merciful spelled out in connection with the Sabbath?

      II. II:4: And what is the point of "dwelling" that the All-Merciful spelled out in connection with the forbidden fat and blood at Lev. 3:17?

      III. II:5: And what is the point of "dwelling" that the All-Merciful spelled out in connection with unleavened bread and bitter herbs for Passover at Ex. 12:20?

      IV. II:6: And what is the point of "dwelling" that the All-Merciful spelled out in connection with the

Chapter Twenty. Qiddushin

phylacteries and the firstling of an ass which are not limited to the Land of Israel?

v. II:7: Now from the viewpoint that "dwelling" means, wherever you live, there are no problems; that is in line with the statement, "And they ate of the new produce of the land on the day after the Passover" (Josh. 5:11). They ate on the day after Passover, but not before, and that proves that the sheaf of first barley was offered and then they ate. But from the perspective of him who maintains that "dwelling" means, after the inheritance and settling down on the Land, why did they not eat the new produce forthwith?

   A. II:8: It has further been taught on Tannaite authority: "And the children of Israel ate the manna forty years, until they came to a land inhabited; they ate the manna until they came to the borders of the land of Canaan" (Ex. 16:35): Well, did they really eat it for forty years? Didn't they eat it for forty years less thirty days?

   B. II:9: It has further been taught on Tannaite authority: "On the seventh of Adar, Moses died, and on the seventh of Adar, he was born. How do we know that on the seventh of Adar, Moses died? "So Moses the servant of the Lord died there" (Deut. 34:5); "And the children of Israel wept for Moses in the plains of Moab thirty days" (Deut. 34:8); "Moses my servant is dead, now therefore arise, go over this Jordan" (Josh. 1:2); "Pass through the midst of the camp and command the people saying, Prepare you food for within three days you are to pass over this Jordan" (Josh. 1:11); "And the people came up out of the Jordan on the tenth day of the first month Nisan." Deduct from the tenth of Nisan the prior thirty-three days, and you learn that on the seventh of Adar, Moses died.

4. II:10: It has been taught on Tannaite authority: R. Simeon b. Yohai says, "Three religious duties were assigned to Israel when they entered the Land, and they apply both to the Land

and abroad: And it is logical that they should apply: If the consideration of new grain to be eaten only after the waving of the sheaf of barley on the fifteenth of Nisan, which is not forbidden forever but only until that rite, and from which it is not forbidden to derive any kind of benefit whatsoever, and from which the prohibition can be raised through the rite, applies both in the Land of Israel and abroad, then the prohibition of mixed seeds, the prohibition of which is permanent, and the prohibition of which extends to deriving any sort of benefit from the crop, and from which it is not possible to raise the prohibition, surely should apply both in the Land and abroad; and the same logic on two grounds applies also to orlah fruit."

5. II:11: R. Eleazar b. R. Simeon says, "Every commandment for which the Israelites became liable before they entered the Land applies in the Land and abroad, and every commandment for which the Israelites became liable only after they came into the Land applies only in the Land, except for the forgiveness of debts, the redemption of fields that have been sold, and the sending forth free of the Hebrew slave in the Seventh Year. For even though they became liable to them only after they had come into the Land, they do apply in the Land and abroad" (T. Qid. 1:12A-C).

   a. II:12: Except for the forgiveness of debts: But that's a personal duty and applies even before entry into the Land!

   b. II:13: The sending forth free of the Hebrew slave in the Seventh Year: But that's a personal duty and applies even before entry into the Land!

6. II:14: We have learned in the Mishnah: Consumption in any locale of new produce, that is, that on behalf of which the omer has not yet been offered, is forbidden by Scripture. And the prohibition against eating produce which is orlah that is, deriving from fruit trees in the first three years of their growth applies outside of the Land of Israel by law. And the prohibition against planting together diverse kinds in a vineyard applies outside of the Land of Israel by authority of the scribes (M. Orl. 3:9Kff.). With reference to the clause, and the prohibition against eating produce which is orlah applies outside of the Land of Israel by law, what is the meaning of by law? Said R. Judah said Samuel, "It means, a law practiced in the province as matter of local

Chapter Twenty. Qiddushin 265

custom." Ulla said R. Yohanan said, "It is a law given to Moses at Sinai."

    a. II:15: Said Levi to Samuel, "Your eminence, provide me with produce that may or may not be orlah fruit and I'll eat it."

    b. II:16: Said R. Assi said R. Yohanan, "The prohibition of orlah produce abroad derives from a law revealed to Moses at Sinai."

    c. II:17: Said R. Assi said R. Yohanan, "By the ruling of the Torah, violators of the prohibition of mixed seeds in the exile are flogged."

        I. II:18: Case.

        II. II:19: Case.

XI. MISHNAH-TRACTATE QIDDUSHIN 1:10A-D

    A. WHOEVER DOES A SINGLE COMMANDMENT – THEY DO WELL FOR HIM AND LENGTHEN HIS DAYS. AND HE INHERITS THE LAND. AND WHOEVER DOES NOT DO A SINGLE COMMANDMENT – THEY DO NOT DO WELL FOR HIM AND DO NOT LENGTHEN HIS DAYS. AND HE DOES NOT INHERIT THE LAND.

    1. I:1: By way of contradiction: These are things the benefit of which a person enjoys in this world, while the principal remains for him in the world to come: Deeds in honor of father and mother, performance of righteous deeds, and acts which bring peace between a man and his fellow. But the study of Torah is as important as all of them together (M. Peah 1:1C-E). Thus only for these is one reward in this world, while the Mishnah says that that is so of any precept.

        a. I:2: Secondary analysis of the solution to the foregoing problem.

            I. I:3: Illustrative story.

    2. I:4: R. Tobi bar R. Qisna contrasted for Raba the following rules: "We have learned in the Mishnah, whoever does a single commandment – they do well for him. So if he does it, that is so, but if not, not, and by contrast: If one sits and does not transgress, they give him a reward like that going to one who does a religious duty!" He said to him, "The latter speaks of a case in which an opportunity to sin comes to hand and he is saved from it."

        a. I:5: Story.

        b. I:6: Story.

    3. I:7: Raba pointed out to R. Nahman the following contrast: "We have learned in the Mishnah: These are things the

benefit of which a person enjoys in this world, while the principal remains for him in the world to come: Deeds in honor of father and mother, performance of righteous deeds, and acts which bring peace between a man and his fellow. But the study of Torah is as important as all of them together (M. Pe. 1:1C-F). And with respect to honor of parents, it is written, 'that your days may be long and that it may go well with you' (Deut. 5:16); of performance of righteous deeds: 'He who pursues righteousness and loving kindness finds life, righteousness, and honor' (Prov. 21:21). As to bringing peace, it is said, 'seek peace and pursue it' (Ps. 34:15), and said R. Abbahu, 'We learn by verbal analogy the meaning of pursuing in two distinct passages; here, 'seek peace and pursue it,' and elsewhere, 'he who pursues after righteousness and loving kindness' (Prov. 21:21). As to study of the Torah: 'For that is your life and the length of your days' (Deut. 30:20). But as to sending forth the dam from the nest it is written, 'that it may be well with you and that you may prolong your days' (Deut. 22:7). So why not add this item to the list?"

4. I:8: Merit has both principal and interest: "Say you of the righteous when he is good that they shall eat the fruit of their doings" (Isa. 3:10). Wickedness has principal but no interest: "Woe to the wicked man who is evil, for the reward of his hands shall be given to him" (Isa. 3:11).

5. I:9: Good intention joins with deeds: "Then they that feared the Lord spoke with one another, and the Lord listened and heard and a book of remembrance was written before him for those who feared the Lord and who thought about his name" (Mal. 3:16).

6. I:10: Said R. Abbahu in the name of R. Hanina, "It is better for someone to transgress in private but not profane the Name of Heaven in public: 'As for you, house of Israel, thus says the Lord God: Go, serve every one his idols, and hereafter also, if you will not obey me; but my holy name you shall not profane' (Ezek. 20:39)."

7. I:11: We have learned in the Mishnah there: They do not allow credit in connection with profaning the name of God, whether it was done unwittingly or intentionally.

8. I:12: Our rabbis have taught on Tannaite authority: One should always see himself as if he is half meritorious and half guilty. If he did a single commandment, happy is he,

for he has inclined the balance for himself to the side of merit. If he committed a single transgression, woe is he, for he has inclined the balance to the side of guilt. Concerning this one it is said, "One sinner destroys much good" (Qoh. 9:18), for on account of a single sin that he commits, much good is lost to him. R. Eleazar b. R. Simeon says, "For the world is judged by the conduct of the majority in it, and an individual is judged by the majority of the deeds that he has done; if he did a single commandment, happy is he, for he has inclined the balance for himself and for the world as well to the side of merit. If he committed a single transgression, woe is he, for he has inclined the balance to the side of guilt for himself and for the world, for it is said, 'One sinner destroys much good' (Qoh. 9:18) – for on account of a single sin that he commits, much good is lost to him and to the whole world." R. Simeon b. Yohai says, "If a man was righteous his entire life but at the end he rebelled, he loses the whole, for it is said, 'The righteousness of the righteous shall not deliver him in the day of his transgression' (Ezek. 33:12). And even if one is completely wicked all his life but repents at the end, he is not reproached with his wickedness, for it is said, 'And as for the wickedness of the wicked, he shall not fall thereby in the day that he turns from his wickedness' (Ezek. 33:12)" (T. Qid. 1:13-15).

XII. MISHNAH-TRACTATE QIDDUSHIN 1:10E-G
   A. WHOEVER HAS LEARNING IN SCRIPTURE, MISHNAH, AND RIGHT CONDUCT WILL NOT QUICKLY SIN, SINCE IT IS SAID, "AND A THREEFOLD CORD IS NOT QUICKLY BROKEN" (QOH. 4:12).
   1. I:1: Said R. Eliezer bar Sadoq, "To what are the righteous compared in this world? To a tree that is standing in a clean place, with its foliage extending from it to an unclean place. What do people say? 'Cut off the foliage from the tree so that the whole of it may be clean, as is its character.' Thus the Holy One, blessed be He, brings suffering upon the righteous in this world so that they will inherit the world to come: 'And though your beginning is small, yet the latter end shall greatly increase' (Job 8:7). To what are the wicked compared in this world? To a tree that is standing in an unclean place, with its foliage extending from it to a clean place. What do people say? 'Cut off the foliage from the

tree, so that the whole of it may be unclean, as is its character' (Abot deR. Nathan XXXIX.X.1).

2. I:2: Once R. Tarfon and the elders were reclining at a banquet in the upper room of the house of Niseh in Lud. This question was raised for them: "Is study greater or is action greater?"

3. I:3: It has been taught on Tannaite authority: R. Yosé says, "Great is study, for it preceded the commandment to separate dough-offering by forty years, the commandments governing priestly rations and tithes by fifty-four years, the commandments covering remission of debts by sixty-one years, the commandment concerning the Jubilee Year by one hundred and three years." The Torah was given to Israel two months after the Exodus from Egypt, but liability to dough-offering came into force forty years later, and so throughout.

B. **AND WHOEVER DOES NOT HAVE LEARNING IN SCRIPTURE, MISHNAH, AND RIGHT CONDUCT HAS NO SHARE IN SOCIETY.**

1. II:1: Said R. Yohanan, "And he is invalid to give testimony."
2. II:2: Our rabbis have taught on Tannaite authority: He who eats out in the marketplace – lo, he is like a dog. And there are those who say, "He is invalid to give testimony."
3. II:3: Expounded Bar Qappara, "A temperamental person gets nothing but his anger. To a good man they feed the good taste of the fruit of his deeds. And whoever does not have learning in Scripture, Mishnah, and right conduct – forbid yourself by a vow from having any good from him: 'Nor sits in the seat of the scorners' (Prov. 1:1) – such a person is the very seat of the scorners.

XIII. MISHNAH-TRACTATE QIDDUSHIN 2:1A-C

A. **A MAN EFFECTS BETROTHAL ON HIS OWN OR THROUGH HIS AGENT. A WOMAN BECOMES BETROTHED ON HER OWN OR THROUGH HER AGENT:**

1. I:1: A man effects betrothal on his own or through his agent: If it is clearly stated that a man effects betrothal through his agent, can there be any question that a man effects betrothal on his own?

2. I:2: It has been stated: A woman may accept a token of betrothal either on her own part or through an agent. If it is clearly stated that A woman may accept a token of betrothal through an agent, can there be any question that it may be done on her own?

Chapter Twenty. Qiddushin

B. A MAN BETROTHS HIS DAUGHTER WHEN SHE IS A GIRL ON HIS OWN OR THROUGH HIS AGENT.

1. II:1: May then he do so when she is prepubescent but not when she is a minor? Then that supports the position of Rab. For said R. Judah said Rab, and some say, R. Eleazar, "It is forbidden for a man to betroth his daughter when she is a minor; he may do so only when she grows up and says, 'I want So-and-so.'"

2. II:2: As to the fact that an agent may participate, how on the basis of Scripture do we know that fact? So we have found the principle of agency in the matter of divorce. How on the basis of Scripture do we find that same principle when it comes to a betrothal?

   a. II:3: Secondary development of the foregoing. And what about that which we have learned in the Mishnah: One who says to his agent, "Go and separate heave-offering for me" – he agent separates heave-offering in accordance with the disposition of the householder. And if he does not know the disposition of the householder, he separates the average amount, one-fiftieth. If the agent unintentionally separated one-tenth less or more than the percentage he needed to separate – that which he separates still is valid heave-offering (M. Ter. 4:4A-G)? Now how do we know this? Should you say, derive the principle from the rule governing writs of divorce, the two processes are to be differentiated, for it is the definitive trait of a writ of divorce that it is a secular issue.

      I. II:4: Expansion of a detail of the foregoing.

      II. II:5: Continuation of II:4.

   b. II:6: Now when we learned in the Mishnah, He who causes a fire to break out through the action of a deaf-mute, idiot, or minor, is exempt from punishment under the laws of man, but liable to punishment under the laws of heaven. If he did so through the action of a person of sound senses, the person of sound senses is liable (M. B.Q. 6:4A-B). But why should this be the case? Why not say, a man's agent is equivalent to the man himself so the sender is liable?

   c. II:7: And as to that which has been taught on Tannaite authority: If the agent did not carry out his errand in committing an act of sacrilege, the agent is responsible and inadvertently has committed the act of sacrilege (M. Me. 6:1C-D) – when the person carried out the commission of the householder, then in any event the householder has performed an act of sacrilege. But why not say, an agent cannot be appointed to carry out a violation of the law?

> I. II:8: Secondary expansion of the foregoing: Now that we have found that that rule applies to the case of sacrifices slaughtered outside of the tabernacle. How do we know that the same rule applies throughout the Torah that an agent who violates the law of the Torah is culpable, not the one who sent him?
>> A. II:9: Exegetical issues contained in the foregoing are now worked out.
> d. II:10: And as to that which is stated as a Tannaite rule: He who says to his agent, "Go kill So-and-so" – the agent is liable if he does so, and the one who sends him is exempt. Shammai the Elder says in the name of the prophet Haggai, "The one who sends him is liable as well: 'You have slain him with the sword of the children of Ammon' (2 Sam. 12:9)."

3. II:11: It has been stated: Rab said, "An agent may serve as a witness." The household of R. Shila say, "An agent may not serve as a witness."

4. II:12: Said Raba said R. Nahman, "If one said to two persons, 'Go and betroth that woman for me,' those who serve as his agents also serve as his witnesses, and so is the law with regard to a writ of divorce, and so is the law with regard to property cases."

> a. II:13: And it was necessary to make mention of all three classes of action.
> b. II:14: And what is R. Nahman's view? If he takes the view, He who lends money to his fellow before witnesses has to collect the money before witnesses as well, still, these are interested parties, for if they should say, "we didn't pay him back," the debtor can say to them, "Then pay me" for he may have entrusted them the money before witnesses, which is the same as lending it to them; they are personally concerned and as such are inadmissible as witnesses. So it must follow that he takes the position, He who lends money to his

fellow before witnesses doesn't have to collect the money before witnesses, for, since they can claim, "We paid it back to the debtor," they also can testify, "We paid it back to the creditor."

5. II:15: A man betroths his daughter when she is a girl on his own or through his agent: There we have learned in the Mishnah: A betrothed girl – she and her father receive her writ of divorce. Said R. Judah, "Two hands together do not make acquisition simultaneously. But her father receives her writ of divorce alone. And any girl who is not able to keep watch over her writ of divorce cannot be divorced" (M. Git. 6:2G-K). Said R. Simeon b. Laqish, "As is the dispute with respect to writs of divorced, so there is a dispute with respect to betrothals." And R. Yohanan said, "There is a dispute as to writs of divorce, but as to betrothals, all parties concur that the father may do so, but she may not."

   a. II:16: And said R. Yosé bar Hanina, "What is the operative consideration behind R. Yohanan's account of the position of rabbis? In the matter of the writ of divorce, she reverts thereby to the domain of her father, so either she or her father may receive the writ; but as to a betrothal, in which case she removes herself from the domain of her father, her father but not she receives the token of divorce."

   b. II:17: Reason supports the response of R. Yohanan the declaration made against her will, since the language is used, which is not the case with respect to tokens of betrothal which only the father can receive. But may one say that that represents a refutation of the position of R. Simeon b. Laqish "As is the dispute with respect to writs of divorced, so there is a dispute with respect to betrothals"?

      I. II:18: Secondary gloss on the dispute.

6. II:19: Raba asked this question of R. Nahman: "Can a prepubescent girl appoint an agent to accept a writ of divorce from her husband? Is she comparable to her father's hand or her father's courtyard? "Is she comparable to her father's hand: Just as her father may appoint an agent, so she, too, has the power to appoint an agent. Or perhaps she is comparable to her father's courtyard: Until the writ of divorce actually reaches her hand, she is not divorced."

7. II:20: It has been stated: A minor who was betrothed without her father's knowledge and consent said Samuel, "She nonetheless requires a writ of divorce and also the exercise of the right of refusal."
   a. II:21: Said R. Nahman, "But that is the case that she requires a writ of divorce only if they negotiated the betrothal afterward with the father." Ulla said, "Even the right of refusal is not required."
8. II:22: It has been stated: If the man who betrothed a minor without her father's knowledge and consent died, and she fell to the lot of the surviving brothers for levirate marriage – Said R. Huna said Rab, "The minor girl may exercise the right of refusal against the statement of the levir that he plans to enter into levirate marriage, but she may not exercise the right of refusal so as to sever the levirate bond itself. How does this work out? If the levir performed the act of bespeaking, she requires a writ of divorce and also has to go through the rite of removing the shoe and also has to exercise the right of refusal. She requires a writ of divorce: perhaps her father was reconciled to the betrothal of the second party the levir; And also has to go through the rite of removing the shoe: Perhaps her father was reconciled to the betrothal of the first party the now deceased brother; And also has to exercise the right of refusal: Perhaps her father was reconciled to the betrothal of neither the second party nor the first, and people may say, the betrothal with her sister is null."
   a. II:23: Case: Two men were drinking wine under the willows in Babylonia. One of them took a cup of wine, gave it to the other, and said, "Let your daughter be betrothed to my son."
   b. II:24: Case. There was a man who in the marketplace betrothed a minor with a bunch of vegetables. Said Rabina, "Even in the view of him who said, 'we take account of the possibility that the father was reconciled,' that is the case only if the act was done in a respectful way and not in a disgraceful way."
   c. II:25: Case. There was someone who said, "She should marry one of my relatives." She said, "She should marry one of my relatives." While they were eating and drinking at the betrothal party, his relative went up to a loft and betrothed her.

Chapter Twenty. Qiddushin

9. II:26: If the daughter of an Israelite became betrothed with her father's knowledge and consent to a priest, and her father went overseas and the girl went and got married consummating the marriage – said Rab, "She may continue to eat food in the status of priestly rations which marriage to the priest confers upon her until her father comes home and protests against the consummation of the marriage." R. Assi said, "She may not eat food in the status of priestly rations, lest her father come and protest the consummation of the marriage, and it will retroactively come about that a non-priest is eating priestly rations."

10. II:27: If she became betrothed with her father's knowledge and consent and she consummated the marriage without, and her father is here at hand – R. Huna said, "She may not eat food in the status of priestly rations." R Jeremiah bar Abba said, "She may eat food in the status of priestly rations."

11. II:28: If she accepted tokens of betrothal without her father's knowledge and consent and consummated the marriage without her father's knowledge and consent, and her father is here at hand – R. Huna said, "She may eat food in the status of priestly rations." R Jeremiah bar Abba said, "She may not eat food in the status of priestly rations."

12. II:29: It has been stated: A minor who accepted tokens of betrothal without her father's knowledge and consent – said Rab, "Either she or her father has the power to repudiate the betrothal." And R. Assi said, "Her father can but she can't."

13. II:30:

XIV. MISHNAH-TRACTATE QIDDUSHIN 2:1D-I

A. HE WHO SAYS TO A WOMAN, "BE BETROTHED TO ME FOR THIS DATE, BE BETROTHED TO ME WITH THIS," IF EITHER ONE OF THEM IS OF THE VALUE OF A PENNY, SHE IS BETROTHED, AND IF NOT, SHE IS NOT BETROTHED.

1. I:1: Who is the Tannaite authority behind the repeated formula, "Be betrothed to me for this date, be betrothed to me with this"?

B. IF HE SAID TO HER, "BY THIS, AND BY THIS, AND BY THIS" – IF ALL OF THEM TOGETHER ARE WORTH A PENNY, SHE IS BETROTHED, AND IF NOT, SHE IS NOT BETROTHED. IF SHE WAS EATING THEM ONE BY ONE, SHE IS NOT BETROTHED, UNLESS ONE OF THEM IS WORTH A PENNY.

1. II:1: To which clause does this statement pertain? Shall we say it is to the first? Then why specify that she was eating them? Even if she put them down, the rule is the same, since he says, "Be betrothed to me for this date"? So it must refer to the concluding clause, and that is so, even if there was a penny's worth in the first date only? But then it is a debt and a betrothal cannot be accomplished through remission of a debt! If he says, be betrothed to me with this one and this one, and she eats them one by one, his statement is considered as a whole; as soon as she eats one, she cannot be betrothed by it, since his statement was as yet incomplete, and it becomes a debt.
2. II:2: It has been stated: He who betroths his sister – Rab said, "The money is returned since the brother has not got the legal right to betroth his sister." Samuel said, "The money is considered a gift."
3. II:3: "By this, and by this, and by this" – if all of them together are worth a penny, she is betrothed, and if not, she is not betrothed. If she was eating them one by one, she is not betrothed, unless one of them is worth a penny: said Raba, "That rule applies only if he made the statement to her, By this, and by this, and by this, but if he said to her, 'By these,' then even if she is then eating them one by one, she is nonetheless betrothed, for what she eats belongs to her."
   a. II:4: Gloss of a secondary statement in the foregoing.
4. II:5: With reference to the phrase in the Mishnah paragraph, unless one of them is worth a penny: That poses no problem to the position of him who said that that language refers to the second clause, and what is the meaning of the language, unless one of them is worth a penny? It means, Unless the last of them is worth a penny. Here, too, then, the sense is, Unless the last of them is worth a penny. But from the perspective of Rab and Samuel, both of whom maintain that it pertains to the opening clause of the Mishnah, being required to state the rule governing eating, then what we have here is comprehensive statements taken into account without detailed enumerations! How do they explain "unless one of them is worthy a penny," for the clause, "with this and this and this" is a comprehensive statement, insofar as it is taught that if they are all together worth that much and so on; there is no clause in the passage cited just now that is

Chapter Twenty. Qiddushin

equivalent to the first clause in the Mishnah; now according to Ammi, there is no problem, since in the Mishnah too, "if she eats" refers to the second clause, that is, to his comprehensive statement; but according to Rab and Samuel, it must refer to a detailed enumeration, for example, "by this by this" but there is no such clause in the cited Tannaite statement.

5. II:6: Said Rab, "He who betroths a woman with a loan remitting a loan she has already received from him – she is not betrothed, for a loan is handed over to be spent" this money that he gives becomes her own and he is not giving her anything at all.

    a. II:7: Secondary development of a subordinate issue.

        i. II:8: Extension of the foregoing.

XV. MISHNAH-TRACTATE QIDDUSHIN 2:2

A. "BE BETROTHED TO ME FOR THIS CUP OF WINE," AND IT TURNS OUT TO BE HONEY – "...OF HONEY" – AND IT TURNS OUT TO BE OF WINE, "...WITH THIS SILVER DENAR" – AND IT TURNS OUT TO BE GOLD, "...WITH THIS GOLD ONE" – AND IT TURNS OUT TO BE SILVER – "...ON CONDITION THAT I AM RICH" – AND HE TURNS OUT TO BE POOR, "...ON CONDITION THAT I AM POOR" – AND HE TURNS OUT TO BE RICH – SHE IS NOT BETROTHED.

1. I:1: Our rabbis have taught on Tannaite authority: "Be betrothed to me with this cup" – One Tannaite formulation: "With it and its contents" is his meaning, and if they are worth a penny in all, the betrothal is valid. And it has further been taught on Tannaite authority: With it, but not what is in it. And it has further been taught on Tannaite authority: with what is in it but not with it itself (T. Qid. 2:3C-F).

B. R. SIMEON SAYS, "IF HE DECEIVED HER TO HER ADVANTAGE, SHE IS BETROTHED."

1. II:1: But doesn't R. Simeon accept the following: Wine, and it turned out to be vinegar; vinegar, and it turned out to be wine – both parties have the power to retract (M. B.B. 5:6K-L)? Therefore, there are people who are perfectly happy with wine, others with vinegar; so here, too, some are happy with silver and not with gold at all.

    a. II:2: Said Abbayye, "R. Simeon, Rabban Simeon b. Gamaliel, and R. Eleazar all take the view that, in a case such as this, in giving these instructions, all he was doing was giving him good advice on how to proceed 'showing him the place'."

2. II:3: Said Ulla, "The Mishnah's controversy concerns only a monetary advantage, but as to a genealogical advantage, all parties concur that she is not betrothed. How come? 'I really don't want a shoe that is bigger than my foot.'"
3. II:4: Our rabbis have taught on Tannaite authority: "On condition that I am able to read the Torah in the synagogue" – once he has read three verses in the synagogue, lo, this woman is betrothed. R. Judah says, "Only if he both reads and interprets."
   a. II:5: Gloss of the foregoing.
      I. II:6: Gloss of the foregoing.
4. II:7: "On condition that I can repeat Mishnah" – Hezekiah said, "This means, laws." R. Yohanan said, "This means, the Torah."
   a. II:8: Gloss.
5. II:9: If he said, "On condition that I am a disciple," they do not say, "A disciple like Simeon b. Azzai or Simeon b. Zoma," but in the case of anyone whom they ask a question concerning any passage in his studies which he can answer, even in tractate Kallah, that would meet the criterion. If he said, "On condition that I am a sage," they do not say, "like the sages of Yavneh, like R. Aqiba and his colleagues," but in the case of anyone whom they ask a question of wisdom in any context and he says the answer that would meet the criterion. If he said, "On condition that I am strong," they do not say, "Like Abner b. Ner or Joab b. Zeruiah," but so long as he is held in awe by his friends because of his strength that would meet the criterion. If he said, "On condition that I am rich," they do not say, "Like R. Eleazar b. Harsom or R. Eleazar b. Azariah," but so long as he is honored by his townsfolk because of his wealth, that would meet the criterion. If he said, "On condition that I am righteous," even if he is completely wicked, she is betrothed, for he may have repented in his heart. If he said, "On condition that I am wicked," even if he is completely righteous, she is betrothed, for he may have considered in his heart the worship of idols.
6. II:10: Ten qabs of wisdom came down into the world, nine were taken by the Land of Israel, and one by the rest of the entire world. Ten qabs of beauty came down into the world, nine were taken by Jerusalem, and one by the rest of the entire world. Ten qabs of wealth came down into the world,

Chapter Twenty. Qiddushin

nine were taken by the earliest Romans, and one by the rest of the entire world. Ten qabs of poverty came down into the world, nine were taken by Babylonia, and one by the rest of the entire world. Ten qabs of arrogance came down into the world, nine were taken by Elam, and one by the rest of the entire world.

XVI. MISHNAH-TRACTATE QIDDUSHIN 2:3

A. "...ON CONDITION THAT I AM A PRIEST," AND HE TURNS OUT TO BE A LEVITE, "...ON CONDITION THAT I AM A LEVITE," AND HE TURNS OUT TO BE A PRIEST, "...A NETIN," AND HE TURNS OUT TO BE A MAMZER, "...A MAMZER," AND HE TURNS OUT TO BE A NETIN, "...A TOWN DWELLER," AND HE TURNS OUT TO BE A VILLAGER, "...A VILLAGER," AND HE TURNS OUT TO BE A TOWN DWELLER, "...ON CONDITION THAT MY HOUSE IS NEAR THE BATH," AND IT TURNS OUT TO BE FAR AWAY, "...FAR," AND IT TURNS OUT TO BE NEAR: "...ON CONDITION THAT I HAVE A DAUGHTER OR A SLAVE GIRL WHO IS A HAIRDRESSER'" AND HE HAS NONE, "...ON CONDITION THAT I HAVE NONE," AND HE HAS ONE; "...ON CONDITION THAT I HAVE NO CHILDREN," AND HE HAS; "...ON CONDITION THAT HE HAS," AND HE HAS NONE – IN THE CASE OF ALL OF THEM, EVEN THOUGH SHE SAYS, "IN MY HEART I WANTED TO BECOME BETROTHED TO HIM DESPITE THAT FACT," SHE IS NOT BETROTHED. AND SO IS THE RULE IF SHE DECEIVED HIM.

1. I:1: There was someone who sold off his property intending to emigrate to the Land of Israel, but when he made the sale, he said nothing whatsoever. Said Raba, "This is a mental stipulation, and a mental stipulation is null."
2. I:2: There was someone who sold off his property intending to emigrate to the Land of Israel, emigrated, but then couldn't settle down. Said Raba, "Whoever emigrates, it is with the intention of settling down, and this man hasn't done it so the sale is null, since it is a prevailing stipulation."
3. I:3: There was someone who sold off his property intending to emigrate to the Land of Israel, but in the end didn't emigrate. Said R. Ashi, "He could have gone if he'd wanted to."

XVII. MISHNAH-TRACTATE QIDDUSHIN 2:4

A. HE WHO SAYS TO HIS MESSENGER, "GO AND BETROTH MISS SO-AND-SO FOR ME, IN SUCH-AND-SUCH A PLACE," AND HE WENT AND BETROTHED HER FOR HIM IN SOME OTHER PLACE, SHE IS NOT BETROTHED. IF HE

SAID, "...LO, SHE IS IN SUCH-AND-SUCH A PLACE," AND HE BETROTHED HER IN SOME OTHER PLACE, LO, SHE IS BETROTHED.

1. I:1: We have learned in the Mishnah precisely the same rule with reference to writs of divorce: He who says, "Give this writ of divorce to my wife in such-and-such a place," and he the messenger delivered it to her in some other place – it is invalid. If he said, "Lo, she is in such-and-such a place," and he gave it to her in some other place, it is valid (M. Git. 6:3G-J).

XVIII. MISHNAH-TRACTATE QIDDUSHIN 2:5

A. HE WHO BETROTHS A WOMAN ON CONDITION THAT SHE IS NOT ENCUMBERED BY VOWS, AND SHE TURNS OUT TO BE ENCUMBERED BY VOWS – SHE IS NOT BETROTHED. IF HE MARRIED HER WITHOUT SPECIFYING AND SHE TURNED OUT TO BE ENCUMBERED BY VOWS, SHE GOES FORTH WITHOUT COLLECTING HER MARRIAGE CONTRACT. ...ON CONDITION THAT THERE ARE NO BLEMISHES ON HER, AND SHE TURNS OUT TO HAVE BLEMISHES, SHE IS NOT BETROTHED. IF HE MARRIED HER WITHOUT SPECIFYING AND SHE TURNED OUT TO HAVE BLEMISHES, SHE GOES FORTH WITHOUT COLLECTING HER MARRIAGE CONTRACT. ALL BLEMISHES WHICH INVALIDATE PRIESTS FROM SERVING IN THE TEMPLE INVALIDATE WOMEN.

1. I:1: We have learned this rule in the Mishnah with respect to marriage contracts!

XIX. MISHNAH-TRACTATE QIDDUSHIN 2:6

A. HE WHO BETROTHS TWO WOMEN WITH SOMETHING WORTH A PENNY, OR ONE WOMAN WITH SOMETHING WORTH LESS THAN A PENNY, EVEN THOUGH HE SENT ALONG ADDITIONAL PRESENTS AFTERWARD, SHE IS NOT BETROTHED, SINCE HE SENT THE PRESENTS LATER ON ONLY BECAUSE OF THE ORIGINAL ACT OF BETROTHAL WHICH WAS NULL. AND SO IN THE CASE OF A MINOR WHO BETROTHED A WOMAN.

1. I:1: He who betroths two women with something worth a penny, or one woman with something worth less than a penny.... And so in the case of a minor who betrothed a woman: It was necessary to state all three cases. For had we been informed only of the rule concerning a penny's worth for two women, I might have thought that, since the money has gone forth from him, he may err thinking that the betrothal was valid; but with regard to use of less than a penny's worth, I might suppose that he obviously knows that the betrothal with less than a penny's worth is null, so

when he sends gifts, it is as part of the token of betrothal. And if these two were covered, it is because one may not be clear on the rule governing a penny's worth or less, but when a minor betroths, everyone knows that the betrothal is null, so, when he sends gifts, I might suppose that these are sent as tokens of betrothal. So we are informed to the contrary.

2. I:2: It has been stated: R. Huna said, "We take account of the provision of gifts" so if a marriage is arranged and the husband to be sends gifts before witnesses, we take account of the possibility that these may be meant as tokens of a betrothal, so she is subject to the doubt as to her status; if someone else should betroth her, both have to divorce her. And so said Rabbah, "We take account of the provision of gifts."

    a. I:3: Gloss.

3. I:4: R. Aha bar R. Huna asked this question of Raba: "If a deed covering the marriage settlement was assumed in the marketplace to be valid though people don't know whether the couple was betrothed, but later on she accepted tokens of betrothal from a third party, what is the law?"

XX. MISHNAH-TRACTATE QIDDUSHIN 2:7

A. HE WHO BETROTHS A WOMAN AND HER DAUGHTER, OR A WOMAN AND HER SISTER, SIMULTANEOUSLY – THEY ARE NOT BETROTHED.

1. I:1: What is the scriptural source of this rule?
    a. I:2: Gloss of a subordinate detail of the foregoing.
2. I:3: Reversion to I:1's exegesis of the Mishnah-rule.
3. I:4: It has been stated: An act of betrothal that cannot lead to sexual intercourse – Abbayye said, "It is a valid act of betrothal." Raba said, "It is not a valid act of betrothal."
    a. I:5: Said Raba, "Bar Ahina explained to me, '"When a man takes a woman and has sexual relations with her" (Deut. 24:1) – a betrothal that can be followed by sexual relations is valid, but a betrothal that cannot be followed by sexual relations is not valid.'"

B. THERE WAS A CASE INVOLVING FIVE WOMEN, INCLUDING TWO SISTERS, AND ONE GATHERED FIGS, AND THEY WERE THEIRS, BUT IT WAS SEVENTH YEAR PRODUCE. AND SOMEONE SAID, "LO, ALL OF YOU ARE BETROTHED TO ME IN VIRTUE OF THIS BASKET OF FRUIT," AND ONE OF THEM ACCEPTED THE PROPOSAL IN BEHALF OF ALL OF THEM – AND SAGES RULED, "THE SISTERS IN THE GROUP OF FIVE ARE NOT BETROTHED."

1. II:1: Said Rab, "Our Mishnah paragraph yields four conclusions," but he had in hand only three of them. Our Mishnah paragraph yields the conclusion that he who betroths with produce of the Seventh Year – the betrothal is valid. Our Mishnah paragraph yields the conclusion that he who betrothed a woman with stolen property – she is not betrothed. And even if the stolen property belonged to her – how so? Since the formulation goes on, and they were theirs, but it was Seventh Year produce. So the operative consideration is that it was produce of the Seventh Year, which is ownerless; lo, if it were of the other years of the seven-year cycle, that would not be the case. Our Mishnah paragraph yields the conclusion that a woman may serve as an agent for another woman, and even in a situation in which she thereby becomes her co-wife.
    a. II:2: When R. Zira came up, he repeated this tradition before R. Yohanan, who said to him, "Well, now did Rab make any such statement?"
        I. II:3: Case illustrating a position of Raba along the lines of II:1. A certain woman was washing her feet in a bowl of water. Someone came along, grabbed a zuz from his neighbor, threw it to her and said, "Lo, you are betrothed to me." That man came before Raba, who said to him, "No one accepts R. Simeon's statement: Robbery in general involves the owner's despair of getting the property back so that if we don't know whether the owner despairs of getting the article back, we assume he does; that ruling is null, the betrothal is invalid."
        II. II:4: Case illustrating a position of Raba along the lines of II:1. That man came before Raba, who said to him, "Who renounced ownership of which the landlord owns half in your favor?"
        III. II:5: Case illustrating a position of Raba along the lines of II:1. A certain contractor for brewing the dates of others betrothed a woman with a measure of beer that he had brewed with someone else's dates, of which he gets a share. The owner of the beer came and found him. He said to him, "Why didn't you give her this beer, which is stronger?" He came before Raba, who said to him, "The consideration of 'you should have gone and taken

Chapter Twenty. Qiddushin 281

better ones' is valid only with regard to the case of heave-offering, because the owner of the field is happy to carry out his religious duty in such a manner. So he may have meant what he said. But in this case, it is merely a matter of courtesy and does not bear the sense of consent for what the agent has done."

XXI. MISHNAH-TRACTATE QIDDUSHIN 2:8
  A. **HE WHO WAS A PRIEST WHO BETROTHS A WOMAN WITH HIS SHARE OF THE PRIESTLY GIFTS, WHETHER THEY WERE MOST HOLY THINGS OR LESSER HOLY THINGS – SHE IS NOT BETROTHED.**
  1. I:1: May we say that our Mishnah paragraph does not accord with the position of R. Yosé the Galilean? For it has been taught on Tannaite authority: "'If a soul sin and commit an act of sacrilege against the Lord and lie to his neighbor' (Lev. 5:21) – this extends the law to Lesser Holy Things, which are classified as the property of the neighbor," the words of R. Yosé the Galilean.
  2. I:2: Our rabbis have taught on Tannaite authority: After R. Meir's death, R. Judah said to his disciples, "Don't let the disciples of R. Meir in here, because they are contentious and don't come to study the Torah but to throw up against me a barrage of trivial laws." Nonetheless Sumkhos forced his way in. He said to them, "This is what R. Meir repeated as a Mishnah teacher: He who was a priest who betroths a woman with his share of the priestly gifts, whether they were Most Holy Things or Lesser Holy Things – she is not betrothed." R. Judah became angry with them and said to them, "Didn't I tell you, 'Don't let the disciples of R. Meir in here, because they are contentious and don't come to study the Torah but to throw up against me a barrage of trivial laws'? So how in the world would a woman end up in the Temple courtyard anyhow? That is the only place where she could receive sacrifices of Most Holy Things!" Said R. Yosé, "Should people say, 'Meir lies in his grave, Judah is outraged, and Yosé kept his silence'? Then what will come of the teachings of the Torah? Can't a man routinely receive tokens of betrothal for his daughter in the Temple courtyard? And can't a woman routinely appoint a messenger to accept tokens of betrothal for her in the Temple courtyard? And, anyhow, what if she pushes herself in one way or the other?"

        a. I:3: It has been taught on Tannaite authority: R. Judah says, "She is betrothed." R. Yosé says, "She is not betrothed."
3. I:4: Continuation of I:2: Said R. Yohanan, "They took a vote and decided: He who was a priest who betroths a woman with his share of the priestly gifts, whether they were Most Holy Things or Lesser Holy Things – she is not betrothed." And Rab said, "The dispute continues even now."
        a. I:5: Gloss of the foregoing.

B. IF ONE DID SO WITH FOOD IN THE STATUS OF SECOND TITHE, "WHETHER INADVERTENTLY OR DELIBERATELY, HE HAS NOT EFFECTED BETROTHAL," THE WORDS OF R. MEIR. R. JUDAH SAYS, "IF HE DID SO INADVERTENTLY, HE HAS NOT EFFECTED BETROTHAL. IF HE DID SO DELIBERATELY, HE HAS EFFECTED BETROTHAL."
1. II:1: What is the scriptural basis for this ruling?

C. AND IN THE CASE OF THAT WHICH HAS BEEN DEDICATED: IF HE DID SO DELIBERATELY, HE HAS EFFECTED BETROTHAL, AND IF HE DID SO INADVERTENTLY, HE HAS NOT EFFECTED BETROTHAL," THE WORDS OF R. MEIR. R. JUDAH SAYS, "IF HE DID SO INADVERTENTLY, HE HAS EFFECTED BETROTHAL. IF HE DID SO DELIBERATELY, HE HAS NOT EFFECTED BETROTHAL."

1. III:1: Said R. Jacob, "I heard from R. Yohanan two considerations in connection with the inadvertent use of tithe, in the framework of the view of R. Judah, and the inadvertent use of what has been consecrated, in the framework of the view of R. Meir, explaining why, in each case, respectively, a woman is not betrothed therewith. First, because the woman doesn't approve; if she knew what it was, she would not have accepted it as a token of betrothal, so it is a betrothal done in error; second, because neither party approves. But I don't know which of the two belongs to which of the named authorities."
2. III:2: As to money that belongs to the sanctuary, from Meir's perspective, Raba asked R. Hisda, "Granted that the woman is not betrothed. Does the money that is consecrated revert to the status of what is unconsecrated?"
3. III:3: R. Hiyya bar Abin asked R. Hisda, "As to a purchase made with the money, what is the law?" As to money that belongs to the sanctuary, from Meir's perspective, what if one unwittingly buys something with that money?
        a. III:4: Gloss of III:1.
4. III:5: Said Ulla in the name of Bar Peda, "R. Meir would say, 'What has been consecrated that is deliberately used

has been made secular, if inadvertently used has not been made secular. But it is only with regard to an offering that they have said, if it is used inadvertently, it is secularized.'"

5. III:6: Said R. Nahman said R. Ada bar Ahbah, "The decided law accords with R. Meir in the matter of tithe, since a Tannaite authority has given without attribution the rule in line with his views, and the decided law accords with R. Judah in regard to what has been consecrated, since a Tannaite authority has given without attribution the rule in line with his views." And the decided law accords with R. Judah in regard to what has been consecrated, since a Tannaite authority has given without attribution the rule in line with his views.

6. III:7: We have learned in the Mishnah elsewhere: Cattle found between Jerusalem and Migdal Eder – and in an equivalent range on all sides of the city – if male, they are deemed to be burnt-offerings; if female, they are deemed to be peace-offerings. R. Judah says, "That which is suitable for Passover-offerings are Passover-offerings if they are found thirty days before that festival" (M. Sheq. 7:4). So can the males be used only for burnt-offerings and not peace-offerings? They certainly can be used for either purpose. So how can they be sacrificed only as burnt-offerings, if they may have been originally consecrated for peace-offerings?

    a. III:8: Gloss of the foregoing.

    b. III:9: As above.

7. III:10: Our rabbis have taught on Tannaite authority: With coins in the status of second tithe having been traded for produce in the status in second tithe, then brought to Jerusalem for the purchase of food, they do not purchase a beast. If one has done so, if this was inadvertently done, the money reverts to its original status to the owner, who made a mistake, since he'd rather take the money to Jerusalem than drive the beast up there; if this was done deliberately, the beast must be brought up to Jerusalem and eaten up there. R. Judah says, "Under what circumstances? If one deliberately bought it to begin with for the sake of using the beast for peace-offerings. But if he bought it for the purpose of turning the money in the status of second tithe into unconsecrated coins, whether he did so inadvertently or deliberately, the money must be returned to its original status,

to the owner" (T. M.S. 1:15A-C). Now, lo, we have learned in the Mishnah: R. Judah says, "If he did so inadvertently, he has not effected betrothal. If he did so deliberately, he has effected betrothal." This shows that we do not take account of the possibility that the woman may spend the money outside of Jerusalem; otherwise what he did would be null; so why do we take account of that possibility in the case of a sale?
    a. III:11: Gloss of the foregoing.

XXII. MISHNAH-TRACTATE QIDDUSHIN 2:9
    A. HE WHO BETROTHED A WOMAN WITH (1) ORLAH FRUIT:
        1. I:1: What is the source in Scripture for this rule?
    B. (2) WITH FRUIT WHICH WAS SUBJECT TO THE PROHIBITION AGAINST MIXED SEEDS IN A VINEYARD:
        1. II:1: What is the source in Scripture for this rule?
    C. (3) WITH AN OX WHICH WAS TO BE STONED:
        1. III:1: What is the source in Scripture for this rule?
           a. III:2: Gloss of the foregoing proof.
               I. III:3: Secondary development of the foregoing.
    D. (4) WITH A HEIFER THE NECK OF WHICH WAS TO BE BROKEN:
        1. IV:1: What is the source in Scripture for this rule?
    E. (5) WITH BIRDS SET ASIDE FOR THE OFFERING OF A PERSON AFFLICTED WITH THE SKIN AILMENT LEV. 13-14:
        1. V:1: What is the source in Scripture for this rule?
        2. V:2: It has been stated: As to the bird-offering of a person healed of the skin ailment, from what point are the birds forbidden for any sort of benefit? R. Yohanan said, "From the moment at which they are slaughtered." R. Simeon b. Laqish said, "From the moment at which they are taken and designated for that purpose."
    F. REVERSION TO IV:1 IN THE SETTING OF THE BIRDS OF THE PERSON HEALED OF THE SKIN AILMENT
        1. V:3: With reference to the heifer the neck of which is to be broken itself, from what point is the beast forbidden as to any sort of secular benefit?
           a. V:4: Gloss of the foregoing.
        2. V:5: A Tannaite authority of the household of R. Ishmael stated, "'And he shall let go the living bird into the open field' (Lev. 14:7) – it is comparable to the field. Just as the field is permitted, so this, too, is permitted."
    G. (6) WITH THE HAIR OF A NAZIR:

Chapter Twenty. Qiddushin

1. VI:1: What is the source in Scripture for this rule?
H. (7) WITH THE FIRSTBORN OF AN ASS:
1. VII:1: Shall we say that our Mishnah paragraph is not in accord with R. Simeon? For it has been taught on Tannaite authority: "It is forbidden to derive benefit from the firstborn of an ass," the words of R. Judah. R. Simeon declares it permitted.
I. (8) WITH MEAT MIXED WITH MILK:
1. VIII:1: What is the source in Scripture for this rule?
2. VIII:2: Our Mishnah paragraph does not accord with the following Tannaite authority, for it has been taught on Tannaite authority: R. Simeon b. Judah says in the name of R. Simeon, "Meat cooked in milk may not be eaten, but one may derive benefit from it for example, by selling it to gentiles to eat, as it is said, 'For you are a holy people to the Lord your God' (Deut. 14:21), which is followed by the prohibition of cooking a kid in its mother's milk, bearing the sense that you may not eat it but you may give it to others to eat. And further, 'And you shall be holy to me' (Ex. 22:30) in regard to terefah-meat. Just as in that latter case, the food may not be eaten but one may derive benefit from it, so here, too, the food may not be eaten but one may derive benefit from it."
J. (9) WITH UNCONSECRATED ANIMALS MEAT WHICH HAD BEEN SLAUGHTERED IN THE COURTYARD OF THE TEMPLE – SHE IS NOT BETROTHED.
1. IX:1: What is the source in Scripture for this rule?
2. IX:2: Mar Judah came across R. Joseph and R. Samuel b. Rabbah bar bar Hannah, who were standing at the gate of the household of Rabbah. He said to them, "It has been taught on Tannaite authority: He who betroths a woman with the firstling of an ass, meat cooked in milk, or unconsecrated beasts killed in the Temple court – R. Simeon says, 'She is betrothed.' And sages say, 'She is not betrothed.' Therefore in R. Simeon's opinion, unconsecrated beasts that are killed in the Temple courtyard are not prohibited by the law of the Torah. In Simeon's view, if the slaughter does not qualify the animal for food, because it is otherwise forbidden, it is not slaughter at all, and no interdict which would normally result from the killing takes effect; therefore one may benefit therefrom and it is valid for betrothal. But by way of contradiction: R. Simeon says, 'Unconsecrated animals that

are slaughtered in the Temple courtyard – the meat is sent off to be burned. And so a wild beast that was slaughtered in the Temple courtyard is treated the same way.'"

K. IF HE SOLD THEM OFF AND BETROTHED A WOMAN WITH THE MONEY RECEIVED IN EXCHANGE FOR THEM, SHE IS BETROTHED.
1. X.1. What is the source in Scripture for this rule?
a. X:2: Secondary development of the exegetical argument.

XXIII. MISHNAH-TRACTATE QIDDUSHIN 2:10
A. HE WHO CONSECRATED A WOMAN WITH FOOD IN THE STATUS OF HEAVE-OFFERING, TITHE, OR GIFTS TO BE GIVEN TO THE PRIEST, PURIFICATION WATER, PURIFICATION ASH – LO, THIS WOMAN IS BETROTHED, AND EVEN IF SHE IS AN ISRAELITE.
1. I:1: Said Ulla, "The good will accruing for the gift of priestly donations to the priesthood is regarded as having no monetary value."
2. I:2: R. Hiyya bar Abin addressed this question to R. Huna: "Is the good will accruing for the gift of priestly donations to the priesthood regarded as having monetary value or is it regarded as not having monetary value?"
a. I:3: May we say that the issue at hand is subject to a conflict of Tannaite versions?
3. I:4: We have learned in the Mishnah: He who consecrated a woman with food in the status of heave-offering, tithe, or gifts to be given to the priest, purification water, purification ash – lo, this woman is betrothed, and even if she is an Israelite. And by way of contradiction: He who takes payment for judging – his judgments are null. He who takes payment for testifying – his testimony is null. He who takes payment to sprinkle purification water on one made unclean by a corpse and to mix ash of a red cow with water for the purpose of making purification water – his water is cave water, and his ash is hearth ash null and useless (M. Bekh. 4:6A-F).

XXIV. MISHNAH-TRACTATE QIDDUSHIN 3:1
A. HE WHO SAYS TO HIS FELLOW, "GO AND BETROTH MISS SO-AND-SO FOR ME," AND HE WENT AND BETROTHED HER FOR HIMSELF – SHE IS BETROTHED.
1. I:1: A Tannaite statement: What he has done is done, but he has treated the other deceitfully.

2. I:2: What differentiates the present case, in which the language is used, He who says to his fellow, from the parallel, He who says to his messenger, "Go and betroth Miss So-and-so for me, in such-and-such a place," and he went and betrothed her for him in some other place, she is not betrothed, in which the language, He who says to his messenger, is used?
   a. I:3: Case. Rabin the Pious went to betroth a woman for his son. He betrothed her for himself.
   b. I:4: Case. Rabbah bar bar Hannah gave money to Rab. He said, "Buy for me that plot of land." He went and bought it for himself.
   c. I:5: Case. R. Giddal was involved with buying a certain field. R. Abba went and bought it. R. Giddal went and complained about him to R. Zira. R. Zira went and complained about him to R. Isaac Nappaha. He said to him, "Wait until he comes up to us for the festival."

B. AND SO: HE WHO SAYS TO A WOMAN, "LO, YOU ARE BETROTHED TO ME AFTER THIRTY DAYS HAVE PASSED," AND SOMEONE ELSE CAME ALONG AND BETROTHED HER DURING THE THIRTY DAYS –
1. II:1: If someone else didn't come along and betroth her during the thirty days, what is the law? Both Rab and Samuel said, "She is betrothed, and that is the case even if the money that was given has already been used up."
2. II:2: If no one else came along to betroth her, but she retracted her agreement in the interim, what is the law? R. Yohanan said, "She may retract: Words can come and wipe out words." R. Simeon b. Laqish said, "She may not retract: Words can't come and wipe out words."
   a. II:3: Another version of the foregoing dispute.
      i. II:4: The decided law accords with the position of R. Yohanan, and that is so even in respect to the first of the two disputes, for even though we may invoke the argument, "Handing money into the woman's hand is tantamount to an action," even so, words can come and wipe out words.

C. SHE IS BETROTHED TO THE SECOND PARTY. IF IT IS AN ISRAELITE GIRL BETROTHED TO A PRIEST, SHE MAY EAT HEAVE-OFFERING. IF HE SAID, "...AS OF NOW AND AFTER THIRTY DAYS," AND SOMEONE ELSE CAME ALONG AND BETROTHED HER DURING THE THIRTY DAYS, SHE IS BETROTHED AND NOT BETROTHED. IF IT IS EITHER AN ISRAELITE GIRL BETROTHED TO A PRIEST, OR A PRIEST GIRL BETROTHED TO AN ISRAELITE, SHE SHOULD NOT EAT HEAVE-OFFERING.

1. III:1: Said Rab, "She is permanently betrothed to the second party." And Samuel said, "She is betrothed to the second party only for thirty days. After thirty days have passed, the betrothal of the second party is dissolved, and the betrothal of the first party takes effect."
  2. III:2: In session R. Hisda raised this difficulty: "But how has the act of betrothal of the second party been removed?"
      i. III:3: What is at issue is what is subject to dispute between the following Tannaite authority,
          A. III:4: Said Abbayye, "Within the theory of Rab, if somebody came along and said to her, 'Behold, you are betrothed to me from now and after thirty days,' and then someone else came along and said to her, 'Behold, you are betrothed to me from now and after twenty days,' and then someone else came along and said to her, 'Behold, you are betrothed to me from now and after ten days,' from the first and third parties she requires a writ of divorce, but from the second party she does not require a writ of divorce. For which way do you want to go? If it was a stipulation, then that of the first is a valid act of betrothal, but not the acts of the second and the third; if it is a withdrawal, then the state of the final party is a valid act of betrothal, but not of the first or the second parties."
  2. III:5: Ulla said R. Yohanan said, "Even the betrothals of a hundred men may take effect on her." And so said R. Assi said R. Yohanan, "Even the betrothals of a hundred men may take effect on her."

XXV. MISHNAH-TRACTATE QIDDUSHIN 3:2
  A. HE WHO SAYS TO A WOMAN, "BEHOLD, YOU ARE BETROTHED TO ME, ON CONDITION THAT I PAY YOU TWO HUNDRED ZUZ" – LO, THIS WOMAN IS BETROTHED, AND HE MUST PAY HER WHAT HE HAS PROMISED.
    1. I:1: It has been stated: R. Huna said, "And she will give the money to him." R. Judah said, "When she gives the money to him."
        a. I:2: Expansion on a detail of the foregoing.

Chapter Twenty. Qiddushin

B. "...ON CONDITION THAT I PAY YOU WITHIN THE NEXT THIRTY DAYS," AND HE PAID HER DURING THE THIRTY DAYS, SHE IS BETROTHED. AND IF NOT, SHE IS NOT BETROTHED.
  1. II:1: Yeah, big deal, so what else is new?
C. "...ON CONDITION THAT I HAVE TWO HUNDRED ZUZ," LO, THIS WOMAN IS BETROTHED, AND IF HE HAS THAT SUM.
  1. III:1: But shouldn't we take account of the possibility that he really does have the money, and, furthermore, it is taught on Tannaite authority: We take account of the possibility that he has the money?
D. "...ON CONDITION THAT I SHALL SHOW YOU TWO HUNDRED ZUZ," LO, THIS WOMAN IS BETROTHED, AND IF HE WILL SHOW HER THAT SUM.
  1. IV:1: A Tannaite statement: She intended only to see money that was his.
E. BUT IF HE SHOWED HER THE MONEY ON THE TABLE OF A MONEY CHANGER, SHE IS NOT BETROTHED.
  1. V:1: Yeah, big deal, so what else is new?

XXVI. MISHNAH-TRACTATE QIDDUSHIN 3:3
A. "...ON CONDITION THAT I HAVE A KOR'S SPACE OF LAND," LO, THIS WOMAN IS BETROTHED, AND IF HE HAS IT.
  1. I:1: "...On condition that I have a kor's space of land," lo, this woman is betrothed, and if he has it: But shouldn't we take account of the possibility that he really does have the money, and, furthermore, it is taught on Tannaite authority: We take account of the possibility that he has the money?
    a. I:2: Why do I have to be given a Tannaite statement with respect both to real estate and ready cash?
B. "...ON CONDITION THAT I HAVE THAT LAND IN SUCH-AND-SUCH A PLACE," IF HE HAS IT IN THAT PLACE, SHE IS BETROTHED, AND IF NOT, SHE IS NOT BETROTHED.
  1. II:1: Well, that's pretty obvious!
C. "...ON CONDITION THAT I SHOW YOU A KOR'S SPACE OF LAND," LO, THIS WOMAN IS BETROTHED, AND IF HE WILL SHOW IT TO HER.
  1. III:1: A Tannaite statement: This woman had the intention only of seeing what belongs to him.
D. BUT IF HE SHOWED HER LAND IN A PLAIN WHICH WAS NOT HIS, SHE IS NOT BETROTHED.
  1. IV:1: Obviously.
  2. IV:2: In respect to consecrated property, we have learned in the Mishnah: He who sanctifies his field at the time of the

Jubilee's being in effect pays the fifty sheqels of silver for every part of a field that suffices for the sowing of a homer of barley. If there were there crevices ten handbreadths deep or rocks ten handbreadths high, they are not measured with it. If they were in height less than this, they are measured with it (M. Ar. 7:1E-H). And in that connection we reflected: Granted that they are not sanctified along with the field, at any rate let them be considered as sanctified as autonomous areas of the field, since they are not regarded as part of the arable field for purposes of redemption, and let them be redeemed on their own. And if you wish to propose that, since they do not take a kor of seed, they are not subject to consecration, has it now been taught to the contrary: "A field..." (Lev. 27:16). Why does Scripture say, "A field"? Since it is said, "Fifty sheqels of silver for every part of a field that suffices for the sowing of a homer of barley" (Lev. 27:16), I know only that the law applies to a case such as is specified in Scripture, that is, to a field of the specified size. How do I know that the law encompasses a field suitable for sowing only a letekh of seed or a half-letekh, a seah of seed or a tirqab or a half-tirqab? Scripture says, "A field" – of any dimensions.

3. IV:3: With respect to a sale we have learned in the Mishnah: He who says to his fellow, "I am selling you a kor's area of arable land – if there were there crevices ten handbreadths deep, or rocks ten handbreadths high, they are not measured with the area. If they were less than the stated measurements, they are measured with the area (M. B.B. 7:1A-D), and said Mar Uqba bar Hama, "That is so even if the crevices are not filled with water."

    a. IV:4: So what's the rule here? Do we invoke the analogy of what has been consecrated or what has been sold?

XXVII. MISHNAH-TRACTATE QIDDUSHIN 3:4

    A. R. MEIR SAYS, "ANY CONDITION WHICH IS NOT STATED AS IS THE CONDITION OF THE SONS OF GAD AND THE SONS OF REUBEN THAT IS, IN BOTH NEGATIVE AND POSITIVE FORMULATIONS, IS NO CONDITION, SINCE IT SAYS, 'AND MOSES SAID TO THEM, "IF THE CHILDREN OF GAD AND THE CHILDREN OF REUBEN WILL PASS OVER" (NUM. 32:29). AND IT IS WRITTEN, "AND IF THEY WILL NOT PASS OVER ARMED" (NUM. 32:20).'" R. HANANIAH B. GAMALIEL SAYS, "THE MATTER HAD TO BE STATED IN JUST THAT WAY, FOR IF NOT, IT WOULD HAVE

BEEN IMPLIED THAT EVEN IN THE LAND OF CANAAN THEY WOULD NOT INHERIT LAND."
1. I:1: So did R. Hananiah b. Gamaliel give a good reply to R. Meir?
2. I:2: It has been taught on Tannaite authority: Said R. Hanina b. Gamaliel, "A parable: To what is the matter comparable? To the case of a man who was dividing up his estate among his sons. He said, 'So-and-so, my son, will inherit such-and-such a field, and So-and-so, my son, will inherit such-and-such a field, and So-and-so, my son, will pay two hundred zuz and inherit such-and-such a field, but if if he doesn't pay, he will inherit a share with his other brothers in the rest of my estate.' Now what causes him to inherit a share with the brothers in the rest of the estate? The father's doubling of the stipulation effects it for him." But for the second statement, it might be said that if he doesn't give the two hundred zuz, he can claim a share only in the third field but receives nothing from the other two fields assigned to his brothers; similarly, in the verses under discussion, but for the second statement, it would be assumed that the Gaddites and Reubenites in the case of their not carrying out of the condition would share with the rest of the tribes the district of Gilead, while forfeiting all claim to the land of Canaan.
   a. I:3: Secondary discussion of the exegetical problem.
   b. I:4: Secondary discussion of the exegetical problem.
   c. I:5: Secondary discussion of the exegetical problem.
   d. I:6: Secondary discussion of the exegetical problem.
      I. I:7: Gloss of the foregoing.
   e. I:8: Secondary discussion of the exegetical problem.
   f. I:9: Secondary discussion of the exegetical problem.
   g. I:10: Secondary discussion of the exegetical problem.
      I. I:11: Gloss of the foregoing.
      II. I:12: As above.

XXVIII. MISHNAH-TRACTATE QIDDUSHIN 3:5

A. HE WHO BETROTHS A WOMAN AND SAID, "I WAS THINKING THAT SHE IS A PRIEST, AND LO, SHE IS A LEVITE," "...A LEVITE, AND LO, SHE IS A PRIEST," "A POOR GIRL, AND LO, SHE IS A RICH GIRL," "A RICH GIRL, AND LO, SHE IS A POOR GIRL," LO, SHE IS BETROTHED, FOR SHE HAS NOT DECEIVED HIM. HE WHO SAYS TO A WOMAN, "LO, YOU ARE BETROTHED TO ME AFTER I CONVERT TO JUDAISM," OR "AFTER YOU

CONVERT," "...AFTER I AM FREED" OR "AFTER YOU ARE FREED," "...AFTER YOUR HUSBAND DIED," OR "...AFTER YOUR SISTER DIES," "AFTER YOUR LEVIR WILL HAVE PERFORMED THE RITE OF REMOVING THE SHOE WITH YOU" – SHE IS NOT BETROTHED. AND SO HE WHO SAYS TO HIS FELLOW, "IF YOUR WIFE GIVES BIRTH TO A GIRL-CHILD, LO, THE BABY IS BETROTHED TO ME" – SHE IS NOT BETROTHED. IF THE WIFE OF HIS FELLOW INDEED WAS PREGNANT AND THE FOETUS WAS DISCERNIBLE, HIS STATEMENT IS CONFIRMED, AND IF SHE PRODUCED A GIRL-CHILD, THE BABY IS BETROTHED.

1. I:1: There we have learned in the Mishnah: They do not separate heave-offering from that which is picked for that which is not picked; and not from that which is not picked for that which is picked. And if they separated heave-offering, that which they have separated is not valid heave-offering (M. Ter. 1:5). R. Assi asked R. Yohanan, "If one said, 'The produce of this furrow that is detached be heave-offering for the produce of that furrow that is attached to the ground or the produce of that furrow that is attached to the ground be heave-offering for the produce of this furrow when it is detached, when it is plucked' – and then it is plucked?" He said to him, "Anything that is in one's power to carry out is not classified as an act that is as yet incomplete since the farmer has the power to harvest the produce, it is regarded as already harvested, so his declaration in this case is valid." An objection was raised: He who says to a woman, "Lo, you are betrothed to me after I convert to Judaism," or "after you convert," "...after I am freed" or "after you are freed," "...after your husband died," or "...after your sister dies," "after your levir will have performed the rite of removing the shoe with you" – she is not betrothed. Now there is no problem in the most of these items, since it is not in his power to fulfil the stated condition, but surely it is in his power to convert!
   a. I:2: Secondary development of the foregoing.
   b. I:3: It has been taught on Tannaite authority in accord with the position of R. Yohanan.
      i. I:4: Said Abbayye, "R. Eliezer b. Jacob, Rabbi, and R. Meir all concur in the theory that one may transfer title to a being that has not yet come into the world. R. Eliezer b. Jacob: as we have just now said...."

Chapter Twenty. Qiddushin   293

XXIX. MISHNAH-TRACTATE QIDDUSHIN 3:6A-C
   A. HE WHO SAYS TO A WOMAN, "LO, YOU ARE BETROTHED TO ME, ON CONDITION THAT I SPEAK IN YOUR BEHALF TO THE GOVERNMENT'" OR, "THAT I WORK FOR YOU AS A LABORER," IF HE SPOKE IN HER BEHALF TO THE GOVERNMENT OR WORKED FOR HER AS A LABORER, SHE IS BETROTHED. AND IF NOT, SHE IS NOT BETROTHED.
      1. I:1: Said R. Simeon b. Laqish, "But that is the case only if he gave her something worth at least a penny."

XXX. MISHNAH-TRACTATE QIDDUSHIN 3:6D-G
   A. "...ON CONDITION THAT FATHER WILL CONCUR," IF FATHER CONCURRED, SHE IS BETROTHED. AND IF NOT, SHE IS NOT BETROTHED. IF THE FATHER DIED, LO, THIS WOMAN IS BETROTHED. IF THE SON DIED, THEY INSTRUCT THE FATHER TO STATE THAT HE DOES NOT CONCUR.
      1. I:1: What is the sense of, "...on condition that father will concur"? Should I say, on the condition that father explicitly said, "Yes"? Then note the middle clause: If the father died, lo, this woman is betroth. And lo, the father never said yes! So it must mean, "on condition that father keeps silent." But then notice the concluding clause, If the son died, they instruct the father to state that he does not concur! So why would that matter, since he had kept silence! So it must mean, "on condition that father does not object in so many words." But in that case, the opening clause presupposes one theory, the middle and concluding clauses, another theory!

XXXI. MISHNAH-TRACTATE QIDDUSHIN 3:7
   A. "I HAVE BETROTHED MY DAUGHTER, BUT I DON'T KNOW TO WHOM I HAVE BETROTHED HER," AND SOMEONE CAME ALONG AND SAID, "I HAVE BETROTHED HER," HE IS BELIEVED. IF THIS ONE SAID, "I BETROTHED HER," AND AT THE SAME TIME, THAT ONE SAID, "I BETROTHED HER," BOTH OF THEM GIVE HER A WRIT OF DIVORCE. BUT IF THEY WANTED, ONE OF THEM GIVES HER A WRIT OF DIVORCE AND ONE OF THEM CONSUMMATES THE MARRIAGE.
      1. I:1: Said Rab, "He is believed – so as to give her a divorce, but he is not believed so as to consummate the marriage. He is believed – so as to give her a divorce: Nobody sins for nothing. But he is not believed so as to consummate the marriage: One might say, his lust is what motivates him." R. Assi said, "He is also believed so as to consummate the marriage."

2. I:2: It has been taught on Tannaite authority in accord with the position of R. Assi: "I have betrothed my daughter and I don't know to whom I have betrothed her," and someone came along and said, "I have betrothed her" – he is even believed to consummate the marriage. If he consummated the marriage and someone else came along and said, "I betrothed her," he does not have the power to forbid her to the first husband. The woman who said, "I have been betrothed and I don't know to whom I have been betrothed," and someone came along and said, "I betrothed her," he is not believed to consummate the marriage, because she will cover for him being eager to marry just anyone at all (T. Qid. 4:10).
3. I:3: The question was raised: "What is the law on stoning her should she commit adultery on the strength of his statement that is, the father's, that he betrothed her, without producing witnesses to that effect?" Is she then a married woman, so that, if she commits adultery, she is stoned to death? Rab said, "They do not stone her under such circumstances." R. Assi said, "They do stone her under such circumstances."

XXXII. MISHNAH-TRACTATE QIDDUSHIN 3:8A-G

A. IF THE FATHER SAID, "I HAVE BETROTHED MY DAUGHTER," "…I HAVE BETROTHED HER AND I HAVE ACCEPTED HER WRIT OF DIVORCE WHEN SHE WAS A MINOR" – AND LO, SHE IS YET A MINOR – HE IS BELIEVED. "I BETROTHED HER AND I ACCEPTED HER WRIT OF DIVORCE WHEN SHE WAS A MINOR," AND LO, SHE IS NOW AN ADULT – HE IS NOT BELIEVED. "SHE WAS TAKEN CAPTIVE AND I REDEEMED HER," WHETHER SHE IS A MINOR OR WHETHER SHE IS AN ADULT, HE IS NOT BELIEVED.

1. I:1: So what's the difference between the first and the second cases?

XXXIII. MISHNAH-TRACTATE QIDDUSHIN 3:8H-I

A. HE WHO SAID AT THE MOMENT OF HIS DEATH, "I HAVE CHILDREN," IS BELIEVED. IF HE SAID, "I HAVE BROTHERS," HE IS NOT BELIEVED.

1. I:1: It follows that he is accorded credence when the result of his action is to release the wife from the levirate bond, but he is not believed to impose upon her the levirate connection. So may we say that the Mishnah rule does not accord with the position of R. Nathan?

Chapter Twenty. Qiddushin 295

XXXIV. Mishnah-Tractate Qiddushin 3:8J, 3:9
- A. He who betroths his daughter without specification — the one past girlhood is not taken into account.
    1. I:1: Since the minors are included in this statement of his, it follows that an act of betrothal that cannot lead to sexual intercourse is a valid act of betrothal.
- B. He who has two groups of daughters by two wives in succession, and who said, "I have betrothed my oldest daughter, but I do not know whether it is the oldest of the older group or the oldest of the younger group, or the youngest of the older group, who is also older than the oldest of the younger group" — "All of them are prohibited to marry without a writ of divorce, except for the youngest of the younger group," the words of R. Meir. R. Yosé says, "They are all permitted, except for the oldest of the older group." "I betrothed my youngest daughter, but I do not know whether it was the youngest of the younger group, or the youngest of the older group, or the oldest of the younger group, who is younger than the youngest of the older group" — "ll of them are prohibited except for the oldest of the older group," the words of R. Meir. R. Yosé says, "All of them are permitted, except for the youngest of the younger group."
    1. II:1: It was necessary for both cases to be set forth, for had we been informed only of the first of the two, I might have supposed that it is in that case in particular that R. Meir took the position that he did, for, since there is still a younger daughter than this one, he might call this one "older," but in the latter clause, I might suppose that he concurs with R. Yosé that he calls only the youngest of them all "young." And if the latter clause alone were stated, I would have imagined that it is only in that instance does R. Yosé take the position that he does, but in the former, he will concur with R. Meir. So both had to be set forth in full.
        a. II:2: Does this dispute bear the implication that R. Meir takes the view that a person will place himself in situation of doubt, while R. Yosé maintains that a person will not place himself in a situation of doubt? But we have a tradition of their opinions that reverses matters.
        b. II:3: Said Abbayye, "The dispute concerns a case in which there are two groups of daughters. But in the case in which there is only a single set of daughters, all

XXXV. MISHNAH-TRACTATE QIDDUSHIN 3:10-11
  A. HE WHO SAYS TO A WOMAN, "I HAVE BETROTHED YOU," AND SHE SAYS, "YOU DID NOT BETROTH ME" – HE IS PROHIBITED TO MARRY HER RELATIVES, BUT SHE IS PERMITTED TO MARRY HIS RELATIVES. IF SHE SAYS, "YOU BETROTHED ME," AND HE SAYS, "I DID NOT BETROTH YOU" – HE IS PERMITTED TO MARRY HER RELATIVES, AND SHE IS PROHIBITED FROM MARRYING HIS RELATIVES.
     1. I:1: It was necessary to list all of these situations. For had we been informed of the rule with respect to his statement that if he said, I betrothed you, his relatives are not forbidden to her, since to a man such a situation makes no difference, so that is how he talks; but as to her, I might suppose, if she were not sure of herself, she would not have made such a statement, so her relatives would be forbidden to him. So we are informed that that is not the case.
  B. "I BETROTHED YOU," AND SHE SAYS, "YOU BETROTHED ONLY MY DAUGHTER," HE IS PROHIBITED FROM MARRYING THE RELATIVES OF THE OLDER WOMAN, AND THE OLDER WOMAN IS PERMITTED TO MARRY HIS RELATIVES. HE IS PERMITTED TO MARRY THE RELATIVES OF THE YOUNG GIRL, AND THE YOUNG GIRL IS PERMITTED TO MARRY HIS RELATIVES.
     1. II:1: So what do I need more of the same for?
  C. "I HAVE BETROTHED YOUR DAUGHTER," AND SHE SAYS, "YOU BETROTHED ONLY ME," HE IS PROHIBITED TO MARRY THE RELATIVES OF THE GIRL, AND THE GIRL IS PERMITTED TO MARRY HIS RELATIVES. HE IS PERMITTED TO MARRY THE RELATIVES OF THE OLDER WOMAN, BUT THE OLDER WOMAN IS PROHIBITED FROM MARRYING HIS RELATIVES.
     1. III:1: So what do I need more of the same for?
     2. III:2: It has been stated: Rab said, "We force him to issue a writ of divorce." And Samuel said, "We induce him to do so."
        a. III:3: To which of the foregoing cases does this dispute make reference? Should I say that it refers to the opening case? But then there is an issue neither of compulsion nor inducement. If it is to the middle clause "You have betrothed me", then, as to inducement, there is no problem, but as to compulsion, on what basis?

Chapter Twenty. Qiddushin

He can object, "But I don't want to be forbidden to marry her relatives as the relatives of a woman he has divorced!"

3. III:4: Said R. Judah, "He who betroths a woman in the presence of only a single witness – they do not take account of the possibility that his act of betrothal is valid."
4. III:5: It has been stated: said R. Nahman said Samuel, "He who betroths a woman in the presence of only a single witness – they do not take account of the possibility that his act of betrothal is valid, and that is the case even if both parties concur."
5. III:6: Said R. Isaac bar Samuel bar Marta in the name of Rab, "He who betroths a woman in the presence of only a single witness – they do not take account of the possibility that his act of betrothal is valid, and that is the case even if both parties concur."
6. III:7: Said Rabbah bar R. Huna, "He who betroths a woman in the presence of only a single witness – the high court rules, 'they do not take account of the possibility that his act of betrothal is valid.'"
   a. III:8: Illustrative case.
7. III:9: Said Abbayye, "If a single witness said to someone, 'You ate forbidden fat,' and the other remains silent, the witness is believed."
8. III:10: And said Abbayye, "If a single witness said to someone, 'Your foods requiring preparation in conditions of cleanness have been made unclean,' and he remains silent, the witness is believed."
9. III:11: And said Abbayye, "If a single witness said to someone, 'Your ox has been subjected to an act of bestiality,' and the other party remains silent, the witness is believed."
   a. III:12: And it was necessary to give the opinions in all three items.
10. III:13: The question was raised: If on the testimony of a single witness it was said that one's wife had committed adultery, and he remained silent, what is the law? Abbayye said, "The single witness is believed and the husband has to divorce the wife." Raba said, "The single witness is not believed, since this is a matter having to do with illicit sex, and a matter involving illicit sex cannot be established with less than two witnesses."
    a. III:14: Secondary gloss of a detail of the foregoing.
    b. III:15: Secondary gloss of a detail of the foregoing.

XXXVI. Mishnah-Tractate Qiddushin 3:12

A. In any situation in which there is a valid betrothal and no commission of a transgression, the offspring follows the status of the male, What is such a situation? It is in particular the situation in which a priest girl, a Levite girl, or an Israelite girl was married to a priest, a Levite, or an Israelite. And any situation in which there is a valid betrothal, but there also is the commission of a transgression, the offspring follows the status of the impaired inferior party. And what is such a situation? It is a widow married to a high priest, a divorcée or woman who has undergone the rite of of removing the shoe married to an ordinary priest, a mamzer girl, or a Netin girl married to an Israelite, an Israelite girl married to a mamzer or a Netin.

1. I:1: In any situation in which there is a valid betrothal and no commission of a transgression, the offspring follows the status of the male: Said R. Simeon b. Laqish to R. Yohanan, "Is it then a governing principle that in any situation in which there is a valid betrothal and no commission of a transgression, the offspring follows the status of the male? Lo, there is the case of proselyte who marries a mamzer girl, in which case there is a valid act of betrothal and no transgression, but the offspring follows the status of the inferior partner. For it has been taught on Tannaite authority: 'A proselyte who married a mamzer girl – the offspring is a mamzer,' the words of R. Yosé (T. Qid. 5.2A)."

   a. I:2: Now if you say that our Mishnah paragraph follows the position of R. Judah, then it must follow, the language, in any situation, used in the opening clause is meant to extend the law to the case of an Israelite who married a woman of profaned priestly status, and the case of Rabbah bar bar Hannah, and the language, It is in particular the situation, serves to eliminate the case of what R. Dimi and Rabin said. Moreover, the language, in any situation, used in the second clause serves to extend the law to a proselyte who marries a mamzer girl. But if you maintain that the Mishnah paragraph follows the position of R. Yosé, then while the language in any situation, used in the opening clause is for the purpose that we have said, and likewise, in any situation is as we have said, but as to the language,

Chapter Twenty. Qiddushin

in any situation used in the later clause, what case is it meant to encompass?
      i. I:3: Gloss of a detail of the foregoing.
         A. I:4: Gloss of the gloss.
   B. AND IN ANY SITUATION IN WHICH A WOMAN HAS NO RIGHT TO ENTER BETROTHAL WITH THIS MAN BUT HAS THE RIGHT TO ENTER INTO BETROTHAL WITH OTHERS, THE OFFSPRING IS A MAMZER. WHAT IS SUCH A SITUATION? THIS IS A MAN WHO HAD SEXUAL RELATIONS WITH ANY OF THOSE WOMEN PROHIBITED TO HIM BY THE TORAH.
      1. II:1: How on the basis of Scripture do we know this fact?
         a. II:2: Same result achieved through an argument a fortiori.
   C. BUT ANY SITUATION IN WHICH A WOMAN HAS NO RIGHT TO ENTER INTO BETROTHAL WITH THIS MAN OR WITH ANY OTHER MAN — THE OFFSPRING IS IN HER STATUS. AND WHAT IS SUCH A SITUATION? IT IS THE OFFSPRING OF A SLAVE GIRL OR A GENTILE GIRL.
      1. III:1: How on the basis of Scripture do we know that that is the case with a Canaanite slave girl that betrothal with her is null?
         a. III:2: Gloss of a detail of the foregoing.
            i. III:3: Gloss of the gloss.

XXXVII. MISHNAH-TRACTATE QIDDUSHIN 3:13
   A. R. TARFON SAYS, "MAMZERIM CAN BE PURIFIED FROM THE TAINT OF BASTARDY. HOW SO? A MAMZER WHO MARRIED A SLAVE GIRL — THE OFFSPRING IS A SLAVE GIRL. IF HE THEN FREED HIM, THE SON TURNS OUT TO BE A FREE MAN:"
      1. I:1: The question was raised: Does R. Tarfon take the position that he does before the fact, or merely after the fact?
   B. R. ELIEZER SAYS, "LO, THIS IS A SLAVE WHO ALSO IS IN THE STATUS OF A MAMZER."
      1. II:1: Said R. Eleazar, "What's the scriptural foundation for the ruling of R. Eliezer? Said Scripture, 'A mamzer even to the tenth generation shall none enter to him into the assembly of the lord' (Deut. 23:3)."

XXXVIII. MISHNAH-TRACTATE QIDDUSHIN 4:1-2
   A. TEN CASTES CAME UP FROM BABYLONIA:
      1. I:1: Ten castes came up from Babylonia: How come the Tannaite formulation prefers the language, came up from Babylonia, rather than saying, came to the Land of Israel?

2. I:2: How come the Tannaite formulation prefers the language, came up from Babylonia, rather than saying, came up to the Land of Israel?
3. I:3: It has been stated: Abbayye said, "We have learned in formulation of the Mishnah, they came up of their own volition." And Raba said, "We have learned in formulation of the Mishnah, he brought them up willy-nilly."

B. (1) PRIESTS, (2) LEVITES, (3) ISRAELITES:
1. II:1: How on the basis of Scripture do we know that they went up?

C. (4) IMPAIRED PRIESTS,
1. III:1: How on the basis of Scripture do we know that fact of the impaired priests?

D. (5) CONVERTS, AND (6) FREED SLAVES:
1. IV:1: How on the basis of Scripture do we know that fact?

E. (7) MAMZERS:
(8) NETINS, (9) "SILENCED ONES" SHETUQI, AND (10) FOUNDLINGS. PRIESTS, LEVITES, AND ISRAELITES ARE PERMITTED TO MARRY AMONG ONE ANOTHER. LEVITES, ISRAELITES, IMPAIRED PRIESTS, CONVERTS, AND FREED SLAVES ARE PERMITTED TO MARRY AMONG ONE ANOTHER. CONVERTS, FREED SLAVES, MAMZERS, NETINS, "SILENCED ONES," AND FOUNDLINGS ARE PERMITTED TO MARRY AMONG ONE ANOTHER.
1. V:1: How on the basis of Scripture do we know that fact?

F. TOPICAL APPENDIX ON THE MAMZER AND THE RESULT OF OTHER INAPPROPRIATE UNIONS
1. V:2: Said Rabbah bar bar Hannah, "Whoever marries a woman who is not genealogically suitable to him – Scripture regards him as though he had ploughed the whole world and sown it with salt: 'And these are the ones who went up from Tel-melah, Tel-harsha.'"
2. V:3: Said Rabbah bar R. Adda said Rab, "Whoever marries a woman for money will have children who are unworthy: 'They have dealt treacherously against the Lord, for they have produced strange children' (Hos. 6:7). And lest you think, at least the money is there, Scripture states, 'Now shall the new moon devour them with their portions' (Hos. 5:7). And lest you think, his, not hers, the language that is used refers to both: 'Their portions.' And lest you think that that is only after a long period, Scripture is explicit: 'The new moon.'"
3. V:4: And said Rabbah bar R. Adda said Rab, and some say,

said R. Sela said R. Hamnuna, "Whoever marries a woman who is not genealogically suitable to him – Elijah binds him to the stock and the Holy One, blessed be He, administers the flogging."
4. V:5: Long story on Mamzerut.
5. V:6: Said R. Judah said Samuel, "Four hundred slaves" – some say, "four thousand slaves" – did Pashur son of Immer have, and they all became mixed up with the priesthood, so every priest who shows arrogance derives only from them."
6. V:7: Said R. Abin bar R. Adda said Rab, "Whoever marries a woman who is not genealogically suitable to him – when the Holy One, blessed be He, brings his divine presence to rest on Israel, he will testify concerning all of the tribes, but he will not testify concerning him: 'The tribes of the Lord are a testimony to Israel' (Ps. 122:4). So when are the tribes 'a testimony to Israel'? When the tribes really are 'tribes of the Lord.'"
7. V:8: Said R. Hama b. R. Hanina, "When the Holy One, blessed be He, brings his divine presence to rest on Israel, he will bring it to rest only on families of proper genealogy in Israel: 'At that time says the Lord will I be the God of all the families of Israel' (Jer. 31:1) – not to 'all Israel,' but to 'all the families of Israel,' 'and they shall be my people.'"
    a. V:9: Gloss of a detail of the foregoing.
8. V:10: Said R. Hama bar Hanina, "When the Holy One, blessed be He, purifies the tribes, he will purify the tribe of Levi first: 'And he shall sit as a refiner and purifier of silver, and he shall purify the sons of Levi and purge them as gold and silver, and they shall offer to the Lord offerings in righteousness' (Mal. 3:3)."
    a. V:11: Gloss of the foregoing.
    b. V:12: Gloss of the foregoing.
9. V:13: Reversion to I:3: Reverting to the body of the foregoing I:3:R. Judah said Samuel said, "All other countries are like gross dough not fine flour in comparison to the Land of Israel, and the Land of Israel is like gross dough by comparison to Babylonia" – In the time of Rabbi, they wanted to declare Babylonia as dough in comparison with the Land of Israel. Since his ancestor, Hillel, had come from Babylonia, he said to them, "You're throwing thorns between my eyes. If you like, R. Hanina bar Hama will deal with you."

10. V:14: n the time of R. Phineas, they wanted to declare Babylonia as dough in comparison with the Land of Israel. He said to his staff, "When I make two statements in the house of study, pick me up in my litter and run like hell." When he came in, he said to them, "On the basis of the law of the Torah, there is no requirement that fowl be slaughtered." So while they were looking into that statement, he said to them, "All other countries are like gross dough not fine flour in comparison to the Land of Israel, and the Land of Israel is like gross dough by comparison to Babylonia." They picked him up in his litter and ran like hell. They ran after him but couldn't catch up. So they went into session and they did thorough genealogical research until they got to some danger spots, and they desisted.
    a. V:15: Gloss.
    b. V:16: Gloss.
        I. V:17: Gloss of the gloss.
            A. V:18: Expansion of the foregoing.
            B. V:19: As above.
            C. V:20: As above.
11. V:21: Said Samuel in the name of an elder, "Any family in Babylonia stands in the presumption of genealogical purity until you have sound evidence concerning how it has been invalidated. Families in all other countries stand in the presumption of being invalid, until you have sound evidence in favor of their validity. In the Land of Israel, a family that is assumed to be invalid genealogically remains so, one that is assumed to be valid genealogically remains so."
    a. V:22: Gloss.
12. V:23: Said R. Joseph, "To someone with a Babylonia accent they marry off a woman of sound genealogy. But nowadays, when there are people who can imitate the accent, we take precautions."
    a. V:24: Story.
    b. V:25: Story.
    c. V:26: As above.
13. V:27: Said Rab, "Irenic conduct in Babylonia is a sign of good genealogy."
14. V:28: Said R. Judah said Rab, "If you see two men quarreling with one another, that is a sign that there is some blemish of genealogical unfitness in one of them, and on that account, they are not allowed to form an alliance with one another."

Chapter Twenty. Qiddushin   303

    15. V:29: Said R. Pappa the Elder in the name of Rab, "Babylonia is genealogically healthy, Mesene is utterly dead, Media is sick, Elam is dying. What's the difference between the sick and the dying? most of the sick get well, most of the dying die."
        a. V:30: What are the geographical limits of the genealogical province of Babylonia?
            I. V:31: Gloss of a detail of the foregoing.
        b. V:32: What are the geographical limits of the genealogical province of the upper Euphrates?
            I. V:33: Gloss of the foregoing.
        c. V:34: Said Abbayye to R. Joseph, "On this side of the Euphrates, how far does it go?"
    16. V:35: Said R. Pappa, "As is the dispute concerning genealogy, so is the dispute as to the delivery of writs of divorce whether or not one has to declare that before him the document was written and signed; the issue of boundaries concerns that matter as well."
    17. V:36: Said R. Ammi bar Abba, "In respect to genealogy, Habil Yamma is the crown jewel of Babylonia, Shunya and Gubya are the crown jewel of Habil Yamma."
        a. V:37: Story.
    18. V:38: R. Iqa bar Abin said R. Hananel said Rab said, "Halwan and Nehawend – lo, these locales in the status of the Exile, so far as genealogy is concerned."
G. TOPICAL APPENDIX ON THE STATUS OF VARIOUS TERRITORIES IN THE IRANIAN EMPIRE
    1. V:39: "And three ribs were in his mouth between his teeth" (Dan. 7:5): Said R. Yohanan, "This refers to Halwan, Adiabene, and Nisibis, which Persia sometimes swallowed but sometimes spit out."
    2. V:40: "And behold another beast, a second, like a bear" (Dan. 7:5): R. Joseph repeated as a Tannaite formulation, "This refers to the Persians, who eat and drink like a bear, are obese like a bear, are shaggy like a bear, and are restless like a bear."
    3. V:41: aid Rabbi to Levi, "Tell me about the Persians." He said to him, "They look like the hosts of the house of David." "Tell me about the Magi." They are like the angels of destruction."
H. REVERSION TO THE PRIOR PROBLEM

1. V:42: When Rabbi was dying, he said, "There is the town of Humanayya in Babylonia, the whole of the population of which is made up of Ammonites; there is the town of Misqarayya in Babylonia, the whole population of which is made up of mamzers; there is the town of Birqa in Babylonia: Two brothers swap wives there; there is the town of Birta diSatayya in Babylonia, only today they have apostatized from following the Omnipresent, for a fish pond overflowed on the Sabbath, so they went and caught the fish on the Sabbath, on account of which R. Ahi b. R. Josiah excommunicated them, and they have apostatized. There is the town of Fort Agama in Babylonia. Adda bar Ahbah is located there. Today he is sitting in the bosom of Abraham being circumcised. Today Rab Judah was born in Babylonia."
   a. V:43: Gloss.
2. V:44: "The Lord has commanded concerning Jacob that they that are round about him should be his adversaries" (Lam. 1:17): R. Judah said, "For instance, gentile Humanayya in relationship to Jewish Pum Nehara."
3. V:45: And it came to pass, when I prophesied, that Pelatiah son of Benaiah died. Then I fell down upon my face and cried with a loud voice and said, 'Ah Lord God'" (Ezek. 11:13): Rab and Samuel – one said, "This was for good in praise of Pelatiah." and the other said, "This was for bad."
4. V:46: Ten castes came up from Babylonia, in line with the interpretation of R. Eleazar, "Ezra did not go up from Babylonia until he had made it pure as sifted flour; then he went up" taking those of inferior genealogy, so that they should not remain in Babylonia): Said R. Judah said Samuel, "This represents the statement of R. Meir, but sages say, 'Israelite residents of all countries are assumed to be valid.'"
   a. V:47: Case.
5. V:48: Our rabbis have taught on Tannaite authority: "Netins and Mamzers will be genealogically purified in the world to come," the words of R. Yosé. R. Meir says, "They will not be clean." Said to him R. Yosé, "But hasn't it been said, 'I will sprinkle clean water upon you, and you shall be clean' (Ezek. 36:25)?" Said to him R. Meir, "When Scripture says, 'And you shall be clean from all your uncleannesses and from all your idols I will cleanse you' (Ezek. 36:25) – it means, but not from the status of mamzer." Said to him R.

Chapter Twenty. Qiddushin 305

  Yosé, "When Scripture says, 'I will cleanse you' it means, also from the status of mamzer" (T. Qid. 5:4A-E).

  a. V:49: Now from the perspective of R. Meir, there is no problem, for that's in line with the verse, "And the mamzer will dwell in Ashdod" (Zech. 9:6), apart from all other Jews, because they will remain forbidden to marry. But from the perspective of R. Yosé, how are we to understand the verse, "And the mamzer will dwell in Ashdod" (Zech. 9:6)?

  b. V:50: Said R. Judah said Samuel, "The decided law is in accord with R. Yosé."

6. V:51: Our rabbis have taught on Tannaite authority: "A proselyte may marry a mamzer girl," the words of R. Yosé. R. Judah says, "A proselyte should not marry a mamzer girl" (T. Qid. 5:2B). "All the same are a proselyte, a freed slave, and a priest of impaired genealogy: They are permitted to marry a priest girl."

  a. V:52: What is the scriptural basis for the position of R. Yosé?

  b. V:53: "All the same are a proselyte, a freed slave, and a priest of impaired genealogy: They are permitted to marry a priest girl": This supports the position of Rab, for said R. Judah said Rab, "Genealogically fit women were not warned against marrying unfit men that is, fit priest girls are not admonished not to marry those who may not marry into the priesthood." While a priest may not marry the daughter of a priest of impaired genealogy, freed man or proselyte, the daughter of a priest may marry one of these.

  c. V:54: R. Zira expounded in Mehoza where there were many proselytes, "A proselyte may marry a mamzer girl."

I. AND WHAT ARE "SILENCED ONES"? ANY WHO KNOWS THE IDENTITY OF HIS MOTHER BUT DOES NOT KNOW THE IDENTITY OF HIS FATHER. AND FOUNDLINGS? ANY WHO WAS DISCOVERED IN THE MARKET AND KNOWS NEITHER HIS FATHER NOR HIS MOTHER.

1. VI:1: Said Raba, "By the law of the Torah, a silenced one is fit. How come? The majority of men are fit to marry the mother, and only a minority would be unfit to marry her, since we know that the mother was unmarried, the only men whose offspring would be a mamzer are themselves mamzers or consanguineous relations, for a gentile or slave doesn't

produce a mamzer; only a minority would be unfit in this regard. So if they went to her, then he who separates himself in such a way separates himself from the majority."

2. VI:2: And said Raba, "By the law of the Torah, a foundling is fit. How come? A married woman ascribes an illegitimate child to her husband and wouldn't throw the child out as a foundling."

3. VI:3: Said Raba bar R. Huna, "If a foundling was found circumcised, he is not subject to the classification of foundling at all. If his limbs are set, he is not subject to the classification of foundling at all. If he has been massaged with oil, fully powdered, has beads hung on him, wears a tablet or an amulet, he is not subject to the classification of foundling at all. If he was hung from a palm tree or located where a wild beast can reach him, he is subject to the classification of foundling, and if not, he is not subject to the classification of foundling at all. If he was left exposed on a sorb bush, if it is near a town, he is subject to the classification of foundling; and if not, he is not subject to the classification of foundling at all. If he is found near a synagogue near a town, where large numbers gather, he is not subject to the classification of foundling at all. And if not, he is subject to the classification of foundling."

4. VI:4: Said R. Hisda, "Three are believed if they give their testimony on the spot, and these are they: Those who state the status of a foundling, a midwife, and one who lifts from her companions the suspicion of having been raped"

5. VI:5: Our rabbis have taught on Tannaite authority. A midwife is believed to testify, "This one is a priest, this one is a Levite, this one is a Netin, this one is a mamzer." Under what circumstances? In a case in which there is no sort of objection. But if someone raises an objection, she is not believed.

   a. VI:6: Gloss.

6. VI:7: A vendor is believed to testify, "To this one I sold it, and to that one I didn't sell it." Under what circumstances? When the object is still in his possession. But if the object is no longer in his possession, he is not believed (T. B.M. 1:11).

   a. VI:8: But why not find out which party's money he has in hand?

7. VI:9: A judge is believed to testify, "This party I declared free of obligation, that party I have declared guilty." Under

what circumstances? When the litigants are standing before him. But if the litigants are not standing before him, he is not believed (T. B.M. 1:12).
   a. VI:10: Well, why not just find out who holds the written verdict in his favor?
8. VI:11: Said R. Nahman, "Three are believed in regard to a firstborn, and these are they: The midwife, the father, and the mother. The midwife is believed if she gives testimony on the spot; the mother, all seven days after birth; and the father, permanently."

J. ABBA SAUL DID CALL A "SILENCED ONE" SHETUQI "ONE WHO IS TO BE EXAMINED" BEDUQI.
   1. VII:1: What's the meaning of "one who is to be examined"? Should we say, they examine his mother, and if she says, "I had sexual relations with a valid person," she is believed? Then in accord with what authority is this unattributed ruling? It is in accord with Rabban Gamaliel, in which case we have already learned this elsewhere in the Mishnah and it does not have to be repeated, for we have learned in the Mishnah: If she was pregnant, and they said to her, "What is the character of this foetus?" and she said, "It is by Mr. So-and-so, and he is a priest" – Rabban Gamaliel and R. Eliezer say, "She is believed." And R. Joshua says, "We do not depend on her testimony. But lo, she remains in the assumption of having been made pregnant by a Netin or a mamzer, until she brings evidence to back up her claim" (M. Ket. 1:9)! And said R. Judah said Samuel, "The decided law accords with Rabban Gamaliel."

XXXIX. MISHNAH-TRACTATE QIDDUSHIN 4:3
   A. ALL THOSE WHO ARE FORBIDDEN FROM ENTERING INTO THE CONGREGATION ARE PERMITTED TO MARRY ONE ANOTHER. R. JUDAH PROHIBITS THEIR MARRYING ONE ANOTHER.
      1. I:1: What is the meaning of, all those who are forbidden from entering into the congregation? Should I say this refers to Mamzers, Netins, silenced ones, and foundlings? Lo, the opening clause states explicitly: Converts, freed slaves, mamzers, Netins, "silenced ones," and foundlings are permitted to marry among one another. And furthermore, with reference to the statement, R. Judah prohibits their marrying one another, to which clause does R. Judah's statement pertain? Should I say, it refers to the marriage of

persons whose status is certain and persons whose status is subject to doubt? Now, since the concluding clause states, R. Eliezer says, "Those who are of certain status are permitted to intermarry with others who are of certain status. Those who are of certain status and those who are of doubtful status, those who are of doubtful status and those who are of certain status, those who are of doubtful status and those who are of doubtful status – intermarriage among persons in such classifications is prohibited," it must follow that R. Judah does not take that position. And should you say R. Judah forbids pertains to the marriage of a proselyte and a mamzer girl, then does the language at hand state, a proselyte with a mamzer girl? What it states is, All those who are forbidden from entering into the congregation!

2. I:2: And is it an encompassing generalization that all those who are forbidden from entering into the congregation are permitted to marry one another? What about a widow, a divorcée, a woman of impaired priestly genealogy, and a whore Lev. 21:7, all of whom are prohibited from entering into the congregation of the priesthood, but who also are forbidden to marry with these others? Furthermore, then is one who is permitted to marry into the priesthood forbidden to marry with these? But what about a proselyte, who is permitted to marry a priest's daughter but also is permitted to marry a mamzer girl?

3. I:3: Our rabbis have taught on Tannaite authority: An Ammonite, Moabite, Egyptian, Idumaean proselyte, Samaritan, Netin, person of profaned priestly genealogy, mamzer, who was nine years and a day old, who had sexual relations with the daughter of a priest, Levite, or Israelite, disqualifies a woman so that, if of Levitical or Israelite caste, she may not marry a priest, and if of priestly caste, may not marry a priest nor eat food in the status of priestly rations. R. Yosé says, "Any whose offspring is unfit – she is rendered unfit; but any whose offspring is fit – she is not disqualified." Rabban Simeon b. Gamaliel says, "Any whose daughter you may marry, his widow you may marry, but if you may not marry his daughter, you may not marry his widow" (T. Nid. 6:1A-C).

   a. I:4: What is the issue between the initial Tannaite authority and R. Yosé?
   b. I:5: Further gloss of I:3.

Chapter Twenty. Qiddushin

          I.   I:6: Further gloss of I:3, developing the results of I:5.
- B. R. ELIEZER SAYS, "THOSE WHO ARE OF CERTAIN STATUS ARE PERMITTED TO INTERMARRY WITH OTHERS WHO ARE OF CERTAIN STATUS. THOSE WHO ARE OF CERTAIN STATUS AND THOSE WHO ARE OF DOUBTFUL STATUS, THOSE WHO ARE OF DOUBTFUL STATUS AND THOSE WHO ARE OF CERTAIN STATUS, THOSE WHO ARE OF DOUBTFUL STATUS AND THOSE WHO ARE OF DOUBTFUL STATUS – INTERMARRIAGE AMONG PERSONS IN SUCH CLASSIFICATIONS IS PROHIBITED." AND WHO ARE THOSE WHO ARE OF DOUBTFUL STATUS? THE "SILENCED ONE," THE FOUNDLING, AND THE SAMARITAN.
  1. II:1: And said R. Judah said Rab, "The decided law accords with R. Eliezer. But when I made that statement before Samuel, he said to me, 'Hillel repeated as a Tannaite statement: Ten castes came up from Babylonia: (1) priests, (2) Levites, (3) Israelites, (4) impaired priests, (5) converts, and (6) freed slaves, (7) mamzers, (8) Netins, (9) "silenced ones" shetuqi, and (10) foundlings (M. Qid. 4:1A) and all of these castes may intermarry,' and you say that the decided law accords with the position of R. Eliezer?!"
  2. II:2: There is a contradiction between two statements of Rab, and there is a contradiction between two statements of Samuel. For it has been stated: A betrothed girl who got pregnant – Rab said, "The offspring is a mamzer." And Samuel said, "The offspring is in the status of one who is silenced when he asks who his father was."
  3. II:3: It has been taught on Tannaite authority: And so R. Eleazar says, "A Samaritan man should not marry a Samaritan woman" (T. Qid. 5:1G).
     - a. II:4: What's the operative consideration?
       - I. II:5: Gloss of the foregoing.
  4. II:6: Said R. Nahman said Rabbah bar Abbuha, "A mamzer by a sister and a mamzer by a brother's wife became mixed up among the Samaritans" and that explains why they may not marry one another.

XL.   MISHNAH-TRACTATE QIDDUSHIN 4:4-5
- A. HE WHO MARRIES A PRIEST GIRL HAS TO INVESTIGATE HER GENEALOGY FOR FOUR GENERATIONS, VIA THE MOTHERS, WHO ARE EIGHT: (1) HER MOTHER, AND (2) THE MOTHER OF HER MOTHER, AND (3) THE MOTHER OF THE FATHER OF HER MOTHER, AND (4) HER MOTHER, AND (5) THE MOTHER OF HER FATHER, AND (6) HER MOTHER,

AND (7) THE MOTHER OF THE FATHER OF HER FATHER, AND (8) HER MOTHER. AND IN THE CASE OF A LEVITE GIRL AND AN ISRAELITE GIRL, THEY ADD ON TO THEM YET ANOTHER GENERATION FOR GENEALOGICAL INQUIRY.
1. I:1: How come the ancestry of women is investigated but not that of men?
2. I:2: R. Adda bar Ahbah repeated as the Tannaite formulation, "Four mothers, which are twelve." In an external Tannaite formulation it is repeated, "Four mothers, which are sixteen."
3. I:3: Said R. Judah said Rab, "This represents the opinion of R. Meir, but sages say, "All families are assumed to be valid."

B. THEY DO NOT CARRY A GENEALOGICAL INQUIRY BACKWARD FROM PROOF THAT ONE'S PRIESTLY ANCESTOR HAS SERVED AT THE ALTAR:
1. II:1: How come?

C. NOR FROM PROOF THAT ONE'S LEVITICAL ANCESTOR HAS SERVED ON THE PLATFORM:
1. III:1: How come?

D. AND FROM PROOF THAT ONE'S LEARNED ANCESTOR HAS SERVED IN THE SANHEDRIN. IT IS TAKEN FOR GRANTED THAT AT THE TIME OF THE APPOINTMENT, A FULL INQUIRY WAS UNDERTAKEN.
1. IV:1: How come?

E. AND ALL THOSE WHOSE FATHERS ARE KNOWN TO HAVE HELD OFFICE AS PUBLIC OFFICIALS OR AS CHARITY COLLECTORS – THEY MARRY THEM INTO THE PRIESTHOOD, AND IT IS NOT NECESSARY TO CONDUCT AN INQUIRY.
1. V:1: Does that bear the implication, then, that we do not appoint judges who derive from genealogically unfit families? But by way of contradiction: All are valid to engage in the judgment of property cases, but all are not valid to engage in the judgment of capital cases, except for priests, Levites, and Israelites who are suitable to marry into the priesthood (M. San. 4:2A-C), and in reflecting on that matter, someone asked, what is the word all meant to encompass? And said R. Judah, "It is meant to encompass a mamzer."
2. V:2: How come?
    a. V:3: Case.
    b. V:4: R. Zira would deal with them and provide honor for them. Rabbah bar Abbuha would deal with them honorably. But in the West, even an inspector of measures were not appointed of them. In Nehardea, even the superintendent of irrigation was not appointed of them.

Chapter Twenty. Qiddushin *311*

    F. R. Yosé says, "Also: He who was signed as a witness in the ancient archives in Sepphoris."
        1. VI:1: How come?
    G. R. Haninah b. Antigonos says, "Also: Whoever was recorded in the king's army."
        1. VII:1: Said R. Judah said Samuel, "This speaks of those who served in the armies of the house of David."

XLI. Mishnah-Tractate Qiddushin 4:6-7
    A. The daughter of a male of impaired priestly stock is invalid for marriage into the priesthood for all time.
        1. I:1: What is the meaning of *for all time*?
    B. An Israelite who married a woman of impaired priestly stock – his daughter is valid for marriage into the priesthood.
        1. II:1: What is the source of this rule?
    C. A man of impaired priestly stock who married an Israelite girl – his daughter is invalid for marriage into the priesthood.
        1. III:1: But that is spelled out in the opening clause: The daughter of a male of impaired priestly stock is invalid for marriage into the priesthood for all time!
        2. III:2: Our Mishnah rule does not accord with the position of R. Dosetai b. Judah.
        3. III:3: Our rabbis have taught on Tannaite authority: "That he may not profane his children among his people": I know only that through such a marriage his children are profaned. How do I know that the woman herself is profaned as to her status within the priesthood? It is a matter of logic: If the children, who have not transgressed, lo, are profaned, she, who has transgressed, surely should be profaned! But he presents an anomaly, for he has transgressed but is not profaned! No, if you invoke the case of a male priest, who is not profaned under any circumstances, will you say the same of a woman, who is profaned under a variety of circumstances for if she has sexual relations with various invalid persons, she is profaned and may no longer be held to be within the priestly caste, for example, as to the right to eat priestly rations is concerned? If you prefer, Scripture itself states, "He will not profane": "He will not profane" even someone who was valid but is then made invalid which is to say, the woman (Sifra Parashat Emor Pereq 2:CCXIV:I.7).

a. III:4: What is the purpose of adding the materials from If you prefer?
4. III:5: Our rabbis have taught on Tannaite authority: What is the definition of one who has been defiled? It is any woman who has been born to any invalid priestly marriage (Sifra Parashat Emor Pereq 2:CCXIV:I.2).
   a. III:6: What is the definition of any invalid priestly marriage? Shall we say, a marriage of persons unfit for him? Then lo, there is the case of one who remarries a woman he has divorced, who is invalid for him, but her offspring with him are valid, since it is written, "She is an abomination" (Deut. 24:4) – She is an abomination – but her children are not an abomination!
5. III:7: Our rabbis have taught on Tannaite authority: If a high priest had sexual relations with a widow, a widow, a widow, he is liable on only a single count; a divorcée, a divorcée, a divorcée, he is liable on only a single count. If a high priest had sexual relations with a widow, a divorcée, a woman of impaired priestly stock, and a whore, if it is in respect to the same woman who has entered these very conditions by actions taken in that exact order, he is liable on each count. If the same woman first of all committed an act of whoredom, then was profaned from priestly stock, then was divorced, and then was widowed, he is liable on only a single count.
   a. III:8: Gloss of a detail of the foregoing.
   b. III:9: As above.
6. III:10: A Tannaite authority repeated the following allegation as to the state of the rule before R. Sheshet, "Any classification of woman who is encompassed under 'a virgin of his own people shall he take to wife' (Lev. 21:14) is encompassed under the language, 'a widow...he shall not take,' but whoever is not encompassed under '...shall he take...,' is not encompassed under '...he shall not take.' The high priest transgresses the latter only on account of a woman who would be permitted to him if she were a virgin. This then excludes a high priest who marries his widowed sister being liable not on the count of her widowhood but only on the count of her being his sister."
7. III:11: Said R. Pappa to Abbayye, "An Israelite who had sexual relations with his sister certainly places her in the classification of a whore; but does he place her in the classification of one impaired for marriage into the

Chapter Twenty. Qiddushin

priesthood or is that not the case is a priest who has sexual relations with her flogged separately on each count? Do we maintain it as an argument a fortiori: If she becomes one impaired for marriage into the priesthood by reason of sexual relations with those forbidden to her merely by negative commandments, how much the more so if the six is those forbidden on the penalty of extirpation? Or maybe, impairment for marriage into the priesthood derives only from sexual relations with one forbidden to her by reason of being a priest?"

    a. III:12: Said R. Ashi, "Therefore a priest who had sexual relations with his sister has made her a whore but hasn't made her a woman of impaired priestly status. If then he went and had sexual relations with her again, he has made her into a woman of impaired priestly status" since as a result of the first act of sexual relations, she becomes forbidden to him also as a whore of the type forbidden only to priests.

    b. III:13: Said Abbayye, "When a high priest or an ordinary priest betroths a woman he is forbidden to marry, he is flogged; when he has sexual relations, he is flogged on that count too. When a high priest or an ordinary priest betroths a woman he is forbidden to marry, he is flogged: on the count of 'he shall not take.' When he has sexual relations, he is flogged on that count too: On the count of 'he shall not profane.'" Raba said, "If he had sexual relations, he is flogged; if he didn't have sexual relations, he is not flogged. For it is written, 'He shall not take in marriage' (Lev. 21:14) so that 'he shall not profane his seed' (Lev. 21:15). The prohibition in the former instance is on account of the latter consideration, which yields the conclusion that one is not liable until he shall actually have had sexual relations."

D. R. JUDAH SAYS, "THE DAUGHTER OF A MALE PROSELYTE IS EQUIVALENT TO THE DAUGHTER OF A MALE OF IMPAIRED PRIESTLY STOCK."

    1. IV:1: It has been taught on Tannaite authority: "Among his people": This serves to encompass under the law the daughter of a male priest who has been profaned, indicating that she is invalid for marriage into the priesthood. R. Judah says, "The daughter of a male proselyte is in the status of the daughter of a male priest who has been profaned" (Sifra Parashat Emor Pereq 2:CCXIV:I.8).

E. R. Eliezer b. Jacob says, "An Israelite who married a female proselyte – his daughter is suitable for marriage into the priesthood. And a proselyte who married an Israelite girl – his daughter is valid for marriage into the priesthood. But a male proselyte who married a female proselyte – his daughter is invalid for marriage into the priesthood. All the same are proselytes and freed slaves, even down to ten generations – the daughters cannot marry into the priesthood unless the mother is an Israelite."

1. V:1: It has been taught on Tannaite authority: R. Simeon b. Yohai says, "A convert who converted at the age of less than three years and a day may marry into the priesthood, as it is said, 'But all the female children who have not known man by lying with him keep alive for yourselves' (Num. 31:18), and Phineas a priest was certainly among them."
   a. V:2: And all parties to the dispute of the Mishnah paragraph interpret the same verse of Scripture, namely: "Neither shall they take for their wives a widow nor her that is put away but they shall take virgins of the seed of the house of Israel" (Ezek. 44:22).
      I. V:3: Said R. Nahman to Raba, "But as to this verse, does the first part refer to a high priest and the second to an ordinary priest" for the first part prohibits marriage to a widow, and the second half "and a widow that is a widow of a priest they shall take" permits it.
   2. V:4: "And a widow that is the widow of a priest they shall take" (Ex. 44:22): only of a priest, not of an Israelite? This is the sense of the statement: "...Of a priest they shall take" – as to those of other priests may take such a woman.

F. R. Yosé says, "Also: A proselyte who married a female proselyte: His daughter is valid for marriage into the priesthood."

1. VI:1: Said R. Hamnuna in the name of Ulla, "The decided law accords with the position of R. Yosé." And so said Rabbah bar bar Hannah, "The decided law accords with the position of R. Yosé.

XLII. MISHNAH-TRACTATE QIDDUSHIN 4:8

A. HE WHO SAYS, "THIS SON OF MINE IS A MAMZER" IS NOT BELIEVED. AND EVEN IF BOTH PARTIES SAY CONCERNING THE FOETUS IN THE MOTHER'S WOMB, "IT IS A MAMZER" – THEY ARE NOT BELIEVED.

Chapter Twenty. Qiddushin 315

    1. I:1: What is the meaning of the clause, even if both parties...?
- B. R. JUDAH SAYS, "THEY ARE BELIEVED."
  1. II:1: That is in accord with what has been taught on Tannaite authority: "He shall acknowledge the firstborn" (Deut. 21:17) – even to others letting the know who is firstborn. In this connection said R. Judah, "A man is believed to state, 'This son of mine is firstborn.' And just as he is believed to state, 'This son of mine is firstborn,' so he is believed to state, 'This son of mine is the son of a divorcée or the son of a woman who has performed the rite of removing the shoe.'" And sages say, "He is not believed."
     a. II:2: Said R. Nahman bar Isaac to Raba, "Well, there is no problem in explaining the position of R. Judah, since that is in line with the verse of Scripture, 'He shall acknowledge the firstborn.' But as to rabbis, what need to I have for that clause, He shall acknowledge the firstborn?"

XLIII. MISHNAH-TRACTATE QIDDUSHIN 4:9
- A. HE WHO GAVE THE POWER TO HIS AGENT TO ACCEPT TOKENS OF BETROTHAL FOR HIS DAUGHTER, BUT THEN HE HIMSELF BETROTHED HER – IF HIS CAME FIRST, HIS ACT OF BETROTHAL IS VALID. AND IF THOSE OF HIS AGENT CAME FIRST, HIS ACT OF BETROTHAL IS VALID. AND IF IT IS NOT KNOWN WHICH CAME FIRST, BOTH PARTIES GIVE A WRIT OF DIVORCE. BUT IF THEY WANTED, ONE OF THEM GIVES A WRIT OF DIVORCE, AND ONE CONSUMMATES THE MARRIAGE. AND SO: A WOMAN WHO GAVE THE POWER TO HER AGENT TO ACCEPT TOKENS OF BETROTHAL IN HER BEHALF, AND THEN SHE HERSELF WENT AND ACCEPTED TOKENS OF BETROTHAL IN HER OWN BEHALF – IF HERS CAME FIRST, HER ACT OF BETROTHAL IS VALID. AND IF THOSE OF HER AGENT CAME FIRST, HIS ACT OF BETROTHAL IS VALID. AND IF IT IS NOT KNOWN WHICH OF THEM CAME FIRST, BOTH PARTIES GIVE A WRIT OF DIVORCE. BUT IF THEY WANTED, ONE OF THEM GIVES A WRIT OF DIVORCE AND ONE OF THEM CONSUMMATES THE MARRIAGE.
  1. I:1: Both cases given in the Mishnah paragraph are required. For if we had been informed of the rule in respect to the father, that might have been because a man is solid in his knowledge of genealogy, but as to a woman, who is not solid in her knowledge of genealogy, I might say that that her act of betrothal is invalid. And if we were told that that is the case of the woman, it is because before a woman accepts a betrothal, she carefully investigates the situation,

but as for the father, I might have supposed he doesn't really care about pure genealogy, in which case he didn't cancel the agent's authority but made a provisional act of betrothal on his own. So both formulations are required.

2. I:2: It has been stated: If her father betrothed her on the road, and in town she betrothed herself to someone else, and now on the very same day she has become pubescent so her father no longer has authority over her – Rab said, "Lo, she is pubescent right in our very presence and her act of betrothal is certainly valid." And Samuel said, "We take account of the possibility that the acts of betrothal of both parties may be valid."
   a. I:3: Gloss.
   b. I:4: As above.
   c. I:5: As above.
   d. I:6: As above.
      i. I:7: The decided law.

XLIV. MISHNAH-TRACTATE QIDDUSHIN 4:10-4:11
   A. HE WHO WENT ALONG WITH HIS WIFE OVERSEAS, AND HE AND HIS WIFE AND CHILDREN CAME HOME, AND HE SAID, "THE WOMAN WHO WENT ABROAD WITH ME, LO, THIS IS SHE, AND THESE ARE HER CHILDREN" – HE DOES NOT HAVE TO BRING PROOF CONCERNING THE WOMAN OR THE CHILDREN. IF HE SAID, "SHE DIED, AND THESE ARE HER CHILDREN," HE DOES BRING PROOF ABOUT THE CHILDREN, BUT HE DOES NOT BRING PROOF ABOUT THE WOMAN. IF HE SAID, "I MARRIED A WOMAN OVERSEAS. LO, THIS IS SHE, AND THESE ARE HER CHILDREN" – HE BRINGS PROOF CONCERNING THE WOMAN, BUT HE DOES NOT HAVE TO BRING PROOF CONCERNING THE CHILDREN. "...SHE DIED, AND THESE ARE HER CHILDREN," HE HAS TO BRING PROOF CONCERNING THE WOMAN AND THE CHILDREN.
   1. I:1: Said Rabbah bar R. Huna, "And all cases address a situation in which the children are minors and clinging to the woman who need not prove her motherhood in any more plausible manner than that."
   2. I:2: Our rabbis have taught on Tannaite authority: "A woman did I marry overseas" – he brings proof concerning the woman, but he does not have to bring proof concerning the children. He brings proof concerning the adults, but he does not have to bring proof concerning the minors. Under what circumstances? In the case of one wife. But in the case of two wives, he has to bring proof concerning both the woman and her children, whether adults or minors.

Chapter Twenty. Qiddushin

a. I:3: Said R. Simeon b. Laqish, "This evidentiary standard applies only in regard to the children's eating Holy Things separated in the provinces so the priest's children are confirmed if the woman cling to the mother, and they may eat priestly rations produced in the provinces, but not in respect to genealogy." And R. Yohanan said, "It pertains even to the matter of genealogy.
   I. I:4: Now R. Yohanan is consistent with opinion expressed elsewhere
   II. I:5: It has been taught on Tannaite authority in accord with the view of R. Yohanan.

XLV. MISHNAH-TRACTATE QIDDUSHIN 4:12
   A. A MAN SHOULD NOT REMAIN ALONE WITH TWO WOMEN:
      1. I:1: What is the operative consideration here? The Tannaite authority of the household of Elijah explained: Because women are lightheaded.
      2. I:2: A man should not remain alone with two women, but a woman may remain alone with two men: What is the scriptural authority for that view? Said R. Yohanan said R. Ishmael, "How on the basis of the Torah do we find an indication that there is a decree against being alone with an Israelite woman? 'If your brother, son of your mother...entice you' (Deut. 13:7). But can there be the son of a mother who is not of the son of the father who is subject to the consideration of enticement by a relative? The meaning is, a son may be alone with his mother, but no one else may be alone with any woman with whom the Torah prohibits him to marry."
         a. I:3: Gloss.
      3. I:4: A man should not remain alone with two women: May we say that our Mishnah passage is not in accord with the position of Abba Saul,
   B. BUT A WOMAN MAY REMAIN ALONE WITH TWO MEN. R. SIMEON SAYS, "ALSO: ONE MAY STAY ALONE WITH TWO WOMEN, WHEN HIS WIFE IS WITH HIM. AND HE SLEEPS WITH THEM IN THE SAME INN, BECAUSE HIS WIFE KEEPS WATCH OVER HIM."
      1. II:1: Said R. Judah said Rab, "This rule applies only to upright persons, but in the case of immoral ones, then even if it were ten, it is not permitted. There was a case in which ten men took out a loose woman on a bier."

2. II:2: Said R. Judah said Rab, "The statement that a woman may be alone with two men pertains only to a town. But as to a trip, there must be three. Perhaps one of them will have to attend to his natural needs, and it will turn out that one of the men the remaining one will be left alone with a woman forbidden to have sexual relations with him."
   a. II:3: Story.
3. II:4: Said Rab, "A flogging is administered on account of her doing into seclusion with another man, but she is not prohibited from her husband on account of seclusion." Said R. Ashi, "That statement concerns only being alone with a free agent, but not with a married woman, so that people won't suspect the parentage over her children."
4. II:5: Said Rab, "A flogging is administered on account of 'it is no good report' (1 Sam. 2:24), as it is said, 'No, my sons, for it is no good report that I hear.'"
5. II:6: Said Rabbah, "If her husband was in town, we do not take precautions on the count of being alone with a man."
   a. II:7: Story.
6. II:8: Said R. Kahana, "If men are outside and women are inside, we do not take precautions on the count of being alone with a man. If men are inside and women are outside, we do take precautions on the count of being alone with a man."
   a. II:9: Said Abbayye, "The year's sorest spot is the festival of Tabernacles."

C. TOPICAL APPENDIX ON RIDICULING SINNERS, ATTACHED TO SUPPLEMENT A DETAIL IN THE FOREGOING
   1. II:10: R. Meir would ridicule sinners. One day Satan appeared to him on the opposite side of a canal in the form of a woman. There being no ferry, he grabbed a rope and got across. As he had reached half way down the rope, temptation released him, saying, "If they had not accounted in Heaven, 'Watch out for R. Meir and his Torah learning,' I would not have valued your life for two maahs."
   2. II:11: R. Aqiba would ridicule sinners. One day Satan appeared to him on the top of a palm tree in the form of a woman. He was climbing up, till he got half way up the palm tree, when temptation released him, saying, "If they had not accounted in Heaven, 'Watch out for R. Aqiba and his Torah learning,' I would not have valued your life for two maahs."

Chapter Twenty. Qiddushin

    3.   II:12: Every day Pelimo would be accustomed to say, "An arrow in the eyes of Satan." One day, the eve of the Day of Atonement, Satan appeared to him in the guise of a poor man. He came and called at the door. They brought food out to him. He said to him, "On a day such as this, when everybody is inside, should I be outside?"

    4.   II:13: R. Hiyya bar Ashi was accustomed, whenever he prostrated himself to his face, to say, "May the All-Merciful save us from the Evil Impulse."

    5.   II:14: So it has been taught on Tannaite authority: "Her husband has made them void and the Lord shall forgive her" (Num. 30:13) – Of whom does Scripture speak? It speaks of a woman who took a vow to be a Nazirite, and her husband annulled the vow for her, but she did not know that her husband had annulled it for her and nonetheless continued to go around drinking wine and contracting corpse uncleanness (M. Naz. 4:3C).

        a.   II:15: When R. Aqiba would come to this verse, he wept, saying, "If someone intended to eat ham and really had in hand veal, yet the Torah has said that he requires atonement and forgiveness, one who intends to eat ham and really had in hand ham – all the more so!"

D.   **A MAN MAY STAY ALONE WITH HIS MOTHER OR WITH HIS DAUGHTER. AND HE SLEEPS WITH THEM WITH FLESH TOUCHING.**

    1.   III:1: Said R. Judah said R. Assi, "A man may be alone with his sister and lie with his mother and daughter alone."

        a.   III:2: Gloss of a detail of the foregoing.

    3.   III:3: Said Raba, "A man may be alone with two levirate widows, or with two co-wives, or with a woman and her mother-in-law, or with a woman and her husband's daughter, or with a woman and a child who knows what sexual relations are all about but will not have sexual relations herself so she can well talk about what she's seen."

E.   **BUT IF THEY THE SON WHO IS WITH THE MOTHER, THE DAUGHTER WITH THE FATHER GREW UP, THIS ONE SLEEPS IN HER GARMENT, AND THAT ONE SLEEPS IN HIS GARMENT.**

    1.   IV:1: What is the definition of growing up?

    2.   IV:2: Said Rafram bar Pappa said R. Hisda, "That rule applies only to a girl who is not embarrassed to stand naked before him, but if she is embarrassed to stand naked before him, it is forbidden."

        a.   IV:3: Illustrative story.

XLVI. MISHNAH-TRACTATE QIDDUSHIN 4:13, 4:14A-C
   A. AN UNMARRIED MAN MAY NOT TEACH SCRIBES. NOR MAY A WOMAN TEACH SCRIBES.
      1. I:1: An unmarried man may not teach scribes: How come? Should we say that it is on account of pederasty? But hasn't it been taught on Tannaite authority: They said to R. Judah, "Israelites are not suspect of sodomy or bestiality." It is unthinkable and so need not be taken into consideration.
   B. R. ELIEZER SAYS, "ALSO: HE WHO HAS NO WIFE MAY NOT TEACH ELEMENTARY SCHOOL."
      1. II:1: The question was raised: Someone who has no wife at all, or someone whose wife is not living with him?
   C. R. JUDAH SAYS, "AN UNMARRIED MAN MAY NOT HERD CATTLE. AND TWO UNMARRIED MEN MAY NOT SLEEP IN THE SAME CLOAK." AND SAGES PERMIT IT.
      1. III:1: It has been taught on Tannaite authority: They said to R. Judah, "Israelites are not suspect of sodomy or bestiality." It is unthinkable and so need not be taken into consideration.

XLVII. MISHNAH-TRACTATE QIDDUSHIN 4:14D-T
   A. WHOEVER HAS BUSINESS WITH WOMEN SHOULD NOT BE ALONE WITH WOMEN. AND A MAN SHOULD NOT TEACH HIS SON A TRADE WHICH HE HAS TO PRACTICE AMONG WOMEN. R. MEIR SAYS, "A MAN SHOULD ALWAYS TEACH HIS SON A CLEAN AND EASY TRADE. AND LET HIM PRAY TO HIM TO WHOM BELONG RICHES AND POSSESSIONS. FOR THERE IS NO TRADE WHICH DOES NOT INVOLVE POVERTY OR WEALTH. FOR POVERTY DOES NOT COME FROM ONE'S TRADE, NOR DOES WEALTH COME FROM ONE'S TRADE. BUT ALL IS IN ACCORD WITH A MAN'S MERIT."
      1. I:1: Our rabbis have taught on Tannaite authority: Anyone whose business is mainly with woman has a bad character, for instance, gold refiners, carders, handmill cleaners, peddlers, wool-dressers, hairdressers, laundrymen, blood letters, bathhouse attendants, and tanners. From such as these they do not appoint either a king of a high priest (T. Qid. 5:14A).
         a. I:2: Our rabbis have taught on Tannaite authority: Anyone whose business is mainly with woman has a bad character, for instance, gold refiners, carders, handmill cleaners, peddlers, wool-dressers, hairdressers, laundrymen, blood letters, bathhouse attendants, and tanners. From such as these they do not appoint either a king of a high priest (T. Qid. 5:14A).

Chapter Twenty. Qiddushin   321

      b. I:3: Bar Qappara expounded, "A person should always try to teach his son a clean and easy trade."
2. I:4: It has been taught on Tannaite authority: Rabbi says, "You have no trade that passes out of the world. Happy is him who sees his parents in an honored profession, woe is he who sees his parents in a mean profession. It is not possible to have a world without either a spice dealer or a tanner. But happy is the one who makes his living as a spice dealer, and woe is the one who makes his living as a tanner. It is not possible to have a world without either males or females, but happy is the one whose children are males, and woe for him whose children are females" (T. Qid. 5:14C-D).
3. I:5: It has been taught on Tannaite authority: R. Meir says, "A man should always teach his son a clean and easy trade. And let him pray to him to whom belong riches and possessions. For there is no trade which does not involve poverty or wealth. For poverty does not come from one's trade, nor does wealth come from one's trade. But it is all from the one to whom wealth and fortunate belong: 'Mine is the silver, mine is the gold, says the Lord of hosts' (Hag. 3:8) (T. Qid. 5:15)."

B. R. SIMEON B. ELEAZAR SAYS, "HAVE YOU EVER SEEN A WILD BEAST OR A BIRD WHO HAS A TRADE? YET THEY GET ALONG WITHOUT DIFFICULTY. AND WERE THEY NOT CREATED ONLY TO SERVE ME? AND I WAS CREATED TO SERVE MY MASTER. SO IS IT NOT LOGICAL THAT I SHOULD GET ALONG WITHOUT DIFFICULTY? BUT I HAVE DONE EVIL AND RUINED MY LIVING." ABBA GURION OF SIDON SAYS IN THE NAME OF ABBA GURYA, "A MAN SHOULD NOT TEACH HIS SON TO BE AN ASS DRIVER, A CAMEL DRIVER, A BARBER, A SAILOR, A HERDSMAN, OR A SHOPKEEPER. FOR THEIR TRADE IS THE TRADE OF THIEVES." R. JUDAH SAYS IN HIS NAME, "MOST ASS DRIVERS ARE EVIL, MOST CAMEL DRIVERS ARE DECENT, MOST SAILORS ARE SAINTLY, THE BEST AMONG PHYSICIANS IS GOING TO GEHENNA, AND THE BEST OF BUTCHERS IS A PARTNER OF AMALEK."

1. II:1: It has been taught on Tannaite authority: R. Simeon b. Eleazar says, "In my whole life I have never seen a deer collecting produce, a lion carrying a load, a fox keeping shop; yet all of them are supported without a whole of of work, and yet they were created only for serve me, and I have been treated to serve my Creator: If these, who were created only to serve me are supported without a whole lot

of trouble, and I am created only to serve my Creator – isn't it logical that I should be supported without a whole lot of trouble! But I acted evilly and so spoiled my living: 'Your iniquities have turned away these things' (Jer. 5:25)" (T. Qid. 5:15Eff.).

C. R. NEHORAI SAYS, "I SHOULD LAY ASIDE EVERY TRADE IN THE WORLD AND TEACH MY SON ONLY TORAH. FOR A MAN EATS ITS FRUITS IN THIS WORLD, AND THE PRINCIPAL REMAINS FOR THE WORLD TO COME. BUT OTHER TRADES ARE NOT THAT WAY. WHEN A MAN GETS SICK OR OLD OR HAS PAINS AND CANNOT DO HIS JOB, LO, HE DIES OF STARVATION. BUT WITH TORAH IT IS NOT THAT WAY. BUT IT KEEPS HIM FROM ALL EVIL WHEN HE IS YOUNG, AND IT GIVES HIM A FUTURE AND A HOPE WHEN HE IS OLD. CONCERNING HIS YOUTH, WHAT DOES IT SAY? THEY WHO WAIT UPON THE LORD SHALL RENEW THEIR STRENGTH (ISA. 40:31). AND CONCERNING HIS OLD AGE WHAT DOES IT SAY? 'THEY SHALL BRING FORTH IN OLD AGE' (PS. 92:14). AND SO IT SAYS WITH REGARD TO THE PATRIARCH ABRAHAM, MAY HE REST IN PEACE, 'AND ABRAHAM WAS OLD AND WELL ALONG IN YEARS, AND THE LORD BLESSED ABRAHAM IN ALL THINGS' (GEN. 24:1). WE FIND THAT THE PATRIARCH ABRAHAM KEPT THE ENTIRE TORAH EVEN BEFORE IT WAS REVEALED, SINCE IT SAYS, 'SINCE ABRAHAM OBEYED MY VOICE AND KEPT MY CHARGE, MY COMMANDMENTS, MY STATUTES, AND MY LAWS' (GEN. 26:5)."

1. III:1: It has been taught on Tannaite authority: R. Nehorai says, "I should lay aside every trade in the world and teach my son only Torah. For every trade in the world stands by a man only in his youth, but in his old age, lo, he is left in famine. But the Torah is not that way. It stands by a man in his youth and gives him a future and a hope in his old age. In the time of youth what does it say? 'Those who hope in the Lord shall renew their strength, they shall mount up with wings as eagles' (Isa. 40:31). And of his old age? 'They shall still bring forth fruit in old age, they shall be full of sap and vigor' (Ps. 92:15)" (T. Qid. 5:16).

My claim that the entirety of the tractate forms a vast construction of Mishnah-exegesis and amplification, with only a few composites serving some purpose other than that of Mishnah-exegesis, is now fully exposed, and this tractate stands for them all. Let us now take up the underlined units and ask why they are included. At issue at each point is whether or not the Mishnah can explain the inclusion of a free-standing topical composite.

1. TOPICAL APPENDIX CONCERNING SEVERANCE PAY: The topical appendix is worked out on its own terms, but its inclusion does not disrupt the flow of Mishnah-

Chapter Twenty. Qiddushin 323

amplification, since the issue of severance pay is explicitly linked to the comparison of the Hebrew slave boy and girl and their emoluments, thus G.VI.2. That is the joining-composition.

    2. TOPICAL APPENDIX ON THE MARRIAGE TO THE CAPTIVE WOMAN OF GOODLY FORM: The reason for the intrusion of this composite is formal, as noted.

    3. MISCELLANY ON THE HONOR OF MOTHER AND FATHER: This composite takes up the Mishnah's theme and enriches it with relevant compositions.

    4. TOPICAL COMPOSITE ON RISING BEFORE ONE'S MASTER: As soon as respect for father and mother enters discussion, respect for the master will surely follow.

    5. TOPICAL APPENDIX ON THE MAMZER AND THE RESULT OF OTHER INAPPROPRIATE UNIONS: This carries forward the Mishnah's own topic.

    6. TOPICAL APPENDIX ON THE STATUS OF VARIOUS TERRITORIES IN THE IRANIAN EMPIRE: This is a subset of the foregoing.

    7. TOPICAL APPENDIX ON RIDICULING SINNERS, ATTACHED TO SUPPLEMENT A DETAIL IN THE FOREGOING: The reason for the inclusion of this item is as specified.

All the indicated composites turn out to complement the Mishnah's statements with topically relevant amplifications or carry forward the Mishnah's principle to new data. We may now state very simply that every composite of Bavli tractate Qiddushin serves a single purpose, Mishnah-exegesis or amplification. None finds necessary that dazzling inquiry into the unity at the level of underlying principle that characterizes discrete topics of law; we find not only no evidence of analytical-dialectical compositions or composites, but also none that signifies work on an exegetical-dialectical problem either.

South Florida Studies in the History of Judaism

240001	Lectures on Judaism in the Academy and in the Humanities	Neusner
240002	Lectures on Judaism in the History of Religion	Neusner
240003	Self-Fulfilling Prophecy: Exile and Return in the History of Judaism	Neusner
240004	The Canonical History of Ideas: The Place of the So-called Tannaite Midrashim, Mekhilta Attributed to R. Ishmael, Sifra, Sifré to Numbers, and Sifré to Deuteronomy	Neusner
240005	Ancient Judaism: Debates and Disputes, Second Series	Neusner
240006	The Hasmoneans and Their Supporters: From Mattathias to the Death of John Hyrcanus I	Sievers
240007	Approaches to Ancient Judaism: New Series, Volume One	Neusner
240008	Judaism in the Matrix of Christianity	Neusner
240009	Tradition as Selectivity: Scripture, Mishnah, Tosefta, and Midrash in the Talmud of Babylonia	Neusner
240010	The Tosefta: Translated from the Hebrew: Sixth Division Tohorot	Neusner
240011	In the Margins of the Midrash: Sifre Ha'azinu Texts, Commentaries and Reflections	Basser
240012	Language as Taxonomy: The Rules for Using Hebrew and Aramaic in the Babylonia Talmud	Neusner
240013	The Rules of Composition of the Talmud of Babylonia: The Cogency of the Bavli's Composite	Neusner
240014	Understanding the Rabbinic Mind: Essays on the Hermeneutic of Max Kadushin	Ochs
240015	Essays in Jewish Historiography	Rapoport-Albert
240016	The Golden Calf and the Origins of the Jewish Controversy	Bori/Ward
240017	Approaches to Ancient Judaism: New Series, Volume Two	Neusner
240018	The Bavli That Might Have Been: The Tosefta's Theory of Mishnah Commentary Compared With the Bavli's	Neusner
240019	The Formation of Judaism: In Retrospect and Prospect	Neusner
240020	Judaism in Society: The Evidence of the Yerushalmi, Toward the Natural History of a Religion	Neusner
240021	The Enchantments of Judaism: Rites of Transformation from Birth Through Death	Neusner
240022	Åbo Addresses	Neusner
240023	The City of God in Judaism and Other Comparative and Methodological Studies	Neusner
240024	The Bavli's One Voice: Types and Forms of Analytical Discourse and their Fixed Order of Appearance	Neusner
240025	The Dura-Europos Synagogue: A Re-evaluation (1932-1992)	Gutmann
240026	Precedent and Judicial Discretion: The Case of Joseph ibn Lev	Morell
240027	Max Weinreich *Geschichte der jiddischen Sprachforschung*	Frakes
240028	Israel: Its Life and Culture, Volume I	Pedersen
240029	Israel: Its Life and Culture, Volume II	Pedersen
240030	The Bavli's One Statement: The Metapropositional Program of Babylonian Talmud Tractate Zebahim Chapters One and Five	Neusner

240031	The Oral Torah: The Sacred Books of Judaism: An Introduction: Second Printing	Neusner
240032	The Twentieth Century Construction of "Judaism:" Essays on the Religion of Torah in the History of Religion	Neusner
240033	How the Talmud Shaped Rabbinic Discourse	Neusner
240034	The Discourse of the Bavli: Language, Literature, and Symbolism: Five Recent Findings	Neusner
240035	The Law Behind the Laws: The Bavli's Essential Discourse	Neusner
240036	Sources and Traditions: Types of Compositions in the Talmud of Babylonia	Neusner
240037	How to Study the Bavli: The Languages, Literatures, and Lessons of the Talmud of Babylonia	Neusner
240038	The Bavli's Primary Discourse: Mishnah Commentary: Its Rhetorical Paradigms and their Theological Implications	Neusner
240039	Midrash Aleph Beth	Sawyer
240040	Jewish Thought in the 20th Century: An Introduction in the Talmud of Babylonia Tractate Moed Qatan	Schweid
240041	Diaspora Jews and Judaism: Essays in Honor of, and in Dialogue with, A. Thomas Kraabel	Overman/MacLennan
240042	The Bavli: An Introduction	Neusner
240043	The Bavli's Massive Miscellanies: The Problem of Agglutinative Discourse in the Talmud of Babylonia	Neusner
240044	The Foundations of the Theology of Judaism: An Anthology Part II: Torah	Neusner
240045	Form-Analytical Comparison in Rabbinic Judaism: Structure and Form in *The Fathers* and *The Fathers According to Rabbi Nathan*	Neusner
240046	Essays on Hebrew	Weinberg
240047	The Tosefta: An Introduction	Neusner
240048	The Foundations of the Theology of Judaism: An Anthology Part III: Israel	Neusner
240049	The Study of Ancient Judaism, Volume I: Mishnah, Midrash, Siddur	Neusner
240050	The Study of Ancient Judaism, Volume II: The Palestinian and Babylonian Talmuds	Neusner
240051	Take Judaism, for Example: Studies toward the Comparison of Religions	Neusner
240052	From Eden to Golgotha: Essays in Biblical Theology	Moberly
240053	The Principal Parts of the Bavli's Discourse: A Preliminary Taxonomy: Mishnah Commentary, Sources, Traditions and Agglutinative Miscellanies	Neusner
240054	Barabbas and Esther and Other Studies in the Judaic Illumination of Earliest Christianity	Aus
240055	Targum Studies, Volume I: Textual and Contextual Studies in the Pentateuchal Targums	Flesher
240056	Approaches to Ancient Judaism: New Series, Volume Three, Historical and Literary Studies	Neusner
240057	The Motherhood of God and Other Studies	Gruber
240058	The Analytic Movement: Hayyim Soloveitchik and his Circle	Solomon

240059	Recovering the Role of Women: Power and Authority in Rabbinic Jewish Society	Haas
240060	The Relation between Herodotus' *History* and Primary History	Mandell/Freedman
240061	The First Seven Days: A Philosophical Commentary on the Creation of Genesis	Samuelson
240062	The Bavli's Intellectual Character: The Generative Problematic: In Bavli Baba Qamma Chapter One And Bavli Shabbat Chapter One	Neusner
240063	The Incarnation of God: The Character of Divinity in Formative Judaism: Second Printing	Neusner
240064	Moses Kimhi: Commentary on the Book of Job	Basser/Walfish
240066	Death and Birth of Judaism: Second Printing	Neusner
240067	Decoding the Talmud's Exegetical Program	Neusner
240068	Sources of the Transformation of Judaism	Neusner
240069	The Torah in the Talmud: A Taxonomy of the Uses of Scripture in the Talmud, Volume I	Neusner
240070	The Torah in the Talmud: A Taxonomy of the Uses of Scripture in the Talmud, Volume II	Neusner
240071	The Bavli's Unique Voice: A Systematic Comparison of the Talmud of Babylonia and the Talmud of the Land of Israel, Volume One	Neusner
240072	The Bavli's Unique Voice: A Systematic Comparison of the Talmud of Babylonia and the Talmud of the Land of Israel, Volume Two	Neusner
240073	The Bavli's Unique Voice: A Systematic Comparison of the Talmud of Babylonia and the Talmud of the Land of Israel, Volume Three	Neusner
240074	Bits of Honey: Essays for Samson H. Levey	Chyet/Ellenson
240075	The Mystical Study of Ruth: *Midrash HaNe'elam* of the Zohar to the Book of Ruth	Englander
240076	The Bavli's Unique Voice: A Systematic Comparison of the Talmud of Babylonia and the Talmud of the Land of Israel, Volume Four	Neusner
240077	The Bavli's Unique Voice: A Systematic Comparison of the Talmud of Babylonia and the Talmud of the Land of Israel, Volume Five	Neusner
240078	The Bavli's Unique Voice: A Systematic Comparison of the Talmud of Babylonia and the Talmud of the Land of Israel, Volume Six	Neusner
240079	The Bavli's Unique Voice: A Systematic Comparison of the Talmud of Babylonia and the Talmud of the Land of Israel, Volume Seven	Neusner
240080	Are There Really Tannaitic Parallels to the Gospels?	Neusner
240081	Approaches to Ancient Judaism: New Series, Volume Four, Religious and Theological Studies	Neusner
240082	Approaches to Ancient Judaism: New Series, Volume Five, Historical, Literary, and Religious Studies	Basser/Fishbane
240083	Ancient Judaism: Debates and Disputes, Third Series	Neusner

240084	Judaic Law from Jesus to the Mishnah	Neusner
240085	Writing with Scripture: Second Printing	Neusner/Green
240086	Foundations of Judaism: Second Printing	Neusner
240087	Judaism and Zoroastrianism at the Dusk of Late Antiquity	Neusner
240088	Judaism States Its Theology	Neusner
240089	The Judaism behind the Texts I.A	Neusner
240090	The Judaism behind the Texts I.B	Neusner
240091	Stranger at Home	Neusner
240092	Pseudo-Rabad: Commentary to Sifre Deuteronomy	Basser
240093	FromText to Historical Context in Rabbinic Judaism	Neusner
240094	Formative Judaism	Neusner
240095	Purity in Rabbinic Judaism	Neusner
240096	Was Jesus of Nazareth the Messiah?	McMichael
240097	The Judaism behind the Texts I.C	Neusner
240098	The Judaism behind the Texts II	Neusner
240099	The Judaism behind the Texts III	Neusner
240100	The Judaism behind the Texts IV	Neusner
240101	The Judaism behind the Texts V	Neusner
240102	The Judaism the Rabbis Take for Granted	Neusner
240103	From Text to Historical Context in Rabbinic Judaism V. II	Neusner
240104	From Text to Historical Context in Rabbinic Judaism V. III	Neusner
240105	Samuel, Saul, and Jesus: Three Early Palestinian Jewish Christian Gospel Haggadoth	Aus
240106	What is Midrash? And a Midrash Reader	Neusner
240107	Rabbinic Judaism: Disputes and Debates	Neusner
240108	Why There Never Was a "Talmud of Caesarea"	Neusner
240109	Judaism after the Death of "The Death of God"	Neusner
240110	Approaches to Ancient Judaism	Neusner
240111	Ecology of Religion	Neusner
240112	The Judaic Law of Baptism	Neusner
240113	The Documentary Foundation of Rabbinic Culture	Neusner
240114	Understanding Seeking Faith, Volume Four	Neusner
240115	Paul and Judaism: An Anthropological Approach	Laato
240116	Approaches to Ancient Judaism, New Series, Volume Eight	Neusner
240119	Theme and Context in Biblical Lists	Scolnic
240120	Where the Talmud Comes From	Neusner
240121	The Initial Phases of the Talmud, Volume Three: Social Ethics	Neusner
240122	Are the Talmuds Interchangeable? Christine Hayes's Blunder	Neusner
240123	The Initial Phases of the Talmud, Volume One: Exegesis of Scripture	Neusner
240124	The Initial Phases of the Talmud, Volume Two: Exemplary Virtue	Neusner
240125	The Initial Phases of the Talmud, Volume Four: Theology	Neusner
240126	From Agnon to Oz	Bargad
240127	Talmudic Dialectics, Volume I: Tractate Berakhot and the Division of Appointed Times and Women	Neusner
240128	Talmudic Dialectics, Volume II: The Divisions of Damages and Holy Things and Tractate Niddah	Neusner

South Florida Academic Commentary Series

243001	The Talmud of Babylonia, An Academic Commentary, Volume XI, Bavli Tractate Moed Qatan	Neusner
243002	The Talmud of Babylonia, An Academic Commentary, Volume XXXIV, Bavli Tractate Keritot	Neusner
243003	The Talmud of Babylonia, An Academic Commentary, Volume XVII, Bavli Tractate Sotah	Neusner
243004	The Talmud of Babylonia, An Academic Commentary, Volume XXIV, Bavli Tractate Makkot	Neusner
243005	The Talmud of Babylonia, An Academic Commentary, Volume XXXII, Bavli Tractate Arakhin	Neusner
243006	The Talmud of Babylonia, An Academic Commentary, Volume VI, Bavli Tractate Sukkah	Neusner
243007	The Talmud of Babylonia, An Academic Commentary, Volume XII, Bavli Tractate Hagigah	Neusner
243008	The Talmud of Babylonia, An Academic Commentary, Volume XXVI, Bavli Tractate Horayot	Neusner
243009	The Talmud of Babylonia, An Academic Commentary, Volume XXVII, Bavli Tractate Shebuot	Neusner
243010	The Talmud of Babylonia, An Academic Commentary, Volume XXXIII, Bavli Tractate Temurah	Neusner
243011	The Talmud of Babylonia, An Academic Commentary, Volume XXXV, Bavli Tractates Meilah and Tamid	Neusner
243012	The Talmud of Babylonia, An Academic Commentary, Volume VIII, Bavli Tractate Rosh Hashanah	Neusner
243013	The Talmud of Babylonia, An Academic Commentary, Volume V, Bavli Tractate Yoma	Neusner
243014	The Talmud of Babylonia, An Academic Commentary, Volume XXXVI, Bavli Tractate Niddah	Neusner
243015	The Talmud of Babylonia, An Academic Commentary, Volume XX, Bavli Tractate Baba Qamma	Neusner
243016	The Talmud of Babylonia, An Academic Commentary, Volume XXXI, Bavli Tractate Bekhorot	Neusner
243017	The Talmud of Babylonia, An Academic Commentary, Volume XXX, Bavli Tractate Hullin	Neusner
243018	The Talmud of Babylonia, An Academic Commentary, Volume VII, Bavli Tractate Besah	Neusner
243019	The Talmud of Babylonia, An Academic Commentary, Volume X, Bavli Tractate Megillah	Neusner
243020	The Talmud of Babylonia, An Academic Commentary, Volume XXVIII, Bavli Tractate Zebahim	Neusner
243021	The Talmud of Babylonia, An Academic Commentary, Volume XXI, Bavli Tractate Baba Mesia	Neusner
243022	The Talmud of Babylonia, An Academic Commentary, Volume XXII, Bavli Tractate Baba Batra	Neusner

243023	The Talmud of Babylonia, An Academic Commentary, Volume XXIX, Bavli Tractate Menahot	Neusner
243024	The Talmud of Babylonia, An Academic Commentary, Volume I, Bavli Tractate Berakhot	Neusner
243025	The Talmud of Babylonia, An Academic Commentary, Volume XXV, Bavli Tractate Abodah Zarah	Neusner
243026	The Talmud of Babylonia, An Academic Commentary, Volume XXIII, Bavli Tractate Sanhedrin	Neusner
243027	The Talmud of Babylonia, A Complete Outline, Part IV, The Division of Holy Things; A: From Tractate Zabahim through Tractate Hullin	Neusner
243028	The Talmud of Babylonia, An Academic Commentary, Volume XIV, Bavli Tractate Ketubot	Neusner
243029	The Talmud of Babylonia, An Academic Commentary, Volume IV, Bavli Tractate Pesahim	Neusner
243030	The Talmud of Babylonia, An Academic Commentary, Volume III, Bavli Tractate Erubin	Neusner
243031	The Talmud of Babylonia, A Complete Outline, Part III, The Division of Damages; A: From Tractate Baba Qamma through Tractate Baba Batra	Neusner
243032	The Talmud of Babylonia, An Academic Commentary, Volume II, Bavli Tractate Shabbat, Volume A, Chapters One through Twelve	Neusner
243033	The Talmud of Babylonia, An Academic Commentary, Volume II, Bavli Tractate Shabbat, Volume B, Chapters Thirteen through Twenty-four	Neusner
243034	The Talmud of Babylonia, An Academic Commentary, Volume XV, Bavli Tractate Nedarim	Neusner
243035	The Talmud of Babylonia, An Academic Commentary, Volume XVIII, Bavli Tractate Gittin	Neusner
243036	The Talmud of Babylonia, An Academic Commentary, Volume XIX, Bavli Tractate Qiddushin	Neusner
243037	The Talmud of Babylonia, A Complete Outline, Part IV, The Division of Holy Things; B: From Tractate Berakot through Tractate Niddah	Neusner
243038	The Talmud of Babylonia, A Complete Outline, Part III, The Division of Damages; B: From Tractate Sanhedrin through Tractate Shebuot	Neusner
243039	The Talmud of Babylonia, A Complete Outline, Part I, Tractate Berakhot and the Division of Appointed Times A: From Tractate Berakhot through Tractate Pesahim	Neusner
243040	The Talmud of Babylonia, A Complete Outline, Part I, Tractate Berakhot and the Division of Appointed Times B: From Tractate Yoma through Tractate Hagigah	Neusner
243041	The Talmud of Babylonia, A Complete Outline, Part II, The Division of Women; A: From Tractate Yebamot through Tractate Ketubot	Neusner
243042	The Talmud of Babylonia, A Complete Outline, Part II, The Division of Women; B: From Tractate Nedarim through Tractate Qiddushin	Neusner

| 243043 | The Talmud of Babylonia, An Academic Commentary, Volume XIII, Bavli Tractate Yebamot, A. Chapters One through Eight | Neusner |
| 243044 | The Talmud of Babylonia, An Academic Commentary, XIII, Bavli Tractate Yebamot, B. Chapters Nine through Seventeen | Neusner |

South Florida-Rochester-Saint Louis Studies on Religion and the Social Order

245001	Faith and Context, Volume 1	Ong
245002	Faith and Context, Volume 2	Ong
245003	Judaism and Civil Religion	Breslauer
245004	The Sociology of Andrew M. Greeley	Greeley
245005	Faith and Context, Volume 3	Ong
245006	The Christ of Michelangelo	Dixon
245007	From Hermeneutics to Ethical Consensus Among Cultures	Bori
245008	Mordecai Kaplan's Thought in a Postmodern Age	Breslauer
245009	No Longer Aliens, No Longer Strangers	Eckardt
245010	Between Tradition and Culture	Ellenson
245011	Religion and the Social Order	Neusner
245012	Christianity and the Stranger	Nichols
245013	The Polish Challenge	Czosnyka
245014	*Gesher Vakesher:* Bridges and Bonds, The Life of Leon Kronish	Green

South Florida International Studies in Formative Christianity and Judaism

242501	The Earliest Christian Mission to 'All Nations'	La Grand
242502	Judaic Approaches to the Gospels	Chilton
252403	The "Essence of Christianity"	Forna Rosa

BM
503.7
.N48
1995
v.1